Predicting through Navamsa and Nadi Astrology

C.S. Patel

Sagar Publications
72, Janpath, Ved Mansion, New Delhi-110001
Tel.: 2332 0648, 2332 8245
E-mail: s.sagarpublications@gmail.com
Website: www.sagarpublications.com

First Published 1996
Reprinted: 1999, 2005, 2010, 2016

Published by Narinder Sagar for Sagar Publications 72, Janpath, New Delhi-1 & Printed at Jay Kay Offset Press, New Delhi.

PREFACE

After the publication of our book "Ashtakavarga" in 1957, I thought to make deep study in Nadi Astrology. With this idea in mind, I placed orders with various libraries, such as G.O.M.L., Adyar; (Madras); Mysore and Tanjore, and collected some manuscripts transcribed into Devanagari from their local languages.

The Nadi Jyotisha is a unique system of astrology. The Nadi Granthas (books) on this system contain readymade horoscopes giving out the whole life-reading with important events in life of the native, as well as his parents, wife etc. and also information about the previous and future births and other matters. Some such books contain certain techniques, usable in predictive astrology which can be rarely found from other sources.

The above manuscripts were collected by 1960. In continuous studies, notes were prepared on important topics from 1960 to 1982. In 1983, I came in contact with Shri K. Aswathappa of Madras (in Ahmedabad), who invited me to deliver lecture on Ashtakavarga in Madras in December 1983.

After completing lecture tour of Madras, I returned to Bombay, thereafter contact with late Shri V.A.K. Aiyar (The great veteran) was established through a common friend of Madras. At times discussions on some of my researches, on important techniques were carried on. In course of time Shri Aiyar suggested to put my researches in writing and publish them in the Astrological Magazine (Bangalore) edited by Dr. B.V. Raman. My first contribution was "Yoga-bhangas or Cancellation of Yogas". (Feb. 1984). This resulted in a series of articles totalling about eighteen till date. Thereafter, I became a regular contributor of this magazine.

In course of time, Shri R. Santhanam (New Delhi) started a new magazine-"The Times of Astrology" from November 1985. He used to request, once in every six months to contribute articles to the "Times of Astrology". The first article for publication, was "New predictive Technique based on Nadi Astrology" (in September 1987). Thereafter about twelve articles have been published, in this magzine so far.

The following techniques were collected from various Nadi Granthas and rare old books, which have proved true in application, and have brought to light for the first time through various articles published in the Astrological Magazine and the Times of Astrology :

(1) Concellation of Yogas; (Feb. 1984);

(2) Use of the Lord of Lagna's Ashtakavarga, (Oct, 1984);

(3) Use of Samundayashtakavarga S.A.V. (Sept. 1985);

(4) Search Light on Navamsa-Navamsa-tulya Rasi (Jan. 1986);

(5) Importance of Rahu/Moon Midpoint from Nandi Nadi (Sept. 1987);

(6) Nadi Principles Behind Saturn's Transit (Jan. 88);

(7) Nadi System of Prediction (July 88);

(8) Relatives from Native's Chart - Deva-keralam (June 89);

(9) Nadi Astrology (Dec. 88);

(10) Eventful Years in One's Life-one Navamsa equals one year of life (Jan. 86 ; Jan. 89; Jan 90);

(11) Pushkara Navamsa, Vidyamadhavium (July 90);

(12) Use of Rahu-Ketu-Transit through "The Sun-Mercury-Venus arc". (Nov. 90);

(13) Navamsa-and Transit of Planets (Jan. 92);

(14) Importance of Deha and Jeeva Rasis (Jan. 93);

(15) Defining - Shubhabde/Krurabde etc. (Jan. 95);

(16) Use of Rekhas in Prognostication (Jan. 96);

(17) Conjunctions of Planets in Transit-use of Rasi and Navamsa Dispositor-(four articles - June 91; Dec. 91; Nov. 92 and July 93);

(18) Rasi-Tulya Navamsa/Navamsa-tulya Rasis (Jan. 96);

In addition to the above many more techniques judiciously culled out from Nadi Granthas have been explained in various chapters. This collection contains many principles not known to many so far (till their publication).

Some of my friends who were deeply impressed by these articles, requested me to compile and publish them all, in a book form for the benefit of posterity.

Meanwhile, a common friend, late Shri N.M. Sethia (Baroda) contacted Shri Narinder Sagar (New Delhi), and talked to him and showed a set of zerox copies of all my articles, who willingly agreed to publish them in the book-form.

A friend Mr. Vladimir Tanchuk, a Russian by birth and a citizen of America, who saw me thrice in Mumbai, wrote on 1-7-1988 from "New York." That coordination of Nadi, Ashtakavarga and Navamsa techniques are really superb, in all your articles. I deeply respect your research, I would say-Meta Astrology."

Another gentleman, Mr. Tommy Larsen from Copen-hegen (Denmark) came to meet me on 27-4-1993, at my residence and requested me to clarify certain points in the articles published in the Astrological Magazine. He came with a bunch of zerox copies of all my sixteen articles published so far, which surprised me, that learned scholars in far-off distant countries study my articles so deligently and meticulously. Another friend from Patna writes-"Mr. C.S. Patel has made a very extensive and intensive study of Navamsa and all his articles are of immense practical utility."

The author, not being a practising astrologer and not equipped with a variety of horoscopes has very often given his own chart as an example to explain certain intricacies of many research principles; deserves to be pardoned by readers, for boring them with the same chart, again and again.

It will be observed, how wonderfully use of Rasi-tulya Navamsa/ Navamsa-tulya Rasi and many other techniques regarding Navamsa is made in Nadi Granthas. The monograph of the book-"Predicting Through Navamsa and Nadi Astrology" is just adequate.

An independent book on principles, use and various techniques of Navamsa is being written and it is hoped to follow shortly probably by December 1996.

I heartily appreciate the interest shown by Shri Narinder Sagar, in bringing out this book attractively on good paper together with all charts in North Indian style alongwith South Indian one, for the benefit of readers. I wish to express my gratitude to (1) Shri N.M. Sethia for contacting the publishers and arranging the publication and (2) Shri Hari Prasad S. Bhatt., for unsolicited help in getting all the thirty two articles zeroxed and similar other jobs.

I shall consider my labour amply rewarded if this work proves helpful in enabling students and practitioners to make predictions with greater confidence and greater success than otherwise.

September 1996

C.S. Patel
29-D, 3rd Floor,
Gandhi Market,
Ghatkopar (E)
Mumbai-400077

CONTENTS

॥ श्रीगणेशाय नमः ॥

अज्ञानतिमिरान्धस्य ज्ञानाञ्जनशलाकया ।
चक्षुरुन्मीलितं येन तस्मै श्रीगुरवे नमः ॥ १ ॥

यथा शिखा मयूराणां नागानां मणयो यथा ।
तद्वद्वेदाङ्गशास्त्राणां ज्योतिषं मूर्धनि स्थितम् ॥ २ ॥

वेदस्य चक्षुः किल शास्त्रमेतत्प्रधानताऽङ्गेषु ततोऽर्थजाता ।
अङ्गैर्युतोऽन्यैः परिपूर्णमूर्तिश्चक्षुर्विहीनः पुरुषो न किञ्चित् ॥ ३ ॥

आरोग्यं सविता तनोतु भवतामिन्दुर्यशोनिर्मलं
भूतिं भूमिसुतस्सुधांशुतनयः प्रज्ञां गुरुर्गौरवम् ।
काव्यः कोमलवाग्विलासमतुलं मन्दो मुदं सर्वदा
राहुर्बाहुबलं विरोधशमनं केतुः कुलस्योन्नतिम् ॥ ४ ॥

अरुणकिरणजालैः रंजिताशावकाशा
विधृतजपवटीका पुस्तिकाभीतिहस्ता ।
इतरकरवराढ्या फुल्लकह्लारसंस्था
निवसतु हृदि बाला नित्यकल्याणरूपा ॥ ५ ॥

1

Use of the 64th Navamsa in Prognostication

Gochara or transit is a topic which has been viewed from various standpoints in astrological classics. The most commonly followed technique of delineating Gochara results is based on transit of slow-moving planets Saturn, Jupiter, Rahu and Ketu in relation to the natal Moon.

Astrological classics, such as *Devakeralam, Brihat Parasara Horasastra, Jataka Parijata, Hora Ratnam, Prasna Marga, Jatakadesamarga* and others speak of certain sensitive areas in a birth chart and transit over these areas by Saturn is said to cause much distress and even death. One such sensitive area is the 64th Navamsa (3° 20' or 200 minutes of arc) from the Navamsa occupied by the Moon or the Ascendant. This article is the result of the writer's research in this virgin area which has remained largely unexplored. The author wishes to discuss in this article certain aspects of the mysterious 64th Navamsa. The 64th Navamsa is nothing but the 210th degree, i.e., the 8th house aspect (dexter quincunx aspect accordig to Western Astrology).

The 64th Navamsa from that occupied by a planet will be the same Navamsa in the 8th sign, in order of sequence. For instnce, a planet is in Aries 8° 30' in the 3rd Navamsa from the beginning of sign Aries, the 64th Navamsa will be the 3rd navsmsa in Scorpio, the 8th sign. The 64th Navamsa will have the same degreecal Navamsa arc, *i.e.*, in the above example the Navamsa of the planet ranges from Aries 6°40' to 10°00' ; and the 64th Navamsa will range in Scorpio from 6°40' to 10°00'. 64, divided by 12. will have balance 4; so the 64th Navamsa sign will be the 4th sign from the planet's Navamsa sign; *i.e.*, in the above example the said planet is in the Gemini Navamsa of Aries sign; so the 64th Navamsa sign will be Virgo in Scorpio sign.

The concept of the 64th Navamsa has been developed by different authors from various standpoints. For instance, *Jataka Parijata* reckons it from the Moon; while *Brihat Parasara Horasastra* reckons it from the Moon and from the Ascendant; while *PrasnaMarga* reckons it from the Moon, the Ascendant and the Sun also.

I. (a). *Jataka Parijata*, Chap. V, verse 56 :

विलग्नजन्मद्रेक्काणाद्यस्तु द्वाविंशतिः(कः?) खरः ।
सुधाकरोपगांशर्क्षात् चतुःषष्ठयंशको भवेत् ॥

— meaning that the 22nd Drekkana from that of the Drekkana occupied by the Ascendant is called Khara. The 64th Navamsa from that of the Navamsa occupied by the Moon is called a Khara Navamsa. Some authors like Vaidyanatha and Ganapati Muni reckon Khara Drekkana from the Ascendant and the 64th Navamsa from the Moon only.

I. (b). Mr. Divakaruni Venkata Subba Rao, the learned scholar of Hyderabad, observes on page No. 31 of the souvenir of All India Astrological Conference—Madras 1982, as follows :

"Ganapati Muni gave interesting details dealing with Khara-grahas, *i.e.*, Khara Drekanadhipati—the lord of the 22nd Drekkana from the Lagna and Khara Navamsadhipati—the lord of the 64th Navamsa from the Moon.

"Whenever the lord of the 22nd Drekkana and the 64th Navamsa lord to the natal Moon happen to be the same planet or when those two Kharas happen to trasit a point deprived of an auspicious *bindu* in Ashtakavarga after two *sodhanas* (reductions) are carried out and if that Kakshya happens to be owned by the transiting Khara, death is unavoidable. This has been observed by me for over a long time and is found to give accurate results."

II. *Jataka Parijata*, Chap. V, verses 52-53 :

रन्ध्रेश्वरो रन्ध्रयुक्तो रन्ध्रद्रष्टा खरेश्वरः ।
रन्ध्राधिपयुतश्चैव चतुःषष्ठयंशनायकः ॥

रन्ध्रेश्वरातिशत्रुश्च सप्तछिद्रग्रहाः स्मृताः ।
तेषां मध्ये बली यस्तु तस्य दाये मृतिं वदेत् ॥

— meaning that the following seven planets are termed as chhidra grahas :

(1) the lord of the 8th house;

(2) the planet occupying the 8th house;

(3) the planet aspecting the 8th house;

(4) the lord of the Khara, *i.e.*, 22nd Drekkana from that of the Ascendant;

(5) the planet in conjunction with the lord of the 8th house;

(6) the lord of the 64th Navamsa from that occupied by the Moon; and

(7) the Atisatru (bitter enemy) of the lord of the 8th house.

The death of a native may be indicated in the Dasa of the strongest planet of the above seven.

III *Jatakadesamarga,* Chap. VII, verse 19 :

जन्मनि लग्नोपगताच्चन्द्रोपगतान्नवांशकाद्वाऽपि ।
चतुरुत्तरषष्ट्यंशकभे लग्ने वा समादिशेन्मरणम् ॥

meaning that death may happen when the Moon in his transit enters the 64th Navamsa reckoned from the Navamsa occupied by the Ascendant at birth or the Moon at birth or when such Navamsa sign is rising at that time. The author of *Jatakadesamarga* reckons the 64th Navamsa both from the Ascendant as well as from the Moon. According to this verse death can happen more specifically within a period of 6 to 7 hours, *i.e.*, the time taken by the Moon to transit one Navamsa sign to rise in the East.

IV. *Brihat Prasara Hora,* Chap. XX, verse 99 :

जन्मलग्नेन्दुगा नंदभागाः क्रमाद्वेदषष्ठ्यंशराशौ प्रयाते तनौ ।
मृत्युजन्मांगनीचोदये शून्यगे दुष्टपाकोदये देहमुक्तिर्भवेत् ॥

meaning that (1) when the sign representing the 64th Navamsa reckoned from the Ascendant or the Moon, is rising; or (2) the 7th house sign from the 8th house (*i.e.*, the 2nd house sign) is rising; or (3) the 7th house sign from the Ascendant is rising : one departs from this world if any one of these rising signs is devoid of *bindus* (has the least number of *bindus)* in the Ashtakavarga of the lord of the Ascendant, and the Dasa during that time is that of an adverse planet.

V. *Prasna Marga*, Chap. IX, verse 61 :

चन्द्रांशेशस्य तद्भूषा नवांशेशोऽथवा रवेः ।
लग्नेशो वापि यद्येवं स्वल्पमध्यचिरायुषः ॥

— meaning that if the lord of Navamsa occupied by the Moon is inimical, neutral or friendly to the lord of the 64th Navamsa therefrom, the longevity of the native will be short, medium or full.

Similarly, reckon the lord of the Navamsa occupied by the Ascendant, with that of the lord of the 64th Navamsa therefrom; and in the same way reckon the lord of the Navamsa occupied by the Sun, with that of the lord of the 64th Navamsa therefrom. It will be noticed that the author of *Prasna Marga* has improved upon the earlier authors by taking into account the relationship—inimical, neutral or friendly—between the lords of the Navamsa occupied by the Moon and the lord of the 64th Navamsa from him; similarly he has taken into account the Ascendant and also the Sun.

VI. *Hora Ratnam*, Chap. VIII, verse 27 :

जन्मलग्नांशकाच्चन्द्रनवांशादथ वापि वा।
राहौ चतुः षष्टिमिते निघनंच विनिर्दिशेत् ॥

meaning that death (of a near relative) should be indicated when Rahu transits the 64th Navamsa either from the Navamsa occupied by the Ascendant or the Moon. *Hora Ratnam's* author goes a step further and states that the death can happen when Rahu transits the 64th Navamsa either from the Ascendant or the Moon (covering a period of about two months).

This pointer made me to investigate the matter further and led me to the conclusion that the transit of Ketu or Saturn also, through the 64th Navamsa from the Moon or the Ascendant, produces similar untoward results and this is the main thrust of this write-up, which you will notice from the examples given, herewith.

The horoscope of our Prime Minister Mrs. Indira Gandhi :

Birth details : November 19th, 1917; at 11-11 p.m. (IST) at Allahabad, Lattitude 25° 27' N, Longitude 81° 51' E (From August 1966 A.M., p. 761).

Planatery Longitudes : The Sun 214° 08'; the Moon 275° 37'; Mars 136° 23' ; Mercury 223° '15'; Jupiter 45° 1'; Venus 261° 00'; Saturn 111° 47'; Rahu 250° 33'; Ketu 70° 33'; Herschel 297° 21';

Neptune 104° 18'; Ascendant 117° 3'; M.C. 00° 25'. Balance of the Sun's Dasa : 1 yr. 11 m. 20 d.

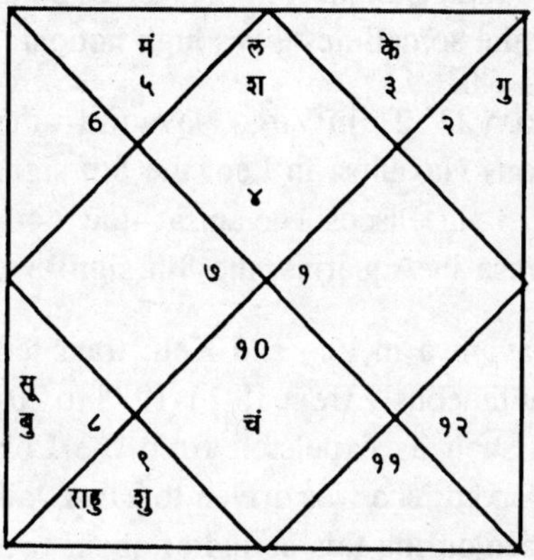

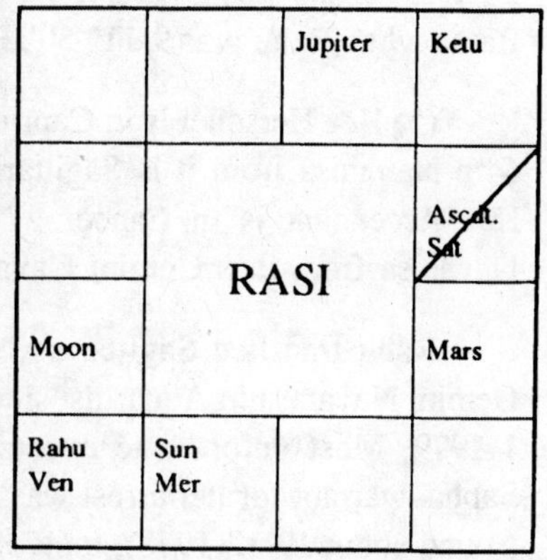

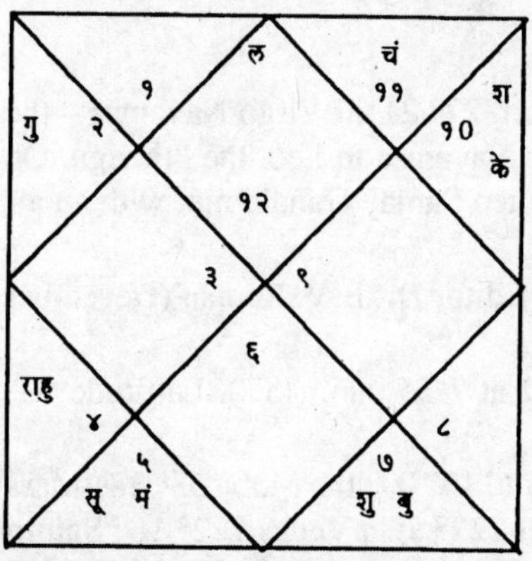

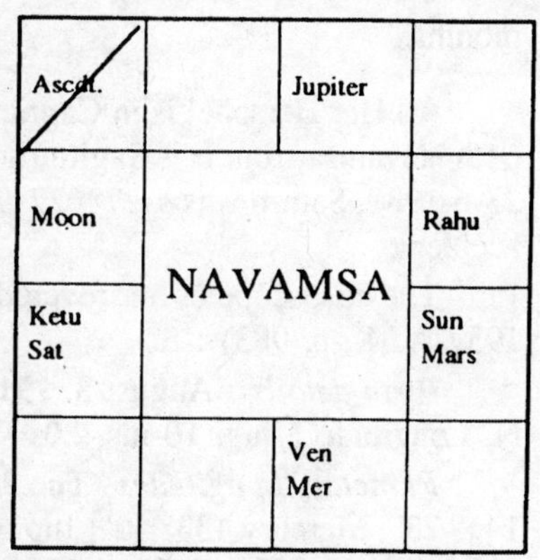

(1) Mrs. Indira Gandhi's Ascendant is Cancer 27° 3' in Pisces Navamsa—the 64th Navamsa from it is Gemini Navamsa in Aquarius, the 8th sign. Saturn was 10-29°-32' when she lost her mother (28-6-1936).

(2) Her Saturn is in Cancer 21°47' in Capcicorn Navamsa - The 64th Navamsa from it is Aries Navamsa in Aquarius, the 8th sign. On 8-9-1960, Ketu was 10-22° 08', when Firoz Gandhi breathed his last.

(3) Her Mercury is in Scorpio 13° 15' in Libra Navamsa—the 64th Navamsa from it is Capricorn Navamsa in Gemini, the 8th sign. On 27-5-1964, Rahu was 2-10°-13', when Jawaharlal Nehru breathed his last.

(4) Her Ketu is in Gemini 10° 33' in Capricorn Navamsa —the 64th Navamsa from it is Aries Navamsa in Capricorn, the 8th sign. On 26-1-1972, she was awarded the country's highest honour of Bharata Ratna when Rahu was 9-11° 50'. Rahu sometimes gives high honours.

(5) Her Herschel is in Capricorn 27° 21' in Virgo Navamsa—the 64th Navamsa from it is Sagittarious Navamsa in Leo, the 8th sign. Her Ascendant is in Cancer 27° 3' in Pisces Navamsa—the 64th Navamsa from it is Gemini Navamsa in Aquarius, the 8th sign.

Rahu transited Sagittarius Navamsa in Leo and Ketu transited Gemini Navamsa in Aquarius, simultaneously from 18-11-1978 to 20-1-1979. Most unfortnuate events, such as expulsion from the Lok Sabha, warrant for her arrest was served; she was driven to Tihar Jail (round about 19-12-1978), took place during this period of about two months.

(6) Her Herschel is in Capricorn 27° 21' in Virgo Navamsa—the 64th Navamsa from it is Sagittarius Navamsa in Leo, the 8th sign. On 23-6-1980, Saturn was 4-27°- 27' when Sanjay Gandhi met with an air accident.

The hososcope of our revered Editor Dr. B.V. Raman (December 1957 A.M., p. 983) :

Birth details : August 8. 1912 at 7-35 p.m. (IST). Lattitude 13° N, Longitude 5 hrs. 10 ms. 20s.

Planetary Longitudes : The Sun 113° 00'; the Moon 53° 38'; Mars 141° 23' ; Mercury 133° 59' ; Jupiter 222° 59' ; Venus 122° 16'; Saturn 40° 11'; Rahu 352° 49'; Ketu 172° 49'; Ascendant 308° 16'; M.C. 222° 49'. Balance of Mars Dasa : 6 yrs. 10 m. 3 d.

Rahu		Sat Moon	
Ascdt.	RASI		Sun
			Ven Mer Mars
	Jup		Ketu

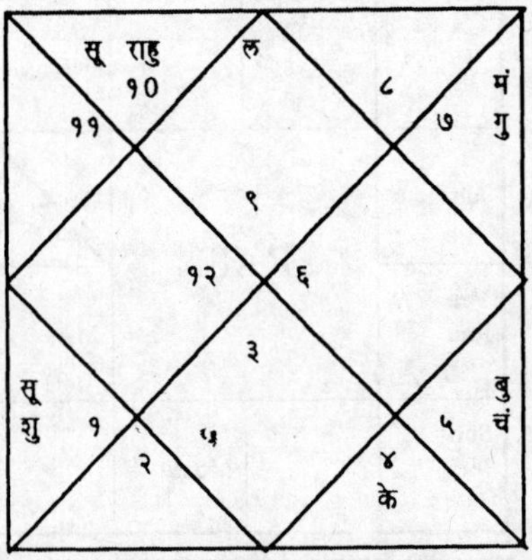

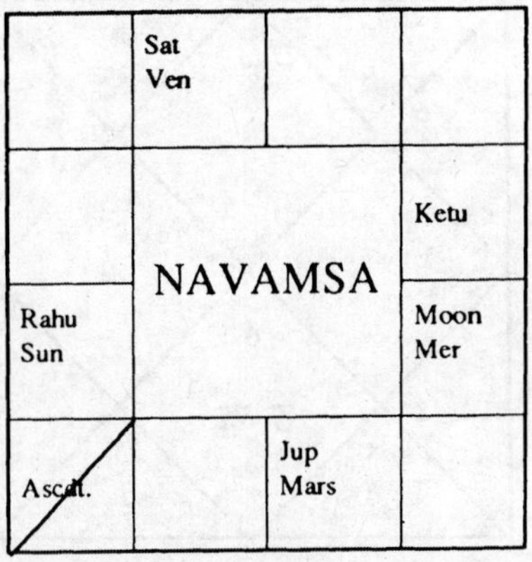

(1) Dr. B.V. Raman's Venus is in Leo 2° 16' in Aries Navamsa—the 64th Navamsa from it is Cancer Navamsa in Pisces. Saturn was 11-2° 16' in March 1937, when his grandfather expired.

(2) His Ascendant is Aquarius 8° 16' in Sagittarius Navamsa—the 64th Navamsa from it is Pisces Navamsa in Virgo, the 8th sign. Rahu was 5-10° 00' to 5-6° 40', when he toured America, England, etc., *i.e.*, from 4-10-1959 to 15-12-1959. Rahu sometimes gives high honours.

(3) (a) His natal Moon is in Taurus 23° 58' in Leo Navamsa—the 64th Navamsa from it is Scorpio Navamsa in Sagittarius, the 8th sign. Ketu was 8-24° 3' on 9-9-1963, when his beloved son Surya Prakash breathed his last.

(b) In Surya Prakash's hososcope—his natal Ketu is in Gemini 24° 40' in Taurus Navamsa—the 64th Navamsa from it is Leo Navamsa in Capricorn, the 8th sign. Saturn was 9-24° 00' on 9-9-1963.

The hosorcope of Mr. Chandulal Sakaralal Patel (myself) :

Birth details : December 31st, 1915 at 7-44 p.m. (IST). Lattitude 23° 02' N, Longitude 72° 39' E.

Planetary Longitudes : The Sun 256° 10'; The Moon 192° 13'; Mars 127° 9'; Mercury 265° 13'; Jupiter 329° 29'; Venus 283° 14'; Saturn 80° 42' (R); Rahu 287° 06'; Ketu 107° 06'; Herchel 291° 00'; Naptune 99° 13' (R); Ascendant 98° 53'; M.C. 04° 08'. Balance of Rahu's Dasa : 10yrs 6m. 3d.

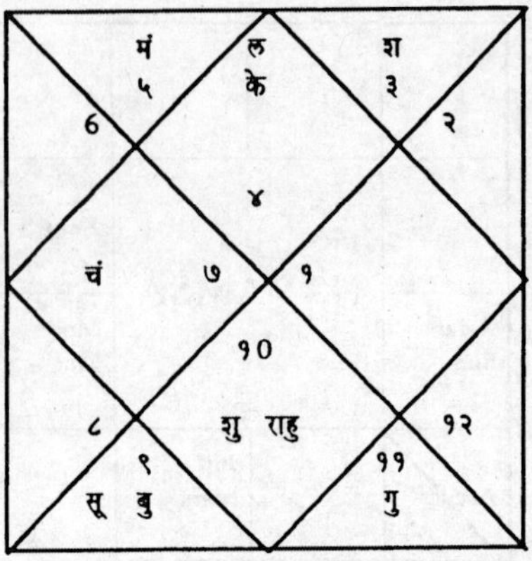

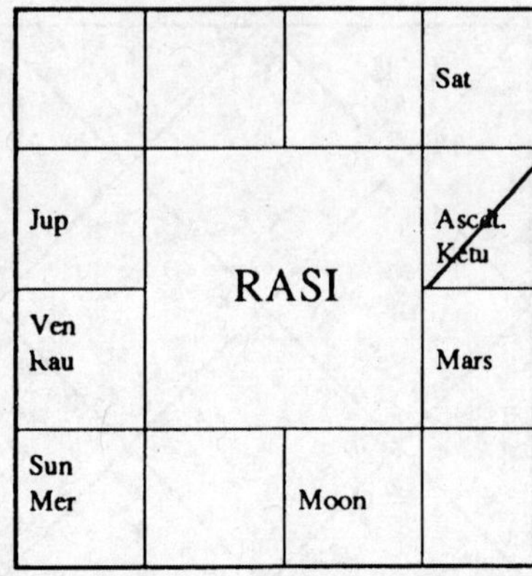

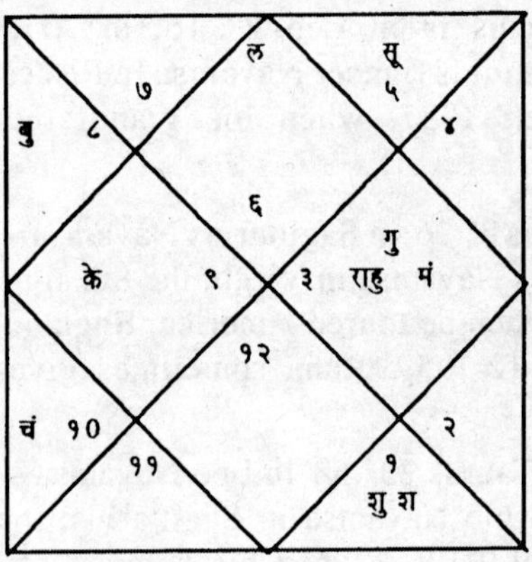

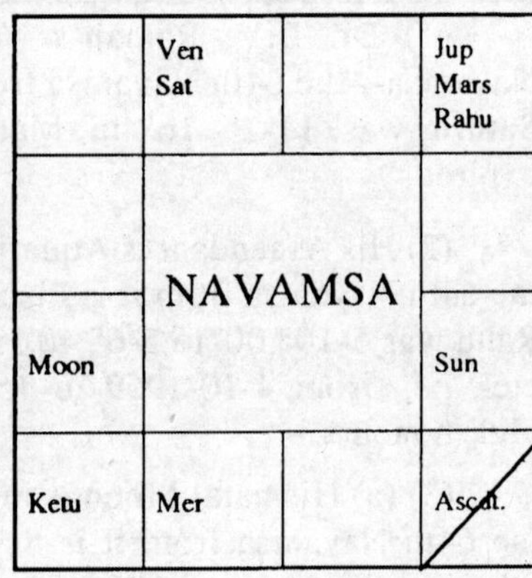

(1) My Herschel is in Capricorn 21° 00' in Cancer Navamsa—the 64th Navamsa from it is Libra Navamsa in Leo, the 8th sign. My marriage took place on 28-5-1933 when Jupiter (a benefic planet) was 4-20° 49'.

(2) M.C. falls in Aries 4° 8' in Taurus Navamsa—the 64th Navamsa from it is Leo Navamsa in Scorpio, the 8th sign. On 9-9-1956 I had a major traffic accident resulting in injuries when Saturn was 7-4° 14'.

(3) My Ascendant is Cancer 8° 53' in Virgo Navamsa—the 64th Navamsa from it is Sagittarious Navamsa in Aquarius, the 8th sign. His Holiness Sri Sankaracharya of Dwaraka Sarada Peetam conferreed on me an honarary degree of "Jyotishalankara" on 10-11-1962 at public function, when Jupiter was 10-9° 43'.

(4) My natal Ketu is in Cancer 17° 6' in Sagittarius Navamsa—the 64th Navamsa from it is Pisces Navamsa in Aquarius, the 8th sign.

On 22-3-1965, I had a major throat operation for cancer, when Saturn was 10-17°- 20'.

(5) (a) My natal Moon is in Libra 12° 12' in Capricorn Navamsa—the 64th Navamsa from it is Aries navamsa in Taurus, the 8th sign. On 30-11-1965, Rahu was 1-10° 58', when I lost my mother.

(b) My natal Ketu is in Cancer 17° 06' in Sagittarius Navamsa—the 64th Navamsa from it is Pisces Navamsa in Aquarius, the 8th sign. On 30-11-1965, Saturn was 10-17° 20' when I lost my mother. Simultaneous transits of Rahu and Saturn may be noted (30-11-1965).

(6) My natal Moon is in Libra 12° 12' in Capricorn Navamsa—the 64th Navamsa from it is Aries Navamsa in Taurus, the 8th sign. On 24-1-1975, I lost my wife when Ketu was 1-13° 10'.

Is is also found in practice that the transits of slow-moving planets through the 64th Navamsa from the remaining five planets, Rahu Ketu, M.C. (Dasamsa Madhyama) and trans-saturnine planets, are also productive of results of a significant nature—favourable or unfavourable. Similarly, transits through the 64th Navamsa of fast-moving planets, such as the Sun, Mars, Mercury, and Venus, also give results, which are of small magnitude.

This principle of the 64th Navamsa, *i.e.*, the transit of any planet on the 210th degree (dexter quincunx aspect) from a natal position can be applied to the Sayana positions also and the effects of transit of the planets can be studied from the Sayana horoscope. The above principle can be extended to even political predictions by referring to the horoscopes of the nations.

Mundane events, such as cyclones, earth-quakes, excessive heat, very heavy rains, devastating floods, excessive cold, droughts, big fires can be predicted by the 64th Navamsa position (dexter quincunx) formed by the fast-moving planets, such as the Sun, Mars, Mercury and Venus with the slow-moving planets such as Saturn, Jupiter, Rahu, Ketu, etc., in transit.

2

Searchlight on Navamsa

There are quite a few verses in Sanskrit astrological classics whose correct impact has eluded the grasp of even seasoned astrological scholars in the past. An in depth study of some of these verses throws a flood of light on a unique technique of prediction based on the concept of Navamsa. Navamsa, as we all know, is one of the 16 vargas (षोडषवर्गाः); whose utility is often limited to weighting the potential of planets and more specifically to study the matrimonial aspect of a native. That, Navamsas have wider application for prognostication on a variety of facets of a person's life has become evident from a critical study of some of the verses from classics, such as *Horasara, Jataka Parijata, Jatakadesamarga* etc., and *Nadi Granthas* like *Dhruva Nadi, Devakeralam,* etc. It is the purpose of this article to elucidate this unique technique of prediction with illustrative examples.

I

Dhruva Nadi, a rare astrological work, is in the possession of the Government Oriental Manuscripts Library, Madras. This work, comprising of 43 volumes, contains about 2,75,000 verses. In this work 12 planetary positions for the hosorcopes discussed are given in a unique manner.

ध्रुवनाड़ी – कन्या लग्नम् (p. 187 of Volume No. R 14, 721) :

रविहोरासमुत्पन्नो द्रेक्काणं मकरं भवेत् ।
नवांशं वृषभञ्चैव गुरुत्रिंशांशजातके ॥
मीने दिनेशे भृगुसंयुतश्च चापांशसूर्ये सुखांशयुक्तः ।

कुंभांशशुक्रे षष्टांशयुक्तः ।
मेषे च सौम्ये वृषभांशयुक्तः भाग्यांशयुक्तः ।
वृषभे च मन्दे शिखिसंयुतश्च सिंहांशमन्दे व्ययांशयुक्तः ।
वृषभांशकेतु वर्गोत्तमांशयुक्तः भाग्यांशयुक्तः ।
सिंहे गुरौ च वर्गोत्तमांशयुक्तः व्ययांशयुक्तः ।
चापे च चन्द्रे वर्गोत्तमांशयुक्तः सुखांशयुक्तः ।
वृश्चिके च कुजे नीचांशयुक्तः लाभांशयुक्तः ।
कीटे च राहौ वर्गोत्तभांशयुक्तः विक्रमांशयुक्तः ॥

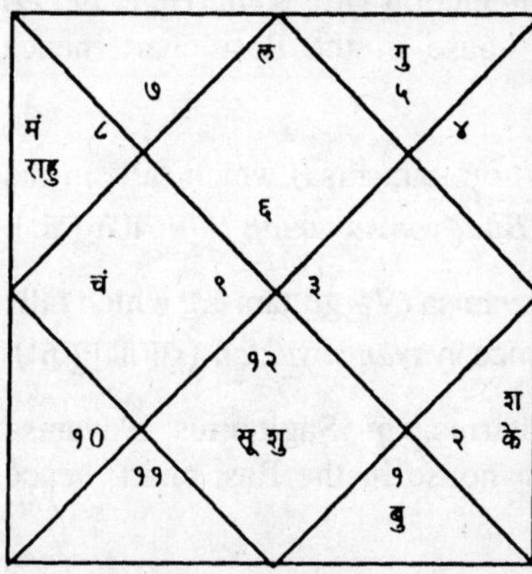

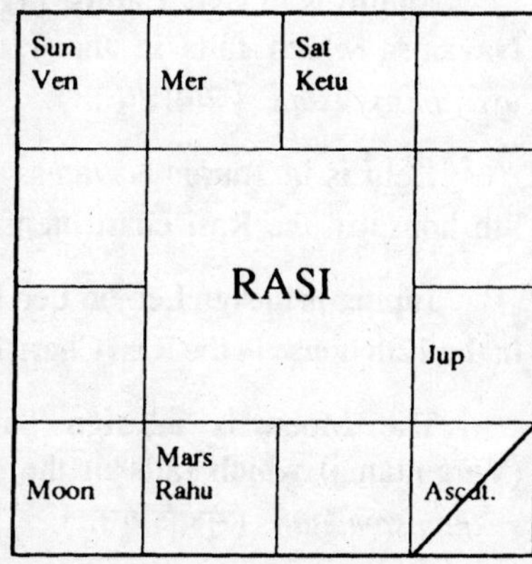

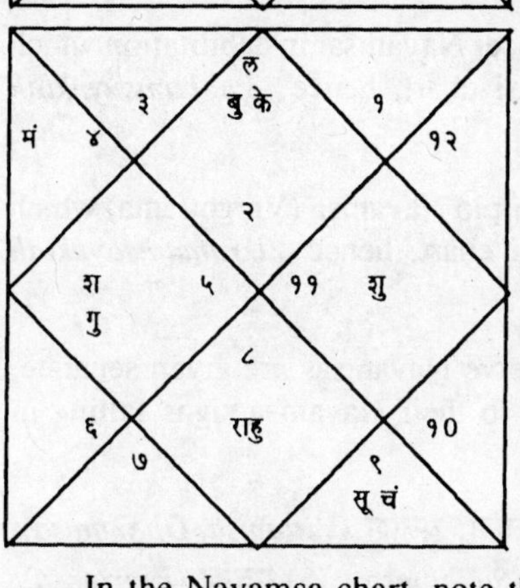

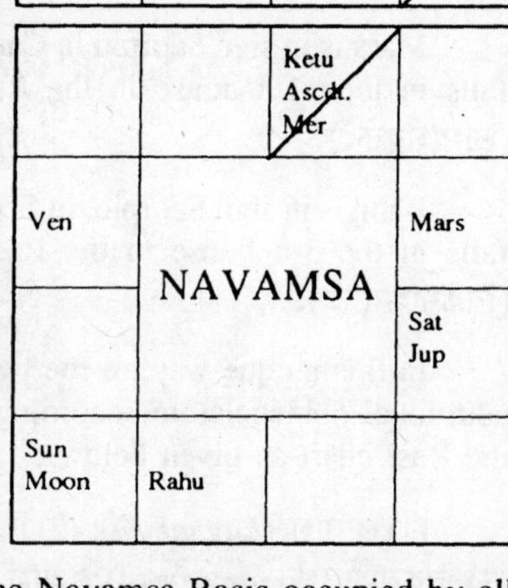

In the Navamsa chart, note the Navamsa Rasis occupied by all the planets. Also note in which houses (Bhavas) in the Rasi chart, these Navamsa Rasis fall. Each planet is given a special nomenclature, according to its Bhava occupation, of Navamsa Rasi, in the Rasi Chart.

Meaning : The native is born in Virgo Ascendant, in the Sun's Hora, in Capricorn Drekkana, in Taurus Navamsa and in Jupiter's Trimsamsa.

The Sun is in sign Pisces in conjunction with Venus. He is in Sagittarius Navamsa, which falls in the 4th house in Rasi chart, hence *sukhamsayuktah* (सुखांशयुक्तः).

Venus is in Aquarious Navamsa which falls in the 6th house in the Rasi chart, hence *shashthamsayuktah* (षष्ठांशयुक्तः).

Mercury is in sign Aries in Taurus Navasmsa, which falls in the 9th house in the Rasi chart, hence *Bhagyamsayuktah* (भाग्यांशयुक्तः).

Saturn is in sign Taurus, in conjunction with Ketu. He is in Leo Navamsa which falls in the 12th house in the Rasi chart, hence *vyayamsayuktah* (व्ययांशयुक्तः).

Ketu is in Taurus Navamsa (Vargottamsmsa) which falls in the 9th house in the Rasi chart, hence *Bhagyamsayuktah* (भाग्यांशयुक्तः).

Jupiter is in sign Leo, in Leo Navamsa (Vargottamsa), which falls in the 12th house in the Rasi Chart, hence *vyayamsayuktah* (व्ययांशयुक्तः).

The Moon is in sign Sagittarius, in Sagittarius Navamsa (Vargottama) which falls in the 4th house in the Rasi chart, hence *sukhamsayuktah* (सुखांशयुक्तः).

Mars is in sign Scorpio in Cancer Navamsa, in debilitation which falls in the 11th house in the Rasi chart, hence *Labhamsuyuktah* (लाभांशयुक्तः).

Rahu is in sign Scorpio, in Scorpio Navamsa (Vargottama) which falls in the 3rd house in the Rasi chart, hence *Vikramamsayuktah* (विक्रमांशयुक्तः).

In this unique way all the twelve Navamsas are given separate, additional nomenclature according to their Navamsa signs falling in the Rasi chart as given below :

(1) लग्नांश (*Lagnamsa*); (2) वित्तांश, धनांश (*Vittamsa, Dhanamsa*); (3) विक्रमांश (*Vikramsa*); (4) सुखांश (*Sukhamsa*); (5) पुत्रांश (*Putramsa*); (6) षष्ठांश (*Shashthamsa*); (7) भार्यांश (*Bharyamsa*); (8) निधनांश रन्ध्रांश (*Nidhanamsa; Randhramsa*); (9) भाग्यांश (*Bhagyamsa*); (10) कर्मांश (*Karmamsa*); (11) लाभांश (*Labhamsa*); and (12) व्ययांश (*Vyanamsa*).

This nomenclature is freely used in *Dhruva Nadi*, sparingly used in *Chandrakala Nadi*, and rarely used in standard works on astrology, where the commentators have mostly not interpreted the terms correctly.

Most of the text books on astrology which are available to astrological readers, say the interpretation of Navamsas with respect to Lagna Navamsa itself, where as in this article, readers may recognise that the interpretations are mainly based on the Lagna of Rasi chart only. Hence the various nomenclatures, *viz.*, *Lagnamsa*, *Vittamsa*, *Vikramamsa*, etc.

II

Here is a verse from *Horosara*, Chapter VI—verse 24 and the same verse from *Jatakadesamarga*, Chapter VI, verse 19, where the authors have used the terms *Nidhanamsa* (निधनांश) and *Lagnamsa* (लग्नांश).

लग्नेशे निधनांशस्थे लग्नांशे निर्धनेश्वरे ।
पापयुक्ते तदाजातः पञ्चाशद्वर्षजीवितः ॥

Meaning : "If the lord of the Lagna be posited inthe Navamsa Rasi owned by the 8th house, and the lord of the 8th house occupy the Navamsa Rasi owned by the Lagna and if they (both) be conjoined with malefic the person concerned will live for 50 years".

Of the above two texts *Horasara* being the earlier one, *Jatakadesamarga* must have adopted the verse from the earlier text.

Other references from standard astrological works:—

सप्तमेशे धनांशस्थे पुंश्चली कामिनी भवेत् ।
शनिशुक्रौ स्मरे यस्य पुनर्भूरङ्गना मता ॥

भावप्रकाश, V Chapter verse 75,

The wife is of loose character because lord of the 7th is in Navamsa Rasi which falls in the 2nd house, *i.e.*, 8th from its 7th.

भौमांशे भौमसंयुक्ते पुत्रांशे सोमनन्दने ।
राहुमन्दयुते लग्ने सर्पशापात्सुतक्षयः ॥

सन्तानदीपिका (Verse 12)

In *Devakeralam—Chandrakala Nadi*—Vol. II, Part II. (वृषभलग्ने

वित्तांष) pages 53 to 61 (Verses 3109 to 3186) the terms वित्तांशे, लग्नांशे, षष्ठांशे, व्ययांशे are used more than fifteen times *e.g.*

वित्तांशे वृषभे लग्ने पूर्वभागे प्रजायते ।
विप्रजन्मा सुखी नित्यं रुपवान् मतिमान् भवेत् ॥ (3108)

लग्ने वर्गोत्तमे चन्द्रे रन्ध्रे लग्नांशगे गुरौ ।
ग्रामाणीर्धनधान्यादि कीर्तिमान् पशुमान् भवेत् (3113)

मारकं लभते तत्र भ्रातृसौख्यं विनिर्दिशेत् ।
विपत्ताराधिपे केतौ व्ययांशे निर्धने स्थिते ॥ (3167)
Jatakaparijata, Chapter V, Verse No. 82.

लग्नेशे निधनांशस्थे मूढे षष्ठगतेऽथवा ।
क्षुद्बाधया च मरणं बन्धुहीने महीतले ॥

The first quarter of this verse 'लग्नेशे निधनांशस्थे' is interpreted incorrectly as – "When the lord of the Lagna occupies the 64th Navamsa from the Lagna..." by Mr. V. Subrahmanya Sastri in his edition (1932). Similarly काशी-संस्कृतग्रन्थमाला (No. 10) edition of *Jataka Parijata*, its commentator has also committed the same error. 'निधनांशस्थे' ....means "posited (a planet) in the Navamsa Rasi owned by the 8th house". The same quarter of the verse 'लग्नेशे निधनांशस्थे' has been correctly interpreted by Mr. V. Subrahmanya Sastri in the previously referred (Ch. VI, verse 24) and जातकदेशमार्ग (Ch. VI—verse 19).

The correct meaning of the above verse is as follows :

"When the lord of the Ascendant is posited in the Navamsa Rasi owned bythe 8th house, or is eclipsed by the rays of the Sun, or is in the 6th house, *the native will die* of starvation or on the bare ground with no blood relations by his side." Let us illustrate this principle.

Chart I is of Mrs. Indira Gandhi born on 19th November 1917, at 11h. 11m. p.m. (IST) at Allahabad (Ref. p. 62 January 1985 A.M.)

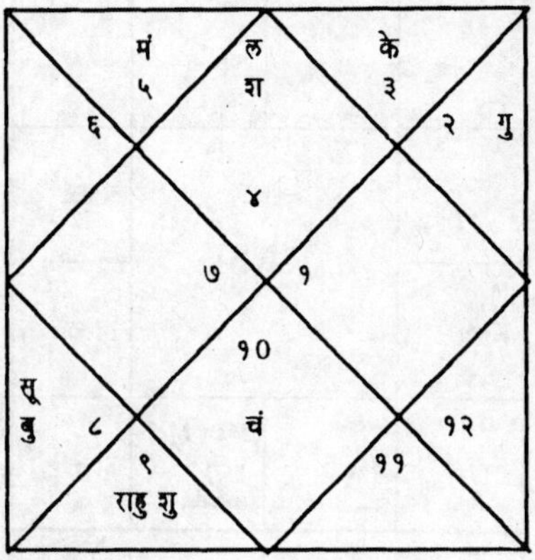

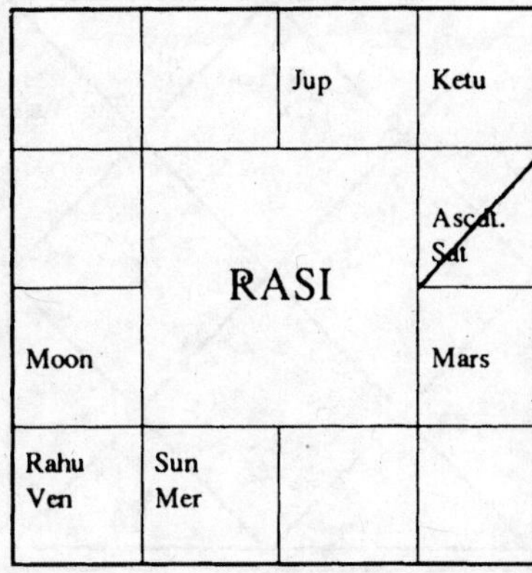

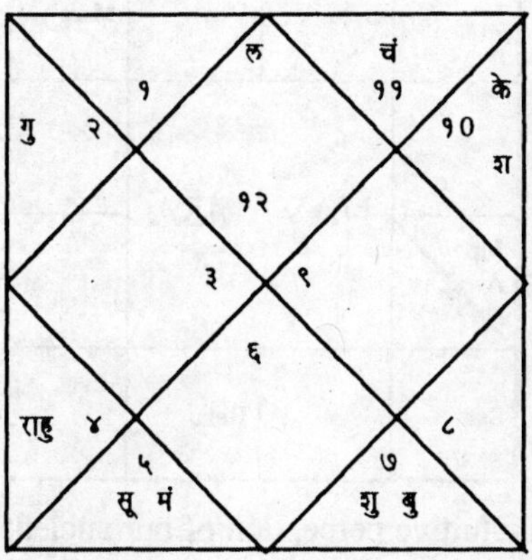

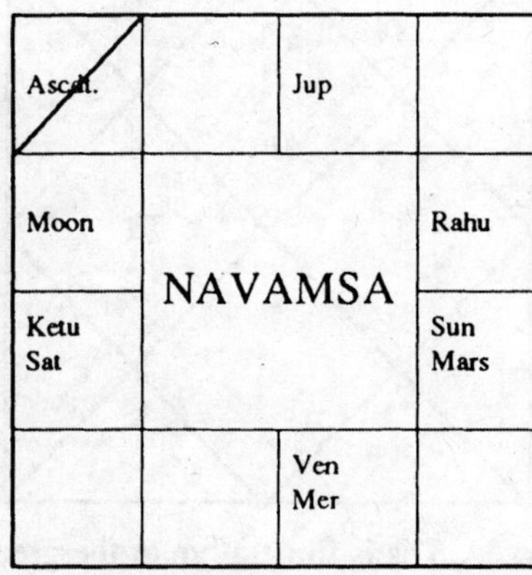

Mrs. Indira Gandhi's Ascendant is Cancer and its lord Moon is in sign Capricorn and in Navamsa Aquarius, which falls in the 8th house in the Rasi chart, hence the Moon is *Nidhamamsashashtah*. She breathed her last on 31-10-1984, on the ground with no blood relations by her side. (मरणं बन्धुहीने महीतले)

Chart 2 is of Mahatma Gandhi (Ref. *Notable Horoscopes*, P. 226) born on 2-10-1869 at 7h. 45m. a.m. (LMT) at Porbandar.

Mahatma Gandhi's Ascendant is Libra and its lord Venus is in sign Libra and in Navamsa Taurus, whch falls in the 8th house in Rasi chart and hence *Nidhanamsashashtah*. Note, in this case, lord of the Ascendant Venus is in her own sign Libra and own Navamsa Taurus. He breathed his last on 30-1-1948 on the ground with no blood relations by his side. (मरणं बन्धुहीने महीतले)

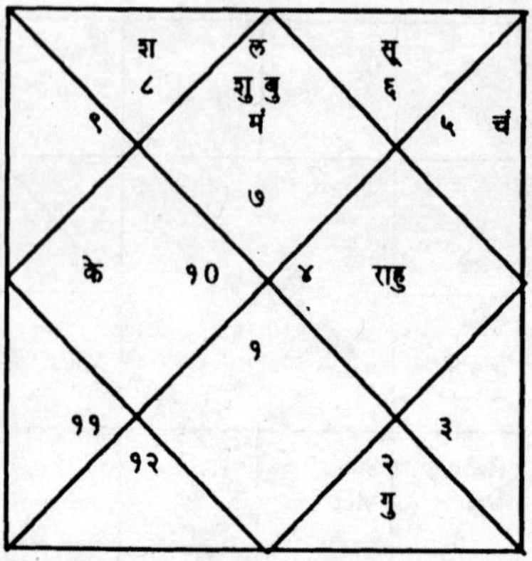

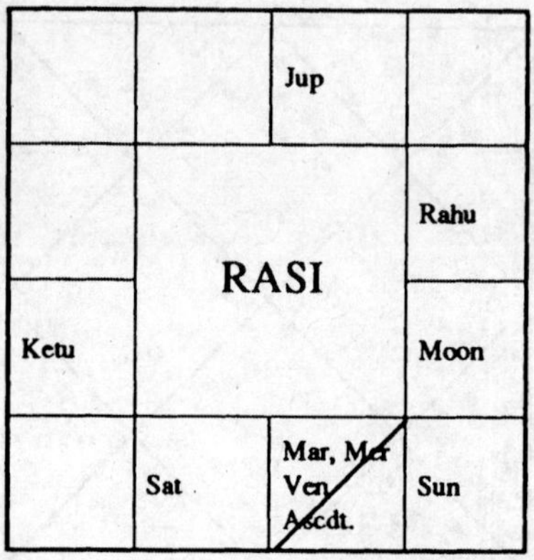

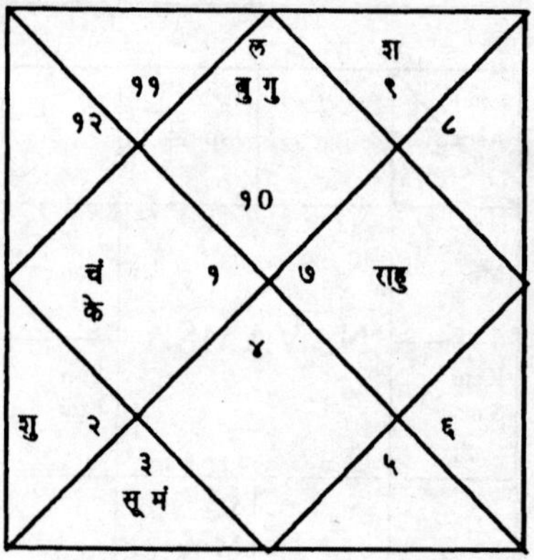

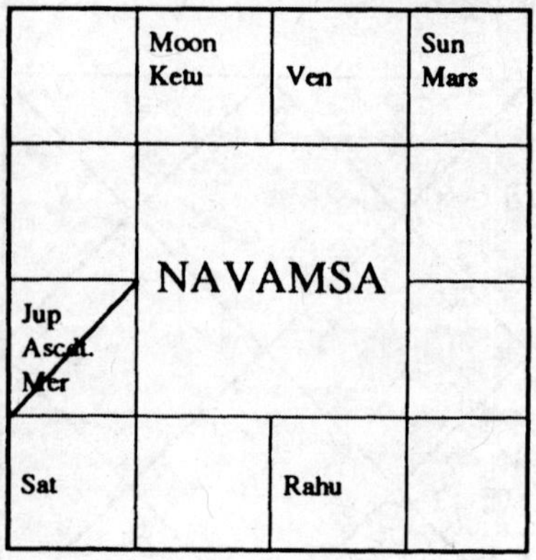

Ths is illustrative of the great intuitive perception of our ancient seers who have authored such invaluable works which throw a flood of light on an important aspect of a person's life.

Fruitful Years of Life :

While studying Nadi literature it is observed that in a particular year of life a favourable or unfavourable event will take place. *Horasara's* author (Prithuyasas) has mentioned one such method, to find the years of life in which good or bad events happen in Chapter XVII, verses 88 1/2 to 91 1/2.

ज्ञेया मन्दादि लग्नान्तनवांशकयुतिर्बुधैः । 89
तद्योगसदृशे वर्षे चायुधक्लेशमादिशेत् ।

This and the subsequent two verses have been incorrectly interpreted in Bangalore (1) and Delhi (2) editions of this book :

(1) Note the Navamsa occupied by Saturn and that of the Lagna.

Find the number of Navamsas revealed by this sum. In the year indicated by this figure, one may expect hurt or hit through a missile or weapon".

(2) "Add the Navamsas of Saturn and Ascendant. The year represented by this figure will cause hurt by weapon."

The correct meaning is :

"Learned men should reckon the number of Navamsas from the Navamsa occupied by Saturn upto the Navamsa occupied by the Ascendant, both inclusive. Injury or wound through a weapon or missile should be feared in the year indicated by that total sum of Navamsas".

राहुभौमादि लग्नान्तमंशयोगसभाब्दके ।90।
विपदस्त्रक्षतायासदु:खादीनि समादिशेत् ।।

Similarly, reckon the number of Navamsas from the one occupied by Rahu upto the Navamsa occupied by the Ascendant, and also from Mars to the Ascendant. In the years indicated by the respective figures, the native concerned meets with some calamity, hit by a weapon, wound, fatigue, sorrow and the like.

शुभग्रहादि लग्नान्तमंशयोगसमाब्दके । 91।
पुत्रवित्तसुखादीनि लभते नात्र संशयः ।

In a similar way, reckon the number of Navamsas from the benefic planets to the Ascendant, during the years, indicated by these sums of Navamsas, the native will be blessed with progeny, wealth, happiness and the like without doubt.

Chart 3 is an example to illustrate these principles. Born on, 31-12-1915 at 19h. 44m. at Ahmedabad

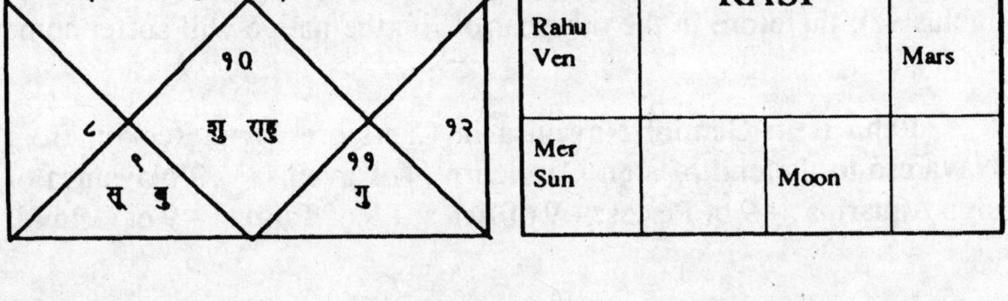

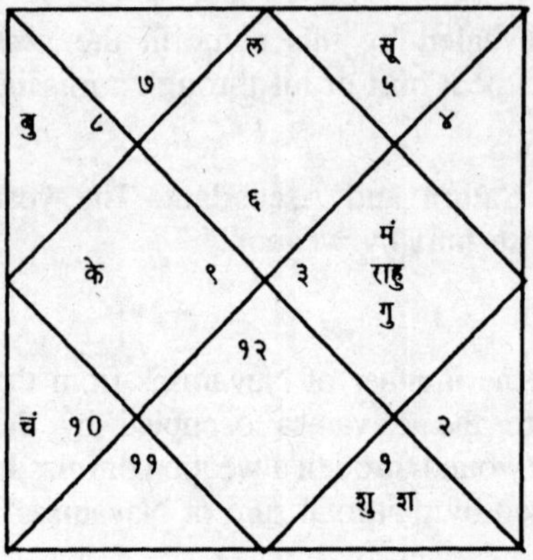

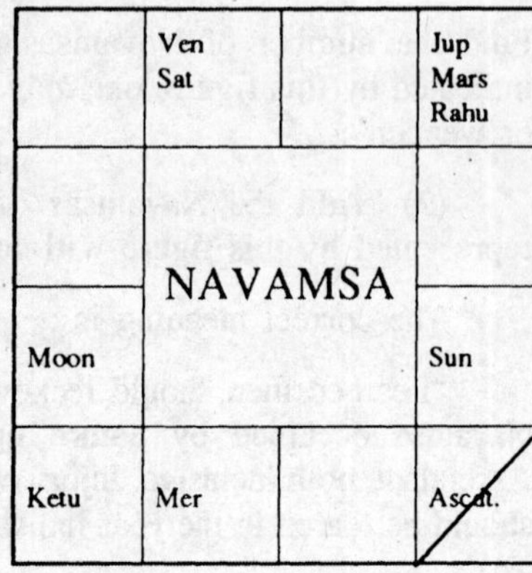

For the sake of convenience, the above square type horoscopes have been shown alongside in a composite circular chart. The outer circle of the disc indicates Navamsas : the third inner circle shows Nakshatras (constellations) and the fifth inner circle indicates signs. Signs and Navamsas are marked numerically as Aries (1), Taurus (2), Gemini (3), Cancer (4), ... Pisces (12) in anticlock-wise direction.

In the example horoscope the Ascendant is in Cancer sign and Virgo Navamsa (3^s 8° 53') and this is indicated by an arrow in the circular chart at its proper place. Similarly, natal positions of all the seven planets and Rahu and Ketu are marked with arrows in their respective Navamsas and signs as shown in the circular chart. This circular diagram with all 108 Navamsas marked along the circumference will be found very useful and convenient for making all kinds of prognositications, including those of the 64th Navamsa. One can immediately find sign, Nakshatra, its pada and Navamsa sign positions occupied by a planet in no time.

Let us apply the principle embodied in the above verses to the example horoscope.

Saturn : Reckon from the Navamsa occupied by Saturn, *i.e.*, Aries Navamsa to the end of the sign Gemini which comes to 3 Navamsas. The Ascendant is in Virgo Navamsa in sign Cencer, third from the beginning of Cancer which also comes to 3; so 3 + 3 = 6 (both inclusive); therefore in the 6th year of life the native will suffer some injury etc.

Rahu is in Gemini Navamsa in Capricorn Sign. Reckon from Navamsa to the end of sign Capricorn (4) Navamsa + 9 Navamsa of sign Aquarius : + 9 of Pisces; + 9 of Aries; + 9 of Taurus; + 9 of Gemini;

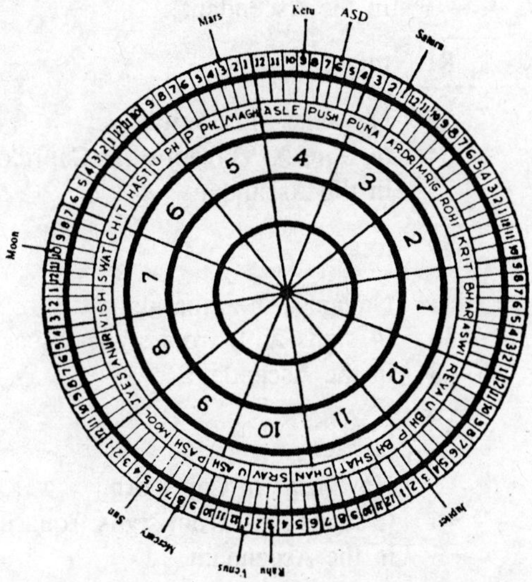

+ 3 Navamsas in Cancer (The Ascendant) = total 52 Navamsas. In the 52nd year the native will have calmity, wound etc. (The native of this chart suffered demotion in service in the 52nd year of life)

Mars in Gemini Navamsa in sign Leo ;

	7	Navamsa to the end of sign Leo;
	+ 90	(10 signs X 9) from signs Virgo to Gemini;
	+ 3	in the Ascendant
	100	Total i.e., in the 100th year, calamity wound, etc.
The Sun =	5	Navamsas in Sagittarius;
	+ 54	(6 signs X 9) from Capricorn to Gemini signs;
	+ 3	in the Ascendant
	62	total, i.e., in the 62nd year

some unfavourable result.

The Moon =	6	Navamsas in Libra
	+ 72	(8 signs X 9) from signs Scorpio to Gemini;
	+ 3	in the Ascendant
	81	total
Mercury =	2	Navamsas in Sagittarius;
	+ 54	(6 signs X 9) from signs Capricorn to Gemini;
	3	in the Ascandant
	59	total
Jupiter =	1	Navamsa in Aquarius
	+ 36	(4 signs X 9) from signs Pisces to Gemini;
	+ 3	in the Ascendant
	40	total
Venus =	6	Navamsas in Capricorn;
	+ 45	(5 signs X 9) from signs Aquarius to Gemini;
	+ 3	in the Ascendant
	54	total

In the years 81st, 59th, 40th and 54th the native will have progeny (grand children), wealth, happiness, notable good events and the like. (The native of this chart published a book on Ashtakavarga in 40th year.)

This confirms that there exists some such unique method of prognostication, independent of transit of planets or Dasas. This system will prove the veracity of the correctness of Navamsa chart. For every addition in a Navamsa of the birth Ascendant (*i.e.*, nearly 13m. 20s. of time) there should be an addition of one year in time of occurrence of the events for each planet. It has been the experience of the author that this technique of timing events has largely come true in a number of cases.

The text suggests reckoning of the Navamsas from each planet to the Ascendant. It is for the research-oriented scholars to experiment and decide as to why one should not also reckon from the Navamsa occupied by the Ascendant to the Navamsas occupied by each planet.

Navamsa in its varied application is a fertile field for research and the author hopes this article would rouse the intelligent interest of scholars on the subject.

3

Eventful Years in One's Life–I

Every one of us undergoes good and bad events in our life. There are several methods of prognostication of good and bad events and one such commonly used method is based on Vimshottari Dasas and Antardasas. The other method is based on transits of major planets using Samudayashtakavarga chart. There is one more simple method to find good and bad events culled from classics like *Janmapradipa, Yavanjataka, Hora-Ratna* and *Hillajataka* which is essentially based on the natal positions of planets in various signs and houses.

In the present write-up the scribe will deal with method of gleaning years of good and bad events in one's life based entirely on Navamsa positions of 9 planets and the Ascendant.

There are two categories of eventful years, *viz.*, fixed and variable ones as described in the classics.

(A) Fixed Years

According to *Horasara* Chap. XXX, the author states that risk; trouble; sickness; disease; danger, unfavourable or doubtful periods; or death will take place in certain fixed years of life, if the native's Ascendant falls in a particular Navamsa :

(1) In Aries Navamsa-12th; 25th; 50th; or 65 year of life;

(2) In Taurus Navamsa-= 10th; 22nd; 32nd; or 72nd year of life;

(3) In Gemini Navamsa- 16th,; 24th; 34th; 40th; or 63rd year of life;

(4) In Cancer Navamsa- 8th; 18th; 21st; 22nd; 72nd or 80th year of life;

(5) In Leo Navamsa- 10th; 20th; 30th; 60th; or 82nd year of life;

(6) In Virgo Navamsa- 20th; 50th; or 60th year of life;

(The native, in example Horoasope, born in Virgo Navamsa had survived from drowning in 20th year; had major cancer operation in 50th year; and had urinary troubles in 60th year).

(7) In Libra Navamsa- 3rd; 23rd; 27th; 38th; 54th; or 76th year of life;

(8) In Scorpio Navamsa- 13th; 18th; 23rd; 28th; 55th; or 70th year of life;

(9) In Sagittarius Navamsa- 4th; 9th; 16th; 36th; 44th; or 72nd year of life;

(10) In Capricorn Navamsa- 19th; 27th; 34th; 49th; 54th; or 68th year of life;

(11) In Aquarius Navamsa- 7th; 14th; 20th; 28th; 32nd or 61st year of life;

(12) In Pisces Navamsa- 10th; 12th; 21st; 26th; 52nd; or 61st year of life;

The 8th; 32nd and 59th years of life are generally periods of sorrow and anxiety to all.

If the rising Navamsa is Vargottama, the favourable effects get enhanced and unfavourable effects get reduced.

When the sub-period of an untoward planet is ruling during the above particular year and the sign-owned or occupied by the planet in question is afflicted, damage to life of the native is indicated or some major ailments are indicated.

(B) Effects of birth for those born in various Navamsas occupied by the Moon

According to *Lagna Chandrika* one born when the Moon is in one of the 12 Navamsas *e.g.*, Aries; Taurus; Gemini; ....upto Pisces; will meet with death (or have severe sufferings), in 8th; 9th; 24th; 22nd; 5th; 1st; 4th; 2nd; 20th; 38th; 21st and 10th year respectively (or in cycles of 12 wherever applicable).

Suppose native is born when the Moon is in Virgo Navamsa, his death is likely to take place in one of the following years-Ist; (1+12) 13th; (1+24) 25th; 37th; 49th; 61st; 73rd or 85th year, etc.

(C) Variable years

According to *Horasara* learned men should reckon the number of Navamsas from the Navamsa occupied by Saturn upto the Navamsa occupied by the Ascendant, both inclusive. Injury or wound through a weapon or missile should be feared in the year indicated by that total sum of Navamsas.

Similarly, reckon the numberof Navamsas from the one occupied by Rahu upto the Navamsa occupied by the Ascendant and also from Mars to the Ascendant. In the years indicated by the respective figures, the native concerned meets with some calamity, hit by a weapon, wound, fatigue, sorrow and the like.

In a like manner, reckon the number of Navamsas from benefic planets to the Ascendant, during the years indicated by these sums of Navamsas the native will be blessed with progeny, wealth, happiness and the like without doubt.

Example Horoscope

The horoscope of this scribe is as follows :

born 31-12-1915, at 7-44 p.m. (IST) at 23° 02' N, 72° 39' E.

Rasi : The Sun 8s- 16° 10'; The Moon 6s 12° 13'; Mars 4s 7° 9'

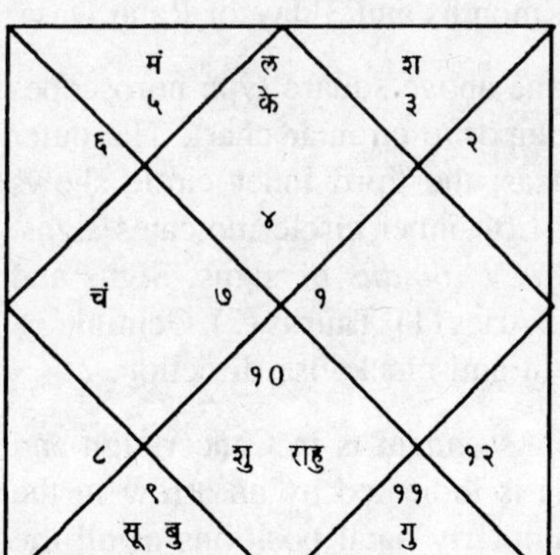

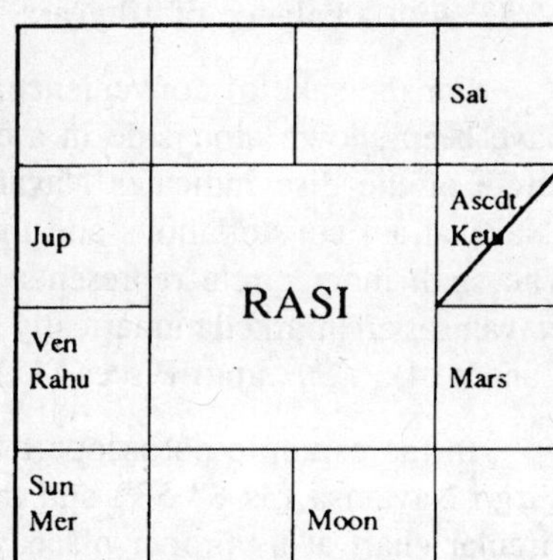

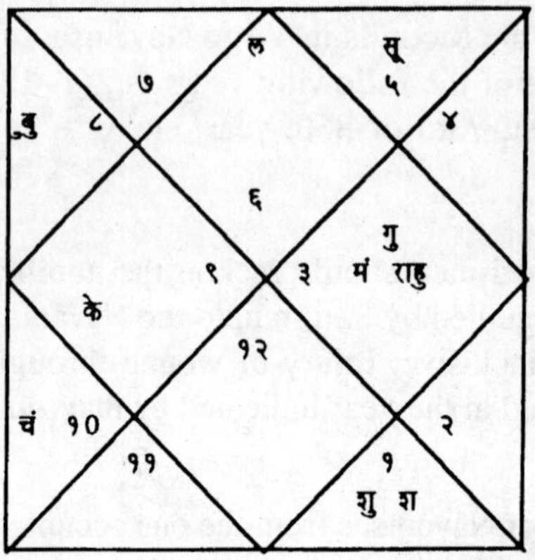

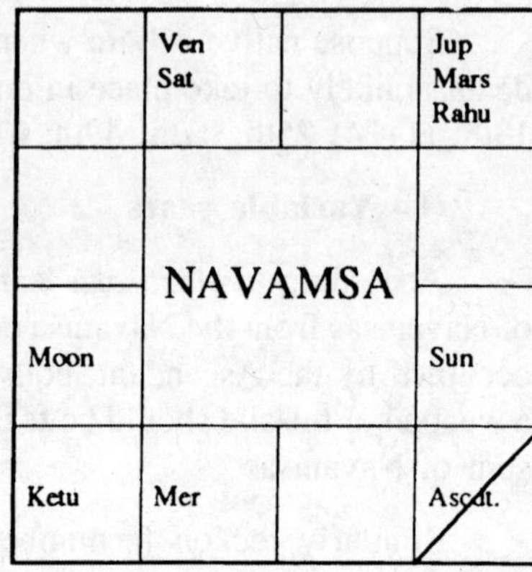

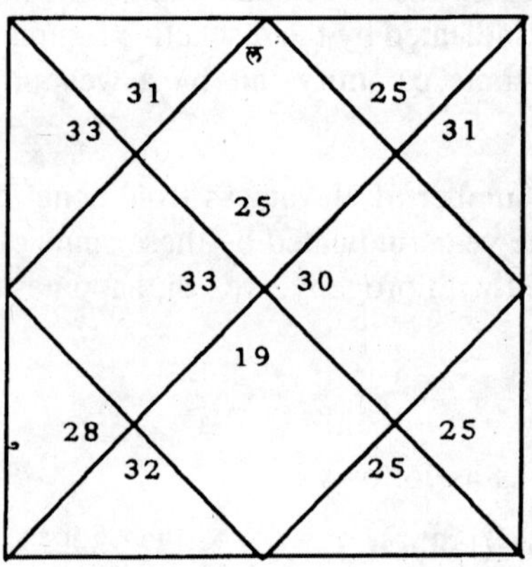

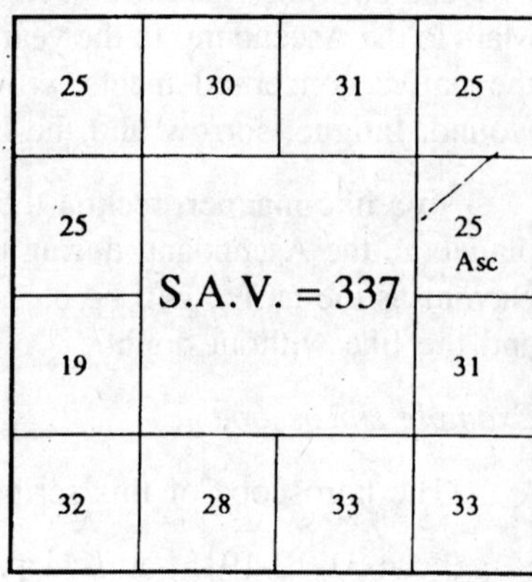

Mercury 8s 25° 13'; Jupiter 10s 29° 29'; Venus 9s 13° 14'; Saturn 2s 20° 42' (R), Rahu 9s 17° 6'; Ketu 3s 17° 6' and the Ascendant 3s 8° 53' with a balance of 10 years, 6 months and 3 daysof Rahu Dasa.

For the sake of convenience, the above square type horoscopes have been shown alongside in a composite circular chart. The outer circle of the disc indicates Navamsas; the third inner circle shows (Nakshatras) constellations and the fifth inner circle indicates signs. The sixth inner circle represents S.A.V. *bindus* of signs, Signs and Navamsas are marked numerically as Aries (1), Taurus (2), Gemini (3), Cancer (4),...........upto Pisces (12) in anti-clockwise direction.

In the example horoscope the Ascendant is in Cancer sign and Virgo Navamsa (3s 8° 53') and this is indicated by an arrow in the circular chart at its proper place. Similarly natal positions of all the seven planets and Rahu and Ketu are marked with arrows in their respective Navamsas and signs as shown in the circular chart. This

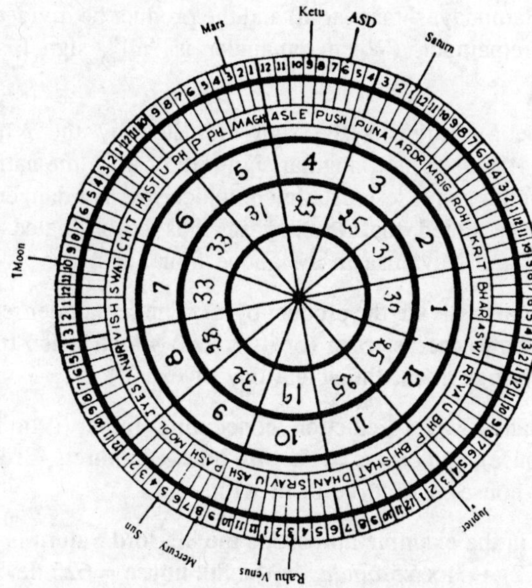

circular diagram with all 108 Navamsas marked along the circumference will be found very useful and convenient for making all kinds of prognostications. One can immediately find sign with S.A.V. *bindus*, Nakshatra, its pada, Navamsa sign position occupied by a planet in no time from the above chart.

Saturn in Aries Navamsa to the end of the sign Gemini 3 Navamsa; Ascendant in Virgo Navamsa in sign Cencer 3 Navamsa; 3 + 3 = 6th year for Saturn.

Rahu	4 + (9 x 5) + 3	=	52	Navamsas	*i.e.,*	52nd year;
Mars	7 + (9 x 10) + 3	=	100	Navamsas	*i.e.,*	100th year;
Sun	5 + (9 x 6) + 3	=	62	Navamsas	*i.e.,*	62nd year;
Moon	6 + (9 x 8) + 3	=	81	Navamsas	*i.e.,*	81st year;
Merc.	2 + (9 x 6) + 3	=	59	Navamsas	*i.e.,*	59th year;
Jupiter	1 + (9 x 4) + 3	=	40	Navamsas	*i.e.,*	40th year;
Venus	6 + (9 x 5) + 3	=	54	Navamsas	*i.e.,*	54th year;

The text suggests reckoning of the Navamsas from each planet to the Ascendant. It is for the consideration of research-minded astrologers to check up and reckon from the Navamsa occupied by the Ascendant to the Navamsa occupied by each planet.

According to *Horasara* the number of the Navamsa reckoned

from the beginning of Aries (zodiac) to the Navamsa occupied by the lord of the 8th house, be multiplied by the *number of bindus in the 8th house* (in Samudayashtakavarga) and the product be divided by 12 and take the remainder. (When remainder is "nil", sign Pisces be taken).

When the Sun transits the sign indicated by the remainder (counted from Aries) or its triangular sign (5th or 9th), the native will have in that month some serious ailment which involve danger to life also. (It may be noted that Pruthuyasas has co-ordinated use of Ashtakagvarga and Navamsa in the above four lines)

(It is logical to divide the product by 27. The remainder reckoned from Aswini shows the asterism (or its trines) which when transited by the Moon brings about the actual day of event.)

In the same way, prediction concerning father (9th house); mother (4th house); and others (wife - 7th house; brethren - 3rd house; children - 5th house) should be dealt with.

For self, in the example horoscope the 8th lord Saturn is in 25th Navamsa (9 x 2) + 7) x 25 *bindus* in the 8th house = 625 devided by 12 leaves "I" remainder *i.e.*, Aries, Leo or Sagittarius.

For father - the 8th house from the 9th house is the 4th house *i.e.*, Libra-lord Venus is in the 85th Navamsa (9 x 9 + 4) x 33 *bindus* in the 4th house = 2805 devided 12 leaves 9 remainder *i.e.*, Sagittarius, Aries or Leo.

For mother - the 8th house from the 4th house is the 11th house *i.e.*, Taurus, Lord Venus is in the 85th Navasmsa x 31 *bindus* in 11th house = 2635 devided by 12 leaves 7 remainder *i.e.*, Libra, Aquarius or Gemini.

For wife - the 8th house from the 7th house is the 2nd house - Leo-lord, the Sun is in the 77th Navamsa (9 x 8 + 5) x 31 *bindus* in the 2nd house = 2387 devided by 12 leaves 11 remainder *i.e.*, Aquarius, Gemini or Libra.

The scribe for the first time in life came across a hososcope, in which, planetary positions in terms of numerical Navamsas, beginning from Aries Navamsa of Aries sign, were given under the columns of planetary positions.

This made him think deeply over the subject and the result is this article.

In example horoscope

The Sun 8s 16° 10'; 8 x 9 + 5 = 77th Navamsa;

The Moon 6s 12° 13'; 6 x 9 + 4 = 58th Navamsa;

In the same way positions of other planets will be :

Mars	in	39th	Navamsa;
Mercury	in	80th	Navamsa;
Jupiter	in	99th	Navamsa;
Venus	in	85th	Navamsa;
Saturn	in	25th	Navamsa;
Rahu	in	87th	Navamsa;
Ketu	in	33rd	Navamsa;

and the Ascendant in the 30th Navamsa.

In the years indicated by the planets' positons, in terms of Navamsas, some good or bad events do take place.

Note in the year 58th (the Moon from Aries sign 58; Rahu from the Ascendant 58) the native had two calamities, *viz.*, his wife suffered from a cholera attack, and the only son had a snake-bite. By God's grace both survived. Both events took place in native's 58th year and that too within 10 days.

Research minded astrologers may try out this method and draw their own conclusions.

In the example horoscope Navamsa occupied by the lord of the 8th house is Aries Navamsa in Gemini sign *i.e.,* 9 x 2 + 7 = 25 Navamsas from Aries sign. Death of the native will occur in 25th year or in cycles of 12, whcih will be 37th, 49th, 61st, 73rd or 85th etc.

It will thus be seen that the Navamsa chart has many potential uses for delineating results. It will be more useful as compared to the Rasi chart.

This article will motivate young research-minded astrologers to do more research on Navamsa chart.

4

Eventful Years in One's Life—II

Since his article "Searchlight on Navamsa" (Chapter-2) mentioning "Fruitful Years in Life" based on one Navamsa, equal to one year of life (1 Navamsa = 1 year), the scribe had continued further research on Navamsa which resulted in the full-fledged article "Eventful Year in One's Life" (Chapter-3), During the current year the scribe had vigorously pursued further research on Navamsa during which he had come across more such methods of arriving at certain eventful years in one's life. The result is the present article.

Till now, five different methods of reckoning the number of Navamsa have been found out.

The First Method : Reckon the number of Navamsas from the Navamsa occupied by various planets (including Rahu), upto the Navamsa occupied by the Ascendant, both inclusive. This method has been fully discussed in the above referred two articles.

(*Horasara*, Chap. XVII, vs. 88 1/2 and 91 1/2).

Example Horoscope

The horoscopeof this scribe is as follows :

Born 31-12-1915 at 7.44 p.m. (IST) at 23° 2' N, 72° 39' E.

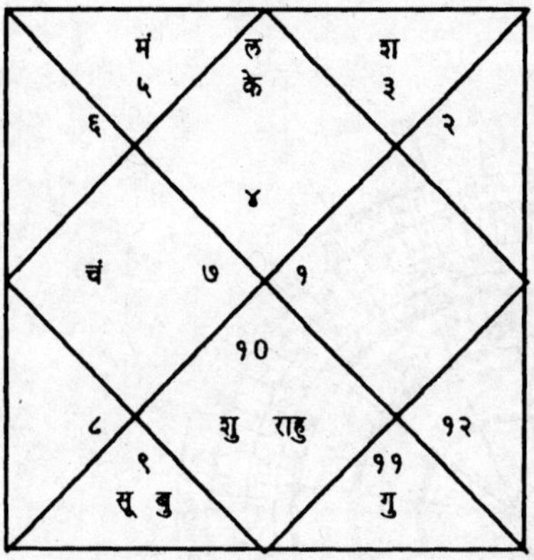

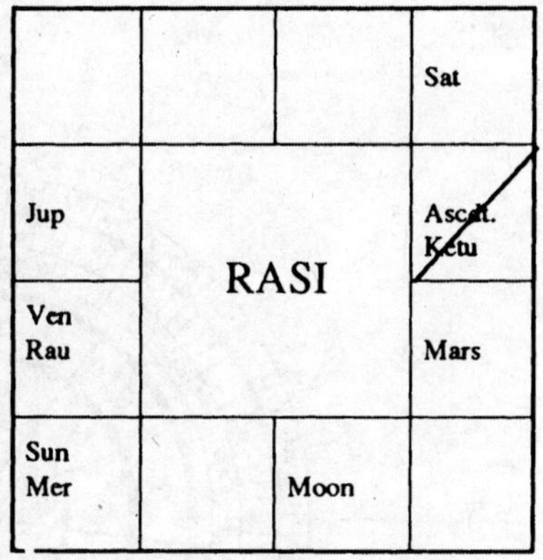

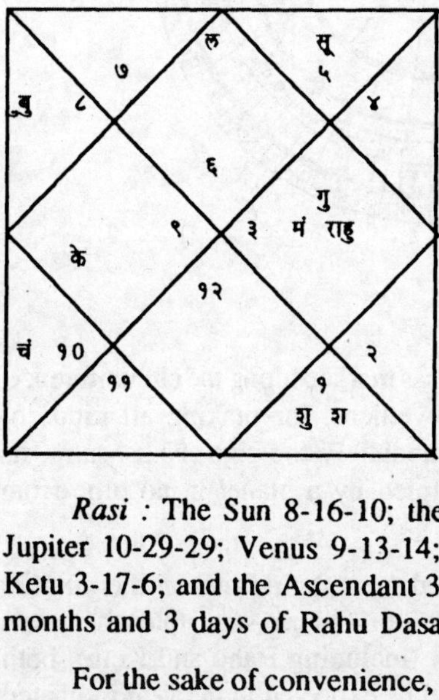

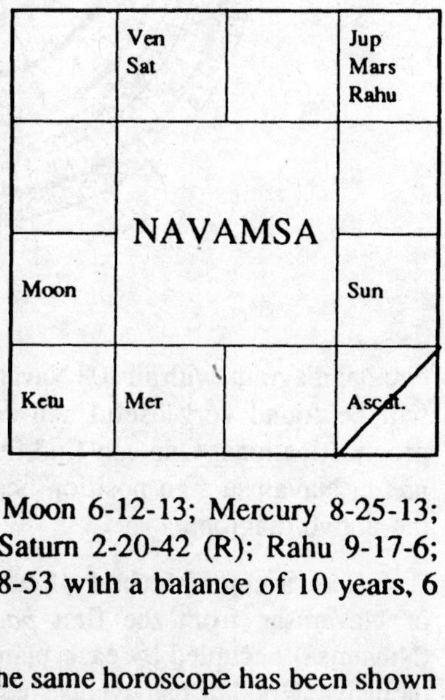

Rasi : The Sun 8-16-10; the Moon 6-12-13; Mercury 8-25-13; Jupiter 10-29-29; Venus 9-13-14; Saturn 2-20-42 (R); Rahu 9-17-6; Ketu 3-17-6; and the Ascendant 3-8-53 with a balance of 10 years, 6 months and 3 days of Rahu Dasa.

For the sake of convenience, the same horoscope has been shown also in a composite circular chart. The outer circle of the disc indicates Navamsas, the third inner circle shows constellations (Nakshatras) and the fifth inner circle indicates signs. Signs and Navamsas are marked numerically as Aries (1), Taurus (2), Gemini (3), Cancer (4), upto Pisces (12) in anticlock-wise direction.

In the example hosorcope the Ascendant is in Cancer sign and Virgo Navamsa (3° 8' 53') and this is indicated by an arrow in the circular chart at the proper place. Similarly natal positions of all the seven planets and Rahu and Ketu are marked with arrows in their respective Navamsas and signs as shown in the circular chart. This

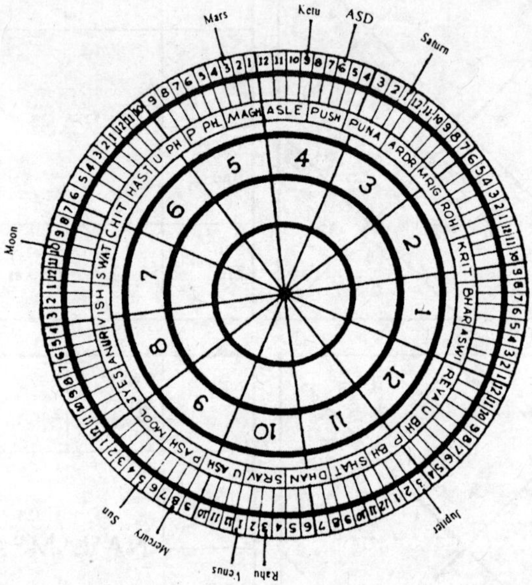

circular diagram, with all 108 Navamsas marked along the circumference, will be found very useful and convenient, for making all kinds of prognostications. One can find immediately the sign, Nakshsatra, its *pada.*, Navamsa sign position occupied by a planet in no time from the above diagram.

The Second Method : Learned men should reckon the number of Navamsas from the first *pada* of Aswini star upto the *pada* (Navamsa) occupied by each planet (including Rahu and Ketu), both inclusive. Good or bad events should be expected in the year indicated by the benefic or malefic planet. (A partial mention of this method is made in *Horasara* XVII, vs 91 1/2 to 93 1/2).

Let us look into the chart of Dr. B.V. Raman as shown in Budha Nadi (Ref. : My Early Experiences in Astrology - XXVII, A.M., April 1989 issue-pages 313 to 316.)

The study of this article gave me a great pleasure to go deep into the subject, because it deals with some secrets of Budha Nadi. The second method as explained earlier has been fully corroborated by Dr. Raman's article.

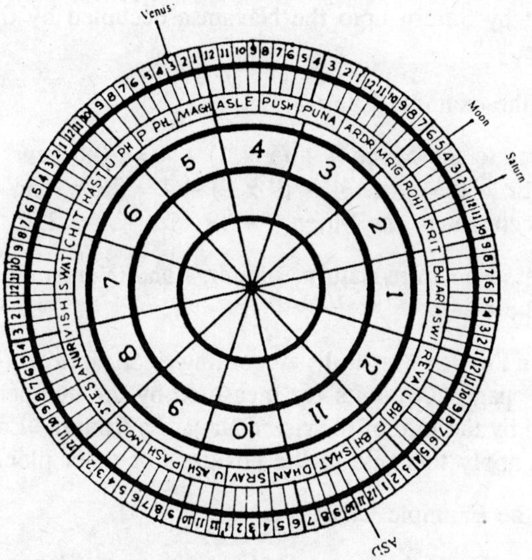

In the circular chart, the Ascendant is in the 95th *pada* from Aries 1st *pada;* so also the Moon is in the 17th *pada* and Venus in the 39th *pada.*

"The Nadi author further suggests that a planet in the 84th *pada* from Saturn's position and 97th *pada* from the Moons' gives Balarishta.

"The mode of direction employed appears to be based on the transits of major planets in certain *padas* (Navamsas) as reckoned from the *padas* in which the planets and the Lagna are situated."

To cite one more example let us look into the chart of our late prime minister Mrs. Indira Gandhi Mercury is 7-13º-15 *i.e.*, in the 3nd *pada* of Anuradha star (Libra Navamsa in Scorpio sign) which is the 67th *pada* from Aswini's 1st *pada.* Date of birth is 19-11-1917 and date of demise is 31-10-1984. She breathed her lasst in the 67th year. May it be, because Mercury is the lord of the 12th house (exit from the world) and lord of the 3rd house *i.e.*, the 8th from the 8th house (house of death)?

The Third Method : Chandrakala Nadi, Part II, Vol. II, page 247, verse 4894—

Sanou janmamsaparyantam pitrusoukhyam na vidyate

Meaning : Reckon the number of Navamsas from the Navamsa occupied by Saturn upto the Navamsa occupied by the Moon, both inclusive.

In the example Chart No. 1;

Mars to the Moon 7 + (9 x 1) + 4 = 20th year
Ketu to the Moon 4 + (9 x 2) + 4 = 26th year
Ascendant to the Moon 7 + (9 x 2) + 4 = 29th year

and so on from Saturn, Jupiter, Rahu, Venus, Mercury and the Sun to the Moon.

The Fourth Method : According to *Sanketa Nidhi,* Chap. VIII, verse 61, page 208, units are measured by the number of Navamsas traversed by the lord of the rising Navamsa from the Lagna Navamsa. One can apply this rule to the positions of other planets.

In the Example Chart No. 1;

Note : From the Lagna in Virgo Navamsa (Cancer sign), its lord Mercury is in Scorpio Navamsa in Sagittarius sign) i.e., from the Lagna to the end of sign 7 + (9 x 4) + 8 = 51st year of life. Ketu to end of sign 4 + (9 x 6) + 9 = 67th year;

Mars to end of sign 7 + (9 x 3) + 8 = 42nd year;
The Moon to end of sign 6 + (9 x 7) + 7 = 76th year;
The Sun to end of sign 1 or 109 because the Sun is in his own Navamsa.
Mercury to end of sign 2 + (9 x 7) + 3 = 68th year;
Venus to end of sign 6 + (9 x 6) + 3 = 63rd year;
Rahu to end of sign 4 + (9 x 10) + 8 = 102nd year;
Jupiter to end of sign 1 + (9 x 9) + 8 = 90th year;
Saturn to end of sign 3 + (9 x 1) + 3 = 15th year.

The Fifth Method : *Prasna Marga* Part I, Chap. X, verse 50, page 325., *Lagnamsakat prabhruti kashtatamo navamsa* second half of 1st line meaning "The number of Navamsa from the Navamsa of the Ascendant upto the Navamsas occupied by the most evil planets *viz.,* Mars, Saturn, Mandi, etc......" Similarly from the Ascendant to Navamsa upto the Navamsas occupied by the benefics. This method is complimentary to the first method.

In example chart No. 1 :

From the Lagna to Mars 7 + 3 = 10th year;

From the Lagna to the Sun 7 + (9 x 4) + 5 = 48th year;
From the Lagna to Saturn 7 + (9 x 10) + 7 = 104th year;

From the Lagna to a benefic planet Jupiter 7 + (9 x 6) + 9 = 70th year.

Similarly for the remainig planets.

Thus it will be clear from the above that reckoning from a starting point to the Navamsa occupied by a malefic planet will give unfavourable results, while upto the Navamsa, occupied by a benefic planet, will bear favourable results.

One more advantage of these methods is that we can cross-check and verify the correctness of Navamsa Ascendant.

The technique of timing events has by and large come true in a number of cases.

The scribe requests the scholars, pandits and advanced students of Asrology to send any literature in Sankrit or in any other language that may be available with them on Budha Nadi etc. to him for further study and research in this virgin field.

5

Pushkara Navamsa

Students of Hindu Astrology are now showing keen interest in the subject of Navamsa. Luckily some rare books like *Chandra Kala Nadi, Vidyamadhaviyam, Dhruva nadi* and *Prasna Marga* have given copious verses dealing with Navamsa which are very useful in delineation without narrowing the spectrum of prediction.

The late Mr. K.M. Kharegat of Bombay had repeatedly requested the students to take up the study of Navamsa seriously.

After reading some of my papers on Navamsa an astrologer friend wrote to me "Your paper is comprehensive, useful and splendid. The paper would have been complete had you touched Pushkaramsa which is important in fixing the Muhurta of any auspicious activity". This induced me to take up further studies when I came across Pushkara Navamsa in *Vidyamadhaviyam,* Part I, pages 30-31, wherein this Navamsas is defined. During the last 44 years I have come across it only once in *Vidyamadhaviyam* (Sarvasiddhih). No standard book has thrown any light on Pushkara Navamsa.

Pushkaramsa has two meanings, depending on the context;

(1) Pushkaramsa is a particular degree (one only) in each of the twelve signs. It is also known as Pushkarabhaga, which is used for auspicious effects when Muhurta, a birth or any other such point is considered. According to *Muhurta Darpana.*

एकविंशो मनुश्चैव जनाश्च मुनयः क्रमात् ।
मेषादिमीनपर्यन्तं पुष्करांशाः प्रकीर्तिताः ॥

meaning "The degrees 21°, 14°, 24°, 7°, 21°, 14°, 24°, 7°, 21°, 14°, 24° and 7° in Mesha and the following signs respectively are called Pushkaramsas (or Pushkarabhaga)". They are useful for fixing Pushkara Muhurta for auspicious activities in general. The same Pushkara degrees are also mentioned in *Vidyamadhaviyam, Kalamritam* and *Kalavidhanam.*

(2) Pushkaramsa also means Pushkara- Navamsa - a particular Navamsa (an arc of 3° 20' as opposed to 1°) in a sign which is very auspicious.

All Pushkaramsas (one particular degree) in the twelve signs fall in Pushkara navamsa which may be noted.

21° Mesha sign falls in Thula Navamsa; 14° in Vrishabha sign falls in Vrishabha Navamsa; 24° in Mithuna sign falls in Vrishabha Navamsa; and 7° in Kataka sign falls in Kanya Navamsa. (Similarly degrees of trine signs fall accorgingly).

Vidhyamadhaviyam Part I p. 30-31.

मेषसिंहचापेषु सप्तमनवमौ ।
वृषकन्यामृगेषु पञ्चंमतृतीयौ ।
मिथुनतुलाकुम्भेष्वष्टमषष्ठौ ।
कर्किकीटमीनेष्वाद्यतृतीयौ ।
एते पुष्करसंज्ञा नवांशाः ॥

In Mesha-Simha and Dhanus signs the 7th Navamsa (Thula) and the 9th Navamsa (Dhanus); in Vrishabha, Kanya and Makara the 5th Navamsa (Vrishabha) and the 3rd Navamsa (Meena); in Mithuna, Thula and Kumbha signs, the 6th Navamsa (Meena) and the 8th Navamsa (Vrishabha); and in Kataka, Vrischika and Meena signs the 1st Navamsa (Kataka) and the 3rd Navamsa (Kanya) are called Pushkara Navamsas.

Rasis (signs)	**Navamsa**
Mesha - Simha	The 7th Navamsa - Thula *i.e.*, from 20° to 23° 20';
and Dhanus signs	The 9th Navamsa - Dhanus *i.e.*, from 26° 40' to 30°

Rasis (signs)	Navamsa
Vrishabha - Kanya	The 3rd Navamsa - Meena *i.e.*, from 6° 40' to 10°
and Makara signs	The 5th Navamsa - Vrishabha *i.e.*, from 13° 20' to 16° 40'
Mithuna - Thula	The 6th Navamsa Meena *i.e.*, from 16° 40' to 20° 00'
and Kumbha signs	The 8th Navamsa Vrishabha *i.e.*, from 23° 20' to 26° 40'
Kataka - Vrischika	The 1st Navamsa Kataka *i.e.*, from 00° to 3° 20'
and Meena signs	The 3rd Navamsa Kanya *i.e.*, from 6° 40' to 10° 00'.

In the composite circular chart, the outer circle of the disc indicates Navamsas, the third inner circle shows constellations (Nakshatras) and the fifth inner circle indicates, signs. Signs and Navamsas are marked numerically as (1) Mesha; (2) Vrishabha; (3) Mithuna; (4) Kataka; upto Meena (12) in anticlock-wise direction.

All the24 Pushakara Navamsas of the zodiac are marked with a dot below the respective Navamsa signs at proper places in the circular chart for convenience.

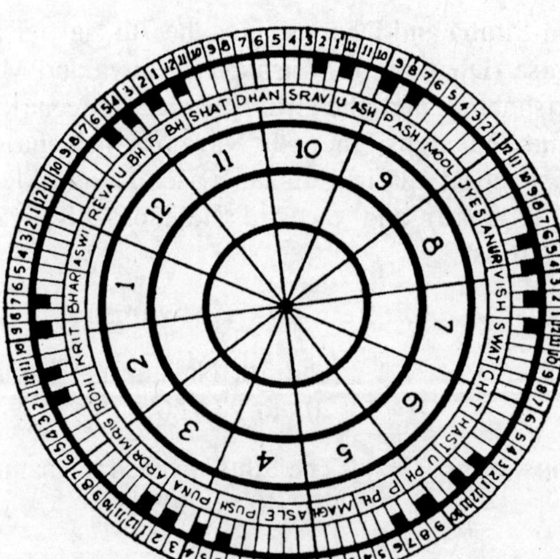

Each sign has two Pushkara Navamsas. There are in all, 12 x 2 = 24 Pushkara Navamsas in the zodiac. They are all *subha* Navamsas, owned by benefic planets and produce auspicious results in Muhurta, natal, *prasna* and other matters.

Out of the 24, three Pushkara Navamsas are Vargottama *viz.*, Vrishabha Navamsa (the fifth one) in Vrishabha sign, Kataka Navamsa (the first one) in Kataka sign and Dhanus Navamsa (the ninth one) in Dhanus sign. Any planet posited therein bestows very good results.

In standard texts Pushkara Navamsas are rarely used while they are freely used in *Chandra kala Nadi*.

1. *Jataka Parijata* Chap. VII, Verse 25—

वर्गोत्तमे वा यदि पुषकरांशे सारेन्दुदेवेन्दगुरौ नृपालः ।
कर्मस्थिते शोभनदृष्टियुक्ते संपुर्णगात्रे शशिनि क्षितिशः ॥

meaning, (1) When Jupiter in conjunction with Mars and the Moon occupies in Vargottama or Pushkara Navamsa, the person born is a king.

(ii) When the full-Moon aspected by benefic planets is posited in the 10th house, a ruler of land is born.

(It may be noted that Pushkara Navamsa is equated with Vargottama).

(b) *Chandrakala Nadi*Vol. II, Part I, page 11 Verse 77—

केन्द्रत्रिकोणगे जीवे पुष्करांशे सुभाग्यवान् ।
षष्ठाष्टमव्ययांशस्थे दुर्बलोपुत्रशोकवान् ॥

meaning, Jupiter in Kendra or Kona in Pushkara Navamsa makes a native very lucky (wealthy). But, if the sign of the Pushkara Navamsa occupied by Jupiter falls in the Rasi chart, in the 6th, the 8th or 12th house (Shastamse, Ashtamse, Vyayamse), the native (in addition to being wealthy) is emaciated (weak in health) and grieves on account of bereavement (death of a son).

(a) Suppose in a chart of Libra Ascendant, Jupiter is posited in the 10th house (in Cancer sign is exaltation) in Virgo Navamsa which falls in the 12th house in the Rasi chart, so both conditions are fulfilled.

(b) Suppose, in a chart of Libra Ascendant, Jupiter is in the 9th house (in Gemini sign) in Taurus Navamsa which is also Ashtamsa-Nidhanamsa.

(c) Suppose, in a chart of Libra Ascendant, Jupiter is in the Ascendant (Libra sign) in Pisces Navamsa which is also Shastamsa.

In all the above three examples, the native will get both good and bad results.

(3) *Chandrakala Nadi* Vol. II Part I p. 12 verse 79—

रव्यादयो ग्रहाः सर्वे पुष्करांशे प्रजायते ।
लक्ष्मीकटाक्षवान् भोगी धनिकः कीर्तिमान् सुखी ॥

meaning, if all the seven planets beginning with the Sun (Sun to Saturn) are posited in Pushkara Navamsa, the native born earns much wealth, enjoys all comforts of life, is very rich, famous (well-known) and happy.

Other verses for reference :

(4) *Chandrakala Nadi* Vol. I page 268 verse 2699—

पुष्करांशगते जीवे राज्येशे कुजवीक्षिते ।
चम्पकांशे प्रजातश्च यावदायुष्यं भाग्यवान् ॥

(5) *Chandrakalsa Nadi* Vol. I, page 272, V. 2737;

पुष्करांशगते जीवे रन्ध्रेशे स्वोच्चराशिगे ।
त्रैलोक्यांशे प्रजातः स यावदायुष्यभाग्यवान् ॥

(6) *Chandrakala Nadi* Vol. I P. 239 V. 2427;

पुष्करांशगते जीवे राज्येशे धनराशिगे ।
जीवे कुजयुते दृष्टे योगश्चामरसंज्ञकः ॥

Examples :

(1) N.T. Rama Rao (Ex-Chief Minister of Andhra) has his Moon, Jupiter and the rising Navamsa in Libra sign, Pisces Navamsa; also Ketu, the Sun and Mercury are in Pushkara Navamsa. The Sun and Mercury are also Vargottama. In all five planets and the rising Navamsa are in Pushkara Navamsa. (It may be noted that rising Navamsa sign falls in Rasi chart in the 6th house — Shastamsa)

(2) Amitabh Bachhan has Jupiter in Cancer sign and Cancer Navamsa, and Venus in Virgo sign in Taurus Navamsa—two planets in Pushkara Navamsa.

(3) K.M. Kharegat has his Sun in Cancer sign, Cancer Navamsa; and Ketu in Leo sign, Libra Navamsa.

(4) Our Prime Minister V.P. Singh has Jupiter in Cancer sign, Cancer Navamsa (Vargottama) and Saturn in Sagittarius sign, Sagittsarius Navamsa (Vargottama) - both planets in Pushkara Navamsa also.

(5) In the scribe's chart the Ascendant falls in Cancer sign, Virgo Navamsa (Pushkara Navamsa)

I have observed that natives having their rising Navamsas (*Uditha Navamsa*) falling either in Vargottama or in Purhkara Navamsa are outstanding in their careers.

I fervently hope that this article will prove useful to all ardentstudents of sidereal Astrology.

6

Navamsa and Transit of Planets

Kerala scholars have contributed many valuable treatises to Hindu Astrology. Amongst them, the most outstanding and unique one is *Chandrakala Nadi* (देच केरलम्) introducing many rare concepts. One such technique is *Navamsa transit* of planets. Secrets of Navamsa transits are hidden in *Nadi granthas.*

Transit is a very important and reliable tool in timing events in the life of an individual. Navamsa transit is a transit of a heavenly body through the zodiacal arc of 3° 20' known as Navamsa or quarter (*pada*), mainly of slow-moving planets such as Saturn, Jupiter, Rahu, Ketu.

In the scribe's earlier articles transit results through the Navamsa with "Use of the 64th Navamsa in Prognostication" (Chapter-I) and Navamsas occupied by natal planets in the "Nadi Principles Behind Saturn's Transit" (Chapter-I!) have

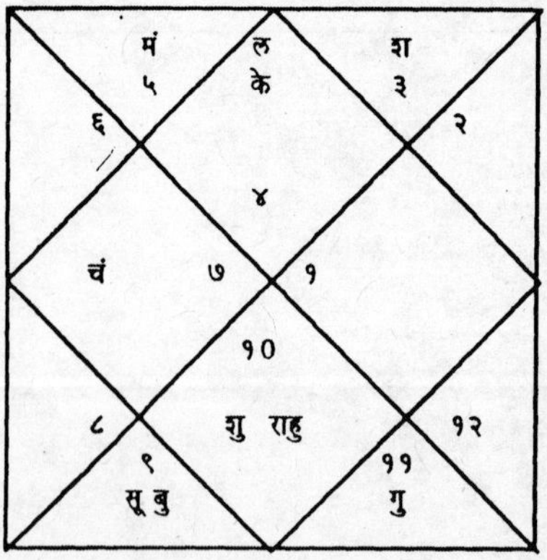

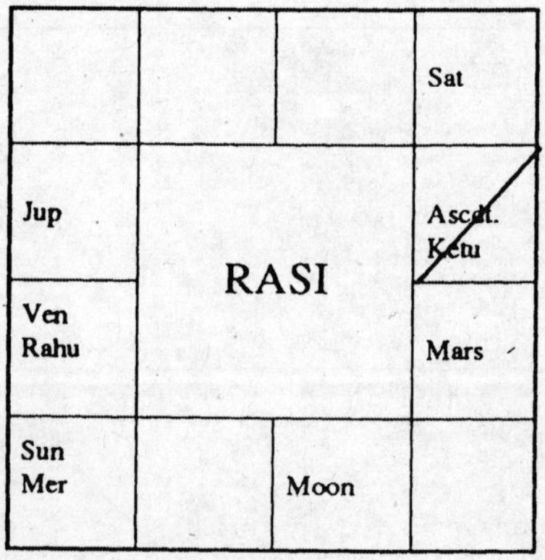

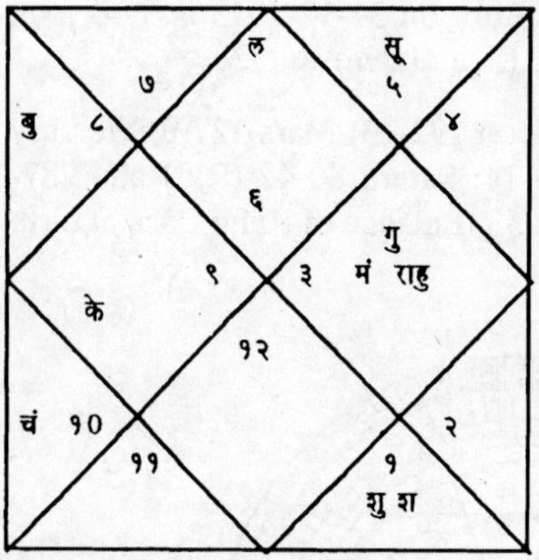

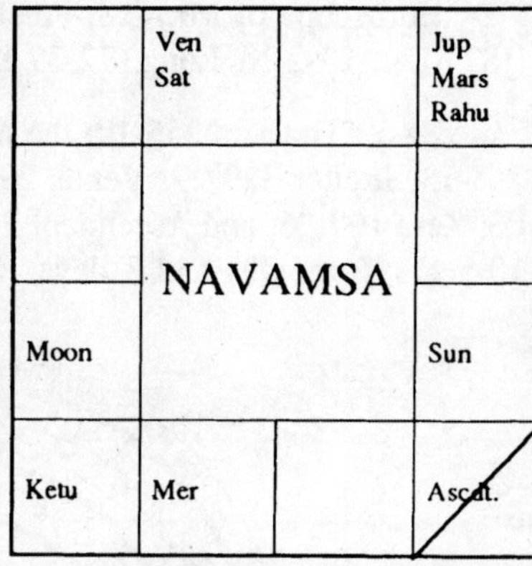

been exhaustively dealth with. There are quite a few verses in *Chandra Kala Nadi* whose correct import has eluded the grasp of many research scholars till date.

In this article an attempt is made to bring to light one more such method of transit, hitherto unnoticed by scholars, from *Chandra Kala Nadi* Volum I page 301 - verses 3018 to 3023 (same versus are again repeated in Vol. II Part I pages 56-57 vesus 465 to 470).

The constellation through which the Moon is passing at the time of birth of a native is reckoned as the first star and is called *Janmarksha;* the 10th star from that is called *Karmarksha,* and the 19th one from that is known as *Adhanarksha.* There are three series of nine asterisms each in the zodiac, totalling 27 stars, their order is from Janma star. (occupied by the Moon at birth).

Janma Series 1st series from Janma Star	**Karma Series** 2nd series from 10th Star	**Adhana Series** 3rd series beginning with 19th Star	**Known as**
1st star	10th star	19th star	Janmatara
2nd star	11th star	20th star	Sampattara
3rd star	12th star	21st star	Vipat-tara
4th star	13th star	22nd star	Kshematara
5th star	14th star	23rd star	Prathyaktara
6th star	15th star	24th star	Sadhakatara
7th star	16th star	25th star	Vadhatara
8th star	17th star	26th star	Maitratara
9th star	18th star	27th star	Parama-maitratara

Horoscope of Mr. C.S. Patel. Born on 31-12-1915 at 7.44 p.m. (IST) Lat. 23-2 N. Long. 72-39 E. (See above)

Rasi : The Sun 256-10; the Moon 192-13; Mars 127-9; Mercury 265-13; Jupiter 329-29; Venus 283-14; Saturn 80-42 (R); Rahu 287-06; Ketu 107-06; and Ascendant 98-53. Balance of Rahu Dasa at birth 10 years, 6 months and 3 days.

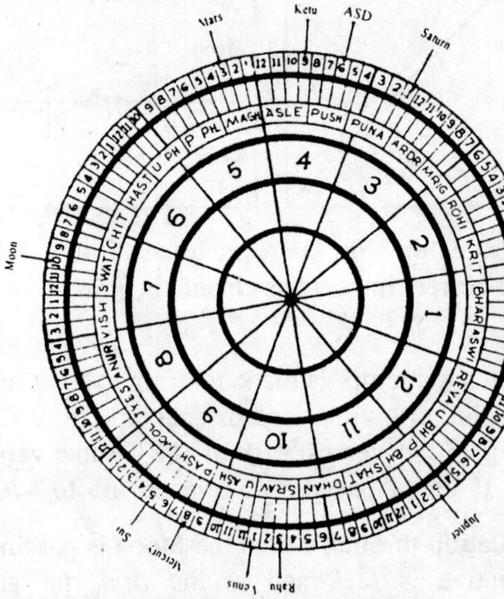

The circular diagram has been explained many times before in previous articles. Each sign is divided into nine equal parts of 3• 20' each, known as Navamsa, which are numerically marked to represent signs occupied by them. Each asterism of 13° 20' is divided into four equal parts of 3° 20' each known as pada or quarter or charan as 1st, 2nd, 3rd or 4th quarter of a star. In short, asterism, its quarters and Navamsa sign position of a transiting or natal planet are noticed in no time from this diagram.

In the example horoscope, the Moon is 6-12°-13' *i.e.*, in Swati asterism 2nd quarter (Capricorn Navamsa in sign Libra). So Swati 2nd quarter is known as Janma-taramsa. The second star from the Moon star, Visakha, is Sampat star and its 2nd quarter is known as Sampat-taramsa. The third star from Swati is Anuradha star and its 2nd quarter is known as Vipattaramsa. Similarly, all the 2nd padas or quarters of all the remaining stars may be termed according. It will be convenient to arrange them in a tabular form as below :

The author Sri Achyuta gives much importance to transit of a planet through a quarter *pada* only in preference to the full transit through a star. Thus from the Table it will be observed that in the above circular diagram all the 9 Taurus Navamsas, all the 9 Virgo Navamsas and all the 9 Capricorn Navamsas are result-oriented. Similarly in all charts under study, quarter-Navamsa whichever it may be, occupied by the Moon at birth and its trine Navamsas are to be considered only, in all totalling 27 quarters *(padas)* charanas Navaṁsas.

Chandrakala Nadi Vol. I page 301 verse 3018—

विपत्तारांशगे मंन्दे गोचरे शत्रुनिग्रहः ।
सम्पत्तारांशगे भीतिर्विपत्प्राणभयं महत् ॥

meaning, when Saturn transits through

(1) Vipat-taramsa, the native suffers defeat [or imprisonment] at the hands of enemy;

(2) Sampat-taramsa-one suffers from fear, calamity or intense possibility of death (The chart discussed by the author in the nadi belongs to some king. In lines there after, the author has shortened the name of Kshemataramsa as just Kshema and Pratyak taramsa as Prathyak etc.)

क्षेमे व्याकुलकार्याणि स्वराज्ये कलहं व्यथाम् ।
प्रत्यरे तु मनस्तापं पाण्ड्यभूपतिविग्रहम् ॥ (V. 3019)

(3) Kshemataramsa-perplexed in his activities, strife in his kingdom and physical pain;

Janma series	Karma series	Adhana series	Taramsas
1 Swati 2nd pada	10. Satabhisha 2nd pada	19. Aridra 2nd pada	Janma - taramsa
2. Visakha 2nd pada	11. Porvabhadra 2nd pada	20. Punarvasu 2nd pada	Sampat-taramsa
3. Anuradha 2nd pada	12. Uttarabhadra 2nd pada	21. Pushyami 2nd pada	Vipat-taramsa
4. Jyeshta 2nd pada	13. Revati 2nd pada	22. Aslesha 2nd pada	Kshema-taramsa
5. Moola 2nd pada	14. Aswini 2nd pada	23. Makha 2nd pada	Prathyak-taramsa

Janma series	Karma series	Adhana series	Taramsas
6. Poorvashadha 2nd pada	15. Bharani 2nd pada	24. Poorvaphalguni 2nd pada	Sadhaka-taramsa
7. Uttsarashadha 2nd pada	16. Krittika 2nd pada	25. Uttaraphalguni 2nd pada	Vadha-taramsa
8. Sravana 2nd pada	17. Rohini 2nd pada	26. Hasta 2nd pada	Maitra-taramsa
9. Dhanishta 2nd pada	18. Mrigasira 2nd pada	27. Chitta 2nd pada	Paramamaitra-taramsa

(4) Prathyak taramsa - mental agony and war with Pandya king.

मण्डलाधिपतेर्मृत्युं बन्धुंक्लेशं विनिर्दिशेत् ।
आधानजन्मकर्मर्क्षे पापाक्रान्ते स्थिते सति ॥ (V. 3021)

meaning, Death of his subordinate king or quarrels with relatives are indicated during transit of malefics through *Adhana, Janma* and *Karma* stars (*i.e.*, through above mentioned quarters).

राजद्वारकलापेन व्याकुलं मनुरबवीत् ।
तदभावे देहजाडयं स्वजनानामुपद्रवम् ॥ (V. 3022)

meaning, Manu has said the king is puzzled with quarrels in his palace, failing that he gains obesity and faces misfortune of his kinsmen.

शुभ्रग्रहाक्रान्तकाले शुभं भवति नित्यशः ।
पापाक्रान्ते मनस्तापं ग्रहो-क्तगुणमार्गतः ॥ (V. 3023)

meaning, When a benefic planet (namely Jupiter) transits (through its above referred quarters) auspicious events take place daily; while transit of a malefic planet results in mental anguish etc., according to the characteristics of the transiting planet.

Benefic results (culed out from Bhukti periods and other sources) for average natives;

Change of residence due to rise in status, job, or line of activity; rise in income; success in endeavours; travel; pilgrimage; gain of land and property; monetary benefits; good fortune; alround improvement in status and living; opening of new sources of income; reward;

appreciation; marriage, birth of child and the like.

Malefic results :

Dishonour, sorrow, trouble, hatred, failure in business, trade etc; threats of intimidation; enemies and troubles through them; loss of property; misunderstanding with own people;wound; sickness; health troubles; disease; hospitalisation; wasteful expenses; fear and anxiety; frustration; loss of position and status; grief; ill-health; chrnoic illness; mental depression; probable death and the like. In short, adverse transit portends results such as death, loss of wealth etc., as indicated in the birth chart. One should ascertain and keep in mind the nature of events and happenings likely to occur in the life of a native.

Jupiter will bestow favourable results while Saturn will bestow unfavourable ones. Rahu will give unexpected, unusual and all of a sudden favourable results while Ketu will give exactly opposite results in the same way. However, the good or bad results will be modified by the simultaneous transits of unfvourable or favourable planets respectively. The transits of Venus and Mercury for favourable results and those of the Sun and Mars for unfavourable results through the *specified quarters of stars* will be useful *to pin-point the probable time of occurrence of events*, during the periods of transit indicated by the four slow-moving planets.

The intensity of the results will vary both on the strength or otherwise of the natal chart as well as of the transiting planets.

While predicting, the astrologer should take into consideration the native's position in life, age, sex, Dasa-Bhukti period, country of origin etc. before coming to any judgement, because all the above-listed results need not materialise at the same tme and in all nativities.

Navamsa transits of major planets for the example chart during coming months; (1) Jupiter will transit Leo, Poorvaphalguni 2nd quarter, Virgo Navamsa (from 4' 20°00' to 4°16°40') during retrograde motion from 23-1-1992 to 23-2-1992. Adhana series in Sadhakataramsa. (2) Jupiter will transit the above quarter (item 1) again in direct motion from 5-7-1992 to 24-7-1992 (3) Rahu will transit Sagittarius sign, Moola star, 2nd quarter Taurus Navamsa (from 8s 6° 40' to 8s 3° 20') from 26-6-1992 to 28-8-1992 Janma series in Prathyak taramsa. (4) Ketu will transit Gemini sign, Aridra star 2nd quarter, Capricorn Navamsa (from 2s 13° 20' to 2s 10° 00') from 21-2-1992 to 24-4-1992, Adhana series in janma-taramsa.

The scribe fervently hopes that research-minded scholars will pay more attention to this old method of Navamsa transit and make further research on this count for the benefit of posterity. The science of Astrology is like a deep ocean.

7

Importance of Navamsa in Prediction–I

It is said that there are 20 or more different *Nadis* prevalent in the South out of which 8 Nadis, I have studied partially — 5 of them in detail (in my possession) and 3 of them through articles and books e.g. *Kaka Bhujander, Budha Nadi.*

Every *Nadi* author uses a particular Navamsa technique in an outstanding way, though basic treatment of Navamsa is common, in the five Nadis, so far studied by me.

(1) *Budha Nadi - (1 Navamsa = 1 year of life)*

I have dealt with five different methods in my articles (explained later in this paper).

(2) *Chandra-Kala Nadi*

Achyuta, the author, deals with Navamsa's transit results of planets through a particular Navamsa, occupied by a planet and its trinal places. He also gives importance to Ashtamamsa, Pushkaramsa, Yogamsa, Vikatamsa etc. Pushkara Navamsa is rarely used in standard texts, but in Chandra-kala Nadi, it is freely used. Persons having Pushkara Navamsa as rising Navamsa (Udit-Navamsa) are outstanding in their careers (explained *infra*).

(3) *Dhruva Nadi of Shri Jaya-Muni*

There are 43 volumes in G.O.M.L. (Madras) comprising about 2,25,000 verses. The scribe has one volume (copied down) having about 10,000 verses (120 Charts are discussed in them). The author,

Shri Jaya Muni deals mostly with Bhavatmaka Navamsas. Results are also given. This method has been already explained in my article "Searchlight on Navamsa" Chapter-2.

(4) *Bhargava Nadi (Adyar Library, Madras)*

(3 verses' translation)

Jupiter in the 10th house :

(i) In Leo Navamsa - native becomes a minister;

(ii) In own (Sagittarius Navamsa) - a learned man;

(iii) In enemy Navamsas (3-6;, 2-7) - native is without learning and happiness;

(iv) In friendly Navamsas (1-8) - becomes well known in government circles;

(v) In Aquarius Navamsa - he is slow-witted and always using harsh words;

(vi) In debilitated Navamsa doing many sins;

(vii) In exalted Navamsa–well-versed in Shastras;

(viii) In own Navamsa (Pisces) - giving shelter to others.

Jupiter's postion in other houses in similar classified Navamsas will give different results. There may be more volumes depicting results of all planets in various houses.

(5) *"Jataka Satyaaschaareeyam" by C.G. Rajan in English*

This book is a translation of a book named *Dhruva-Nadi - Antargata-Satya-Samhita* = a Sanskrit book but published in Telugu script (about 450 verses).

Results of every bhava lord posited in each of the 12 Bhavas are given in about 450 verses (12 Lagnas x 12 Bhavas = 144 possibilities).

E.g. "If the Lord of the 3rd Bhava is posited in the 9th Bhava, some good results for native's brother and father are indicated. .....If the Lord of the 9th Bhava is weak, the native will have some misunderstanding with his father. ..... If the lord of the 3rd Bhava (of Rasi Chart) is posited in the 6th, the 8th or the 12th place from Navamsa-Rasi of the lord of the 9th Bbava (of Rasi Chart) in Navamsa, results contrary to those mentioned above may be predicted".

In the example chart, in Navamsa, Mercury (lord of the 3rd Bhava in Rasi) is in Scorpio Navamsa which is the 6th place from Gemini Navamsa occupied by Jupiter, 9th lord in Rasi.

In other Naid Granthas, some other Navamsa techniques might have been used. The scribe has not come across them so far.

Navamsa Literature

PART - A : *Jaimini System, Kalachakra Dasa, Sarvatobhadra-Chakra, and Ankana-Shastra* (by Vyaghra-Pada) are all based on "Navamsa-Division".

PART - B : Practically every standard text of Astrology, right from *Vraddha-Yavana Jataka* till the 18th century, various authors such as MeenaRaja, Sphujidwaja, Varaha Mihira, Pruthuyasas, Kalyana Varma, author of*Mana-Sagari*, Vaidyanatha, Gunakara, Mantreshwara, author of *Vidya-Madhaviya*, Balabhadra, Dhundi-Raja, Kamalakara and other authors have dealt with Navamsa results in one or more chapters and/or partially here and there in their respective books. If one collects all these verses, the Sangraha would go upto 2000 or more verses.

Big Chapters on Navamsa Results

Some authors give importance to the rising Navamsa and others to the Navamsa occupied by the Moon.

[*Saravali;* (Kalyana Varma) in Chapter-50, (1 + 108 = 109 verses)] gives reslts about the nature, traits, physical features etc., of the native, one verse for each Navamsa *i.e.*, 108 verses for 108 Navamsas.

Nashta-jataka : (from a Tamil Jataka work based on axioms from Nadi-granthas covers 108 Navamsas in Ascendant showing place of birth (North-South street or East -West street), adjacent houses of the birth house, surroundings etc. for 108 Navamsas.

Yavana-Jataka : of Sphuji Dhvaja (1 + 108 = 109) deals with the Navamsa occupied by the Moon describing colour, nature, form and characteristic marks on the body (moles, etc.) of a native for each of the 108 Navamsas.

Nakshatra-Chudamani describes traits, etc., of a native on the basis of the Moon's 108 different Navamsa positions.

Bhava-Madhya Navamsa

The Ascendant Navamsa is known as the rising Navamsa or Udaya Navamsa or Lagna-Navamsa. It is a Navamsa of Bhavamadhya of the first house or Lagna or the Ascendant degree.

In the example chart, Cancer is the Ascendant 3s-8°-53' *i.e.*, Navamsa occupied by Lagna is Virgo). On the basis of this Navamsa sign, the Navamsa Kundali is prepared. Putting this Navamsa sign in the 1st house, all planets are placed in their respective Navamsa signs.

When the first house Bhavamadhya is given so much importance, why not other mid-points of houses such as the 10th, the 7th, the 4th and other houses?

Jataka Tatva G-216, page 184 (by Sri V. Subrahamanya Sastri) refers to Putrasthanavamsa the Navamsa indicated by the centre of the 5th Bhava. S. Krishna Iyengar had written a series of 20 articles on the "Use of Navamsa in Prognostication" from November 1968 to March 1971. He has referred to this midpoint at many places :

(i) "The 2nd house midpoint will join some Navamsa and that Navamsa is occupied by Mercury;

(ii) If Mars, the midpoint of the 3rd house and the lord of the 3rd house, all fall in even Navamsa, the native will be blessed with a number of sisters;

(iii) If the midpoint of the 7th bhava falls in the Navamsa of Venus and several other Venusian Vargas, the native is likely to have many wives.

(iv) If the 5th house midpoint be a Navamsa of Venus, the native will have many children.

So, the Navamsa of the midpoint of a Bhava is used for :

(a) placement of planets in it in Navamsa Chart;

(b) midpoint falls in an odd or even Navamsa;

(c) midpoint falls in a particular planet's Navamsa;

(d) whether, a midpoint Navamsa has an aspect (benefit on malefic); etc.

The midpoints of the opposite Bhavas *e.g.*, of the 1st and the 7th Bhavas; of the 2nd and the 8th Bhavas; of the 3rd and the 9th Bhavas, etc. will fall in the 7th Navamsa from each other; (*e.g.*, in example chart 1st house 3s-8-53' Virgo Navamsa x ofthe 7th bhava 9s-8-53' is Pisces Navamsa).

Midpoints of the 2nd and 6th houses, of the 8th and the 12th houses; of the 3rd and the 11th houses and of the 5th and the 9th houses, are of the same Navamsa signs.

Dispositors

(1) *Chandra kala nadi;* Vol. II, Part II, Page 71, Verse 3272;

मेषे चापांशगे शुक्रे कुलीरे च प्रजायते ।
जीवे कुजयुते काले बहुवित्तयुतः सुखी ॥

Meaning, "A native born in Cancer Ascendant, with Venus occupying Sagittarius Navamsa in Aries sign (both neutral planets), will have much wealth and be happy, during the period of conjunction in transit of Jupiter and Mars."

Note that Venus, a benefic planet is posited in the 10th house, occupying Pushkara Navamsa *i.e.*, Sagittarius Navamsa in Aries sign. It may be noted that Mars is the sign dispositor (Aries) and Jupiter is Navamsa dispositor (Sagittarius). These two planets whenever they conjoin in transit, they produce certain favourable results to the native.

Venus, in Cancer Ascendant, is the lord of the 11th house and the 4th house, hence he bestows wealth (the 11th house) and happiness (the 4th house) as per houses owned by him. The sign conjunction between Jupiter and Mars takes place roughly once every two years (*i.e.*, 24 months). This period of conjunction varies from 1.5 months to 6 months, depending on their speed.

Conjunction of Jupiter and Mars in Cancer, Sagittarius, Pisces, Aries, Scorpio and Capricorn signs are productive of more good results because either of them becomes powerful in each of these six signs. Only, in Cancer or Capricorn, one is exalted and the other is debilitated, simultaneously.

One research scholar has successfully applied this principle of Navamsa dispositor and sign dispositor of Mandi and confirmed the demise of Mahatma Gandhi in the Dasa of Rasi lord Venus and in Bhukti of Navamsa lord Jupiter.

In application of this rule to Dasa/Bhukti, stellar-dispositor of a planet can also be taken into account for inclusion of Dasa/Bhukti of Rahu and Ketu.

A very important rule can be deduced from the above verse - as follows :—

"Two planets, one Navamsa dispositor (Jupiter in this case) and the other Rasi-dispositor (Mars in this case), during their conjunction in transit produce results pertaining to sign/s (houses) owned by the disposited planet (Venus).

How many possibilities are there?

Venus in different signs 12, Venus in different Navamsa 9, different Ascendants 12, Seven Planets 7 That is,

12 x 9 x 12 x 7 = 9072

There can be 9072 different possibilities of results, taking into account all the seven planets in different signs, Navamsas and the Ascendant.

One very important event took place in my life on 10-10-1989 (at Ahmedabad). My tenant vacated my bungalow after 19 years' occupation on Tuesday 10-10-1989 at 12.40 p.m.

Example horoscope

Born on December 31, 1915 at 7.44 p.m. (IST) at 23-2' N and 72-39 E. with a balanceof Rahu Dasa 10 years, 6 months, 3 days.

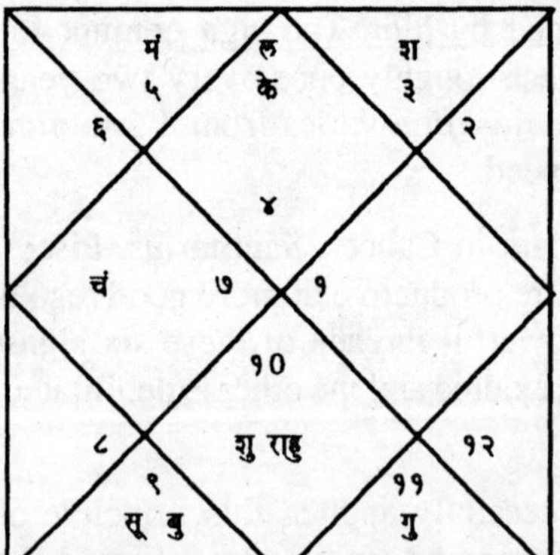

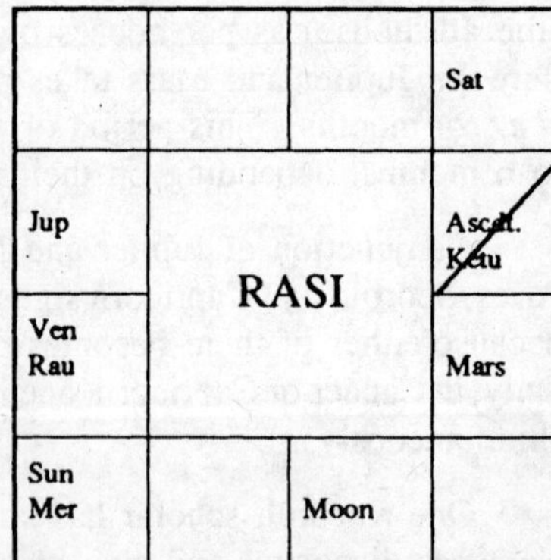

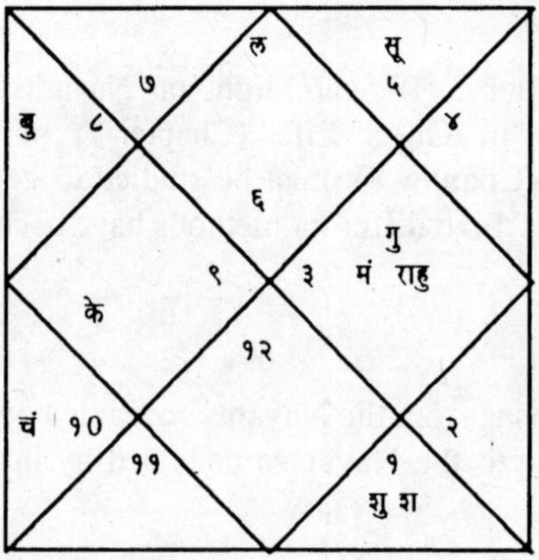

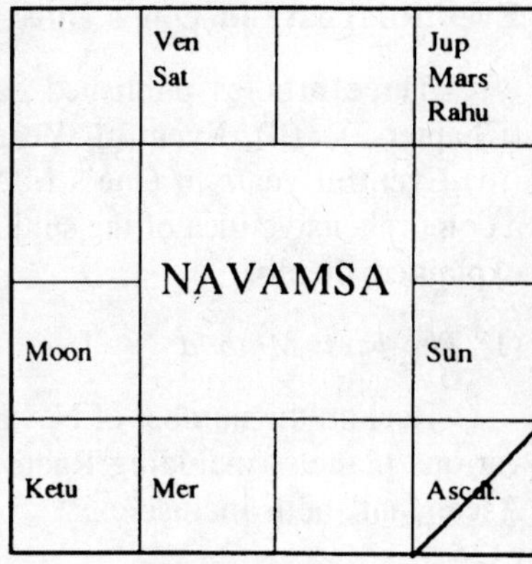

Note

(i) Mars-karaka for landed property is posited in the 2nd house in Leo;

(ii) Sign dispositor of Mars is the Sun; and

(iii) Navamsa dispositor of Mars is Mercury.

A transit conjunction of these three planets - Mars, the Sun and Mercury was in operation from 16-9-1989 to 17-10-1989 in Virgo - *which is Udaya Navamsatulya sign or Navamsa Ascendant sign,* also a Pushkara Navamsa. The event took place when the Moon was passing through the sign Capricorn—Chandra Navamsatulya Rasi, trine to sign Virgo in which the conjunstion of these planets took place. It may be noted that on that day, one of these three planets Mercury, was powerful occupying his own sign Virgo (Moola Trikona 5^s-5°-15') having the maximum number of 33 *bindus* (in S.A.V.).

(2) The Ascendant or Lagna is a very important point in the Chart.

Lagna *dispositor* is the Moon and *Navamsa dispositor* is Mercury. Whenever a conjunctionof these two planets takes place, something (good) happens. This conjunction takes place every month for 2 1/2 days.

(3) Another important point is the Moon's Rasi dispositor is Venus. Navamsa dispositor of the Moon is Saturn. This conjunction takes place once every year.

Results can be checked when they conjoin at least every year.

Eventful Years in One's Life

Three articles published earlier : (i) Searchlight on Navamsa (Chapter-2), (ii) Eventful Years in One's Life (Chapter-7) and (iii) Eventful years in One's Life (Chapter-8) must be studied to get a comprehensive idea of the subject. Five different methods have been explained therein.

(1) *The First Method*

Reckon the number of Navamsas from the Navamsa occupied by various planets (including Rahu) upto the Navamsa occupied by the Ascendant, both inclusive.

(2) *The Second Method*

Reckon the number of Navamsas from the first *pada* (Navamsa) of Aswini Star upto the *pada* occupied by each planet including Rahu/ Ketu) both inclusive.

(3) *The Third Method*

Reckon the number of Navamsas from the Navamsa occupied by Saturn upto the Navamsa occupied by the Moon, both inclusive (and so on, from all the planets to the Moon).

(4) *The Fourth Method*

Reckon the number of Navamsas trsaversed by the lord of the rising Navamsa from the Lagna Navamsa. One can apply this rule to the Navamsa positions of other planets, both inclusive.

(5) *The Fifth Method*

Reckon, the number of Navamsas from the Navamsa of the Ascendant upto the Navamsa occupied by all the 9 planets, both inclusive.

One more advantage of these methods is that one can cross-check and verify the correctness of the Ascendant Navamsa. This is a unique system of delineation, independent of planetary transits and Dasas.

All the above five methods are fully discussed in the above three articles. **This system is the backbone of Budha-Nadi.**

Navamsa Progression

One Navamsa equals one year. This theory will give the year in which an event is likely to take place. But during that particular year, in which month and which day the event occurs, is a subject for research.

Calculate from one planet to another planet (indicating an event) the degree distance, convert the difference into degrees and find out complete Navamsas and the balance. *This balance will indicate the month and day of the event.*

One Navamsa = 3° 20' = 200 minutes = 1 year = 360 days. One should find from the balance degrees and minutes, probable month and day of the event.

E.g. Refer my article "Eventful Years in One's Life" II, (Chapter-8)

In the case of Mrs. Indira Gandhi.

Her Mercury is 7ˢ-13°-15' from Aries

7 Signs	=	63	Navamsas
10 degrees	=	3	Navamsas
	=	66	Navamsas
			Years
Balance 0-3°-15'	=	195	minutes;

For 200' = 360 days; for 195' = 351 days = 11 months and 21 days.

Date of Birth	=	19-11-1917
	+	21-11-0000
Years (Navamsas)	+	00-00-0066
		10-11-1984

She breathed her last on 31-10-1984. Adjustment of 5" five seconds of arc in Mercury's position would give correct result. Mercury is the lord of the 12th house (exit from the world) and the lord of the 3rd house *i.e.*, 8th from the 8th house (house of death).

8

Importance of Navamsa in Prediction II

Pushkara Navamsa

Readers can also refer to a full-fledged article on the subject published in July 1990 in THE ASTROLOGICAL MAGAZINE. (Chapter-5)

Each sign has two Pushkara Navamsas. There are in all 12 x 2 = 24 Pushkara Navamsas in the Zodiac. They are all benefic Navamsas, owned by benefic planets and produce auspicious results in Muhurta, Natal, Prasna and other matters.

Chandra Kala Nadi : Vol. II, Part I, Verse 77, Page 11.

केन्द्रत्रिकोणगे जीवे पुष्करांशे सुभाग्यवान् ।
षष्ठाष्टमव्ययांशस्थे दुर्बले पुत्रशोकवान् ॥

Meaning, Jupiter in Kendra (1-4-7-10th house) or Kona (5-9th house) in Pushkara - Navamsa, makes a native very lucky (wealthy). But, if the sign of Pushkara Navamsa occupied by Jupiter falls in the Rasi in the 6th, the 8th or the 12th hose, one (in spite of being wealthy) is emacilated (weak in health) and grieves on account of bereavement — death of a son.

The next verse No. 78 has been left out as being incorrect. The correct verse has been now traced from *Kerala-Nadi* and is as follows :

एकविंशमनुश्चैव चतुर्विंशति सप्त च ।
मेषादिमीनपर्यन्तं त्रिकोणानां यथाक्रमम् ॥

Meaning, The above refered Jupiter, if posited in Aries triad (1-5-9 signs), in Taurus triad (2-6-10 signs), in Gemini triad (3-7-11 signs) and the Cancer triad (4-8-12 signs), starts giving results of yoga (सुभाग्यावान्) from the 21st, the 14th, the 24th and the 31st (24 + 7) year of life respectively.

Rasi-Tulya Navamsa And Navamsa-Tulya Rasi

(As opposite or reverse position)

Aries sign : There are 9 Navamsas in Aries sign (from Aries to Sagittarius Navamsa).

Rasi :	1	1	1	1	1	1	1	1	1	Aries
	1	2	3	4	5	6	7	8	9	Navamsas

Reverse/Opposite or R/N = N/R = position will be :

1	2	3	4	5	6	7	8	9	Various signs to
1	1	1	1	1	1	1	1	1	have Aries Navamsas

Opposite possibilities : in the following way :

(i) 1/1 this is Vargottama;

(ii) 4/1 in sign Cancer there is no Aries Navamsa.

(iii) 8/1 in sign Scorpio also there is no Aries Navamsa.

In short, only six signs, opposite possibilites will be there for Aries signs.

i.e.,	2	3	5	6	7	9	Sign;
	1	1	1	1	1	1	Navamsas;

Similarly in all other signs, there will be only *six opposite* possibilities.

In the example chart :

The Sun	9th sign — 5th Navamsa	reverse is	5th sign 9th Navamsa	(Yes)
The Moon	7th sign — 10th Navamsa	reverse is	10th sign — 7th Navamsa	(No.).

Mars-Leo sign/Gemini Nav. Reverse is Gemini sign/Leo Nav. (No)

Mercury Sagi./Scorpio Nav. Reverse is Scrorpio Sign/Sag. Nav. (Yes)

Jupiter Aqua. sign/Gem. Nav. Reverse is Gem. sign/Aquarius Nav. (Yes)

Venus in Capri. sign/Aries Nav. Reverse is Aries sign/Cap. Nav. (No)

Saturn in Gemini Sign/Aries Nav. Reverse is Aries sign/Gemini Nav. (Yes)

Rahu in Capri. Sign/Gem. Nav. Reverse is Gemini sign/Capri. Nav. (Yes)

Ketu in Cancer sign/Sagitt. Navamsa Reverse is Sagit. sign/ Cancer Nav. (Yes)

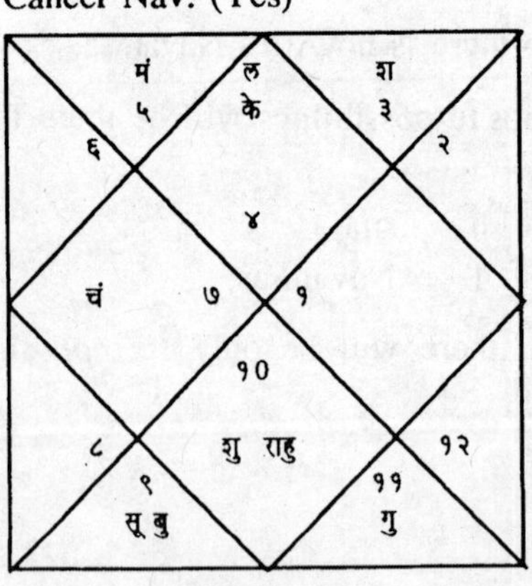

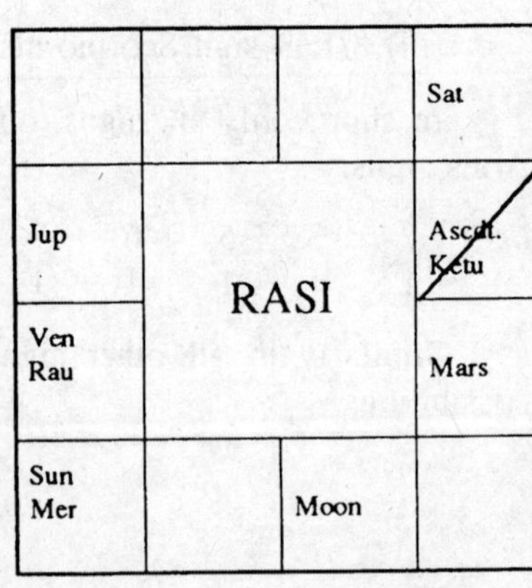

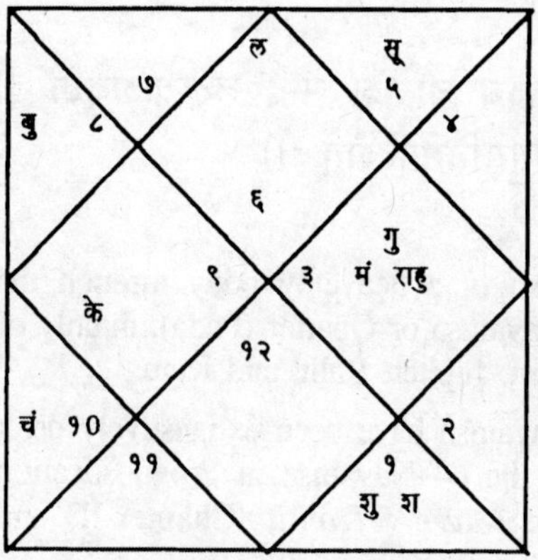

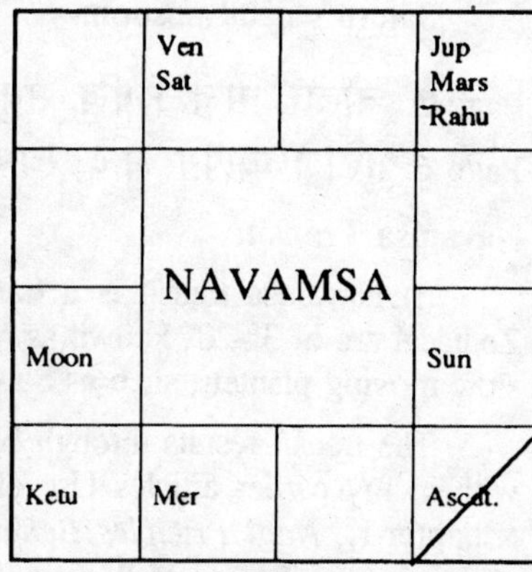

In the example chart Jupiter is in Aqiuarius sign/Gemini Navamsa opposite Gemini sign/ Aquarius Navamsa. This position occurs once every 12 years. Last time, Jupiter passed through Aquarius Navamsa in Gemini sign *i.e.*, from 2s-13°-20° to 2s-16°-40' from 9-9-1989 to 11-10-1989. I got possession of my bungalow on 10-10-1989, a rare event. In the past, whenever Jupiter had passed trough this Navamsa in Gemini sign, every time some good rare event took place in my life. *e.g.*, Saturn in Gemini sign/Aries Navamsa opposite - Aries sign/Gemini Navamsa *i.e.*, from 0s-6°-40' to 0s-10°-00'. I had suffered much when Saturn transited through this Navamsa. This happens once every 30 years. All planets - opposite - Navamsa transits may be studied accordingly.

This is one more method of Navamsa transit. For this theory two authorieies are quoted below :

(1) Cross Positions of Planets

In the Chart under discussion (Page 216 - Aquarius Ascendant *Chandra Kala Nadi* - Vol. I) full details of planets are not given. Venus is posited in the 11th house, in sign Sagittarius - *i.e.*, Venus is aspected by Saturn from the 9th house. From these scant references Verse No. 2191 on Page no. 216 can be interpreted as under :

मेषांशे तौलिगे मन्दे तुलांशे मेषराशिगे ।
भ्रातृ:प्राबल्यकाल: स्यात् स्वप्राबल्यमत: परम् ॥

Meaning, when, Saturn posited in Libra sign, Aries Navamsa in Natal Chart, tansits (throug exactly opposite position) i.e., in Aries Sign andLibra Navamsa, it is high time for native's brother to prosper; also it is high time for the native to prosper still more.

(2) In *Dhruva Nadi* (Saskrit) - G.O.T.N.L. No. R14721.

Mesha Lagnam - Kusumamsa:-

Saturn's natal postion:-

Page 2: तौलोच मन्दे शिखि संयुतश्च चापांश मन्दे लक्ष्म्यांशयुक्ते ॥

Page 6: तुलांशे चापगे मन्दे स्वमातुर्मृतिमादिशेत् ॥

Navamsa Transit

(i) Navamsa transit is a transit of a heavenly body through the Zodiacal arc of 3°-20', known as Navamsa or Quarter (Pada), mainly of slow moving plantets, such as Saturn, Jupiter, Rahu and Ketu.

The transit results through Navamsa have been exhaustively dealt with in my earlier articles Use of the 64 Navamsa in Prognostication (Chapter-I), *Nadi Priciples Behind Saturn's Transit* (Chapter-II) and *Navamsa and Transit of Planets* (Chapter-6).

In the 3rd article above, an attempt is made to bring to light one more such method of transit. The Nadi author gives much importance to transit of a planet through a quarter (Pada) only, in preference to the transit of a star (13°-20'). In all charts Navamsa (Quarter) whichever it may be, occupied by the Moon at birth, is very important. In the example chart, Swati 2nd quarter is known as Janmataramsa. The second star from the Moon star, Visakha, is Sampat star and the 2nd quarter is known as Sampattaramsa etc. One Navamsa in every star (the 2nd one in this case) will be result-bearing. In all 27 Navamsas are to be considered -9 Taurus Navamsas, 9 Virgo Navamsas and 9 Capricorn Navamsas.

When a benefic planet transits through this quarter, auspicious events take place, malefic planet results in metal anguish, etc. according to the characteristics of the transiting planet. The transit of Venus and Mercury for favourable results and those of the Sun an Mars for unfavourable results through specified quarters of stars concurrently with slow moving planets, will be useful to pinpoint the probable time of occurrence of events.

(2) One more Method of Navamsa Transit

(In the example chart)

Now look to Rasi-Tulya-Navamsa of 7 planets.

The Sun is in sign Sagittarius, hence all 9 Sagittarius Navamsas for the Sun's transit. The Moon is in sign Libra, hence all 9 Libra Navamsas for the Moon's transit. Mars is in sign Leo, hence all 9Leo Navamsas for the Mar's transit. Mercury is in sign Sagittarius, hence all 9 Sagittarius Navamsas for Mercury's transit. Jupiter is in sign Aquarius - hence all 9 Aquarius Navamsas for Jupiter's transit. Venus is in sign Capricorn - hence all 9 Capricorn Navamsas for Venus transit. Saturn is in sign Gemini - hence all 9 Gemini Navamsas for Saturn's transit.

(3°20') x 9 = 30 Total = 1 full sign.

All the abvoe cited Navamsas are result-bearing for the native.

(3) The 64th Navamsa

Important points to be noted for research :

(i) When a conjunction of major planets takes place in the 64th Navamsa (3°-20') of a nativity, either from the Ascendant or the Moon or the Sun, major outstading events take place in one's life for good or bad.

(ii) In the case of Amitabh Bachhan, Mars (5-22°-41') in *Natal Chart is posited in the 64th Navamsa from the Ascendant* (10-21°-38') and hence serious injury on 24-7-1982.

(iii) Recently, I came across a chart in which *Ketu was posited in the 64th Navamsa from his natal Jupiter.*The native lost his grown-up son (38 years old) in a car accident.

Can this principle be not applied to other karakas such as, the Sun for father, the Moon for mother, Mars for coborn or Venus for wife?

Difference Between Nidhanamsa And Ashtamamsa

(i) When the lord of Bhava (any planet) is posited in a Navamsa owned by the 8th house (in Rasi chart), that planet is said to be in Nidhanamsas. Suppose in the example chart, Lagna lord Moon is posited in any of the nine Aquarius Navamsas (in any sign), the Moon is said to be Nidhanamsasthah because Aquarius is the 8th Bhava or Rasi.

(2) A planet in any sign occupied by him, if placed in a Navamsa which falls in the 8th house therefrom, is said to be Ashtamamsasthah:-

e.g. (i) Suppose the Moon in Libra is posited in Taurus Navamsa, it is said to be Ashtamamsasthah. (ii) Suppose, Saturn in Gemini is placed in Capricorn Navamsa, it is said to be Ashtamamsasthah.

Karaka planets posited in Nidhanamsa in a chart cause unnatural deaths of relatives indicated by them. *There can be 9 Nidhanamsas in a chart in nine diferent signs.* But Ashtamamsa is only one, it refers to the sign position of a planet. *Fixed signs (2-5-8 and 11 signs) have no Ashtamamsa in them which may be noted.*

e.g. Leo sign does not have Pisces Navamsa.

Chadra Kala Nadi Vol. II, Part-I, Verse 80, Page 12 :—

युग्मे नक्रांशगे सूर्ये चापे कर्कटकांशगे ।
मीने जूकांशगे कन्ये मेषांशे स्वल्पमायुषः ॥

A native born with the Sun :

(i) in Gemini sign - Capricorn Navamsa

(ii) in Sagittarius sign - Cancer Navamsa.

(iii) in Pisces sign - Libra Navamsa.

(ibv) in Virgo sign - Aries Navamsa; will have short life.

All Navamsas referred in the above verse are Ashtamamsa, in their respective signs.

Terminology

In all signs the 1st, the 4th & the 7th Navamsas are Chara, in all signs the 2nd, the 5th & the 8th Navamsas are Sthira, in all signs the 3rd, the 6th & the 9th Navamsas are Dwiswabhava. Every sign begins with a Chara Navamsa and ends with a Dwiswabhava Navamsa.

Every odd sign has five odd Navamsas and four even Navamsas. Every even sign has five even Navamsas and four odd Navamsas.

ओजे ओजांशे means (a planet) in odd Navamsa in odd sign. युग्मे युग्मांशे means (a planet) in even Navamsa in even sign. चराधिभागा: first navamsa of 1-4-7-10 signs. स्थिरमध्यभागा: the middle Navamsas of 2-5-8-11 signs. द्विस्वभावन्तयभागा: the last Navamsas of 3-6-9-12 signs are Vargottamamsas.

Every sign has one Vargottamamsa, one Bhagyamsa and one Putramsa. A planet in own-sign in Bhagyamsa is Yogamsayuktasha.

A planet in own-sign in debilitated Navamsa is Vikatamsayuktah;

In every sign, the middle 3 Navamsas are not found in its opposite sign 3°-20'.

नीचांक्षांशे शुक्रे Venus in Virgo sign (30) or in any one of the remaining eight (3°-20' x 8° = 26°-40') Virgo Navamsas in other signs.

Every star has 4 padas (Navamsas) 1st one is Dharmanavamsa, the 2nd is Arthanavamsa, the 3rd is Kamanavamsa and the 4th is Mokshanavamsa.

1-5-9 signs are Dharma signs 2-6-10 signs are Artha signs; 3-7-11 signs are Kama signs 4-8-12 signs are Moksha signs. The first pada of every star is 1st, 5th or 9th Navamsa, The second pada of every star is 2nd, 6th or 10th Navamsa, the third pada of every star is 3rd, 7th or 11th Navamsa and the fourth pada of every star is 4th, 8th or 12th Navamsa.

One can judge the life mission of a native from *e.g.,*

In my chart the Ascendant Navamsa (Pushya 2 - Virgo Navamsa is, Artha Navamsa. The Moon's Navamsa (Swathi - 2 - Capricorn Navamsa is also Artha Navamsa.

9

Rasi & Navamsa : Interchanging Identicalness

The Zodiac is a circle of 360° having no beginning or end. In order to measure the distance, it is divided into 12 equal parts of 30° each, known as signs or Rasis, beginning with the first point of Aries - (Aries, Taurus .... Pisces). Again, the zodiac is divided into 27 equal parts of 13° 20' each, known as asterisms beginning with Asvini etc. ..... ending with Revathi.

Each sign is further divided into 9 equal parts of 3° 20' each known as "Navamsa". Similarly each asterism is further divided into four equal parts of 3° 20' each known as 'Padas' or quarters. Thus each sign comprises 9 quarters i.e. two-and-a-quarter constellations.

It is very significant that Nakshatra quarter is identified with "Navamsa". Both are not only of the same arc but their lines of demarcation are also identical i.e., each Navamsa corresponds to one Nakshatra Pada or quarter. It is for this reason that the Navamsa division is the most important of the 16 divisions (Vargas). In southern India, no astrologer would look at a Rasi chart without Navamsa.

A cycle of 12 Navamsa will repeat after an interval of 40° each (3° 20' x 12 = 40°). So Aries Navamsa will repeat 9 times in the Zodiac, similarly all other Navamsas will repeat 9 times.

Part - I

Rasi Tulya Navamsa

Dhruva Nadi, is a rare astrological work. In all the charts discussed in this Nadi, the planetary positions are given in the following unique manner :

ध्रुवनाडी - कन्या लग्नम् ।
रविहोरासमुत्पन्नो द्रेष्काणम् मकरं भवेत् ।
नवांशं वृषभञ्चैव गुरुत्रिंशांश जातके ।।
मीने दिनेशो भृगु संयुतश्च चापांश सूर्ये सुखांशयुक्ते ।
कुंभांश शुक्रे षष्ठांश युक्तः ।
मेषे च सौम्ये वृषभांशयुक्तः भाग्यांशयुक्तः ।
वृषभे च मन्दे शिखिसंयुतश्च सिंहांशमन्दे व्ययांशयुक्तः ।
वृषभांशकेतु वर्गोत्तमांशयुक्तः भाग्यांशयुक्तः ।
सिंहे च गुरौ च वर्गोत्तमांशयुक्तः व्ययांशयुक्तः ।
चापे च चन्द्रे वर्गोत्तमांशयुक्तः सुखांशयुक्तः ।
वृश्चिके च कुजे नीचांशयुक्तः लाभांशयुक्तः ।
कीटे च राहौ वर्गोत्तमांशयुक्तः विक्रमांशयुक्तः ।।

Virgo Ascendant 5s 0° 00' to 6s 0° 00'
The Sun's Hora 5s 15° 00' to 6s 00° 00'
Capcirocn Drekkana 5s 10° 00' to 5s 20° 00'
Taurus Navamsa 5s 13° 20' to 5s 16° 40'
Jupiter Trimsamsa 5s 12° 00' to 5s 20° 00'

So, the Ascendant falls between 5s 15° 00' to 5s 16° 40' i.e., within 1°-40' (half Navamsa).

The Sun in Pisces along with Venus, in Sagittarius Navamsa (which falls in the 4th in Rasi chart from Virgo Ascendant) is *sukhamsayuktah.* Venus also in sign Pisces in Aquarius Navamsa, falling in the 6th house in Rasi chart is *shasthamsayuktah.* Mercury in Aries with Taurus Navamsa is *Bhagyamsayuktah.* Saturn in Taurus with Ketu in Leo Navamsa is *Vyayamsayyuktah.* Ketu also in Taurus sign. Taurus Navamsa, Varottamsamsa, is *Bhagyamsayuktah.* Jupiter in Leo with Leo Navamsa is *Vyayamsayuktah* (Vargottamamsa). The Moon in the sign Sagittarius, in same Navamsa (Vargottamsamsa) is *sukhamsa yuktah.* Mars in Scorpio in Cancer Navamsa, in debilitation is *Labhamasayuktah.* Rahu also in Scorpio, in same Navamsa (Vargottama) is *Vikramamsayuktah.* The Ascendant in sign Virgo in Taurus Navamsa falling inthe 9th house is *Bhagyamsayuktah.*

(The above identicalness is reflected in Rasi and Navamsa charts, marked as "A" and "B" for an easy grasp by the reader.)

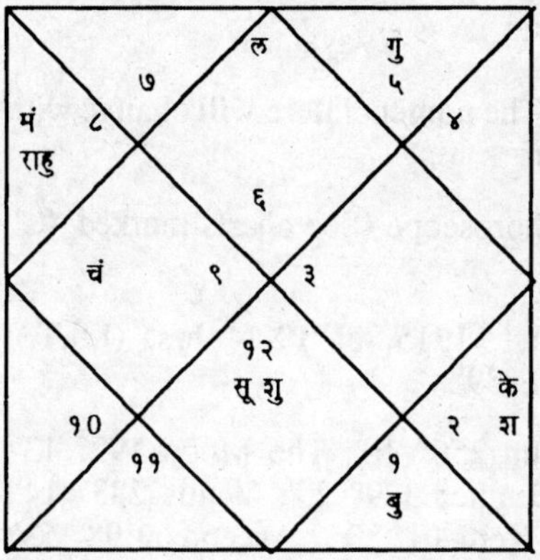

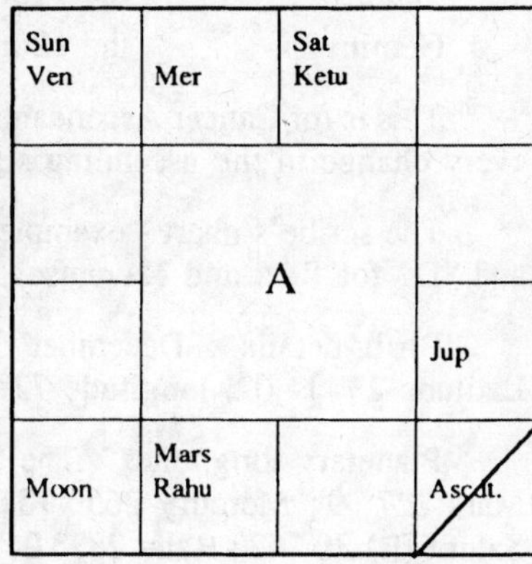

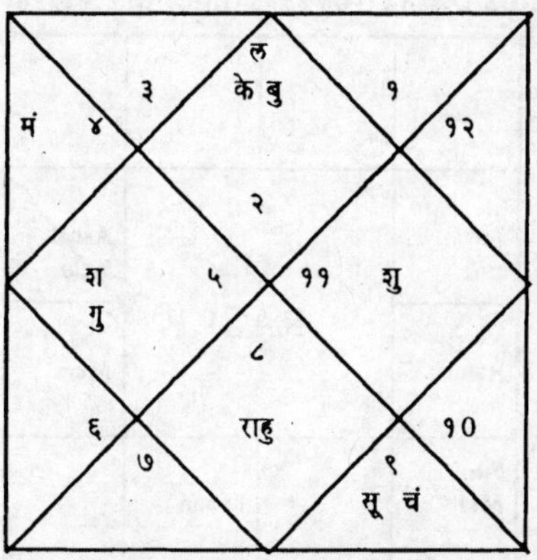

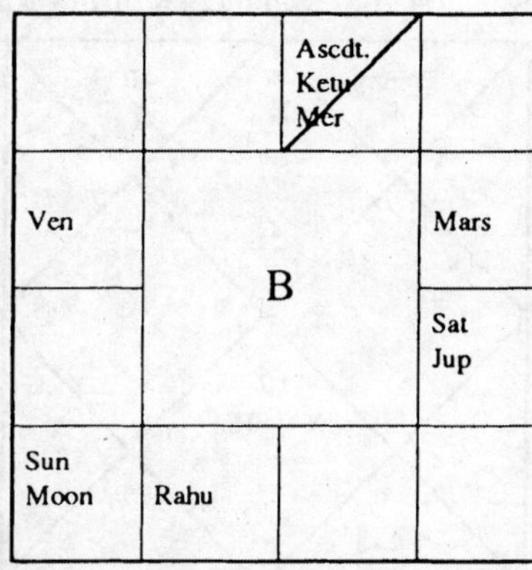

The scribe's chart (Rasi and Navamsa charts shown as "C" and "D" had Cancer Ascendant; so the Rasi Tulya Navamsa is Cancer Navamsa. There are in all nine Cancer Navamsas in the Zodiac. They are known as Lagnamsas for this chart. The second house is Leo, so all nine Leo Navamsas are Vittamsas. The third house is Vigro, so all nine Virgo Navamsas are Vikramamsas. Similarly, others for this chart are known as under :

Scorpio	the 5th	Putramsa
Sagittarius	the 6th	Shashtamsa
Capricorn	the 7th	Bharyamsa
Aquarius	the 8th	Nidhamamsa

Pisces	the 9th	Bhagyamsa
Aries	the 10th	Karmamsa
Taurus	the 11th	Labhamsa
Gemini	the 12th	Vyayamsa

This is for Cancer Ascendant. The nomenclature will change with every change in the ascending sign.

The scribe's chart - example horoscope (See charts marked "C" and "D" for Rasi and Navamsa) :

Birth details : December 31st. 1915, at 19.44 hrs. (I.S.T.); Latitude 23° N 02; longitude 72° E 39'.

Planetary longitudes : The Sun 256° 10'; The Moon 192° 13'; Mars 127° 9'; Mercury 265° 13'; Jupiter 329° 29'; Venus 283° 14'; Saturn (R) 80° 42'; Rahu 287° 06'; Ketu 107° 06'; Ascendant 98° 53'; M.C. 04° 08'. Balance at birth - Rahu's Dasa : 10years 6months 3days.

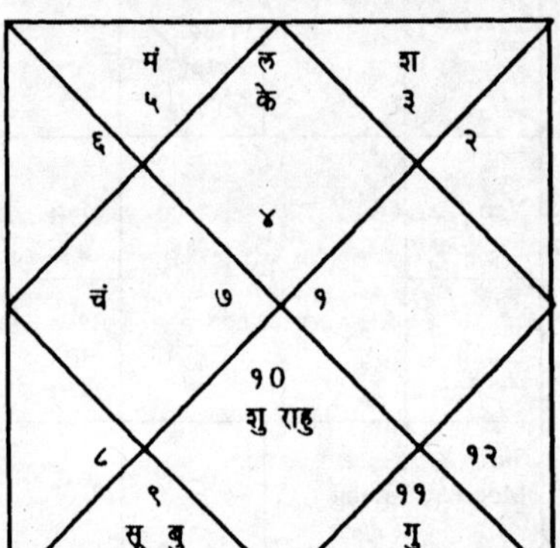

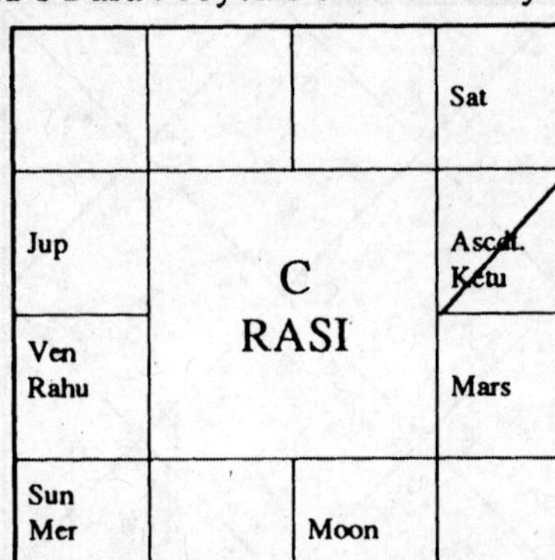

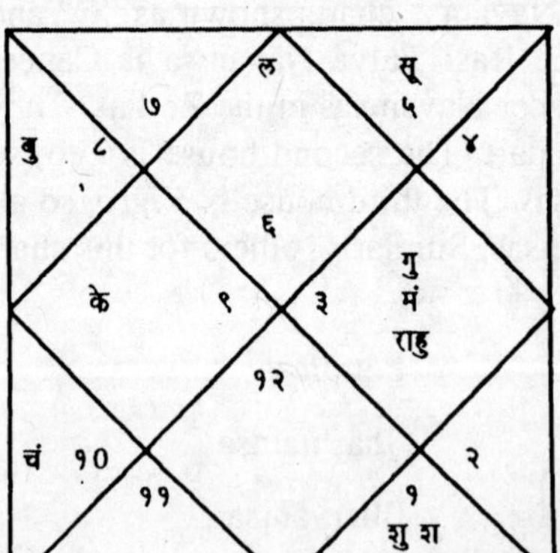

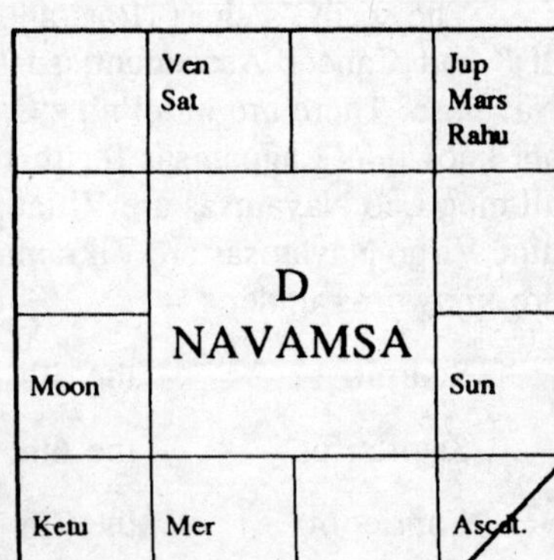

In the scribe's chart following are the Navamsas :

The Sun in Leo Navamsa - in *Vittamsa.*

The Moon in Capricorn - in *Bharyamsa.*

Mars in Gemini - in *Vyayamsa.*

Jupiter in Gemini - in *Vyayamsa.*

Rahu in Gemini - in *Vyayamsa.*

Mercury in Scorpio - in *Putramsa.*

Venus in Aries - in *Karmamsa.*

Saturn in Aries - in *Karmamsa.*

Ketu in Sagittarius - in *Shashtamsa.*

The Ascendant in Virgo - in *Vikramamsa.*

This technique is knwn as Rasi Tulya Navamsa. An authoritative example is given above from *Dhruva Nadi* of Jaya Muni. In this way, all the 9 planets have been given separate additional nomenclature according to this Navamsa Rasi falling in various houses in Rasi chart pertaining to Bhava occupied. This Rasi Tulya Navamsa technique is freely used in Dhruva Nadi. Almost in all charts discussed in the text, the planetary positions are given in this style. It is sparingly used in *Deva Keralam* and rarely used in the standard texts.

Reference *Jataka Parijata,* Chapter V, verse 82 (in Kashi Sanskrit series No. 10 and Mr. V.S. Sastri's English edition, Bangalore, Part-I. The word *"Nidhamamsasthe"* is wrongly interprected as 'when the lord Ascendent occupies 64th Navamsa from the Ascendant...." while its correct meaning is "when the lord of the Ascendant posited in Navamsa Rasi owned by the 8th house....."

Mahatma Gandhiji - Libra Ascendant, its lord Venus in sign Libra and in Navamsa Taurus owned by the 8th house in Ṛasi chart, hence his Venus is *"Nidhamamsa"*.

Mrs. Indira Gandhi (our late Prime Minister) : Cancer Ascendant, its lord Moon in sign Capricorn in Rasi chart and in Aquarius Navamsa, owned by the 8th house in Rasi chart hence Moon is in *"Nidhamamsa."*

Jataka Parijata, chapter 5, verse 82 says :

लग्नेशो निधनांशस्थे ....

.....................मरणं बन्धुहीने महीतले ॥

Both of them breathed their last, on the bare ground, with no blood relations near them.

Part - II
Navamsa Tulya Rasi

Deva Kerlam gives exhaustive details about the effects of Saturn's transits through signs identical with the Navamsa occupied by the lords of all twelve bhavas, or their trines, in about 600 (six hundred) verses out of total 9152 verses.

1. Saturn's Transit Results :

तत्तद्भावाष्टमेशांशे त्रिकोणेवाऽथवा भवेत् ।
स्फुटयोगं गते मन्दे तत्तद्भावविनाशनम् ॥

Saturn's transit in the sign identical with the Navamsa occupied by the lord of the 8th from a given Bhava of a trine thereof on the degree of that sign lord will destroy the good effects due to that Bhava. (Deva Keralam, Book 3, p. 87, verses 3151 - 52.)

लग्नेशांशे तत्त्रिकोणे स्फुटयोगं गते शनौ ।
मातुलारिष्टमाप्नोति मातुर्माता मनोव्यथां ॥

"When Saturn transits the sign represented by the Navamsa occupied by the lord of the ascendant, ora trine thereof, on the degree of that sign lord, one's maternal uncle with face evils and maternal grand-mother wil be mentally disturbed" (Deva Keralam - Book 3, p. 216, v. 4909)

Additional results (from other verses-the first line of the verses being common) are : *Native's father will be grieved due to loss of co-born; loss of a friend; fear from thieves; injury by weapon; loss of maternal brother or sister etc.*

धनेशांशे तत्त्रिकोणे स्फुटयोगं गते शनौ ।
धनेशदृष्टिरासौ तु दारहानिं विनिर्दिशेत् ॥

"Saturn moving in sign denoted by the Navamsa occupied by the lord of the 2nd house or a trine thereof, on the degree of that sign lord, will kill one's wife." (Deva Keralam, Book 3, page 177, verses 4357-58)

Additional results : *Want of marital felicity; obstructions in native's progress; death or calamity in wife's paternal family; loss in profession; wife gaining obesity and consequent disabilities; worries (mental tension) to wife.*

No full verse is traced in the text (*Deva Keralam*) regarding the third house(*Sahodara Sthana*); it being 8th from the 8th house, matters pertaining to that house be looked into, such as medical operation; debts; poverty; ill-health; anguish; inheritance, accident; gaining obesity etc.

सुखेशांशे तत्त्रिकोणे स्फुटयोगं गते शनौ ।
स्वपितुर्देहजाड्यादि दृष्टिराशौ महाविपत् ॥

"One's father will fall ill when Saturn transits in the sign caused by the Navamsa occupied by the 4th lord or a trine thereof, on the degree of that sign lord. Saturn's journey in the signs aspected by the 4th lord will cause great danger to father. (Deva Keralam, Book 3, page 177, verses 4363-64)

Additional results; Mother grieved,grief to father due to loss of his wife; calamity to father's co-born; father's sickness; death of father and consequent mental agony to mother, paternal relatives etc.

सुतेशांशे तत्त्रिकोणे स्फुटयोगं गते शनौ ।
प्रत्यग्दाये सोदरस्य सन्तानारिष्टमादिशेत् ॥

"Saturn arriving in the sign represented by the Navamsa of the5th lord, or a trine thereof, on the degree of that sign lord, will produce evils to the progeny of one's brothers. This transit should be in the native's 5th dasa." (Deva keralam, Book 3, page 95, verses 3246-47)

Additional results : *Death in wife's paternal family, death of a child in one's own family; loss of paternal wealth; serious sickness of friends; ill-health or death of mother-in-law; disease to elder co-born etc.*

षष्ठेशांशे तत्त्रिकोणे स्फुटयोगं गते शनौ ।
स्वपिता मित्रवर्गेषु क्लेशं प्राप्नोति भूरिशः ॥

"When Saturn arriving in the sign represented by the Navamsa of the 6th lord; or a trine thereof, on the degree of that sign lord, one's father will face much anguish through his friends" (Deva Keralam, Book 3, page 216, verse 4914.)

Additional results : *Many difficulties; leaving own's birth place; miseries to ordeath of elder co-born; loss of position; great mental anguish and much fear to native; death of father's co-born etc.*

मदेशांशे तत्त्रिकोणे स्फुटयोगं गते शनौ ।
मदेशदृष्टिराशौ तु मातामहविनाशनम् ॥

Saturn's sojourn in the sign identical with the Navamsa of the 7th lord, or a trine thereof, or the signs aspected by 7th lord, on the degree of that sign lord, will endanger one's maternal granted father.

Additional results : *Paternal grand-mother will be destroyed provided at the time 7th lord's Dasa is in progress; unexpected and heavy expenditure; death of maternal uncle or aunt or afflictions to them.*

रन्ध्रेशांशे तत्त्रिकोणे स्फुटयोगं गते शनौ ।
रन्ध्रेशदृष्टिराशौ वा स्वजनारिष्टमादिशेत् ॥

"Evil to one's kinsman will result during Saturn's transit in the sign identical with the Navamsa occupied by the 8th lord or a trine thereof or in the sign aspected by the 8th lord, on the degrees of that sign lord." (Deva Keralam, Book 2, page 241, verse 1772-73)

Additional results : *Native's health will suffer distress to his father and other elders; fear of untimely death; one's own death; fear of accident; native feels exhausted and becomes emaciated; loss of wealth; calamity in family; worries on account of children; death of a close friend; native confined to hospital; fear from opponents etc.*

भाग्येशांशे तत्त्रिकोणे स्फुटयोगं गते शनौ ।
स्वमातृभगिनीपुत्रनाशं च मनुरब्रवीत् ॥

"Saturn's journey in the sign identical with Navamsa position of the 9th lord, or a trine thereof, on the degree of that sign lord, will destroy progeny of mother's sister.

Additional results : *Quarrels; disease in eyes and throat; loss of wealth; mental agony etc.*

कर्मेशांशे तत्त्रिकोणे स्फुटयोगं गते शनौ ।
श्वसुरस्य प्रपीडादि तद्वर्गे वा ह्यपद्रवः ॥

"When Saturn moves inthe sign denoted by the Navamsa position of thelord of the 10th house, or a trine thereof, on the degree of that sign lord, there will be troubles to native's father-in-law or to his people." (Deva Keralam Book 2, Page 231, verse 1663)

Additional results : *Native's co-born will be in grief due to illness of a child in his family; afflictions to or deathof father-in-law; mental anguish; or pain to a brother or sister; native himself will be hospitalized etc.*

लाभेशांशे तत्त्रिकोणे स्फुटयोगं गते शनौ ।
मातृवंशे जनारिष्टं क्लेशं प्राप्नोति भूरिशः ॥

"Saturn's sojourn in the sign identical with Navamsa of the 11th lord or a trine thereof, on the degree of that sign lord, will produce much grief in mother's family and the native himself will have mental agony." (Deva Keralam. Book 3, page 167, verse 4336-37.)

Additional results : *Anguish to mother on account of her co-born going to a foreign land: the native's relatives will be greatly endangered; mother will face violent death; desertion of one's native place; quarrels on account of landed property etc.*

व्ययेशांशे तत्त्रिकोणे स्फुटयोगं गते शनौ ।
व्ययेशदृष्टिराशौ तु सन्तानारिष्टमादिशेत् ॥

"One will incur evils to his progeny when Saturn transits in the sign identical with the Navamsa occupied by the 12th lord or a trine thereof or the signs aspected by the 12th lord or on the degree of that sign lord."
(Deva Keralam, Book 3, P.177 verse 4358-59)

Additional results : *Paternal grand-father will be endangered; failure in examination; sickness of elder sister's husband or elder brother's wife, loss of wealth; grief to native due to loss of progeny; professional enmity; paternal uncle will incur evils.*

2. Jupiter's Transit Results :

युद्धावेशस्थितर्क्षांशत्रिकोणस्थे गुरुर्यदा ।
गोचरे तस्य भावस्य फलप्राप्तिं विनिर्दिशेत् ॥

"Find out the Rasi and Navamsa occupied by the lord of the Bhava under consideration. When Jupiter in transit comes in trine only

to his sign or the sign identical with the Navamsa occupied, the realisation of the good effects of that Bhava be expected." (Phala Dipika, ch 16, sloka 32.)

विपत्तारदशाकाले लग्नेशांशत्रिकोणगे ।
स्फुटयोगं गते जीवे पुत्रलाभं विनिर्दिशेत् ॥

"Jupiter'stransit in the sign equal to Navamsa occupied by Ascendant lord or a trine thereof on the degree of that sign lord, will cause birth of a son in the 3rd Dasa." (Bhrigu Nadi.)

Notes : In the scribe's chart, the lord of the Ascendant - the Moon - occupies Capricorn Navamsa (Libra 12° 13'). Its trinal signs are Taurus and Virgo. Inthe 3rd Dasa (of Saturn), when Jupiter was transiting Virgo, on its lord Mercury's dgree 8-25° 13', a son was born. On son's birth date, i.e., 19th November, 1945. Jupiter was 5s 25° 0' 57".

धनेशांशे तत्त्रिकोणे लाभेशांशत्रिकोणगे।
स्फुटयोगं गते जीवे पुत्रलाभं विनिर्दिशेत् ॥

"Wealth will come to pass when Jupiter transits the sign identical with the Navamsa occupied by the 2nd lord or the 11th lord, or the trines thereof, on the degree of that sign lord." (Deva Keralam, Book 3, page 37 verse 2518).

"Note the Navamsa occupied by the 5th lord, or the significator (Jupiter). When transit Jupiter comes with sign identical with the said Navamsa, on the degrees of that sign lord one will be get a son."

Notes : In the chart of scribe's son (date of birth - 19th November, 1945). with Gemini Ascendant, the lord of the 5th Venus (6^s 16° 15') is in Libra, own sign, in Aquarius Navamsa. Its trine signs are Gemini and Libra. When Jupiter was transiting sign Gemini, on its lord Mercury's degree 7-26° 7', two sons (twins) were born on 23rd July 1978, when Jupiter was 2^s-27°-05'.

दारेशांशत्रिकोणेषु गोचरे देवपूजिते ।
दारलाभं भवत्येव कारकस्य फलं वदेत् ॥

"Jupiter's sojourn in the sign described by the Navamsa of the 7th lord or of Venus (Karaka) or a trine therof, marriage (Dara Labham) will take place." (Ref. Ansha Nadi.)

Cf. भृगुनाडी

दारेशांशगते जीवे गोचरे दारलाभवान् ।

लाभाधिपांशगे जीवे भाग्येशांशकगेऽथवा ।
गोचरे सौख्यमाप्नोति ह्युद्योगधनवान् भवेत् ॥

"When Jupiter transits the sign identical with the Navamsa occupied by the 11th lord or the 9th lord, happiness, employment and wealth will occur." (Deva Keralam, Book 3, p.37, verse 2517.)

Full verses for Jupiter's transit through all the 12 signs are not traced as yet; whatever verses have been found out are given above.

3. Planet-Occupied Navamsa Positions :

(a) The Sun :

सूर्यांशगे तत्त्रिकोणे शुभेशांशत्रिकोणगे ।
स्फुटयोगं गते मन्दे पितृनिर्याणमादिशेत् ॥

"Saturn transiting a sign identical with the Navamsa occupied by the Sun or the 9th lord or a trine thereof, on the degree of the lord of that sign will promote father's death." (Deva Keralam, Book 3, p. 163, verse 4171.)

(b) The Moon

चन्द्रांशगे तत्त्रिकोणे स्फुटयोगं गते शनौ ।
स्वपितुर्देहजाड्यादि योगकाले विनिर्दिशेत् ॥

"When Saturn transits the sign identical with the natal Moon's Navamsa or a trine threrof, on the degree of the sign lord, his father will incur trouble from fever etc." (Deva Keralam, Book 3, p. 182, verse 4433-44)

बुधांशगे तत्त्रिकोणे षष्ठेशांशत्रिकोणगे ।
स्फुटयोगं गते मन्दे ह्यतिमित्रजनावधि ॥

"Saturn's transit in the sign denoted by Mercury's Navamsa position or the 6th lord's Navamsa position or a trine thereof on the degree of the lord of that sign will trouble dear friends." (Deva Keralam, Book 3, p. 238, verses 5230-31).

शुक्रांशे त्रिकोणर्क्षे स्फुटयोगे गते शनौ ।
स्वदारदेहजाड्यादि दारवंशे ह्यरिष्टजम् ॥

"Saturn arriving in transit the sign identical with the Navamsa occupied by Venus at birth or a trine thereof on the degrees of the lord of that sign, will cause physical sickness etc. to one's spouse. His in-law's family will be subjected to evils." (Deva Keralam, Book 3, page 94, verse 3233.)

For Mars, Jupiter and Saturn, full verses are not traced but a combined verse for the results of Mars, Venus, and Mercury is stated below (vide Deva Keralam, Book 3, page 94, verse 3234), which can be interpreted on the above lines :

भौमांशगे पित्ररिष्टं मातुश्च भार्गवांशे ।
सौम्यांशगे तत्त्रिकोणे सोदरारिष्टमादिशेत् ॥ (Verse 3234)
स्वर्भानुरंशगे कोणे स्फुटयोगं गते शनौ ।
सोदरारिष्टमाप्नोति प्रत्यग्दाये फलं स्मृतं ॥

"Saturn in transit in the sign identical with the Navamsa occupied by Rahu or a trine thereof, on the degree of that sign lord, will destroy co-born in the 5th Dasa." (Deva Keralam, Book 3, p. 27, verse 2362)

केतुक्रान्तांशगे मन्दे स्वदेहे जायते गदः ।
विण्मूत्रदेहबाधादेः क्षिप्रेणारोग्यमादिशेत् ॥

"When Saturn comes to the sign denoted by the Navamsa occupied by Ketu, diseases will strike the native including impure excretion, physical pain etc. Health will however be recovered early." (Deva Keralam, Book 2, page 141, verse 602.)

Deva Keralam (Book 3) in particular excels in applying transits with reference to the sign caused by certain Navamsa positions. Most of the verses quoted in Part-II of the write-up are from that book. One can very well observe this fact, while going through it, dealing with transit of Saturn or Jupiter through signs directed by Navamsa positions of planets.

This technique is dealt with in three different ways :

(i) Transit through signs denoted by Navamsa positions of the lords of all the twelve bhavas (Saturn's transit).

(ii) Transit through signs identical with Navamsa positions of lords of certain bhavas (Jupiter's transit).

(iii) Transit through similar signs denoted by Navamsa positions of various planets e.g. the Sun, the Moon, Mars, Mercury, Venus, Rahu and Ketu.

All these transits discussed in this Part-II of this write up, can be observed with the help of the Navamsa chart only and not from Rasi chart which may be noted.

One who uses such techniques frequently will be able to issue successful predictions.

(All references of verses are from Devakeralam Chandra-Kala Nadi-Books. 1-2 and 3 by Shri R. Santhanam.)

10

Yoga-bhangas or Cancellation of Yogas

Indian Astrology has the following five unique features : (1) Dasa system : (2) 16/20 kinds of sub-divisions of signs (vargas); (3) Ashtakavarga system; (4) Yogas; and (5) use of Rahu and Ketu for prognostication.

The present article deals with an important aspect—the 4th item—yogas. Yogas can be briefly defined as specific planetary combinations. Several yogas are described in Indian Astrology. Dr. B.V. Raman, the great scholar, has written a book describing critically about 300 yogas. *Bhrigu Samhita Yogavali* (Venkateshwar Press, Bombay) contains more than 1000 yogas.

There are many Raja Yogas and Avayogas. The writer does not wish to describe the benefic or malefic results of yogas mentioned in standard astrological works, but will instead focus the attention of scholars on yoga-bhangas (nullifications) of some important yogas.

Results of yogas (good or evil) are generally experienced by the native during the Dasas or Bhuktis of the yoga-causing planets. In some cases, the Dasas of yoga-causing planets come to pass in childhood or at the fag end of life, or sometimes they do not come to pass at all, during the native's life-span. These Dasa periods should operate in the prime of youth in the native's life, in order to have maximum effects. The effects of some yogas are life-long too.

Every horoscope will have some favourable as well as some unfavourable yogas. Sometimes horoscopes may apear to have many benefic yogas in it, yet the good resuls anticipated may not be perceptible because of the presence of nullifying factors. For example, the evil effects of Kemadruma Yoga are not felt, if there is Kemadruma-yoga-bhanga. Similarly, evil effects of Kalasarpa Yoga are not felt if there is Kalasarpa-yoga-bhanga.

Five Mahapurusha Yogas are discussed in every standard book (Ruchaka—Mars; Bhadra—Mercury; Hamsa—Jupiter; Malava—Venus; and Sasa—Saturn) where each of these planets occupies respectively a kendra identical with own house or house of exaltation.

Venus transits Taurus, Libra (own signs) and Pisces (exaltation sign), roughly speaking for a period of three months in a year. During these periods, daily Venus comes four times in kendra (*i.e.*, 8 hours a day); all children, born during these eight hours daily for three months in one cycle of Venus, will have Malava Yoga.

At present, Saturn's transit of Libra is from 6-10-1982 to 20-12-1984; so all children, born in Aries, Cancer, Libra or Capricorn ascendants, in a period of eight hours daily, for a little more than two years and two months, will have Sasa Yoga.

Similarly, in one cycle of Mars, round the zodiac children born in Aries, Scorpio and Capricorn ascendants, daily for a period of six hours, will have Ruchaka Yoga. Similarly for Bhadra—Mercury and Hamsa—Jupiter. Thus these five Mahapurusha Yogas are not very uncommon. In short, roughly speaking 5 out of 12 born will have one of the five Mahapurusha Yogas. While in actual practice we do not see 5 out of 12 nativities having beneficial results as signified by these yogas !

Chandrakala-Nadi (देवकेरलम्), Vol. II, Part I, page 5, verse No. 26 describes Malavya Yoga and its good results. The next verse No. 27 reads as under :

जीवे शनियुते दृष्टे मालवीयोगभङ्गवान् ।
भृगुरूच्चफलं व्यर्थं ग्रहच्छिद्रेण कर्शितः ॥

In a nativity, if Jupiter is associated with or aspected by Saturn, Malava yoga is nullified (bhanga). The good results of Venus are not experienced and the native is troubled by blemish.

Kerala-nadi (University of Mysore), page 7 goes a little further and adds one more condition.

जीवे शनियुते दृष्टे मालवीयोगभङ्गवान् ।
शुक्रे केतुयुते चेत्तु मालवीयोगभङ्गवान् ॥

In a nativity, if Jupiter is associated with or aspected by Saturn and/or Venus is associated with Ketu, the Malava Yoga is nullified.

Probably, the association or aspect of Saturn over Jupiter or conjunction of Ketu with yoga producing planet stunts the growth of beneficial results, in spite of the Mahapurusha Yogas. This gives a clue as to why Mahapurusha Yogs, sometimes, do not give prescribed results in some nativities.

In the April 1983 issue of A.M., page 372, a corresopondent, Mr. T.S. Muthukrishnan (Karatkudi) has raised a question regarding the horoscope of a native born on 28/29-11-1954 in Libra Lagna (Chart 1)

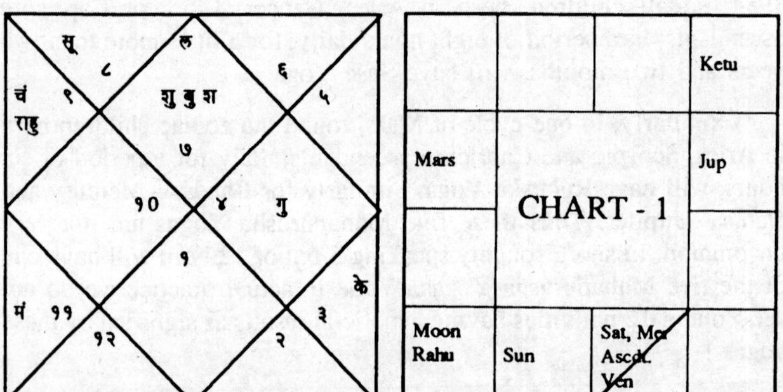

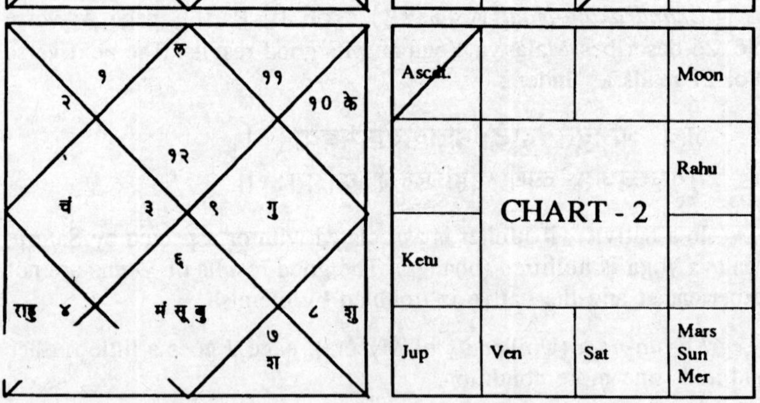

Saturn exalted in the ascendant Libra—Sasa Yoga; Jupiter exalted in the 10th—Hamsa Yoga; and Venus in Libra in the ascendant—Malava Yoga.

The native of Chart 1 is B.Sc. and only a medical representative. Hamsa Mahapurusha Yoga has become defunct, because of the10th aspect of Saturn over Jupiter.

Another correspondent Mr. S.H. Gokhale (Sangli) has also made a reference to this matter under "Defunct Yoga" (August 1983 issueof A.M., page 658).

In another case—May 1982, issue of A.M., page 408, Case II—male born on 8-10-1925 (Chart 2).

Mercury in Virgo in the 7th,Bhadra Yoga; and Jupiter in Sagittarius in the 10th—Hamsa Yoga.

The native of Chart 2 is an ordinary railway employee in spite of two Mahapurusha Yogas. Saturn's 3rd aspect on Jupiter has nullified the yoga.

Another case—July 1983 issue of A.M., page 570—Chart 3 (Article by J.N. Bhasin)

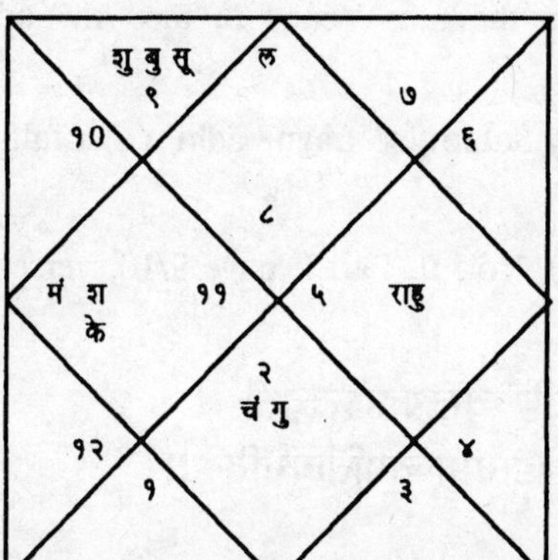

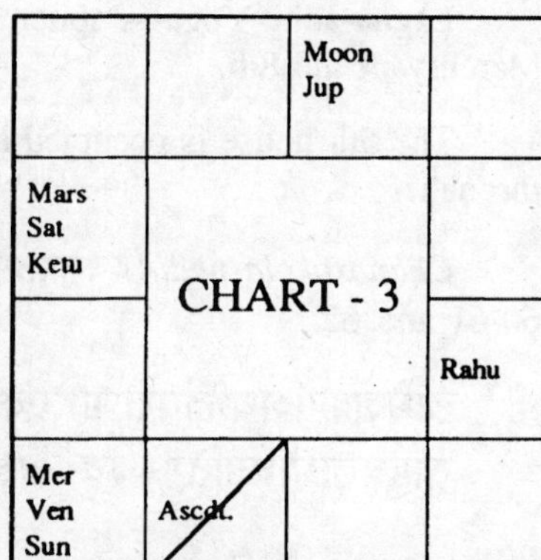

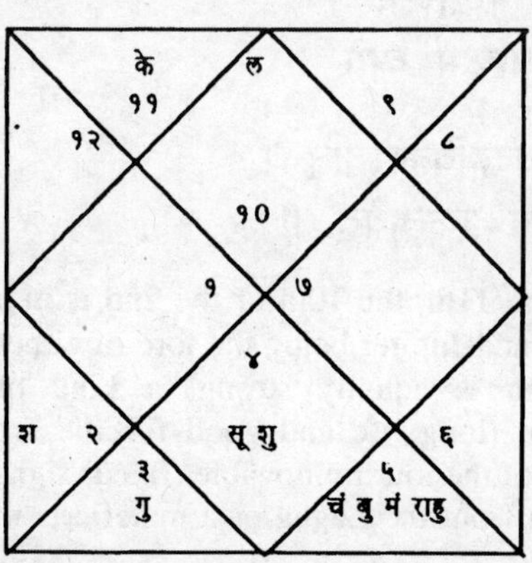

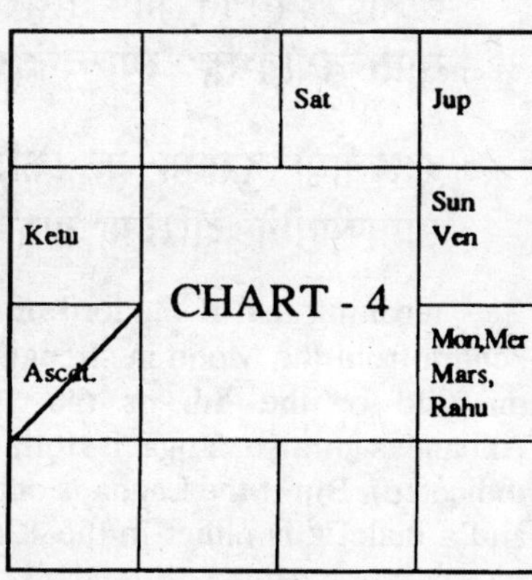

Saturn in Aquarius in the 4th—Sasa Yoga; and Saturn is associated with Ketu—Sasa Yoga is nullified. This is a horoscope of a girl who has married an orphan boy.

Chandrakala-nadi (देवकेरलम्), Vol. II, Part I, page 6/7, verse no. 35 describes Lagna/Chandra-nadi Yoga and its good results. The next verse No. 36 reads as :

लग्नाच्चंद्राधियोगेषु पंचमे तत्त्रिकोणगे ।
शुभेवा त्वशुभेवापि अधियोगो न विद्यते ॥

In the case of Lagna-nadi or Chandra-adhi Yoga, if the 5th or the 9th house from it is occupied by a planet, malefic or benefic, the Adhi Yoga does not exist.

Example (Chart 4)—April 1982 issue of A.M. page 350—Question No. 7

Lagna-adhi Yoga—Jupiter in the 6th; Venus in the 7th and Mercury in the 8th.

The 5th house is occupied by Saturn; so Lagna-adhi Yoga falls through.

Chandrakala-nadi (देवकेरलम्), Vol. II, Part I, page 9/10, verses 60-61 and 62.

लाभेशकर्मेशधनेश्वराणां एकोपि चन्द्रग्रहकेन्द्रवर्ती ।
स्वपुत्रलाभधिपतिर्गुरूश्च अखण्डसाम्राज्यपतित्वमेति ॥

लग्नाद् व्ययगते पापे स्थिरलग्नचतुष्टये ।
साम्राज्ययोगभङ्गः स्याच्चन्द्रलग्नाष्टमे व्यये ॥

दुःखजीवो दुरात्मा वा किञ्चिदङ्गविकारवान् ।
साम्राज्ययोगे दारिद्रयं योगहीन प्रकल्पयेत् ॥

meaning that if the lord of the 11th, the 10th or the 2nd is in a kendra from the Moon in strength and Jupiter being the lord of either the 2nd or the 5th or the 11th is equally strong, a kind of Akhandasamrajya Yoga is formed (long life and good fortune are indicated). But if the Lagna is one of the four immovable (fixed) signs and a malefic is either in the 12th from the Lagna or a malefic is in the 8th or in the 12th from the Moon, there is nullification of Samrajya Yoga. The native is unhappy, a cruel man or one of his limbs is defective or he is miserable.

All the above bhangas (nullifications) are collected from *Nadi* literature and not from standard astrological books.

The printed Sanskrit astrological books with English or vernacular translations form roughly 20% of the total Sanskrit literature on the subject, while 80% still remain hidden or unprinted in manuscript form in big government and private libraries, such as, at Triplicane—Madras; Adayar—Madras; Tanjore; University of Mysore Library; the Kerala University Library—Trivandrum; Sampurnanand Sanskrit University Library—Varanasi; Bhaudaji Collections; Asiatic Library—Bombay; Bhanderkar Oriental Research Institute—Poona; Baroda Oriental Institute—Baroda etc. .... where many rare manuscripts on astrology by ancient masters are stored. God knows, when this literature will see the light of the day.

It is fervently hoped that intelligent studetnts of Indian Astrology will after satisfying themselves make use of the above nullifications while making predictions on nativities.

11

Nadi Principles Behind Saturn's Transit

Saturn is the farthest planet in the solar system, other than the outer planets being 1, 418 million kilometers away from the Sun. It is also the slowest moving planet among the Nava Grahas and takes about 29 1/2 years to go round the Sun and transits each sign of the zodiac for an average period of 2 1/2 years.

In Hindu Astrology Saturn is dreaded as a first-rate malefic. The transit phenomenon of *Sade-sathi* - 7 1/2 year of *Panoti* (in the south known as *elarata*) which occurs in everyone's life at some time or other, when Saturn transits the 12th, the 1st and the 2nd houses from the Moon (Janma Rasi), is well known to students of Astrology and many laymen dread to hear the very words *sadesathi* from the astrologer's mouth.

It is very interesting to note that many secrets of predictive Hindu Astrology are found abundantly in *Nadi-Granthas*. We call these secrets as *Nadi* principles. The research-minded students of Hindu Astrology can study these principles and apply them in their horoscopic analysis.

According to ancient *Nadi Granthas* Saturn's transit results can be delineated from four different phases of Saturn as follows :

I. House-wise transit results of Saturn;

II. Transit results of Saturn through or from certain houses as counted from its *Chandra Navamsa Rasi*.

III. Degreewise transit results of Satrurn over and in trines to the 7 planets and the nodes; and

IV. Degreewise transit results of Saturn over the lords of the 8th house its trines from each house.

Phase I :

House-wise transit result of Saturn :

Chandrakala Nadi (Madras Government Oriental Series 1952 and 1956) gives the following verse at many places.

यद् भावस्याष्टमे मन्दे यद् भावस्याष्टमेक्षिते ।
तद् भावः क्लेशमाप्नोति मूर्त्यादिफलमीरयेत् ॥

Vol. I, P100 Vs. 1058; Vol. II, Part I, P. 106, Vs 913; and Vol. II Part II P. 240, Vs 4827.

Meaning, the house from which the 8th house when transited by Saturn and the other thrree houses from which the respective 8th houses when aspected by Saturn, suffer afflictions. One has to obtain Saturn's transit reslts from the Ascendant onwards, in the same way.

In order to understand the above verse we have to take first the house through which Saturn is transiting and the three houses which Saturn aspects. The suffering and afflictions are felt on account of those houses from which the above four places become the 8th houses.

The whole *Nadi* principle of the verse could be explained clearly as follows :

(1) When Saturn transits the Ascendant, it is the 8th from the 6th house; Saturn's 3rd house aspect falls on the 3rd house, it is the 8th from the 8th house. Saturn's 7th house aspect falls on the 7th house, it is the 8th from the 12th house; and Saturn's 10th house aspect falls on the 10th house, it is the 8th from the 3rd house. Therefore, the native who has the transit of Saturn in the Ascendant, will suffer unfavourable results in matters connected with the 6th, the 8th, the 12th and the 3rd houses.

(2) When Saturn transits the 2nd house, it is the 8th house from the 7th house; 3rd house aspect falls on the 4th house; it is the 8th from the 9th house; Saturn's 7th house aspect falls on the 8th house, it is the 8th from the Ascendant; Saturn's 10th house aspects falls on the 11th

house, it is the 8th from the 4th house. Therefore the native will suffer afflictions in matters connected with the 7th, the 9th, the Ascendant and the 4th houses.

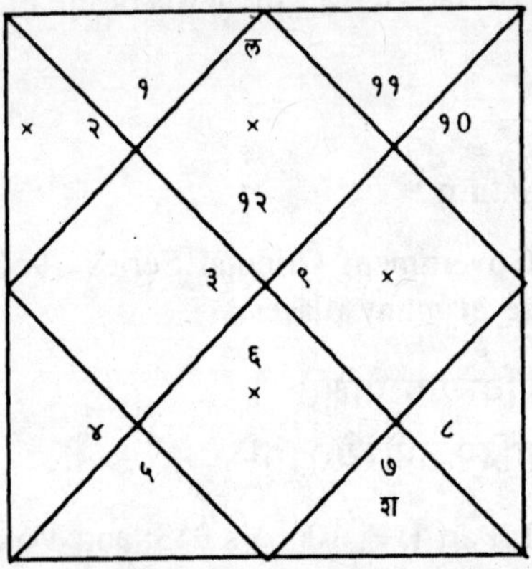
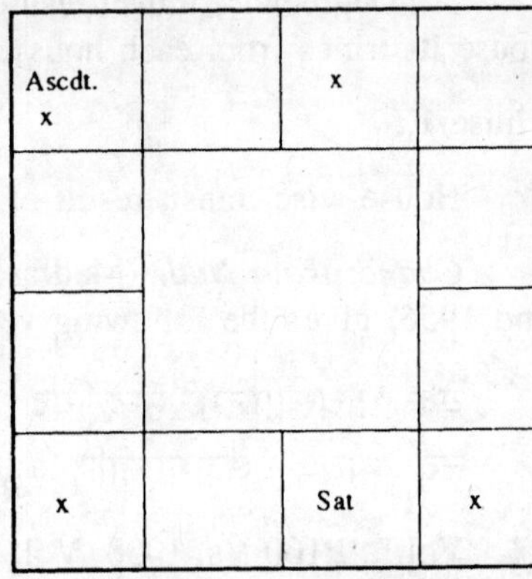

In the same way, Saturn's transit and its influences from the 3rd house onwards to the 12th house can be judged. It may be emphasized here that the above transit results are to be borne by the native throughout the transit of Saturn in a particular sign. Our learned readers very well know, in Indian Astrology, the transit aspects are from sign position to sign position.

Example; Date of birth 28-11-1935 at 15 h, 11 m at Ahmedabad. Saturn's transit results through the 8th house (Libra) i.e. from 6-10-1982 to 20-12-1984 when Saturn transited the 8th house (Libra) the Ascendant, the 3rd, the 7th and the 10th houses were afflicted.

(1) the Ascendant - worries on account of progeny; health complaints, becoming angry soon;

(2) the 3rd house - failure in enter-prise; ear troubles now and then; mental delusion;

(3) the7th house - wife's sickness; theft of silver vessels from residence; small pilgrimages; loss in partnership business.

(4) the 10th house - mother-in-law sick; loss in business; complaints about spinal cord.

The Nadi author Shri Achyuta has succinctly given so much information about transit results of Saturn **in only one single verse as above.**

Phase II :

Transit results of Saturn through or from certain houses are counted from the *Chandra Navamsa Rasi.*

शत्रुभीतिर्मनस्तापमन्तश्छिद्रकलापवान् ।
चन्द्रांशराशिगे मन्दे गोचरे जन्मगेऽथवा ॥

Chandrakala Nadi Part I P. 314, verse 3124.

Meaning, when Saturn transits *Chandra Navamsa Rasi (Rasi represented in the natal chart by the Moon's occupied Navamsa Rasi)* or the sign occupied by the Moon (in Rasi chart), the native suffers fear from enemies, mental anguish and humiliation from secret blemish.

चंद्रांशराशिमारभ्य गोचरे त्वष्टमे शनौ ।
राहुदाये महत्कष्टं योगभङ्गं विनिर्दिशेत् ॥

Chandrakala Nadi Part I, P. 201, Verse 2044/45.

Meaning, When Saturn transits the 8th sign from the *Chandra Navamsa Rasi,* the native will suffer great calamity during Rahu's period and will have termination of some runnng favourable yogaphala or *yogabhanga results.*

चन्द्रांशराशिमारभ्य गोचरे सप्तमे शनौ ।
राहुदाये वक्रभुक्तौ देहजाड्यं विनिर्दिशेत् ॥

Chandrakala Nadi Part I., P. 235, Verse. 2385.

When Saturn transits the 7th sign from the *Chandra Navamsa Rasi, the native gains obesity during Mar's Antara* in Rahu's period (if it coin-cides).

The above rules give us a clue to study transit results of other slow-moving planets through the *Chandra Navamsa Rasi.* Similarly, their transits through *Navamsa* signs occupied by the remaining 6 planets should be looked into. More research is necessary.

Phase II :

Degreewise transit results of Saturn over and in trines to the 7 planets and the nodes :

When Saturn transits over a position which is identical degree-wise to the natal position of any planet or its trine positions, it gives unfavourable results pertaining to :

(i) that natal planet (as significator);

(ii) the house/s owned by that planet; and

(iii) the house occupied by that planet.

1. The Sun :

रवित्रिकोणगे मन्दे पितृपीडा
भवेत् कष्टं पितृवर्गेऽरिष्टदम् ।

meaning, when transit Saturn coin-cides identically with the natal position of the Sun or its trines, the native's father's health will be afflicted or the native himself will be troubled or death of some elderly male relative will take place.

Additional results : Grief on account of demise of a close relative; misunderstanding with father or reproaches from him; mental anguish to father; heavy expenditure; one becomes indebted; prestige at stake; demise of father; troubles in vocation or service; setback in service or business; change of place of residence etc.

2. The Moon :

चन्द्रत्रिकोणगे मन्दे मातृपीडा
भवेत् कष्टं मातृवर्गेऽरिष्टदम् ।

meaning, when transit Saturn coin-cides identically with the natal position of the Moon or its trines, the native's mother's health will be afflicted or the native himself will be troubled or death of some elderly female relative will take place.

Additional results : Mental agony to mother due to misdeeds of her breathern; loss of status; loss of wealth; sickness of mother causing worries to father; mental agony; demise of mother; misunderstanding with mother; devaluation of landed property etc.

3. Mars :

कुजत्रिकोणगे मन्दे भ्रातृपीडा भवेत् कष्टं
भ्रातृवर्गेडरिष्टदम् ॥

meaning when transit Saturn coin-cides identically with the natal position of Mars or its trines, the native's brother's (or sister's) health is afflicted or the native himself will be troubled or death of brother (or sister) will occur.

Additional results : Blood impurities, humiliation, fear of criminal proceedings; quarrels for assets; low ebb in buriness activities; demotion; worries on account of brethren; loss of wealth or property; wound by weapon or physical injury; fear of accident etc.

4. Mercury :

When transit Saturn coincides identically with the natal position of Mercury or its trines, the native's maternal uncle's or aunt's health will suffer.

Additional results : Increase in debts, financial stringency, in business or trade; misfortune or death in mother's paternal family; hindrances in education and mental anguish on account of it; sickness of a close friend; mental disorders; etc.

5. Jupiter :

गुरुत्रिकोणगे मन्दे पुत्रपीडा भवेत्कष्टं पुत्रवर्गेऽरिष्टदम् ।

meaning, when transit Saturn coincides identically with the natal position of Jupiter or its trines, health of the native's son (or daughter) is afflicted or the native himself is troubled or death of son (or daughter) takes place.

Additional results : Worries or troubles from family members; mental anxiety and anguish on account of one's children; hindrance in religious pursuits or studies; demise of son or daughter, etc.

6. Venus :

शुक्रत्रिकोणगे मन्दे कलत्रपीडा महद्भयम् ।

meaning, when transit Saturn coincides identically with the natal position of Venus or its trines, the native's wife will have major health problems or great fear is impending.

Additional results : Disgrace on account of wife and consequent mental anguish; obstacles from inlaws; separation from wife; demise of wife; absence of reciprocal love; marital relations strained; troubles in wife's paternal family, etc.

7. Saturn :

When, transit Saturn coincides identically with its natal position or its trines, the native will experience major physical ailments lasting over long duration.

Additional results : Disputes with and troubles from family members; absence of peace of mind on account of problems concerning landed property and great loss of money; abnormal increase in miseries and sufferings; demise of native himself, etc.

8. Rahu :

राहुत्रिकोणगे मन्दे देहपीडा मनोव्यथा स्वसमानजनावधि :

Meaning, when transit Saturn coincides identically with the natal position of Rahu or its trines, the native is grieved by physical pain or mental agony or death of some nearer relative occurs.

Additional results : Relations with Government strained; setback in health; reputation at stake; happening of some untoward incident in his own family; death of a close friend or a cousin; performs obsequies for a dead relative; food poisoning; snake or insect bite; shifting of residence to a distant place; etc.

9. Ketu :

When transit Saturn coincides identically with the natal position of Ketu or its trines, the health of the native himself is likely to be afflicted seriously *(Swadehe jayate gadah).*

Additional results : Quarrels in family; demise in maternal uncle's family; mental tension due to family dispute over inheritance; kidney disorders; calamity; hospitalization etc.

Phase IV :

Degreewise transit results of Saturn over the lord of the 8th house or its trines from each house.

तत्तद् भावाष्टमेशांशे गोचरे शनि संस्थिते ।
तत्तद् भावविनाशेन क्लेशं प्राप्नोति भूरिशः ॥

तत्तद् भावाष्टमेशांशे त्रिकोणेवाऽथवा भवेत् ।
स्फुटयोगं गते मन्दे तत्तद् भावविनाशनम् ॥

meaning, (of two verses) : When transit Saturn concides identically with the natal position of the lord of 8th house from a particular house or its trine positions, the native will experience mental upsets due to denial of results signified by that particular House (these two verses are complimentary to each other).

A

Bhrugu Nadi, in possession of Theosophical Society's Library, Adyar, Madras-20, contains about 8650 verses. Transit results of Saturn over the lords of the twelve houses only :

लग्नेशांशे शत्रुपीड़ा स्वमातुलजनावधिः ।
धनेशांशे दारपीडा, सोत्थांशे देहजाड्यता ।।
सुखेशांशे पितारिष्टं स्वप्रभोश्च तथा भवेत् ।
सुतेशांशे मित्रपीड़ा राजराष्ट्र विनाशकृत् ।
षष्ठेशांशे पितृव्यस्य देहबाधा भविष्यति ।
दारेशांशे प्रवासं स्यात् मातामहजनावधिः ।।
रन्ध्रेशांशे देहपीड़ा भाग्येशांशे धनक्षयम् ।
कर्मेशांशे व्ययाधिकयं श्वशुरारिष्टमादिशेत् ।।
लाभेशांशे मातृहीनः व्ययेशांशे पुत्रपीड़ा ।
मृर्त्यदिव्ययभावन्तं शनिचारवशात्फलम् ।।

When transit Saturn conicides identically with the natal position of the lord of :

(1) the first house the native will be subjected to trouble from his enemies or the maternal relatives will be afflicted. (1st house being the 8th from the 6th house).

(2) the 2nd house—native's spouse will be subjected to trouble (2nd house being the 8th from the 7th house).

(3) the 3rd house—the native will suffer from some sluggishness (3rd house being the 8th the 8th house).

(4) the 4th house—native's father or employer will be subjected to trouble and affliction (4th house being the 8th from the 9th house).

(5) the 5th house—native will be subjected to trouble from friends or trouble from government or state agencies (5th house being the 8th from the 10th house).

(6) the 6th house—native's paternal uncle or aunt will be

physically injured (6th house being the 8th from the 11th house).

(7) the 7th house—native will undergo unneccessary journeys or will get news about the demise of materinal grandfather (7th house being the 8th from the 12th house).

(8) the 8th house—native's health will be afflicted (8th house being the 8th from the 1st house).

(9) the 9th house—native will experience reduction in his assets or properties (9th house being the 8th from the 2nd house).

(10) the 10th house—native will experience increase in expenditure or health problem concerning his father-in-law (the 10th house being the 8th from the 3rd house).

(11) the 11th house—native may lose his mother (affliction to her) (11th house being the 8th from the 4th house).

(12) the 12th house—native will experience problems concerning his childredn (12th house being the 8th from the 5th house).

Transit results for Saturn are to be judged beginning from the 1st house upto the 12th house. In the *Bhargu nadi* only transits over its natal planets are considered.

Phase IV :

B

Chandrakala Nadi gives exhaustive details of the effects of Saturn's transit, in about 350 verses out of a total of 9512 verses. There are two improvements in this masterpiece as compared with *Bhrugu Nadi*.

(a) the author gives importance also to the trine positions of a natal planet; and

(b) Saturn's transit effects through sign/s aspected by natal planet are also taken into account as stated below :

लग्नेशांशे तत्त्रिकोणे स्फुटयोगं गते शनौ।
मातृलरिष्टमाप्नोति मातुर्माता मनोव्यथाम् ।।

meaning, when transit Saturn coincides degree-wise with the lord of the Ascendant or its trine positions, there will be affliction to one's maternal uncle and consequently maternal grandmother will have mental agony.

Additional results : Physical injury from a weapon; native's father grieved due to loss of his brother or sister; grief to native's mother or maternal grandmother; worries to maternal uncle or aunt; one becomes indebted; loss or fear from thieves; etc.

धनेशांशे तत्त्रिकोणे स्फुटयोगं गते शनौ ।
धनेशदृष्टिराशौ तु दारहानिं विनिर्दिशेत् ॥

meaning, when transit Saturn coincides degree-wise with the lord of the 2nd house or its trine positions or passes through sign/s aspected by that lord (on the same degree) there will occur death of native's wife.

Additional results : Loss in vocational activities, death of someone in wife's paternal family; wife gaining obesity so as to obstruct free movement of her body; worries to wife; death of wife; want of marital happiness; etc.

Regarding the 3rd house or *Sahodarasthana*, no specific verse is found in the text. The 3rd house being the 8th from the 8th house, matters connected with that house will be involved such as illhealth; gaining obesity;' grief; inheritance; accident; debts; poverty; medical operation etc., can be looked into.

सुखेशांशे तत्त्रिकोणे स्फुटयोगं गते शनौ ।
स्वपितुर्देहजाड्यादि दृष्टिराशौ महाविपत् ॥

meaning, when transit Saturn coincides degree-wise with the lord of the 4th house or its trine positions; native's father will gain obesity and when Saturn passes through sign/s aspected by that lord, he will suffer major calamity.

Additional results : Death of native's father and consequent mental agony to mother and to paternal uncle or aunt; mother much worried; grief to father due to loss of spouse; calamity to father's brethren; father's sickness etc.

सुतेशांशे तत्त्रिकोणे स्फुटयोगं गते शनौ ।
प्रत्यग्दाये सोदरस्य सन्तानारिष्टमादिशेत् ॥

meaning, when transit Saturn coincides degree-wise with the lord of the 5th house or its trine position, there will be death of brothers or sister's child provided at that time native's running *Dasa* is the 5th one (Pratyaridasa) from birth Dasa.

Additional results : Loss of paternal wealth; serious sickness of a friend; ill-health or death of wife's mother; death in wife's paternal family; death of a child in one's own family etc.

षष्ठेशांशे तत्रिकोणे स्फुटयोगं गते शनौ ।
षष्ठेशदृष्टिराशौ तु सोदरस्य मनोव्यथा ॥

meaning, when transit Saturn coincides degree-wise with the lord of the 6th house or its trine positions or passess through sign/s aspected by that lord, the native's brother or sister will suffer mental agony.

Additional results : Death of elder brother or sister; loss of status or position; change of place of residence; great mental agony and much fear to native; death of paternal relative (i.e., father's brother or sister); miseries to elder brethern, etc.

मदेशांशे तत्रिकोणे स्फुटयोगं गते शनौ ।
मदेशदृष्टिराशौ तु मातामहविनाशनम् ॥

meaning, when transit Saturn coincides degree-wise with the lord of the 7th house or its trine positions or passes through sign/s aspected by that lord, death of native's maternal grandfather is indicated.

Additional results : Unexpected and heavy expenditure; death of maternal uncle or afflictions to or death of native's father's mother.

रन्ध्रेशांशे तत्रिकोणे स्फुटयोगं गते शनौ ।
रन्ध्रेशदृष्टिराशौ तु स्वजनारिष्टमादिशेत् ॥

meaning, when transit Saturn coincides degree-wise with the lord of the 8th house or its trine positions or passes through sign/s aspected by that lord, death of a nearer relative (family member) takes place.

Additional results : One's own death; fear from opponents; native suffers from severe diseases and is confined to hospital; wife's health suffers; death of a bosom friend; worries on account of children; blemish to family; loss of property or wealth; native feels exhausted and becomes emaciated; fear of death due to accident etc.

Note : My horoscope has Cancer Ascendant. Lord of the 8th house—Saturn is in Gemini (in the 12th) and its trine positions are Libra and Aquarius signs aspected by Saturn are Leo, Sagittarius and

Pisces. I lost (i) my daughter on 30-4-1954 (Saturn in Libra) (ii) my mother on 30.11.1965 (Saturn in Aquarius);' (iii) my father on 15-6-1968 (Saturn in Pisces) and (iv) my wife on 24-1-1975 (Saturn in Gemini).

भाग्येशांशे तत्त्रिकोणे स्फुटयोगं गते शनौ ।
स्वमातृभगिनी पुत्रनाशं च मनुरब्रवीत् ॥

meaning, when transit Saturn coincides degree-wise with the lord of the 9th house or its trine positions, demise of son of native's mother's sister, will occur, so says the great seer Manu.

Additional results : Quarrels with bad people (Goondas); eye disease; disease in throat; loss of wealth; quarrels in family; mental disability, etc.

कर्मेशांशे तत्त्रिकोणे स्फुटयोगं गते शनौ ।
कर्मेशदृष्टिराशौ तु भगिन्याश्च मनोव्यथा ॥

meaning, when transit Saturn coincides degree-wise with the lord of the 10th house or its trine positions or passes through sign/s aspected by that lord, the native's sister suffers mental anguish.

Additional results : Calamity in wife's paternal family; native himself hospitalized; severe sickness or death of brother or sister and consequent grief to native; affliction to or death or wife's father etc.

लाभेशांशे तत्त्रिकोणे स्फुटयोगं गते शनौ ।
लाभेशदृष्टिराशौ तु मातृपीडा विनिर्दिशेत् ।

meaning, when transit Saturn concides degree-wise with the lord of the 11th house or its trine positions or passes through sign/s aspected by that lord, trouble to native's mother is indicated.

Additional results : Desertion of one's birth place; sickness of friend's wife; quarrels on account of or loss of landed property; grief to mother due to death of maternal uncle or aunt; death of a maternal relative; overworried; mental agony to mother; afflictions to or death of mother, etc.

व्ययेशांशे तत्त्रिकोणे स्फुटयोगं गते शनौ ।
व्ययेशदृष्टिराशौ तु सन्तानारिष्टमादिशेत् ॥

meaning, when transit Saturn coincides degree-wise with the lord of the 12th house or its trine positions or passes through signs aspected by that lord, demise of native's child is indicated.

Additional results : Set-back in studies or failure in examination; sickness of elder brother's wife or elder sister's husband; sickness of children; demise of grandfather; loss of wealth; afflictions to son or daughter or misunderstanding with them. etc.

While studying a chart, the astrologer should take into account the native's position in life, age, sex, Dasa period, country of origin etc., before coming to any judgement, because all the results listed above against each transit need not materialise at the same time.

The transit effect of Saturn over a natal position or its trines commences nearly 100 Kalas prior to that degree-wise position and lasts till 100 Kala beyond it (100 kalas + 100 Kalas = 200 Kalas = 3° 20' = 1 Navamsa), but the main event takes place immediately after Saturn has crossed natal or trine position.

Threrfore, while interpreting the transit results of Saturn, the above four methods may be employed and a balanced judgement be arrived. The strength and position of the transited planet, house transited etc., as well as those of transiting Saturn should be considered. One should also see as to whether Saturn is in direct or retrograde motion or is stationary at that time.

The above article is the result of an indepth study of over 30,000 (thirty thousand) Sanskrit verses from *Nadi Granthas*. Hindu Astrology is like a deep ocean, containing many valuable pearls hidden in *Nadi Granthas*. The deeper one dives, the better chances of getting more pearls. May this write-up motivate ardent students of sidereal astrology to study and digest more and more such principles.

12

Nadi System of Prediction

Use of Navamsa Tulya Rasi

It is a well-established fact that in Indian Astrology, the Navamsa chart is of great utility for delineation purposes. The scribe had made a passing reference to this in his article "Use of Collective Ashtakavarga in Prognostication" (Chapter-18) *Samudayashtakabvarga and Navamsa strength.* The present write up is the result of further research in that direction.

1. According to *Ankan Sastram* (p. 14, v. 8) if Jupiter and the Moon were to be together (in one Navamsa), the native will be Kubera, provided this conjunction is in the last quarter of Aslesha star or in the last quarter of Moola star.

Aslesha's last quarter is Pisces Navamsa in Cancer sign and Moola's last quarter is Cancer Navamsa in Sagittarius sign, *i.e., the conjunction takes place in own Navamsa of one planet and in own sign of the other planet.* This yoga, in fact, is Gajakesari Yoga. To have a successful yoga, the author Vyaghrapada gives importance to Navamsa conjunction only (*i.e.*, within 3° 20') and to the sign strength of both planets.

2. Planets posited in natal chart get their effects enhanced or reduced by their placements in Navamsa chart.

According to *Chandrakala Nadi,* Vol. II, Part I, page 5, verse 29, "If an exalted planet in Rasi chart is positioned in a debilitated Navamsa, the native is unhappy; if a debilitated planet in Rasi chart is exalted in Navamsa, the native is happy; while a planet in own Navamsa or in *vargottama* confers enjoyments and a kind of Rajayoga is formed.

Planets, otherwise powerful and well situated in Rasi chart, do not give favourable results, if they are weak in Navamsa chart. The above verse gives too much importance to Navamsa strength of planets.

3. Moreover in our book *Ashtakavarga* on page 206, there is a dictum No. 13-"A *vargottama* planet in any Bhava, with 30 or more *bindus*, advànces the happiness of that Bhava to the greatest extent" (in proportion to increasing number of *bindus).*

A *vargottama* planet, in same sign and in same Navamsa, *i.e.*, being powerful by position and also associated with higher number of *bindus* in Rasi chart as well as in Navamsa chart, gives very favourable results.

From the above three points, it can be concluded that *a planet associateed with higher or lower number of* bindus *in Rasi chart becomes powerful if he gets higher numberof* bindus *in Navamsa sign occupied by that planet.* It is also true that the same planet gives adverse results if he gets lower number of *bindus* in Navamsa sign. These points are well-substantiated in the following four examples.

Chart I. Birth details; July 4/5, 1944 (Tuesday) at 2h, 52m, a.m. (IST), Lat. 23° 24' N; Long. 72° 45' E. *Planetary longitudes* : The Sun 2s 19° 36'; the Moon 8s 2° 2'; Mars 4s 2° 48'; Mercury 2s 23° 44'; Jupiter 4s-2°-48'; Venus 2s-21°-44'; Saturn 2s 8° 48'; Rahu 3s 5° 15'; Ketu 9s 5° 15'; and the Ascendant 0s 16° 45'. balance of Ketu Dassa; 5 years, 11 months and 7 days at birth.

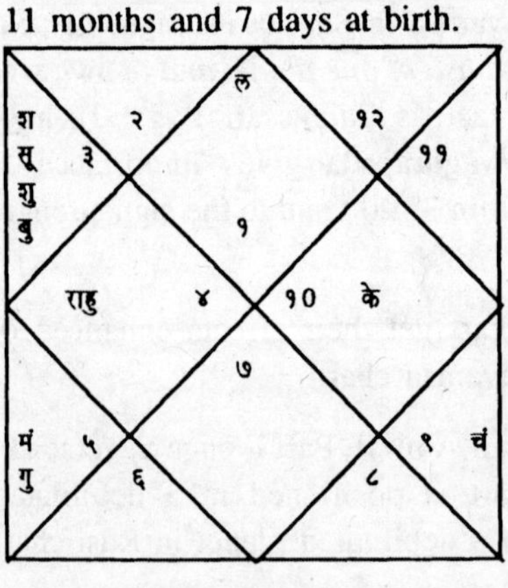

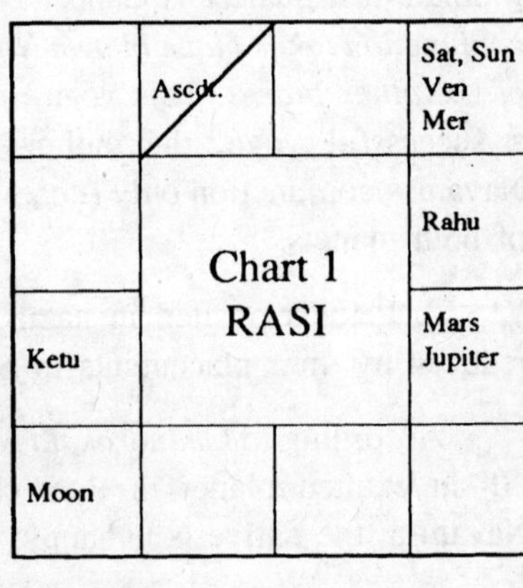

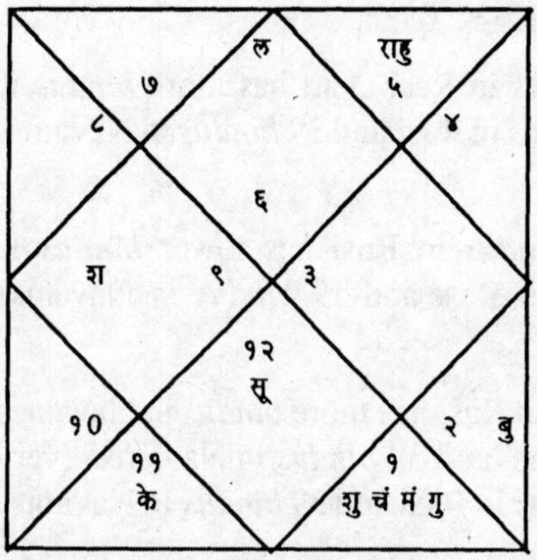

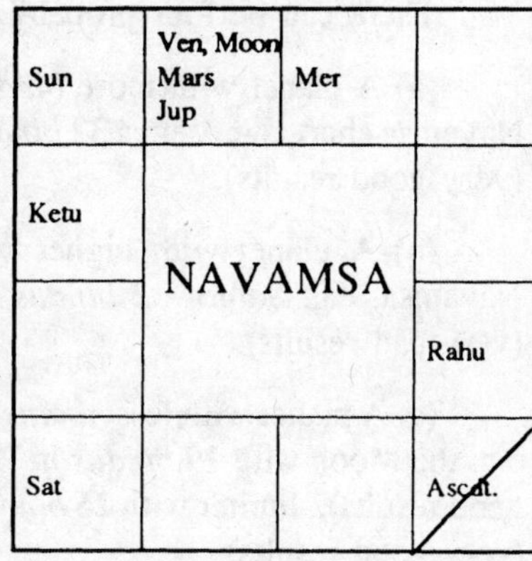

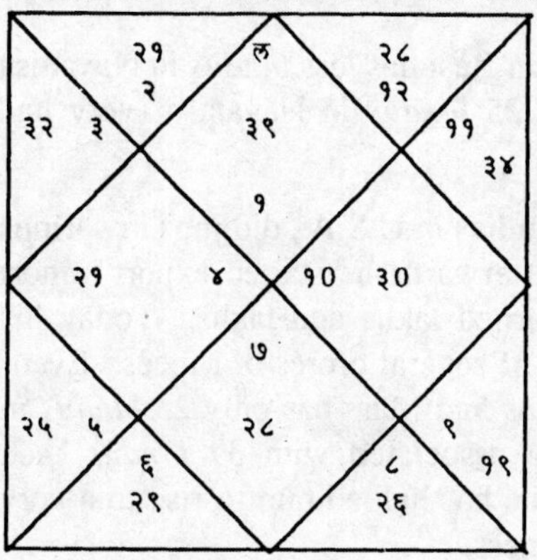

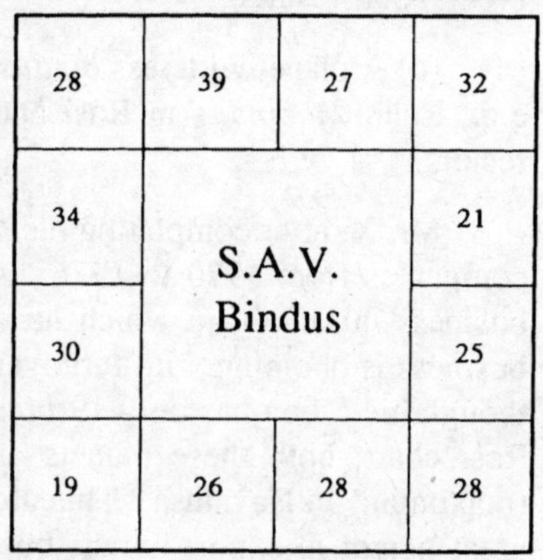

In the Navamsa chart, note the Navamsa positions occupied by all the planets. Also note in which houses (Bhavas) in the Rasi chart, these Navamsa positions fall. Each planets will be associated with certain number of *bindus* [in the *samudayashtakavarga* (S.A.V.) chart] in both Raṣi chart as well as in Navamsa chart.

A table of all planets showing S.A.V. strength in Rasi chart as well as in Navamsa chart **in Vimshottari Dasa order** is given below for guidance.

Planets	Sun	Moon	Mars	Rahu	Jup.	Sat.	Merc.	Ketu	Ven.
Rasi S.A.V. bindus	32	19	25	21	25	32	32	30	32
Nav. S.A.V. bindus	28	39	39	25	39	19	27	34	39

There can be four probabilities:-

(a) A planet with more *bindus* in Rasi chart has more *bindus* in Navamsa chart, e.g. Venus 32 *bindus* in Rasi and 39 *bindus* in Navamsa (very good results).

(b) A planet with higher *bindus* in Rasi has lower *bindus* in Navamsa, e.g. Saturn 32 *bindus* in Rasi and 19 *bindus* in Navamsa (very bad results).

(c) A planet with less *bindus* in Rasi has more *bindus* in Navamsa e.g. the Moon with 19 *bindus* in Rasi and 39 *bindus* in Navamsa (very good results). Jupiter with 25 *bindus* in Rasi and 39 *bindus* in Navamsa (very good results).

(d) A planet with less *bindus* in Rasi has less *bindus* in Navamsa e.g., Rahu 21 *bindus* in Rasi and 25 *bindus* in Navamsa (very bad results).

Mr. X, after completing his studies in U.S.A., did jobs in various companies from 1970 to 1976. Afterwards he started export-import business in U.S.A. in which he earned lakhs and lakhs. Today his business is booming with turnover of several crores of rupees. Eventhough his Moon has only 19 *bindus* and Mars has only 25 *bindus* in Rasi chart, both these planets are associated with 39 *bindus* each (maximum) in Navamsa. This alone has helped him to rise to a very great height in export-import business.

Dasas

D.M. Y.

7-11-5 **balance**

5- 7- 1944
....
12-6-1950 } Ketu (34 *bindus* in Navamsa)

0- 0- 20
....
12-6-1970 } Venus (39 *bindus* in Navamsa)

0-0- 6 12-6-1976	Sun (28 *bindus* in Navamsa)
0-0- 10 12-6-1986	Moon (39 *bindus* in Navamsa)
0-0- 7 .... 12-6-1993	Mars (39 *bindus* in Navamsa)

The above Navamsa bindu strength can be applied to Dasa periods as well as to Bhukti (Antara) periods. The scribe has tested it successfully in many charts.

The horoscope (Chart 2) of N.T. Rama Rao (Chief Minister of Andhra Pradesh) is as follows:

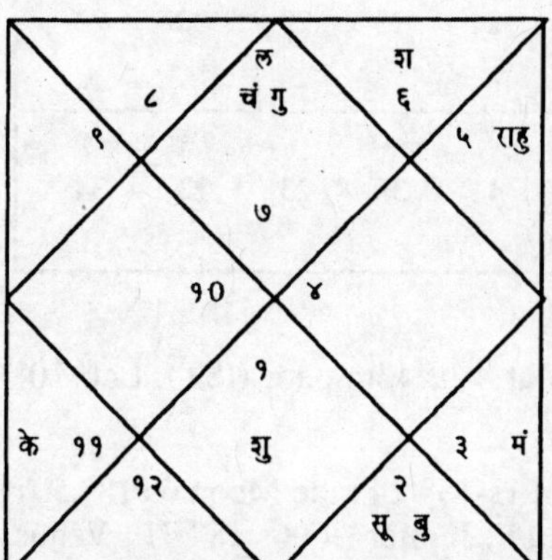

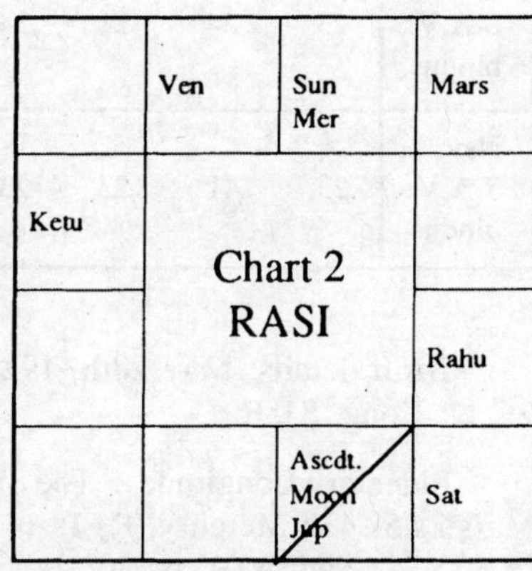

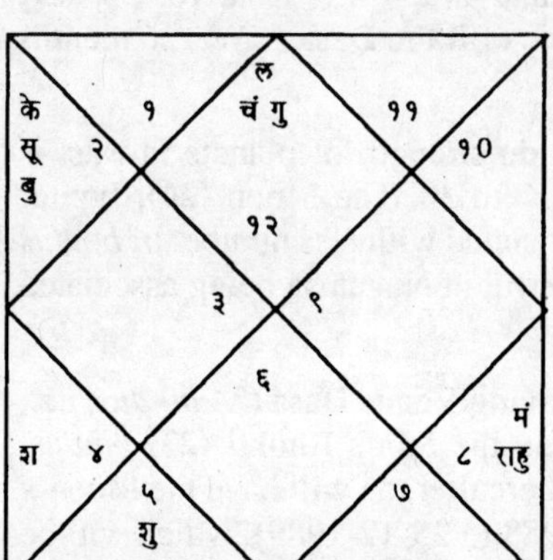

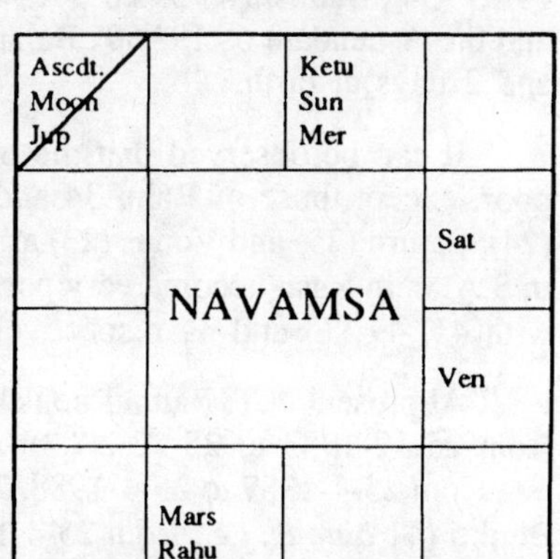

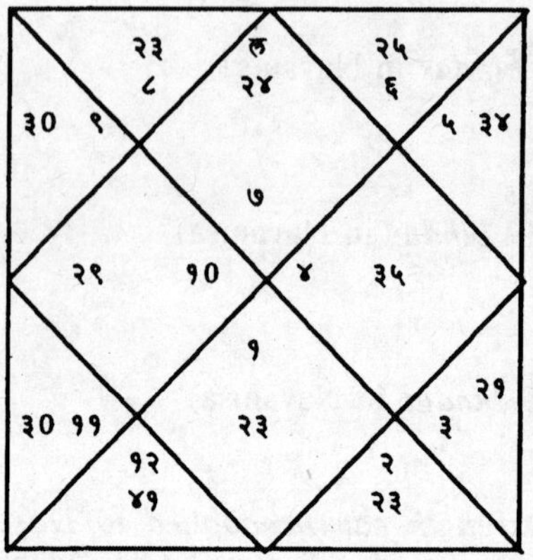

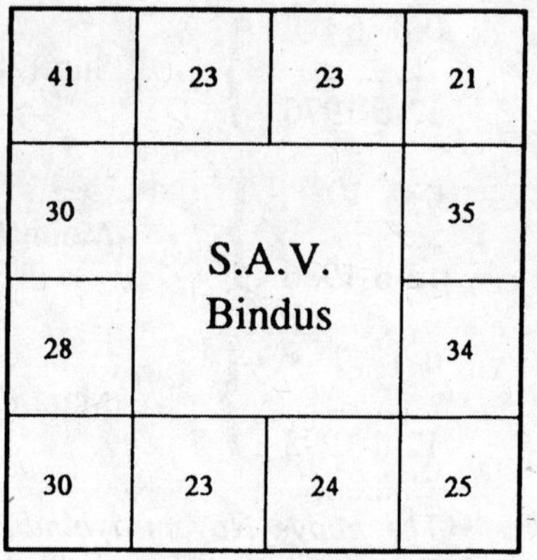

Planets	Sun	Moon	Mars	Rahu	Jup.	Sat.	Merc.	Ketu	Ven.
Rasi S.A.V. bindus	23	24	21	34	24	25	23	30	23
Nav. S.A.V. bindus	23	41	23	23	41	35	23	23	34

Birth details: May 28th, 1923 at 4 h. 43m.p.m. (IST), Lat. 10° 25' N; Long. 81°E.

Planetary Longitudes: The Sun 1s-13°-24'; the Moon 6s 18° 50'; Mars 2s 5° 41'; Mercury (R) 1s 14° 14'; Jupiter (R) 6s 18° 31'; Venus 0s 15° 34'; Saturn (R) 5s 20° 44'; Rahu 4s 23° 45'; Ketu 10s 23° 45'; and the Ascendant 6s 19° 50'. Balance of Rahu Dasa; 1 year, 6 months and 2 days at birth.

It can be observed that the bindu strength of planets in Rasi is poor, except those of Rahu 34 and Ketu 30. The Moon (24), Jupiter (24), Saturn (25) and Venus (23) associated with less number of *bindus* in S.A.V. in Rasi, become very powerful in Navamsa being associated with 41, 41, 35 and 34 respectively.

At present N.T. Rama Rao is having Venus Dasa (34 *bindus, i.e.*, from 25-12-1983 to 25-12-2003); and the Sun's Bhukti (23) *bindus, i.e.*, from 25-4-1987 to 25-4-1988. Thereafter, he will have the Moon's Bhukti (41 *bindus, i.e.*, from 25-4-1988 to 25-12-1989), which will be grand period.

The horoscope (Chart 3) of Amitabh Bachan is as follows :

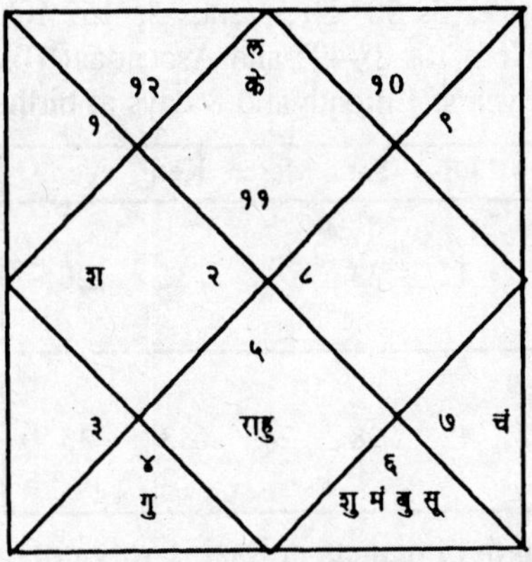

		Sat	
Ascdt. Ketu	Chart 3 RASI		Jup
			Rahu
		Moon	Ven, Mars Mer, Sun

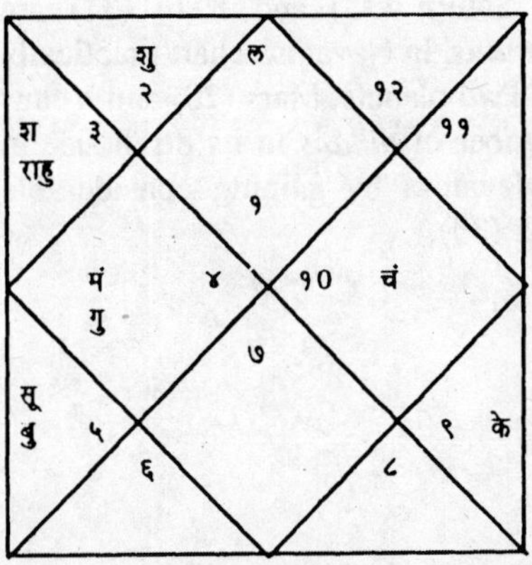

	Ascdt.	Ven	Sat Rahu
	NAVAMSA		Mars Jup
Moon			Sun Mer
Ketu			

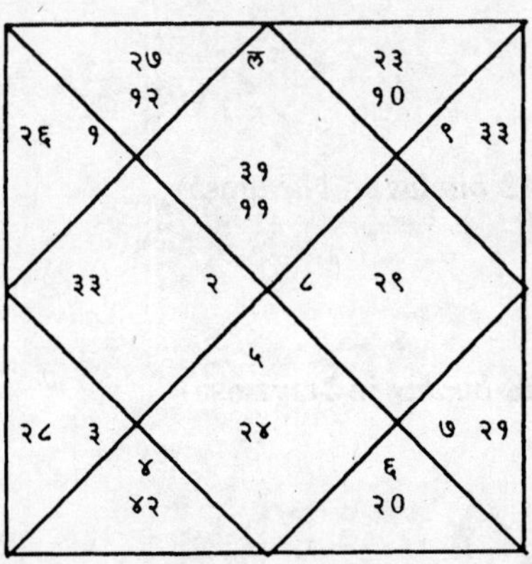

27	26	33	28
31	S.A.V. Bindus		42
23			24
33	29	21	20

Birth details : October 11th 1942 at 4h-00m. p.m. (IST), Lat. 25° 28' N; Long. 81° 52' E.

Planetary Logitudes : The Sun 5s 24° 25'; the Moon 6s 11° 2'; Mars 5s 22° 41'; Mercury 5s 23° 36'; Jupiter 3s 00° 30'; Venus 5s 15° 10'; Saturn 1s 19° 13'; Rahu 4s 8° 49'; Ketu 10s-8°-49'; and Ascendant 10s 21° 38'. Balance of Rahu Dasa : 12 years, 1 month and 8 days at birth.

Planets	Sun	Moon	Mars	Rahu	Jup.	Sat.	Merc.	Ketu	Ven.
Rasi S.A.V. bindus	20	21	20	24	42	33	20	31	20
Nav. S.A.V. bindus	24	23	42	28	42	28	24	33	33

It is found that the *bindu* strength of planets in Rasi is very poor. Only three planets Jupiter (42), Saturn (33) and Ketu (31) are associated with higher number of *bindus*. In Navamsa chart practically every planet has obtained strength. Two planets, Mars (20) and Venus (20), associated with minimum number of *bindus* in its 8th house in Rasi, become very powerful in Navamsa by gaining considerable strength, *i.e.*, Mars (42) and Venus (33).

Dasas

D.M.Y.

8 - 1 - 12	Balance
11-10-1942 19-11-1954	Rahu (28 bindus in Navamsa)
0 - 0 - 16 19-11-1970	Jupiter (42 *bindus* in Navamsa)
0 - 0 - 19 19-11-1989	Saturn (28 *bindus* in Navamsa)

0 - 0 - 17 ⎫
.... ⎬ Mercury (24 *bindus* in Navamsa)
19-11-2006 ⎭
....

At the time of the shooting of the film "Coolie" the Moon's Bhukti (23 *bindus*) was in progress in Saturn's Dasa, *i.e.*, from 22-10-1981 to 22-5-1983. The injury took place on 24-7-1982 when transit Saturn was (5s 22° 53') degreecally crossing over the natal Mars in the 8th house, having minimum 20 *bindus*. At present he is having Saturn's Dasa (28). Jupiter's Bhukti (42) the last one in Dasa, from 7-5-1987 to 19-11-1989.

The horoscope (Chart 4) of Mr. Y is as follows :

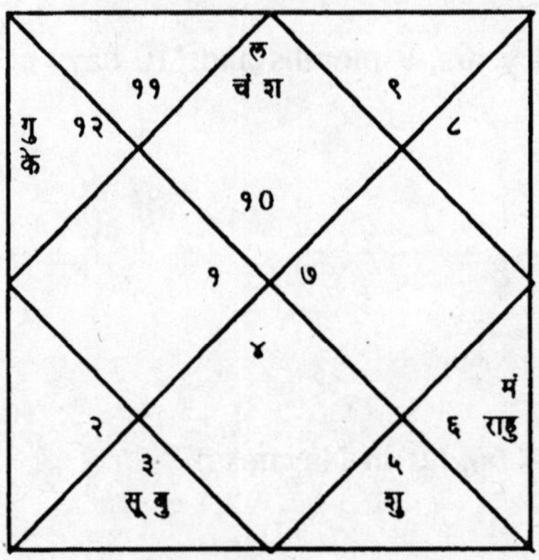

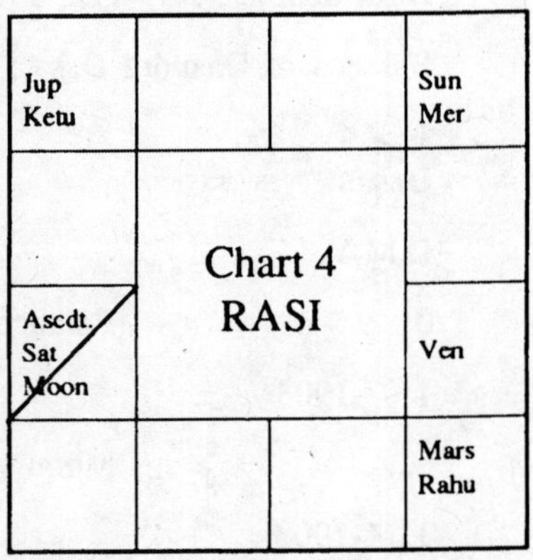

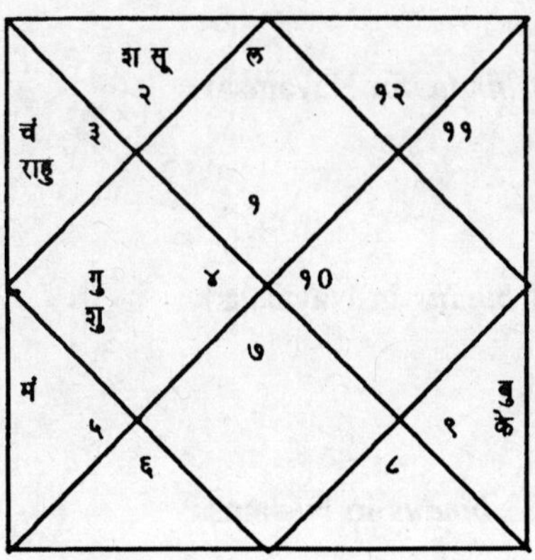

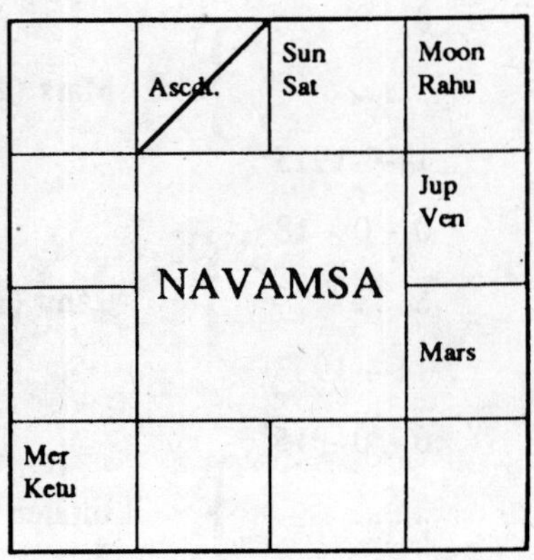

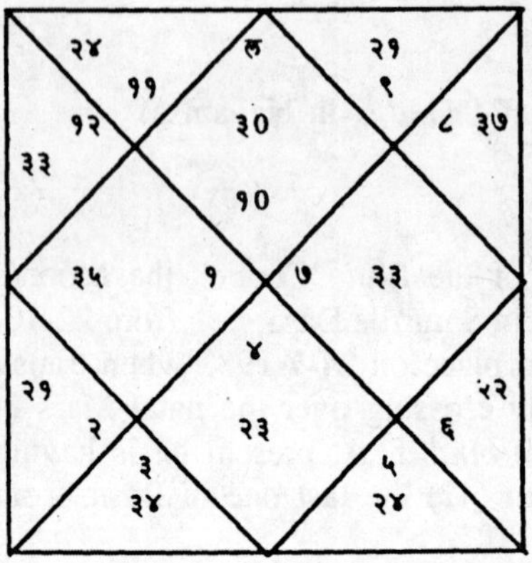

33	35	21	34
24	S.A.V. Bindus		23
Ascdt. 30			24
21	37	33	22

Birth details : July 11th 1903 at 6h, 36m p.m. (IST).

Balance of Chandra Dasa : 4 years, 9 months and '10 days at birth.

Dasas

D.M.Y.

0 - 9 - 4	Balance
11-7-1903 11-4-1908	Moon (34 *bindus* in Navamsa)
0 - 0 - 7 11-4-1915	Mars (24 *bindus* in Navamsa)
0 - 0 - 18 11-4-1933	Rahu (34 *bindus* in Navamsa)
0 - 0 - 16 11-4-1949	Jupiter (23 *bindus* in Navamsa)

0 - 0 - 19
.... } Saturn (21 *bindus* in Navamsa)
11-4-1968

0 - 0 - 17
.... } Mercury (21 *bindus* in Navamsa)
11-4-1985

....

Note that in Rasi chart, six planets are associated with more than 30 *bindus* each, *viz.*, the Sun (34); the Moon (30); Jupiter (33); Saturn (30); Mercury (34); and Ketu (33). Out of these six planets, five planets, *viz.*, the Sun, Jupiter, Saturn, Mercury and Ketu become associated with very less number of *bindus* in Navamsa signs, occupied by them, *i.e.*, 21, 23, 21, 21 and 21 respectively. The native was a successful broker of the Bombay Stock Exchange and had minted money but in 1967 March in Saturn's Dasa (21) and Jupiters' Bhukti (23) he was declared insolvent. In Mercury Bhukti (21) the native expired in October 1968.

Planets	Sun	Moon	Mars	Rahu	Jup.	Sat.	Merc.	Ketu	Ven.
Rasi S.A.V. bindus	34	30	22	22	33	30	34	33	24
Nav. S.A.V. bindus	21	34	24	34	23	21	21	21	23

The scribe on account of his old age and other preoccupations is not in a position to devote more time and energy, on further research in this subject. Ardent research scholars of Astrology may study the horoscopes of smugglers, dacoits, murderers, murdered persons, involvents; persons dead by burns, hypocrites, rapers; persons suffering from incurable diseases and the like.... and try to develop the point as revealed in Chart 4, *viz.*, planets associated with higher number of *bindus* in Rasi chart become associated with minimum or less number of *bindus* in Navamsa.

13

New Predictive Technique Based on Nadi Astrology

Readers are aware of the several methods of prognostication as given in classics like—Brihat Parasara Hora, Brihat Jataka, Jataka Parijata, Phaladeepika, Uttarakalamrita, Saravali, etc. Many are unaware of the principles adopted in Nadi Astrology, some of which are not found in our standard texts. One such principle is prediction of transit results of a planet on an imaginary mid-point between Rahu and the Moon, which is known as Bhrigu-bindu.

One of the passages of 'Bhrigu-Nandi Nadi' reads as under :

".... The native suffers from Meha and phlegmatic troubles. He will get rid of the troubles with the aid of a friend...This happens when Jupiter transits the mid-point of Rahu and Moon Axis." (Ref. page No. 363 of the cyclostyled translation of "Bhrigu-Nandi Nadi" by Shri R. G. Rao, Bangalore).

Why too much importance is given to Rahu? Rahu (the Moon's ascending node) and Ketu (the Moon's descending node) are neither visible planets, nor bodies of matter. They are mere points of intersection in space of the orbit of the Moon and the celestial ecliptic. Rahu is the northern point of intersection while Ketu is the southern one. Their motion is always continuous and retrograde. They take nearly 18.6 years (18y - 7m - 6d) to complete one round of the Zodiac. Formerly the Western astrologers were not giving any importance to these nodes but of late, during the last 50 years or so, a number of books had been published in Western countries on Rahu and Ketu, while much importance had been given to the predictive utility of these nodes in Indian Astrology, since times immemorial.

When a conjunction of Rahu and the Moon takes place, the longitudes and latitudes of both are the same. This perhaps may be the reason, as to why Rahu-Moon axis has been given great importance in Bhrigu Nandi Nadi. The same will be the case when the Sun conjoins Rahu. While the remaining five planets (Kujadi) i.e., Mars, Mercury, Jupiter, Venus and Saturn, when conjoining nodes, there is no difference in longitudes but latitudes differ.

Chart No. 1—Calculation of mid-point of Rahu-Moon axis :

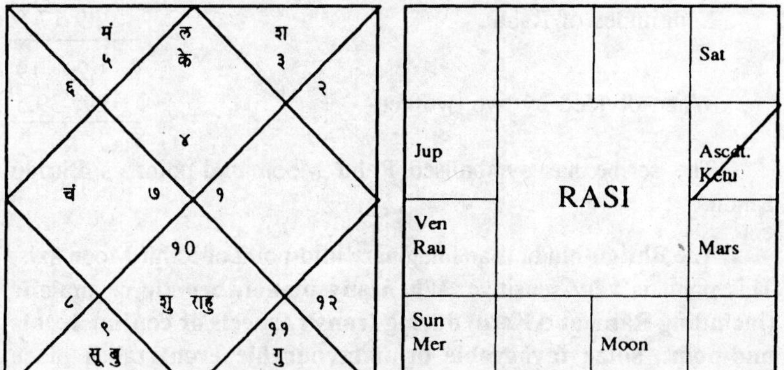

Mr. Chandulal S. Patel (the scribe) was born on 31-12-1915 at 7h 44m P.M. (IST).

Latitude 23° 2N and Longitude 72° 39E. Full details about other planets are not given, in any of the charts discussed, as they are not necessary for this write-up.

One has to find out how far the Moon has progressed from Rahu, after the last conjunction in the natal chart.

1. First method :

Deduct the longitude of Rahu from those of the Moon. The difference be divided by two. Add the quotient to Rahu's natal position. The result will be Rahu-Moon mid-pioint.

in Chart No. 1—

Longitudes of the Moon (+ 12 signs) 6-12°-13'

—Less Longitude of Rahu	9-17° 6'
	8-25°-7'
When divided by 2, we get	4-12°-33.5'
Add it to the natal position of Rahu	9-17°-6'
Mid-point of Rahu-Moon axis	1-29°-39.5'

2. Second method :

Add the longitude of the Moon to Rahu and divide that total by two.

Longitudes of the Moon	6-12°-13'
Longitudes of Rahu	9-17-6'
	3-29°-19'
When divided by two, we get—	1-29°-39.5'

The scribe has symbolised Rahu Moon mid-point as Bhrigu Bindu.

The Bhrigu-bindu is an imaginary mid-point of Rahu-Moon axis. This point is very sensitive. **When any planet, benefic or malefic (including Rahu and Ketu) during transit aspects or conjuncts this mid-point, some favourable or unfavourable event takes place respectively.**

The Moon will form one such aspect (the 7th one) and a conjunction, only two results every month. The Sun, Mercury or Venus will similarly form one aspect each (the 7th one) and one conjunction each, only two results every year for each of them. Mars will form three such aspects (the 4th, the 7th and the 8th) and a conjunction only four results during 18 months or so. Jupiter will form three such aspects (the 5th, the 7th and the 9th) and a conjunction, only four major results during his round through zodiac in 12 years. Saturn will form three such aspects (the 3rd, the 7th and the 10th) and a conjunction, only four major results during his round of about 30 years. Rahu and Ketu will have each two aspects (the 5th and the 9th) and one conjunction each, in all three results each, during 18 1/2 years. **However, it should be borne in mind that the effects of transit by conjunction are more potent than those by aspect.**

A benefic planet such as Jupiter, during transit, as referred above will give favourable results such as progress in studies; birth of brethern; getting employment; marriage; birth of a child; promotion in service; profits in business; expansion of industry; pilgrimage; recovery from long-standing sicknesses; **fulfilment of long cherished desires (depending on age of native) etc.**

Fast moving benefic planets, such as Mercury or Venus will cause benefic results, such as, meeting relations after long time; small gains of wealth; short pilgrimages; festivities and rejoicings with close relation etc.

Saturn, a slow moving planet will produce unfavourable results, such as long sicknesses; disagreement with spouse; her sickness or separation; sudden loss of wealth; death of near relations; one's own death (provided it is indicated by directions) etc.

Fast moving malefic planets such as Mars and the Sun will cause unfavourable results such as, minor sickness or injury; temporary separation from nearer relatives; loss of money; quarrels or misunderstandings etc.

The transit of Rahu or Ketu will cause favourable or unfavourable **results all of a sudden, on a very big scale and from unexpected sources;** bite by snake or poisonous insects; mental sufferings; income-tax, sales-tax or enforcement raids; theft of valuables; harassment, degradation in or termination of service; family dissensions; misunderstanding with wife or husband. In short these types of sufferings are more or less mental causing much anguish and uneasiness.

Sometimes, it so happens that Jupiter and Venus or Jupiter and Mercury or Venus, and Mercury both or seldom all the three planets, simultaneously transit over, or aspect to this mid-point, increasing the magnitude of the favourable result to a very great extent.

Sometimes, it so happens that the Sun and Mars; or the Sun and Saturn or Saturn and Mars, both or seldom all the three planets, simultaneously transit over or aspect to this point, increasing the magnitude of the unfavourable results to a very great extent.

In the example of chart No. 1 given above Saturn has 3rd aspect to and Mars and the Sun transit over the mid-point simultaneously and hence the worst result (death of father) occurred.

Duration of result : The transit effect of a planet by aspect or conjunction over Bhrigu Bindu commences neary 100 kalas prior to it and lasts till 100 kalas beyond it [100 kalas + 100 kalas = 200 kalas = 3° — 20' = 1 Navamsa] but its main effect is felt immediately the planet has crossed that position.

Now I give a few examples below to prove the above points :

[1] Chart No. 1 [of the scribe] above : Mid-point 1 - 29° - 39.5'

A. My father expired on 15.6.68. Mars was 1- 29° - 41° on 11.6.68 when his condition was precarious. The Sun was 1 - 29° - 34° on 14.6.68. Saturn was 11 - 29° - 50° on 15.6.68. Mars and the Sun had just crossed the mid-point and Saturn was having his 3rd house aspect on the mid-point. It may be noted that all the three malefics had this combined effect. Venus also was 1-29°-03° on 15-6-68, a benefic transit which made me to inherit some paternal property.

B. Mercury was - 2-00° - 39° on 19.6.71 and Venus was 1 - 29° on 1.7.71. This period from 19.6.71 to 1.7.71 brought me big financial gains in speculation.

C. My wife had Cholera infection and she was hospitalised on 26.5.73 where her condition was declared serious. My only son had a snake bite on 1.6.73 when Saturn was 1-28° -46'. Note that Mercury was 2-00°-25' and Venus was 2-00° -37' on that day. They had just crossed the Mid-point [1-29° -39,]. My wife's health started improving from 1.6.73. Just on account of bad transit of Saturn both of them suffered but due to favourable transits of Mercury and Venus both of them survived the troubles.

Chart No. 2

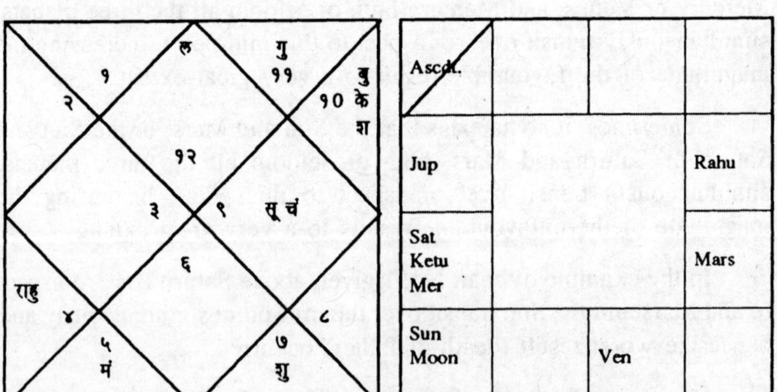

A boy born on 28.12.62 at 1h 10m p.m. (IST) in Bombay.
Natal position :
The Moon 8-29°-26'
Rahu 3-7°-33'
Rahu/Moon mid-point is 6-3° - 28.5'

The young boy met with a railway accident on 7.7.83 and died immediately. Saturn was 6-4° 8' i.e., just transited over the mid-point.

Chart No. 3

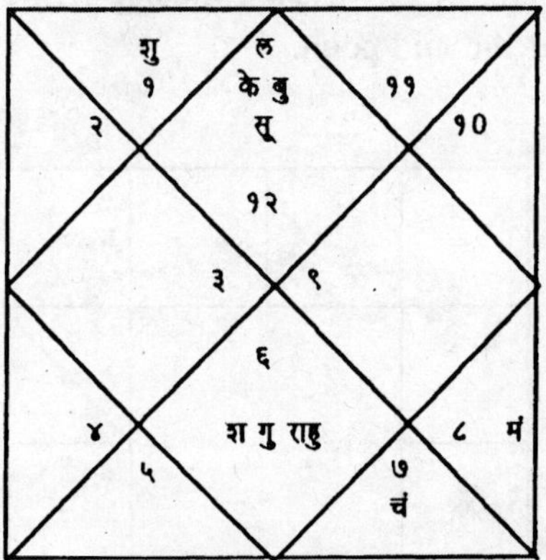

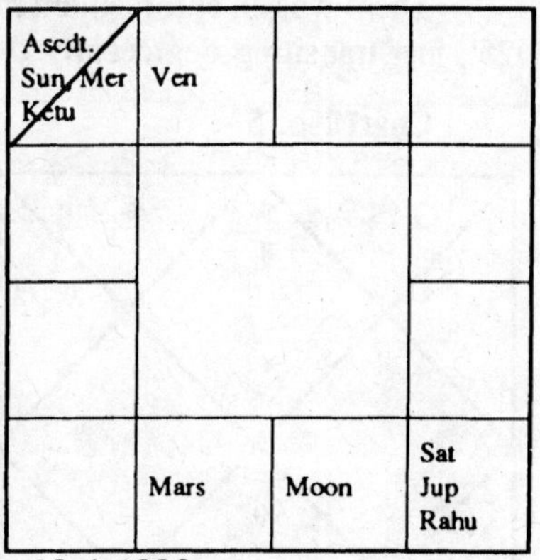

A multimillionaire - birth date 12-4-1922
Natal position :
The Moon 6 - 0° - 26'
Rahu 5 - 15° - 33'
Rahu/Moon mid-point is 5 - 22° - 58.5'

The gentleman died of heart failure on 8.11.1981. Saturn was 5 - 23° - 09' just transited over the mid-point.

Chart No. 4

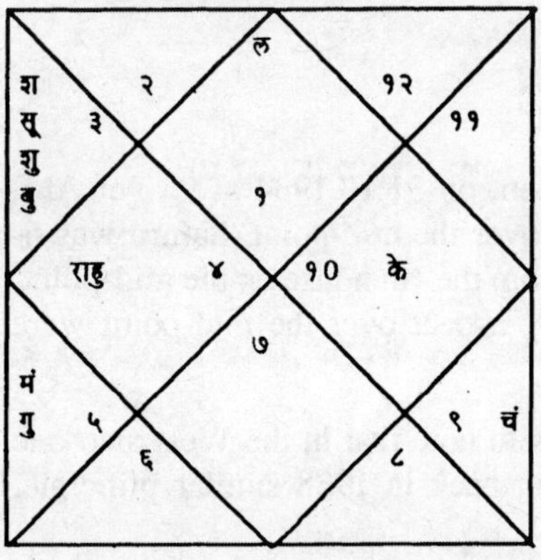

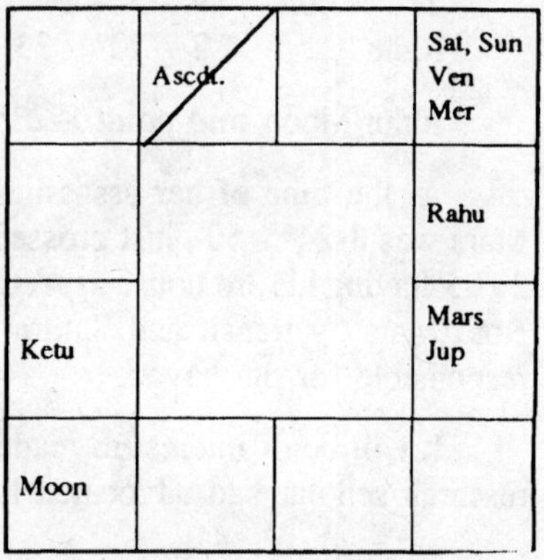

[A very rich man born on 4/5 July 1944 at 2h - 52m A.M. (IST) at Vijapur - North Gujarat]

Natal position :

The Moon 8 - 2° - 2'

Rahu 3 - 5° - 15'

Rahu/Moon midpoint 5 - 18° - 38.5'

There was an enforcement raid on 25.3.87 when Ketu was 5-18°-25', just transiting degreecally over the mid-point.

Chart No. 5

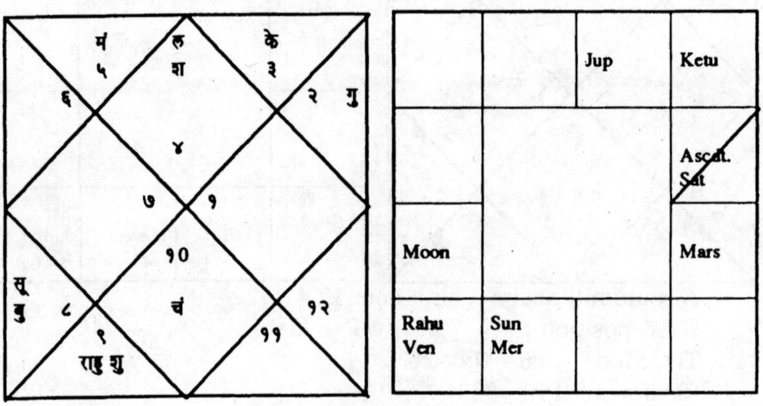

Mrs. Indira Gandhi (late Prime Minister of India) born on 19-11-1917 at 11h - 11m PM (IST) at Allahabad.

Natal positions :

The Moon 9 - 5° - 37'
Rahu 8 - 10° - 33'

Rahu/Moon mid-point 8-23°-5'

At the time of her assassination, on 31.10.1984 at 9h 9m AM, Mars was 8-24° - 50', just crossed over the mid-point. Saturn was 6-24°-5' having his 3rd house aspect from the 4th house on the mid-point. Both Mars by transit and Saturn by aspect over the mid-point were responsible for the havoc.

It will be of interest to readers to note that in the West also one research scholar had advocated long back in 1938 similar principle.

Alfred Witty, a German scholar in his book called "Uranian System of Astrology" [1938] has advocated that one should fix imaginary mid-points between Sun - Moon; Sun - Mars; Sun - Mercury; Sun - Jupiter; Sun - Venus; Sun - Saturn; Sun - Rahu; Sun - Ketu, etc. which according to him, will total about 78 imaginary mid-points. Accordingly when any planet, either slow moving or fast moving transits over one such mid-point in a nativity, a certain favourable or unfavourable event takes place in the life of the native. It will thus be seen that the German scholar had a similar approach to the principle enunciated in Nadi Astrology. There is one draw-back in this system. There are many mid-points and when a particular event has occured, more planets than one, transit over many mid-points simultaneously. It is very difficult to pin point which particular transit is responsible for the result.

I have tested this principle in cases where birth date was accurate and birth time was approximately known. Even here the results were very encouraging. I would recommed to the readers to use this method also in prognostication of both good or bad events in life.

While studying the results as above an idea struck to the mind of the scribe, as to why not investigate and apply this principle to Rahu-Sun Axis, because when the Sun transits over Rahu, the longitudes as well as the latitudes of them both are the same.

शनिचारवशात् क्लेशम् राहुचारवशात् भ्रमम्
गुरुचारवशात् सौख्यम् फलानि परिचिंतयेत् ॥

Chandra Kala nadi, Vol, II Part I Verse 404 (p. 49).

In conclusion one may say that the Science of Astrology is like a deep ocean. The deeper you go the chances of getting big pearls are brighter.

Scholars and research minded students are requested to make deep research in Nadi Astrology and unravel the mysteries of various predictive techniques suggested by great sages, centuries and centuries back. Even today there are many valuable manuscripts collecting dust in oriental libraries at Baroda, Pune, Madras, Mysore, Trivandrum, Benares and at many other places. By doing systematic research into these ancient Granthas, one can enrich one's knowledge in predective techniques. It is suggested that National bodies like the Indian Council of Astrological Sciences and other institutions should take up such assignment for the benefit of the astrological world as a whole.

Chart No. 6

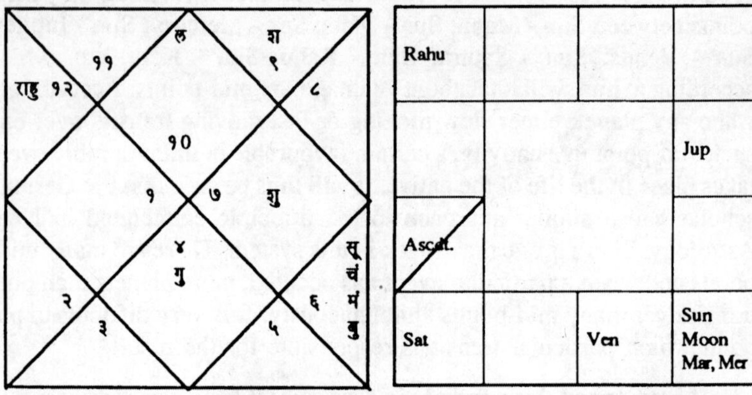

Shri K.S. Krishnamurthy severaly cricisied 'Traditional Astrology' in his book "Transit" [Gocharapala Nirnayam] as under p. No. XXXII] :

Most of the traditional astrologers are not unaware that the Gochara transit systems advocated by various sages, saints, and scholars in different text-books are useless, meaningless and not universally applicable.

This chart reproduced here is from page no. XXXII of the above book, K.B. Jagdish Rapid born at 1h 11m PM (13° - 04'N - 80° -16'E) on 10.10.1931.

Natal positions :

The Moon 5 - 5° - 51'
Rahu 11 - 11° - 52'
Rahu Moon mid-point 2-8°-51.5'

Native's marriage took place on 1.9.1950. The positions of other planets are not necessary. At the time of mariage Jupiter was 10-8°-39' having his 5th house full aspect on Rahu-Moon mid-point. How very convincing? The proof of the pudding lies in the eating.

14

Relatives from the Native's Chart

Very often, the astrologers are confronted with clients who insist on prediction to be given to them in regard to their relatives based on their hosorsopes. Our ancient Rishis, who were past-masters in delineating results have evolved simple techniques by which one can delineate results for practically any relative of the native, based on his horoscope only.

The Nadi literature is full of many such references and Sanskrit trerms denoting relatives. Deva Keralam (Chandra Kala Nadi) was published by the Government Oriental Manuscripts Library, Madras in 2 volumes (Vol. I-1952 and Vol. 2, part I and part 2 in 1956) containing about 9200 Sanskrit verses, the author, Sri Achyuta has shown in detail which house represents which relative of the native. The scribe has made a collection in this write up, which will be useful to the students of astrology. Arabic numerals in chart 1 represent signs, Roman numerals in chart No. 2 represent houses.

House of near relatives;

The 1st house - the native himself

The 9th house - the father

The 4th house - the mother

The 3rd house - the brother

The 7th house - the wife

The 5th house - the children

I. The lagna (the ascendant) - body - the native himself) - the 1st house.

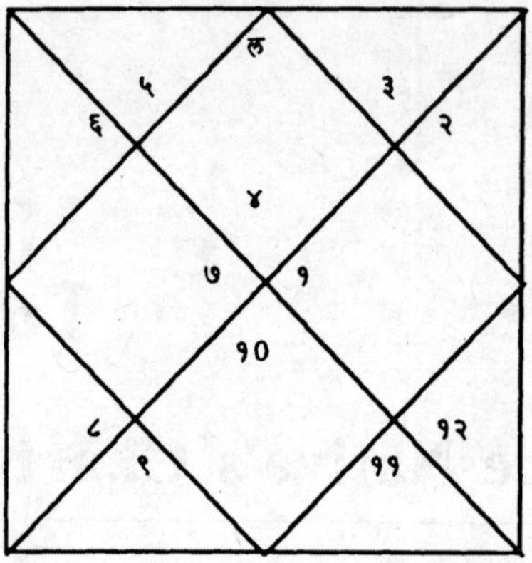

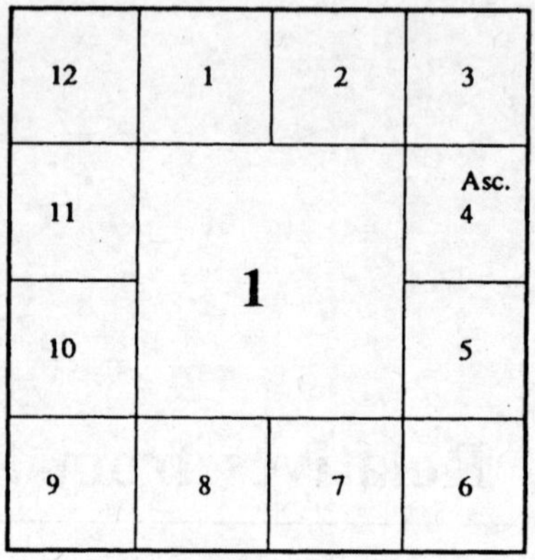

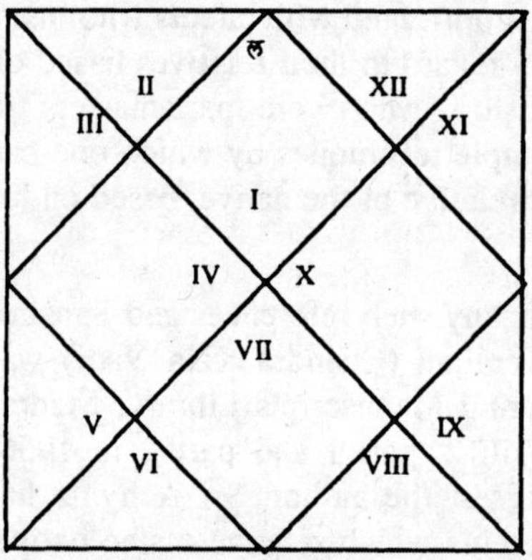

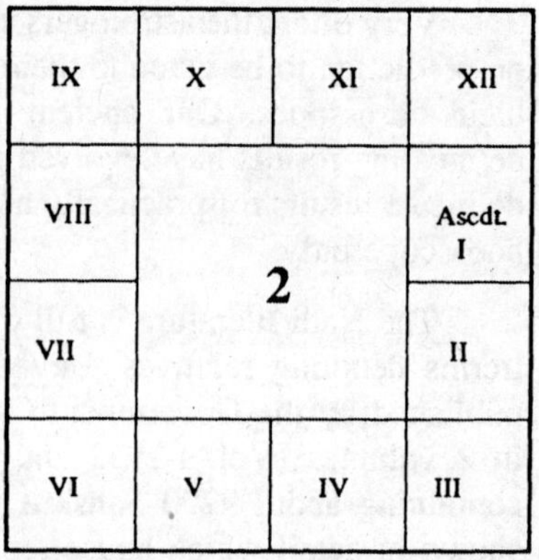

II. Relative through father (Pita) - the father :

(a) Pitru sthana - the 9th house from the lagna

(b) Pitamaha - father's father (grand father) - the 9th house from the 9th house = the 5th house.

Prapitamaha - father's grand father - the 9th house from the 5th house = the 1st house.

Pitamahi - father's mother - the 4th house from the 9th house = the 12th house.

Pitamaha bhratru - grand father's brother - the 3rd house from the 5th hose = the 7th house.

(c) Pitruvya - father's brother - the 3rd house fron the 9th house = 11th house.

Pitruvyee (Pitrubhagini) - father's sister - the 3rd house from the 9th house = 11th house.

Pitruvya Bhaaryaa - father's brother's wife - the7th house from the 11th house = the 5th house.

Pitruvya Bhartru - fathers; sister's busband - the 7th house from the 11th house = the 5th house.

Pitruvya putra putree - father's brother's son/daughter - the 5th house from the 11th house = the 3rd house,

Pitruvyee putra putree - father's sister's son/daughter - the 5th house from the 11th hiouse = the3rd house.

Pitruvya Putra vadhu - wife of father's brother's son - the 7th house from the 3rd house = 9th house.

III. Relative through mother (Matru) :

(a) Matru sthaana - the 4th house from the lagna.

(b) Matamaha - mother's father (maternal grand father) - the 9th house from the 4th house = the 12th house.

Matamahi - mother's mother (maternal grand mother) - the 4th house from the 4th house = the 7th house.

Matamahabharatru - mother's father's brother (maternal grand uncle) - the 3rd house from the 12th house = the 2nd house.

(c) Matula - mother's brother (maternal uncle) - the 3rd house from the 4th house = the 6th house.

Matrusvasu (bhagini) - mother's sister - the 3rd house from the 4th house = the 6th house.

Matula pathni (matulaani) - mother's brother's wife - the 7th house from the 6th house = the 12th house.

Matrusvasu bhartru (mother's sister's husband) - the 7th house from the 6th house = the 12th house.

Matula putra putree - maternal uncle's son/daughter - the 5th house from the 6th house = the 10th house.

(d) Bheda matru (Saapatni matru) - step mother - the3rd house from the 4th house = the 6th house.

Bheda Bhratru bhagini - step brother or step sister - the 5th house from the 6th house = the 10th house.

Bheda Bhratru bharya - step brother's wife - the 7th house from the 10th house = the 4th house.

Bheda bhaginee bhartru - step sister's husband - the 7th house from the 10th house = the 4th house.

IV. Relatives through brethern :

(a) Jyeshta Bhratru Bhagini - elder broter or sister = the 11th house.

Jyeshta bhratru bharya - elder brother's wife - the 7th house from the 11th house = the 5th house.

Jyeshta Bhagini bhartru - elder sister's husband - the 7th house from the 11th house = the 5th house.

Jyeshta bhratru putra putri - elder brother's son/daughter - the 5th house from the 11th house = the 3rd house.

Jyeshta bhagini putra putri - elder sister's/son/daughter = the 3rd house.

(b) Kanishta bhratru - Bhagini - younger brother/sister = the 3rd house.

Kanishta bhratru bharya - younger brother's wife - the 7th house from the 3rd house = the 9th house.

Kanishta bhagini bhartru - younger sister's husband - the 7th house from the 3rd house - the 9th house.

Kanishta bhratru putra-putri - younger brother's son/daughter - the 5th house from the 3rd house = the 7th house.

V. Relatives through wife :

(a) Patni - wife = 7th house.

(b) Svasura - wife's father - the 9th house from the 7th house = the 3rd house.

Svasru - wife's mother - the 4th house frm the 7th house = the 10th house.

Patni pitruvya - wife's father's brother - the 3rd house from the 3rd house = the 5th house.

(c) Syalaka (patni bhratru) - wife's brother - the 3rd house from the 7th house = the 9th house.

Bharya bhagini - wife's sister - the 3rd house from the 7th house = the 9th house.

Syalaka patni - wife's brother's wife - the 7th house from the 9th house = the 3rd house.

Bharya bhagini bhartru - wife's sister's husband - the 7th house from the 9th house - the 3rd house.

(d) Dwiteeya bharya - the 2nd wife - the 3rd house from the 7th house - the 9th house.

Trutiya bharya - the 3rd wife - the 3rd house from the 9th house = the 11th house.

VI. Relatives through son/daughter

Putra-putri - son/daughter = the 5th house.

Putra vadhu - son's wife (dauhter-in-law) - the 7th house from the 5th house = the 11th house.

Jamatru - daughter's husband (son-in-law) - the 7th house from the 5th house = the 11th house.

(b) Pautra/Pautri - son's son; son's daughter (grand-child), the 5th house from the 5th house = the 9th house.

Dohitra-Dohitri-daughter's son, daughter's daughter - the5th house from the 5th house = the 9th house.

(c) Putra svasura - son's wife's (daughter-in-law's) father - the 9th house from the 11th house = the 7th house.

Putri svasura - daughter's husband's (son-in-law's) father - the 9th house from the 11th house = the 7th house.

Putri svasru - daughter's husband's mother (daughter's mother-in-law) - the 4th house from the 11th house = the 2nd house.

VII. Mitra sthana = the tenth house.

Mitra patni - friend's wife - the 7th house from the 10th house = the 4th house.

VIII. Relative's of wife in husband's family (in her horoscope);

Pati jyeshta bhratru - husband's elder brother - the 11th house from the 7th house = the 5th house.

Pati jyeshta bhratru patni - husband's elder brother's wife- the 7th house from the 5th house = the 11th house.

Pati Kanishta bharatru - husband's younger brother - the 3rd house from the 7th house = the 9th house.

Pati kanishta bhratru bharya - husband's younger brother's wife - the 7th house from the 9th house = the 3rd house.

Mostly all the relatives of a native are covered in the above explanations.

Astrologers in north India, Gujarat, Maharashtra and other places consider the 10th house, as the house representing father (Pitrusthana). While in all the four States of southern India, they consider the 9th house as the house for the father. The scribe follows the later view.

Example :

(1) The 5th house represents the son. The native is the father of the son, so the native's house is the 9th house from the 5th house, i.e., Lagna (the native himself).

(2) The 5th house represents grandfather. The native is the grandson of the grand father. So the native's house is the 9thhouse from the 5th house, i.e, Lagna (the native himself).

(3) The 3rd house represents the father-in-law. The native's is son-in-law of the father-in-law, so the native's house is the 11th house from the 3rd house, i.e., the lagna (native himself).

From the above it can be concluded that the 9th house represents the father, in contrast to the 10th house.

Verification :

In the scribe's chart (1989 - running 74th year) the 7th house has 19 bindus (SAV) the minimum and the 3rd house and 4th house have 33 bindus each, the maximum.

1. (a) - The native will have some trouble, deficiency in happiness, delays in fulfilment of aims, unfair behaviour etc. from the

relatives indicated by the 7th house, e.g., Matamahi, Kanishta bhratru, Bhagini putra-putri, patni, putra svasura, putri svasura;

(1) Matamahi - My mother had lost her mother when she was a girl of 15 years.

(2) Kanishta bhratru//Bhagini putra putri-relations with them are not so cordial as they ought to be.

(3) Patni - She was always complaining about her health. She breathed her last in 1975 when she was 58 years old.

(4) My daughter-in-law had lost her father when she was 4 years old.

(5) Putri svasura - my son-in-law had lost his father when he was 10 years old.

Thus it can be observed that the native had deficiency or denial of happiness from relatives indicated by the 7th house.

(b) Another point to be noted is that whenever any slow moving planet transits this house (having 19 bindus) some worry, financial loss or heavy expenditure, hospitalisation, mental anguish etc. *on account of these relatives* do take place. The native has to bear them all.

II. (a) The 3rd house (maximum bindus 33); Conversely, favourable results were experienced by the native from the relatives indicated by the 3rd house, i.e., from brethern, father-in-law lived till 1958. Syalakapatni (wife's brother's wife) is still alive, having cordial relations with the native.

(b) The 4th house (matru sthana) - 33 bindus maximum : The mother happiness lasted till 1965, till the native was 50.

(c) Mitra patni - relations with wives of three bossom friends are very cordial even today.

When slow moving planets transited through these houses some good or favourable events did take place, from or on account of these relatives.

By going through the whole article a good student of astrology can easily trace the thin thread connecting all relatives with the native and he can use the mechanics of the houses more meaningfully while giving prognostication. Again he may recheck any point of doubt at certain required stages to give forth a coherent picture of the native.

It will be seen that one's birth chart would reveal to the experienced eye of astrologer, not only the broad pattern of one's destiny; it would also throw revealing light on the fortunes of near and distant relatives as well.

15

Timing of Events as per Nadi Texts

The most difficult task of an astrologer is to predict an event correctly in advance before it takes place. In Western astrology, use of Primary and Secondary Directions is resorted to, in Timing of an event. While in India astrologers take help of Dasa systems (particularly the Vimsottari Dasa) combined with gochara (transit) and Ashtaka varga.

Most of the practising astrologers in India consider the contacts (conjunctions) of nine transiting planets i.e., from the Sun to Saturn and Rahu/Ketu, with natal positions of these nine planets and the ascendant in the chart as indicative of times when events may be expected. Even the Western astrologers follow this method partially.

The timing of an event becomes a matter of simplicity if methods prescribed by Nadi Astrology are followed. The scribe has come across only three different methods of timing events during his study of last 35 years of Nadi literature.

1. Nandi Nadi :

Many are unaware of the principles adopted in Nadi Astrology, some of which are not found in standard texts. One such principle is prediction of transit results of a planet on an imaginary mid-point between Rahu and the Moon, which is known as "Bhrigu Bindu" in Nandi Nadi (Bhrigu Nandi Nadi by Shri R.G. Rao, Bangalore).

Calculation of midpoint of Rahu-Moon axis (Example chart stated in the middle of the article) :

Deduct the longitude of Rahu from that of the Moon. The difference be divided by two (2). Add the quotient to Rahu's position. The result will be Rahu-Moon midpoint i.e., "Bhrigu-Bindu." -

Longitude of the Moon

(+ 12 signs) (+ 12) = 6s 12° - 12'

Less Longitude of Rahu = 9s 17° 5'

=8s 25° 7'

8s 25° 7' + 2 = 4s 12° -33.5'

Add 4s 12° 33.5' to the natal position of Rahu. The answer is = 1-29° -39.5'

This Bhrigu Bindu is an imaginary midpoint of Rahu-Moon axis. This point is very sensitive. When any planet, benefic or malefic (including Rahu and Ketu) during transit aspects or conjuncts this midpoint, some favourable or unfavourable event takes place respectively. However, it should be borne in mind that the effects of transit by conjunction are more potent than those by aspect.

A benefic planet, such as Jupiter, during transit will give favourable results such as progress in studies, birth of brethern; getting employment; marriage; birth of child; promotion in service; profits in business; expansion of industry; pilgrimage; recovery from long standing sickness; fulfilment of long cherished desires (depending on native's age) etc...

Fast moving benefic planets such as Mercury or Venus will cause benefic results such as meeting relations after long time; small gains in wealth; short pilgrimages; festivities and rejoicings with close relatives and friends etc...

Sometimes, it so happens that Jupiter and Venus or Jupiter and Mercury, or Venus and Mercury both or seldom all these three planets simultaneously transit or aspect this point, increasing the magnitude of the favourable event to a very great extent.

Saturn, a slow moving planet will produce unfavourable results such as long-sickness; disagreement with spouse; her sickness or separation; sudden loss of wealth; death of near relations; one's own death (provided it is indicated by directions) etc....

Fast moving malefic planets, such as Mars and the Sun will cause unfavourable results such as minor sickness or injury; temporary separation from nearer-relatives; loss of money; theft; quarrels, misunderstandings; tooth-ache; eye or ear troubles etc.

Sometimes, it so hapens that the Sun and Mars or the Sun and Saturn; or Saturn and Mars; both or seldom all these three planets simultaneously transit or aspect this point, increasing the magnitude of the unfavourable results to a very great extent (subject to directions).

The transit of Rahu or Ketu will cause results all of a sudden, on a very large scale and from unexpected sources; such as bite by snake; or poisonous insects mental sufferings; income-tax, sales tax or enforcement raids; thefts of valuables and cash harassment; degradation in or termination of service; injury by fall or accident; family dissentions; misunderstandings with wife or husband. In short, these type of sufferings are more or less mental causing much anguish and uneasiness.

II. Dhruva Nadi :

Dhruva Nadi, a voluminous book, containing about2,50,000 (two lakhs fifty thousand) verses in 43 different granthas, is in the possession of Government Oriental Manuscripts Library, Madras.

The following few verses are referred to practically in most of the nativities discussed in Dhruva Nadi.

Page 174.

रवित्रिकोणे मन्दे पितृपीडा भवेत्कष्टं
पितृवर्गेऽरिष्टदम् ॥

Meaning : "When Saturn in transit coincides degreecally with the natal position of the Sun, or its trine positions (120° - 240°), the native's father's health will suffer or the native himself will suffer illness or death of some elderly male relative (some uncle) will take place."

चन्द्रत्रिकोणगे मन्दे मातृपीडा भवेत्कष्टम् मात्रुवर्गेऽरिष्टदम् ॥

"When Saturn in transit coincides degreecally with the natal position of the Moon, or its trine positions, the native's mother's health will suffer or the native himself will suffer illness or death of some elderly female relative (some aunt) will take place."

कुजत्रिकोणगे मन्दे भ्रातृपीडा भवेत्कष्टम् भ्रातृवर्गेऽरिष्टदम् ॥

"When Saturn in transit coincides degreecally with the natal position of Mars or its trine positions, the native brother or sister will suffer or the native himself will suffer illness or death of some cousin will take place."

शुक्रत्रिकोणगे जीवे विवाहं लभते नरः ।

"When Jupiter transits over natal Venus or its trine positios, the native's marriage takes place."

गुरुत्रिकोणगे जीवे पुत्रीपुत्रस्य लाभवान् ॥

"When Jupiter transits over natal Jupiter or its trine positions, birth of a son or a daughter is expected."

Similarly, transits of Saturn or Jupiter may be considered (from natal position and its trines) of the remaining planets for unfavourable and favourable results respectively.

III. Deva Keralam (Chandra Kala Nadi) :

Example Chart : .scribe's chart —

born on 31-12-1915 at 7-44 P.M. (IST) lat 23-2N, Long 72-39E.

Planetary positions : The Sun 256-10; the Moon 192-13; Mars 127-9; Mercury 265-13; Jupiter 329-29; Venus 283-14; Saturn 80-42 (R); Rahu 287-06; Ketu 107-06 and Ascendant 98-53.

Navamsa : Aries : Venus, Saturn; Gamini - Jupiter, Mars, Rahu; Leo - Sun; Virgo - Ascendant; Scorpio - Mercury; Sagittarius - Ketu; Capricorn - Moon.

Balance of Rahu Dasa at birth : 10y-6m-3d.

Reference Deva Keralam, Book 2, P 123 - V 417.

भिन्नाष्टवर्गे लग्नेशे फलहीनस्यराशीषु ।
स्फुटयोगं गते जीवेत्वल्पसौख्यम् विनिर्दिशेत् ॥

Meaning : When Jupiter transits a sign without a bindu (or minimum 1 or 2) in the Bhinnashtakavarga of the lord of the Ascendant (the Moon in example chart) **on the degrees of the lord of that sign,** the native has very little happiness."

In the example chart, the Ascendant lord, the Moon has 6,5,3,4,3,6,6,3,5,1,3 and 4 bindus (Total 49 bindus), from sign Mesha onwards in her Ashtakavarga. The sign Makara has 1 - one bindu (minimum) only. When Jupiter transits Makara sign on the degrees of its lord (sign dispositor) i.e., Saturn's degree 20° 42', the native will have little happiness.

This principle can be applied conversely i.e., when Jupiter transits - (a) sign Mesha (6 bindus) on the degrees of its lord Mars i.e., 7° 9';

(b) sign Kanya (6 bindus) on the degrees of its lord Mercury i.e. 25° - 13'; and

(c) sign Tula (6 bindus) on the degrees of its lord Venus 13°-14' the native will have maximum happiness on all the above three occasions.

Deva Keralam Book 2 P 109 V (282 1/2 - 283 1/2).

सुखेशांशे तत्त्रिकोणे सुखेशाक्रान्तराशिगे
स्फुटयोगं गते जीवे विद्यारंभं विनिर्दिशेत् ॥

Meaning : "The native's (child's, education wil commence when Jupiter transits over the degree of the lord in the following signs :

(1) the sign occupied by the 4th lord;

(2) the sign identical with the 4th lord's occupied Navamsa sign;

(3) & (4) its trtine signs (2nd item)."

In the example chart, when Jupiter transits :

(1) sign Makara on 20°–42' (sign occupied by the 4th lord);

(2) sign Mesha on 7° 9' (4th lord's occupied Navamsa sign);

(3) sign Simha on 16° 10' (trine sign of Mesha); and

(4) sign Dhanus on 29° 29' (trine sign of Mesha); native's education begins.

Deva Keralam Book 2 P111 V. 300 :

.... चन्द्रेशांशत्रिकोणगे ।
स्फुटयोगं गते मन्दे देहोपद्रवमादिशेत् ॥

Meaning : "Saturn's transit over the degrees of the lord of the sign represented by Navamsa occupied by the Moon's dispositor at birth or a trine thereof, will cause physical ailments."

In the example chart the Moon's dispositor is Venus, who occupies Mesha Navamsa - hence Mesha, Simha and Dhanush signs.

In the example chart when Saturn transits :

(1) sign Mesha on 7°9';

(2) sign Simha on 16° - 10' or

(3) sign Dhanus on 29° - 29';

- the native is likely to suffer physical ailments.

स्फुटयोगं

Mesha	Mars	7°-9'
Vrishabha	Ven	13°-14'
Mithuna	Merc	25°-13'
Karkataka	Moon	12°-13'
Simha	Sun	15°-10'
Kanya	Mer	25°-13'
Tula	Venus	13°-14'
Vrischika	Mars	7°-9'
Dhanus	Jup	29°-29'
Makara	Sat	20°-42'
Kumbha	Sat	20°-42'
Meena	Jup	29°-29'

When any planet benefic or malefic transits 7°-9' in signs Mesha, the native gets good or bad result as the case may be. Similarly, any planet, transiting 13°-14' in sign Vrishabha, some result is expected. In the same way transits, through all the remainng ten signs, on their respective degrees of their lords (dispositors) will have some results in the example chart.

Mesha sign - its lord Mars - degreecal position - 7° - 9'

The Moon will transit this point once every month; the Sun,

Mercury and Venus will transit over this point once every year; Mars once in one and half years; Jupiter once in 12 years; Saturn once in 30 years and Rahu or Ketu once in 18.1/2 years roughly.

Some events in scribe's life for verificatiion :

1. Nandi Nadi : On 26-5-1973 scribe's wife had cholera infection. She was hospitalised and on 1-6-73, his son had snake bite - both survived. They were alright after 10-6-1973. (Saturn was transiting from 1-28°-46' to 1-29°-55' - during this period (Rahu-Moon midpoint).

II. Dhruva Nadi : scribe's wife expired on 24-1-75 - Saturn was passing over natal Saturn (2-20°-30' on 24-1-1975).

III. Deva Keralam :

(1) Scribe came to Bombay for the first time in life on 15-6-1937 for post-graduate studies (running year 22nd), when Jupiter was 8-29°-35' (sign Dhanus- on Jupiter's degree);

(2) Scribe lost his father on 15-6-1968 (running year 53rd) when Saturn was 11-29°-50' (sign Meena- on Jupiter's degree);

(3) Scribe had started on pilgrimage on Uttara Khanda for the first time (running year 79th) on 23-5-1994 when Jupiter was 6-13°-13' (sign Tula - on Venus' degree)

Time of fruition on an event :

दिनकर रुधिरौ प्रवेशकाले ...

..... फलदस्तु सर्वकालम् ।

(Brihat Jataka, Ch. 22, s.6)

Also Kala Prakasika, ch 36, s.13 and Muhurtamala, Ch. 5, sloka 20.

The gist of meaning :

"The Sun and Mars give results before touching a natal position; Venus and Jupiter at the time of crossing a natal position; Saturn and the Moon at the time of separating from a natal point, while Mercury throughout crossing a natal point during transit."

Suppose a natal position of a planet is 6s-12°-13'. The Sun and Mars will give results before touching the natal position (applying aspect); Venus and Jupiter, exactly at the time of crossing over it (crossing aspect); Saturn and the Moon after separating from a natal position (separating aspect); and Mercury will give results during all these three positions.

"Late Shri K.M. Kharegat (of Bombay), a great research scholar, observed that our predictions as regards Timing of an event often go wrong. It has been noticed that effect of a transit involving Saturn takes place some time later than the exact time of conjunction, while that of Mars is to time or occur even before due date."

Timing of events is perhaps the most important and yet the most difficulat part of the predictive astrology. This article presents to the students of astrology, a variety of techniques of prediction based on rare Nadi granthas, not accessible to many.

(Deva Keralam references are—from Shri R. Santhanam's edition.)

16

Nadi Astrology

There are many Nadi texts, such as Chandra Kala Nadi, Dhruva Nadi, Bhrigu Nadi, Septarashi Nadi, Suka Nadi, Kapila Nadi, Agastya Muni Nadi, Kaka Bhujandar Nadi and many others, most of which are in Sanskrit but not in Devanagari script.

Out of the many valuable contributions of Kerala scholars, to Indian Astrology, the most outstanding and unique is देवकेरलम् चन्द्र कला नाड़ी. It is full of raredicta for assessing the worth of a horoscope usually not found in classical texts. Even for seasoned astrological scholars, it is difficult to understand some terminology used and to interpet rules mentioned there in. It offers a virgin field for fruitful research.

There valuable books, (Chandra Kala Nadi) Vol. I (1952); Vol. II - Part I and Part II (1956) have been published by the Government Oriental Manuscripts Library, Madras, comprising about 9182 verses. The celebrated authors' names are Shri Achuta and Venkatesha Part II.

These 3 volumes carry a list of names of Nadi Amsas, amended in every volume. Adyar Library (Madras) has a volume of Chandra Kala Nadi, in which these 150 names are given in verses. The correct text of these verses was published for the first time, by the scribe in Janma - Bhumi Almanac, in the uear 1968.

The very word "CHANDRA KALA" represents its samkhya (number) "16". It has been found that the basis of Chandra Kala Nadi is "16-Vargas" of Parashar. If one prepares a table of Shodasha-vargas of a sign, the total number of sub-divisions will be "150" only in each sign. These are the Nadi-amsas. In the annual number of the

Astrological Mazazine of January 1984, page 27 - Shri V.A.K. Aiyer, has thrown some light on this point.

They have distinctive names and sequence. The term "Nadi Amsa" appears to have been used in the sense of a small unit of zodiacal arc and consequential time taken to rise in the east by it. Nc doubt, it is little difficult to correctly pinpoint the Nadi-amsa.

Longitudes of Nadi-amsas :

They begin with वसुधा with and end with परमेश्वरी

खपञ्चेन्दुमिता नाडयश्चरभे व्यत्यये स्थिरे ।
षट्सप्ततिं समारभ्य द्विस्वभावेषु राशिषु ।।

These Nadies are counted in the given order in movable signs; in the reverse order in fixed signs; and from 76 onwards to 150 and 1 to 75, in duel signs.

चर 1 to 150; स्थिर 150 to 1; द्विस्वभाव 76 to 150 and 1 to 75.

So the same Nadi amsa can have different longitudes in different signs as follows :

वसुधा in चरराशि 00°-00'-00" to 00°-30'-00';

वसुधा in स्थिरराशि 29°-30'-00" to 30°-00'-00';

वसुधा in द्विस्वभावराशि 15°-00'-00" to 15°-20'-00"

It may be noted that these Nadi-amsas are not of uniform longitudes (arcs).

They are unequal.

(1) वसुधा (चर) :	परमेश्वरी (स्थिर)	सुशीतला (द्वि.)	
1	150	76	00°-00'-00" to 00°-30'-00';
(2) वसुधा (") :	पंकजा (")	सुखदा (")	
2	149	77	00°-00'-00" to 00°-30'-00';
(2) ब्राह्मी (") :	नागा (")	सुप्रभा (")	
3	148	78	00°-40'-00" to 00°-45'-00';

पूर्वार्धभाग – उत्तरार्धभाग

Usfully the scholars take 150th part of a sign of 30° i.e. 12 minutes of arc to rise, as a Nadi-amsa (time covered is 48" seconds of time). This is again divided into 2 parts of 6' minutes of arc each as पूर्वार्ध and उत्तरार्ध (i.e. 24" seconds of time). After detailed study of Nadi-amsas, I have come to believe that पूर्वार्ध and उत्तरार्ध apply to the Moon's position in a Navamsa. There are many references to this effect in the text. उत्तरांशे निशानाथे । निशाना थे पूर्व भागे । पूर्व भागे चन्द्रे... etc. Vol. I P. 228-229 (Verses-2319, 2321, 2326) and many others.

For the Moon to cover 3°-20' of arc i.e., one Navamsa, it takes nearly 6 hs. - 40 ms. roughly. During this period, one चर one स्थिर and one द्वि स्वभाव signs rise in the East as ascendants; so पूर्वार्ध means, the Moon is in the first half of Navamsa and उत्तरार्ध means the Moon is in the 2nd half of Navamsa.

e.g. the Moon is 6-12°-12'-56" } 1st half of न. will be 6-10°-00' to 6-11°-40' पूर्वार्ध
2nd half न. will be 6-11°-40' to 6-13°-20' उत्तरार्ध
—so the Moon is in उत्तरार्ध

e.g. the Moon is 1-4°-20'-8" } 1st half न. will be 1-3°-20' to 1-5°-00' पूर्वार्ध
2nd half न. will be 1-5°-00' to 1-6°-40' उत्तरार्ध
—so theMoon is in पूर्वार्ध

The above are my observations, during my research. It is left to the research minded scholars to accept them or not or suggest their own findings.

17

Periods of Fortune and Calamity

According to *Saravali*, one's birth chart is a blue print of destiny which a *daivajna, i.e.*, an erudite astrologer will be able to decipher with his clear vision of Hora Sastra. It is only natural that mortal man faced with the propblems of life would like to peep into his future. Whether the period ahead promises prosperity or threatens adversity; whether his life's course would be smooth or beset with obstacles, etc. The question which a person asks the astrologer must often relate to the financial prospects.

Among the many techniques available to an astrologer to answer the queries of the consulatant, perhaps the more reliable one is the Ashtakavarga System of Prediction. In the hands of an accomplished astrologer Ashtakavarga unerringly indicates the nature of events which are likely to occur in future and the time of fruition.

In all standard works on Indian Astrology, nowhere is importance given to the Ashtakavarga of the lord of the Ascendant, except in *Vidhamadhaviya*—University of Mysore, Oriental Library Publications, where stray references are there as *Lagneshasyashtavargetu*—Part I, p. 252 and *Lagnanathashvargeshu*—Part III, p. 14.

Chandrakala Nadi (Devakeralam), Madras Governmetn Oriental Series., Vol. II, Part I, page 51, verses 417 to 420 :

भिन्नाष्टवर्गे लग्नेशे फलहीनस्य राशिषु ।
स्फुटयोगं गते जीवे त्वल्पसौख्यं विनिर्दिशेत् ॥

When Jupiter transits a sign without a bindu in the Bhinnashtakavarga of the lord of the Ascendant, on the degrees of the

Ascendant lord (स्फुटयोगं) the native has little happiness.

एकद्वित्रिफलान्यस्मिन् लग्नेशाष्टकवर्गके ।
अतीव क्लेशकार्याणि तद्राशौ गोचरे शनौ ॥

When Saturn transits a sign having 1, 2 or 3 bindus in the Bhinnashtakavarga of the lord of the Ascendant, the native will suffer, much agony on account of quarrels.

पञ्चबिन्दुसमायुक्ते लग्नेशाष्टकवर्गके ।
शुभग्रहस्थिते काले ह्यतीव श्रियमादिशेत् ॥

When a benefic planet transits a sign having 5 bindus in the Bhinnashtakavarga of the lord of the Ascendant, the native will earn much wealth.

पञ्चमादिफलाधिक्ये पापाक्रान्तस्य कालगे ।
योगदाये महाभाग्यं गृहे गोधनसंकुलम् ॥

Even when a malefic planet transits a sign, having 5 or more bindus (in the Bhinnashtakavarga of the lord of the Ascendant) and if at that time there is Dasa of a planet causing yoga, the native has great luck and a number of cows etc. (In olden days, when these verses were composed, cattle, houses and agricultural land were main items of wealth.)

	bindus	**average**
The Sun's Ashtakavarga	48 ÷ 12 = 4	"
The Moon's Ashtakavarga	49 ÷ 12 = 4 1/12	"
Mars' Ashtakavarga	39 ÷ 12 = 3 1/4	"
Mercury's Ashtakavarga	54 ÷ 12 = 4 1/2	"
Jupiter's Ashtakavarga	56 ÷ 12 = 4 2/3	"
Venus' Ashtakavarga	52 ÷ 12 = 4 1/3	"
Saturn's Ashtakavarga	39 ÷ 12 = 3 1/4	"

From the above, it is observed that there is much variation in the averages of the bindus of the seven planets. In Ashtakavargas of Mars and Saturn, there may be signs having no bindus, while in the Ashtakavargas of the remaining planets, it is rare to have a sign without a bindu. Hence it is essential to render the above translation more practical.

1. Three signs having less bindus (unfavourable results).

2. Three signs having more bindus (favourable results).

3. Six signs having middling (average) bindus (mixed results).

For practical purposes 12 signs may be classified as under :

1. When a benefic planet transits a sign, having less bindus, the native gets little happiness, in proportion to the number of bindus.

2. When a malefic planet transits a sign, having less bindus, the native gets great agony on account of quarrels, in reverse proportion to the number of bindus.

3. When a benefic planet transits a sign, having more bindus, the native earns much wealth.

4. When a malefic planet transits a sign having many bindus (6 or more) and also Dasa is a favourable one, at that time, the native will have great luck.

Example : Chart No. 1, January 1984 issue of A.M., page 19, Question No. 12 :

Mars' Ashtakavarga—39 bindus.

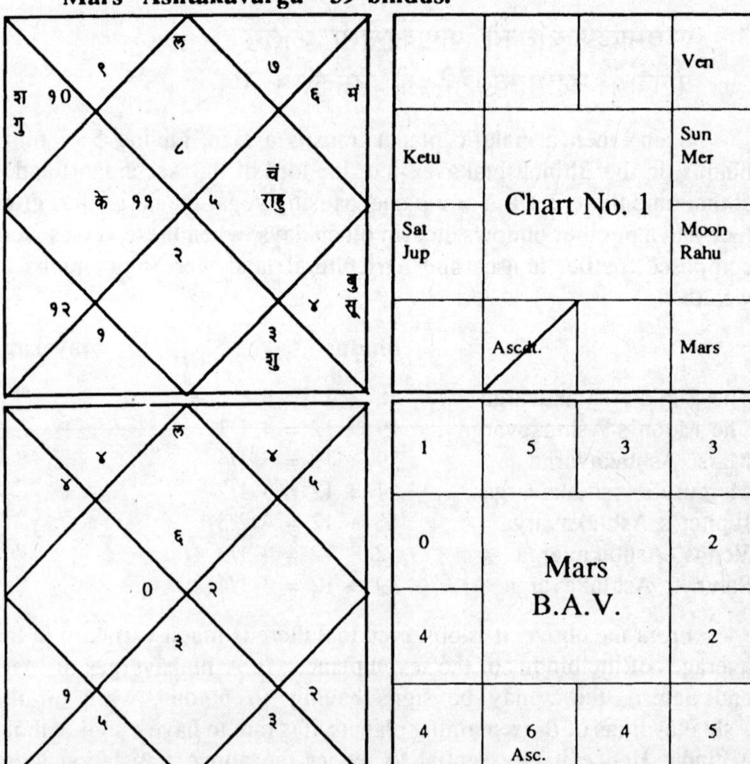

Favourable signs : The 1st house (Scorpio—6 bindus); the 6th house (Aries—5 bindus); the 11th house (Virgo—5 bindus).

Unfavourable signs : The 4th house (Aquarius —0—nil bindu); the 5th house (Pisces—1 bindu); the 9th house (Cancer—2 bindus); aspected by Saturn and occupied by the Sun).

The remaining six signs give mixed results.

When there are more signs than one with the same number of bindus, the favourable sign may be found out by an aspect and/or occupation of a benefic planet; similarly, when there are more signs with the same lesser number of bindus, the unfavourable sign may be found out by an aspect and/or occupation of a malefic planet.

Some horoscopes will have 8 (maximum) bindus in a particular sign. In such cases the quantum of favourable result will be maximum, when a benefic planet transits through it; while some other horoscopes will have 0- (nil) bindu in a particular sign (Ref. Chart No. 1, the 4th house—Aquarius); in such cases the quantum of unfavourable result will be maximum during transit of a malefic planet through that sign. Chart No. 2, January 1984 issue of A.M., page 118—Question No. 6;

Saturn's Ashtakavarga—39 bindus.

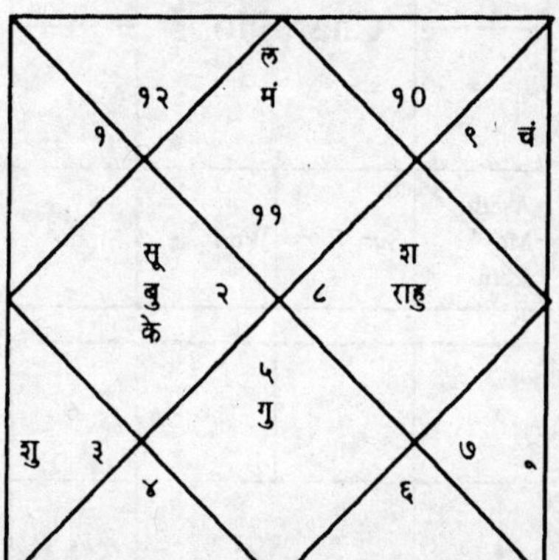

		Sun Mer Ketu	Ven
Mars Ascdt.	Chart No. 2		
			Jup
Moon	Sat Rahu		

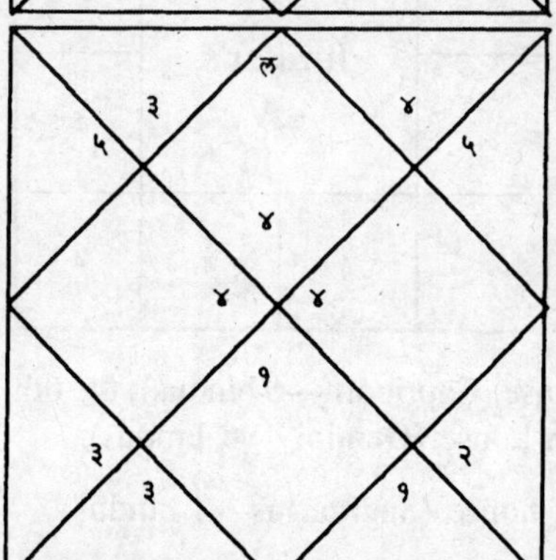

3	5	4	3
4 Asc.	Saturn A.V.		3
4			1
5	4	2	1

Favourable signs : The 3rd house (Aries—5 bindus); the 11th house (Sagittarius—5 bindus); the 1st house (Aquarius—4 bindus); aspected by Jupiter.

Unfavourable signs : The 7th house (Leo—1 bindu); the 8th house (Virgo—1 bindu) and the 9th house (Libra—2 bindus).

The remaining six signs are to give mixed results.

Chart No. 3. January 1984 issue of A.M., page 119—Question No. 14;

Jupiter's Ashtakavarga—56 bindus.

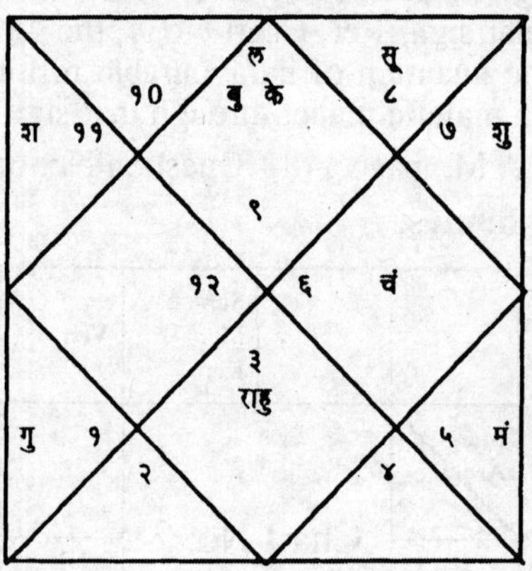

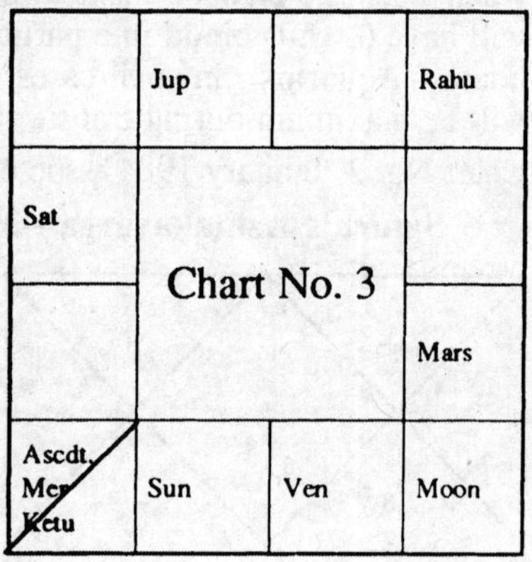

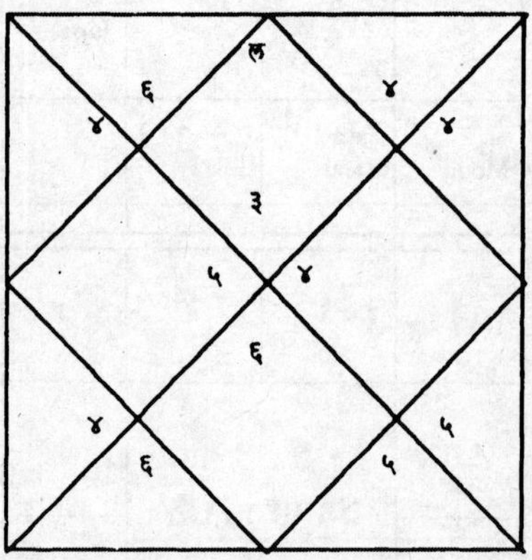

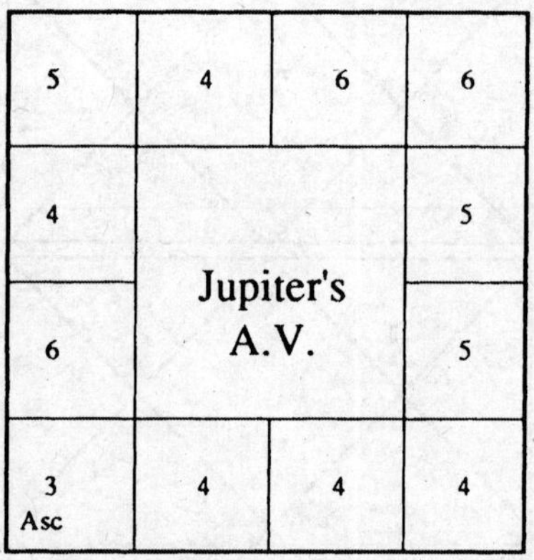

Favourable signs : The 2nd house (Capricorn—6 bindus); the 6th house (Taurus— 6 bindus); the 7th house (Gemini— 6 bindus).

Unfavourable signs : The 1st house (Sagittarius—3 bindus).

There are five signs having 4 bindus each. The 3rd house

(Aquarius—4 bindus; occupied by Saturn and aspected by Mars); the 12th house (Scorpio—4 bindus; occupied by the Sun and aspected by Mars and Saturn both).

The remaining six signs are to give mixed results.

Chart No. 4 : January 1984 issue of A.M., page 120—Question 18 :

Mercury's Ashtakavarga (54 bindus)

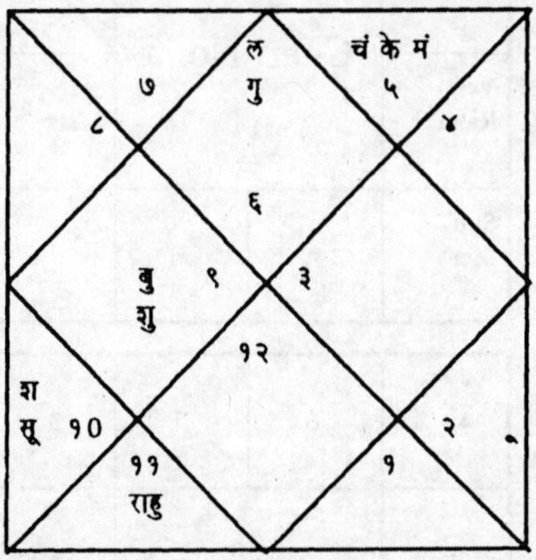

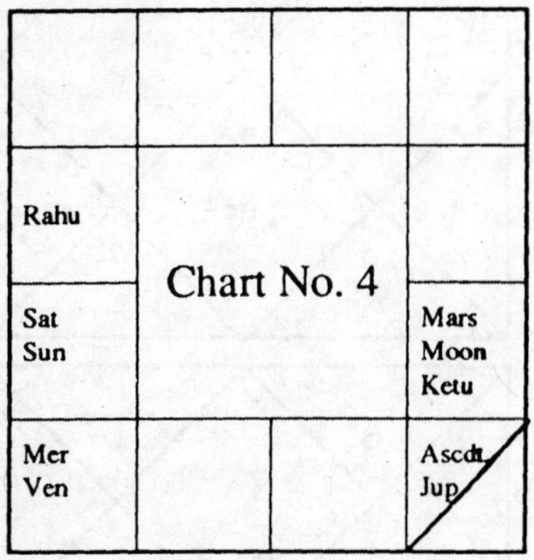

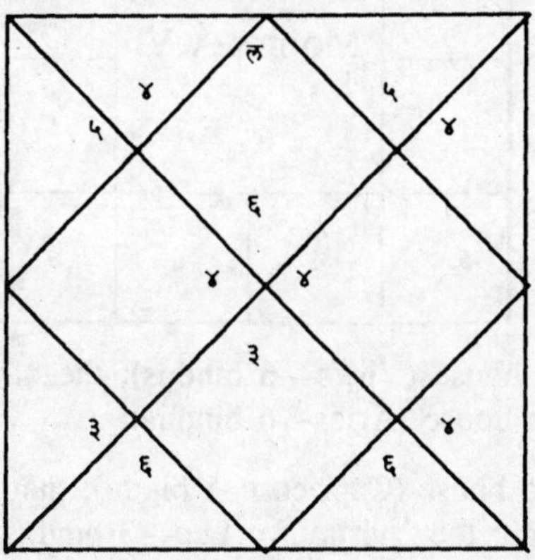

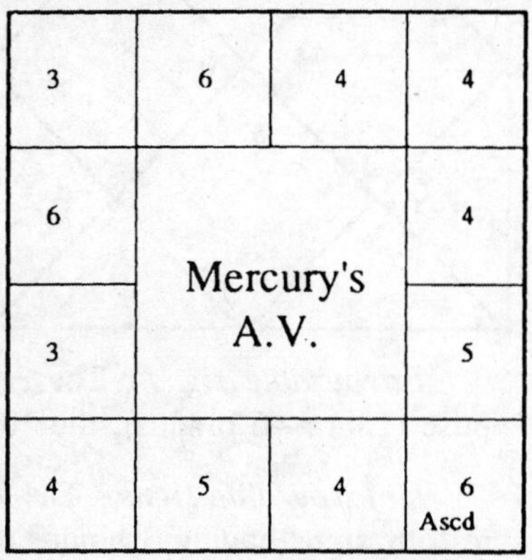

Favourable signs : The 1st house (Virgo—6 bindus); the 6th house (Aquarius—6 bindus); the 8th house (Aries—6 bindus).

Unfavourable signs : The 5th house (Capricorn—3 bindus); the 7th house (Pisces—3 bindus).

There are five signs having 4 bindus each; the 11th house (Cancer—4 bindus; aspected by the Sun and Saturn both).

The remaining six signs will give mixed results.

Chart No. 5 Time 7–45 p.m. Ahmedabad, 31-12-1915 :

The Moon's Ashtakavarga (49 bindus)

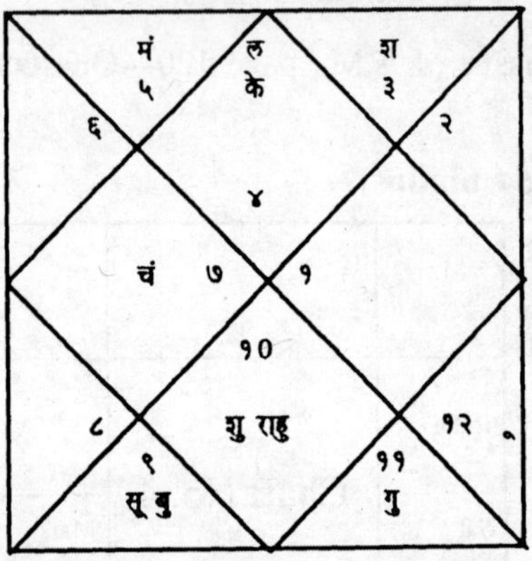

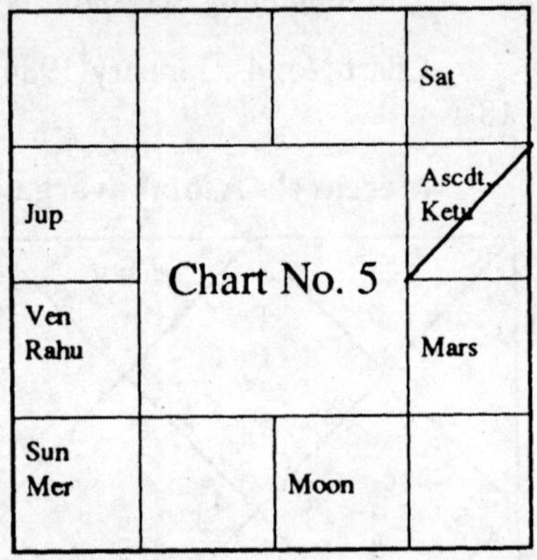

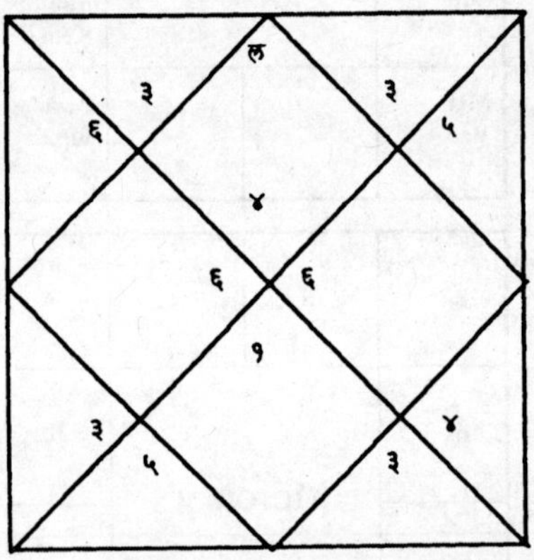

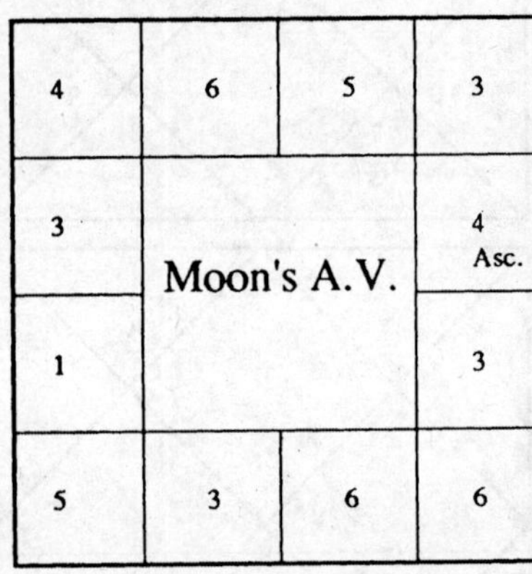

Favourable signs : The 3rd house (Virgo—6 bindus); the 4th house (Libra—6 bindus); the 10th house (Aries—6 bindus).

Unfavourable signs : The 7th house (Capricorn–1 bindu); there are four signs having 3 bindus each; the 2nd house (Leo—3 bindus; occupied by Mars and aspected by Saturn); the 12th house (Gemini—3 bindus; occupied by Saturn and aspected by the Sun).

The remaining six signs are to give mixed results.

The native of example 5 had big monetary gains during Jupiter's transit through Libra (*i.e.*, from 12-11-1969 to 11-12-1970). Jupiter's transit through Libra covers a period of 12 months. During this period of one year, whenever Mercury and/or Venus transits either Virgo, Libra or Aries, the native gets higher monetary gains through ways more than one. During these periods of higher gains, the transit of the Moon through the said three favourable signs indicates specific days. Jupiter's transit through Aries and Virgo should be examined in the same way.

Saturn takes 2 1/2 years to transit a sign. *e.g.*, Capricorn with 1 bindu. During Saturn's transit through Capricorn, when Mars and/or the Sun transits through Gemini, Leo or Capricorn, the native suffers from much anguish and quarrels. Similarly transit through Gemini and Leo should be examined in the same manner.

To what extent the native will get good or bad results, depends much on the intrinsic worth of the horoscope; but as far as the periods (good or bad) are concerned the rules mentioned above have proved fruitful.

The aim of this write-up is to put before the ardent students of Indian astrology, certain principles which are helpful to find out favourable periods, long and short, for getting maximum financial success as stated in Nadi literature (Granthas).

18

Use of Collective Ashtakavarga in Prognostication

The Ashtakavarga system appears to have originated in the very remote past. It is quite likely that the system was initiated even centuries before Christ (B.C.). The Ashtakavarga is recognised as an outstanding system of prediction among the many advocated in the standard works of astrology. This system provides certain keys for judging the strength of the houses (*bhavas*) and planets; and also evaluating the potency of transits. No doubt, this system is rather intricate and laborious. Of late, some students of astrology have started taking keen interest in Ashtakavarga. With the help of the contrivance containing Ashtakavarga plates, it is easy to prepare (1) the Bhinnashtakavarga : (2) the Prastarashtakavarga and (3) the Samudayashtakavarga or the Sarvashtakavarga. Of all the various chapters of Ashtakavrga, the most important for prognostication purposes is the chapter on Samudayashtakavarga (collective Ashtakavarga). The great scholar, Dr. B.V. Raman, has expressed his appreciation of its importance in his book on the subject by saying—"Years ago I had come across a pandit who could give a snapshot interpretation of a horoscope merely on the basis of Sarvashtakavarga, with considerable accuracy".

Those students, who do not possess the above contrivance, can well prepare Samudaya figures in each (house) sign without recourse to summing up their individual Ashtakavarga figures, by the use mnemonic verses

'बालो बलिष्ठो .... तीर्थकृत्'

mentioned in *Horasara, Phaladeepika, Prasnamarga, Jatakadesamarga, Ashtakavarga,* etc.

(1) Samudayashtakavarga—planets associated with more or less bindus :

(a) Planets, in the12th, 6th, 8th or 7th house; or in debilitation, in *vargas* of malefic and inimical planets; or associated with the lord of the house occupied by Mandi, are obstructors (of good results). Those, associated with more bindus, are capable of giving all important good results.

(b) Planets in exaltation, their own, a friend's house, in a trikona, a kendra (the 1st, 4th, 7th or 10th house) or an Upachaya house or powerful by position in benefic *vargas* are not effective, if they are associated with less number of bindus.

The grand total number of Samudayashtakavarga bindus is 337, divided by12 (signs), gives 28 as quotient (average) and leaves 1 as balance. Great teachers of astrology say that houses (signs) containing 31 or more bindus are very auspicious; those having 25 or less bindus produce bad effects.

(2) Samudayashtakavarga and Gochara (transit) results :

The interpretation of its transit results, from the Samudayashtakavarga, gives greater precision in respect of time and greater accuracy in respect of shape of events. Since 337 is total number of bindus, the average for each house is 28. The houses containing 28 or more bindus are auspicious while those with less than 28 bindus are inauspicious.

Again the Samudayashtakavarga is very helpful in estimating the periods of great prosperity and adversity from the transit of planets through houses containing the highest or the lowest number of bindus. If one house has the minimum bindus (*e.g.*, 18) and the very next house has the maximum bindus (*e.g.*, 36) the person experiences sudden rise in life. Conversely, if one house has the maximum bindus (*e.g.*, 36) and in the next house there are the minimum bindus (*e.g.*, 18) the person experiences sudden fall or calamity in life.

Chart No. 1 : Born on 2-6-1933 at 13h 15m at Bombay.

The native, during Saturn's transit through Gemini, earned rupees

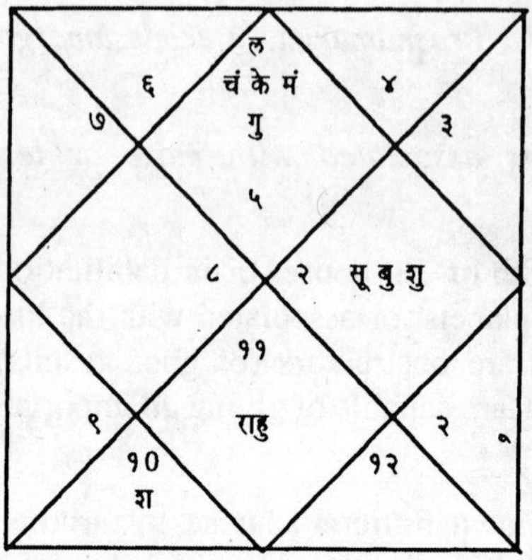

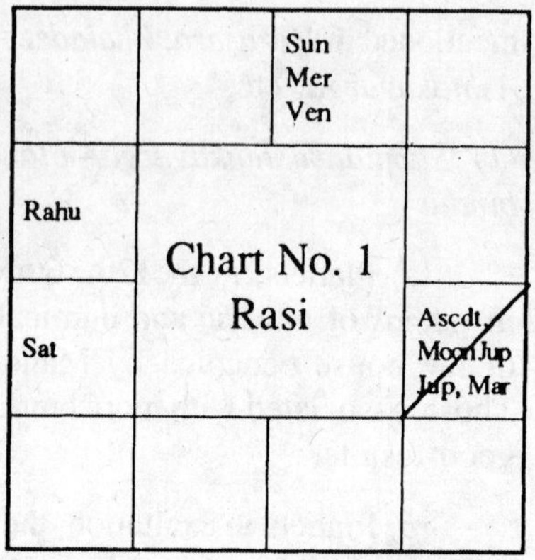

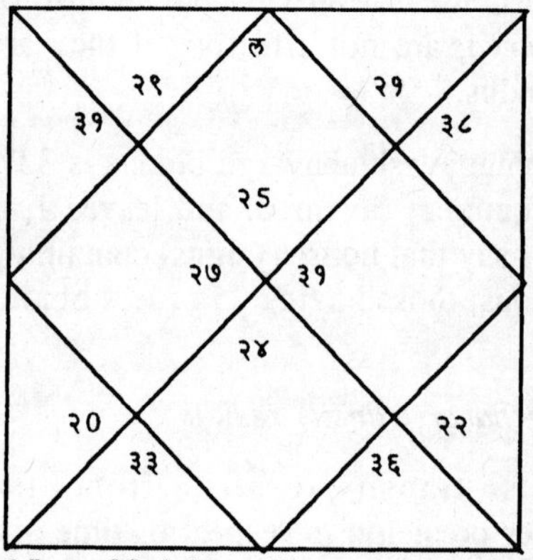

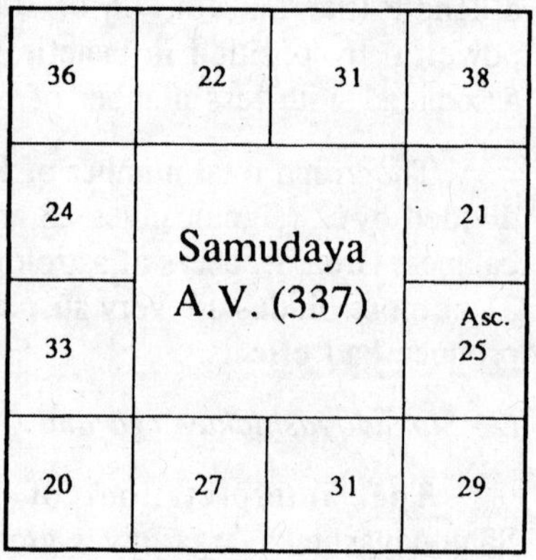

15 to 20 lakhs. The moment Saturn entered Cancer and advanced further, his downfall began and before Saturn came to Leo, he lost more than what he earned previously.

Chart No.2 : Born on 31-12-1915 at 19h 44m at Ahmedabad.

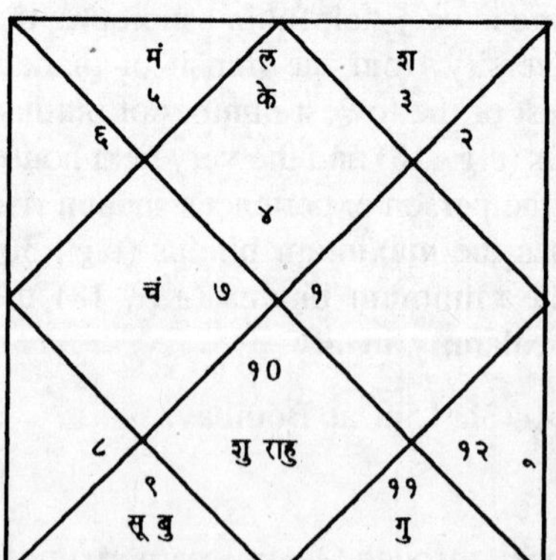

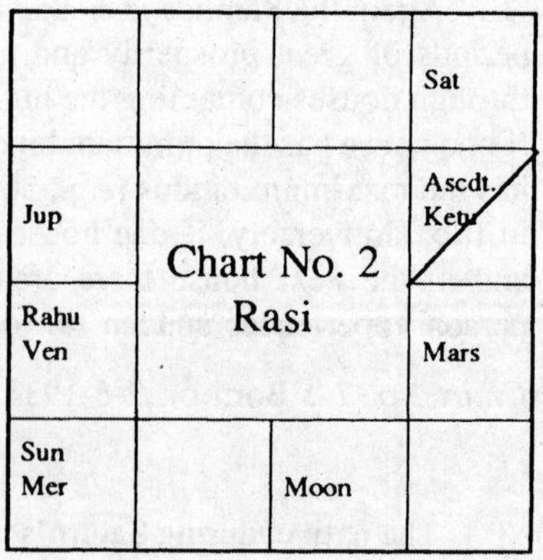

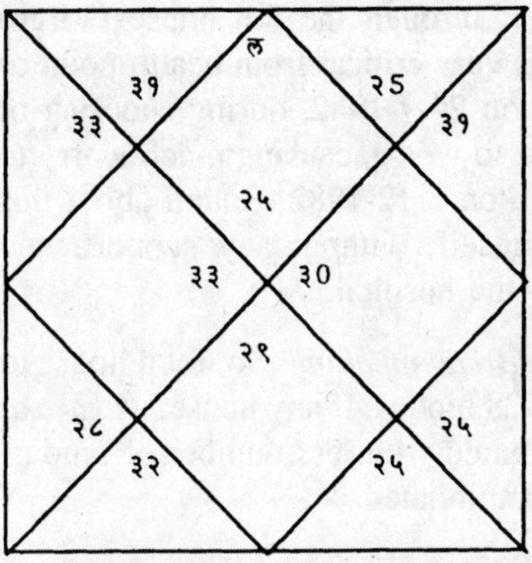

25	30	31	25
25	Samudaya	A.V. (337)	Asc. 25
19			31
32	28	33	33

As long as Saturn was trnsiting Sagittarius the native was in a high position in service. The moment Saturn enetered Capricorn (19 bindus), he was degraded and transferred to a lower position, from which he was not upgraded until his retirement from service.

Chart No. 3 : Born on 11-10-1042 at 16h 00m at Allahabad.

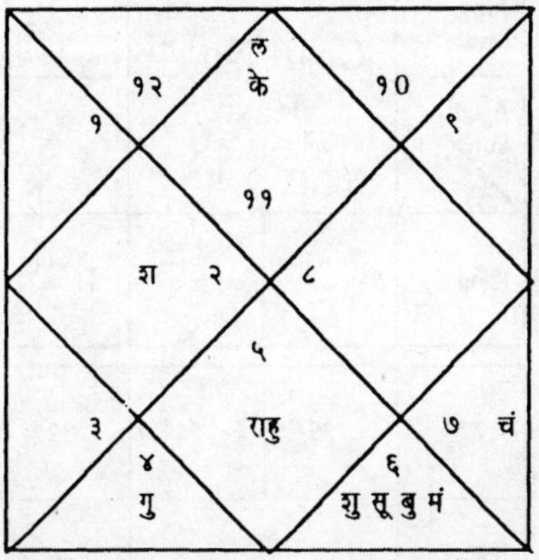

		Sat	
Ketu Ascdt.	Chart No. 3	Rasi	Jup
			Rahu
		Moon	Ven Mars Sun, Mer

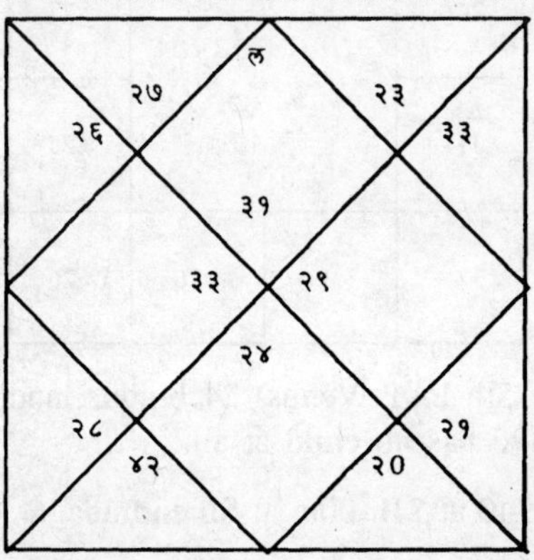

27	26	33	28
Asc. 31	Samudaya	A.V.	42
23			24
33	29	21	20

The period of Saturn's transit through the 8th house (Virgo) having the minimun 20 bindus, was very critical from health point of view. He was injured in the belly on 24-7-1982, during shooting of a picture. His health went from bad to worse, causing much worry to all converned. Saturn entered Libra on 6-12-1982. Round about this date, he was able to walk by himself, without any support, and thereafter he was discharged from the hospital.

(3) *Samudayashtakavarga and Bhavaphalam* : So, for a house to prosper, it must have on average of 28 bindus. If any house, its *karaka* and the lord, each of them is associated with less number of bindus, the good efects of that house are annihilated.

Chart No. 4 : Born on 6-2-1927 at 7h 19m at Ahmedabad.

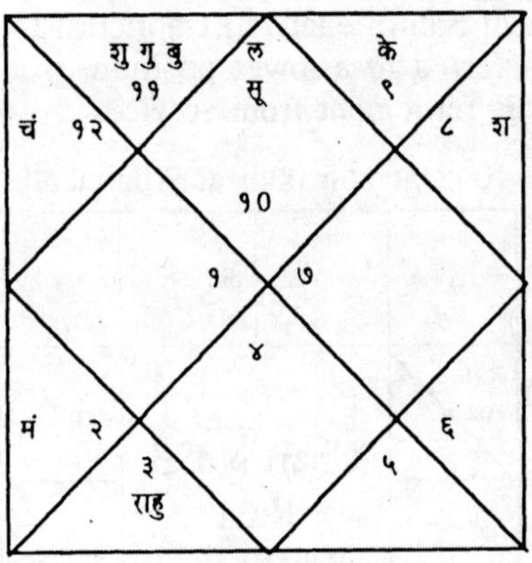

Moon		Mars	Rahu
Ven Jup Mer	Chart No. 4 Rasi		
Ascdt. Sun			
Ketu	Sat		

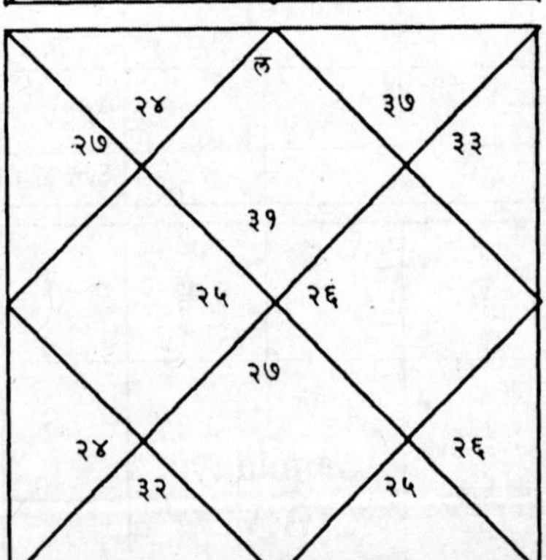

27	25	24	32
24	Samudaya A.V. (337)		27
Asc. 31			25
37	33	26	26

The 5th house 24 bindus; the 5th lord (Venus) 24 bindus, and Karaka Jupiter 24 bindus. The native has no child at all.

Chart No. 5 : Born on 18-2-1940 at 21h-00m at Surendranagar.

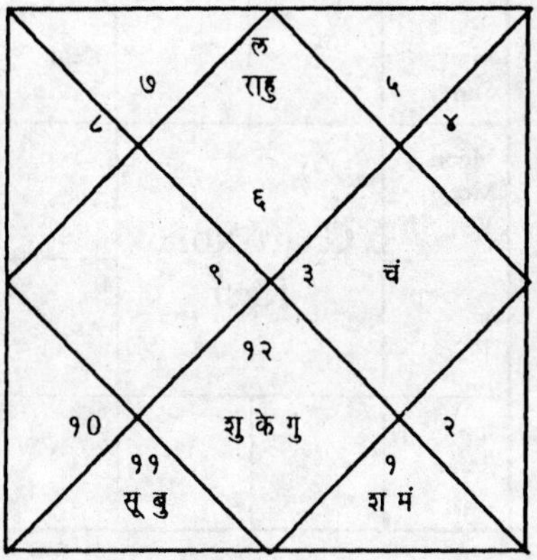

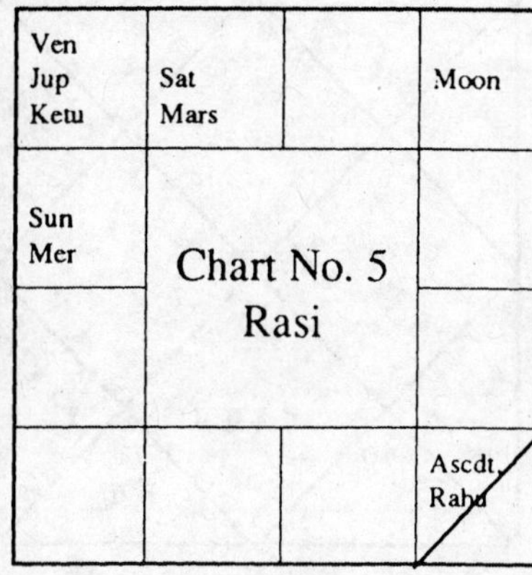

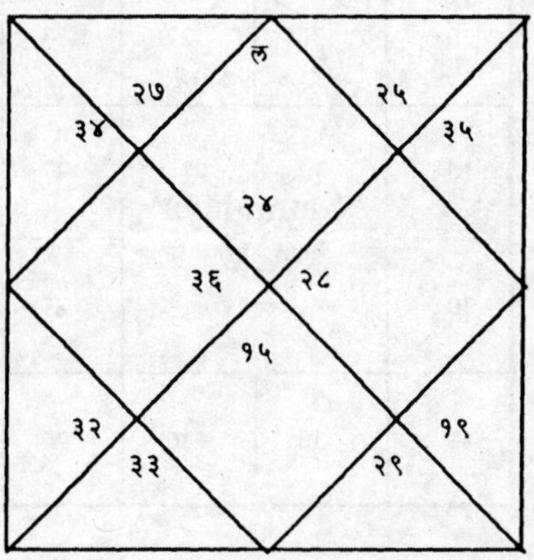

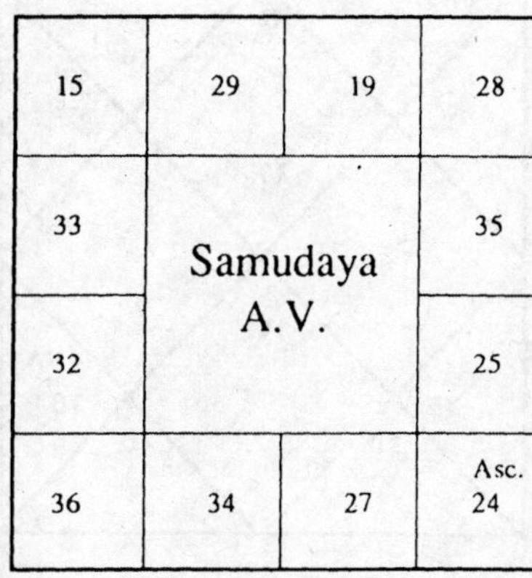

The 7th house 15 bindus; the 7th lord (Jupiter) 15 bindus and Karaka (Venus) 15 bindus.

The native is still unmarried. There is no possibility of his marriage. Malavya Yoga (Venus in Pisces in the 7th) and Hamsa Yoga (Jupiter in Pisces in the 7th) are nullified by the presence of Ketu in the 7th house.

Chart No. 6 : Born on 22-3-1936 at 17h 15m at Ahmedabad.

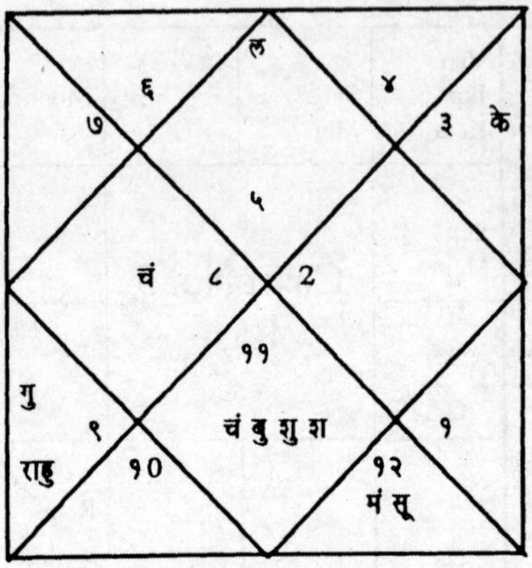

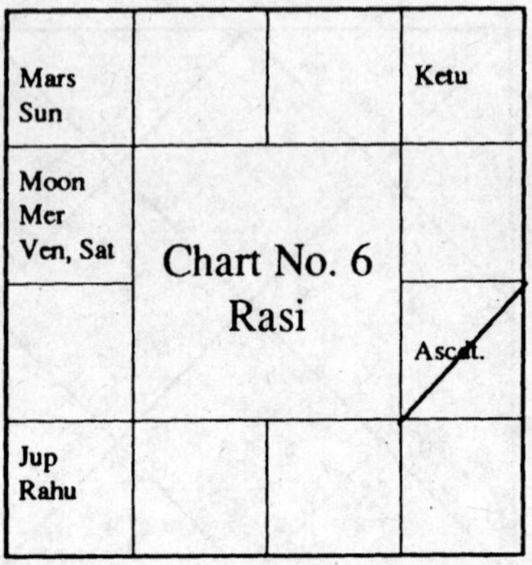

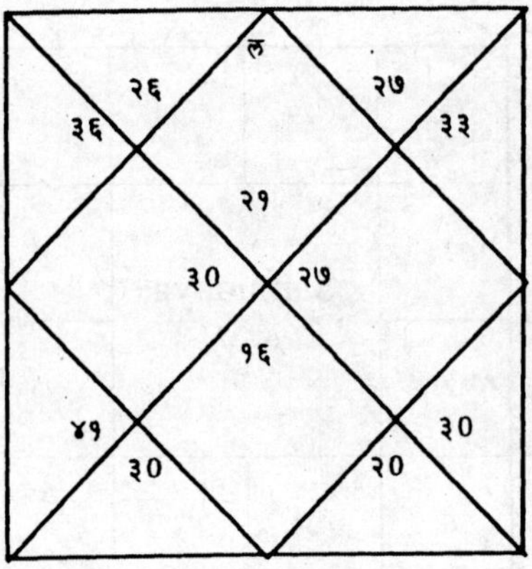

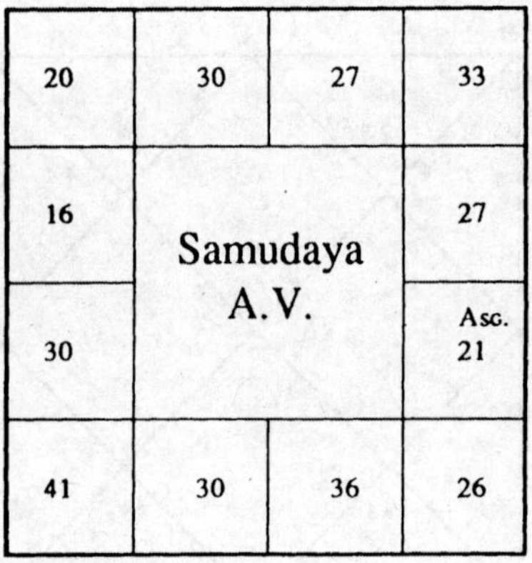

The Ascendant 21 bindus; the lord of Ascendant (the Sun) 20 bindus; and karaka (the Sun) 20 bindus. The first house is annihilated. The native breathed his last in the 29th year.

Since, 28 bindus are an average, so far a house to prosper, it must have more than 28 bindus. If any house, its Karaka and its lord, each of them is associated with more bindus, the good effects of that house are multiplied.

Chart No. 7 : Born on 16-10-1930 at 22h 55m at Virpur (Saurashtra).

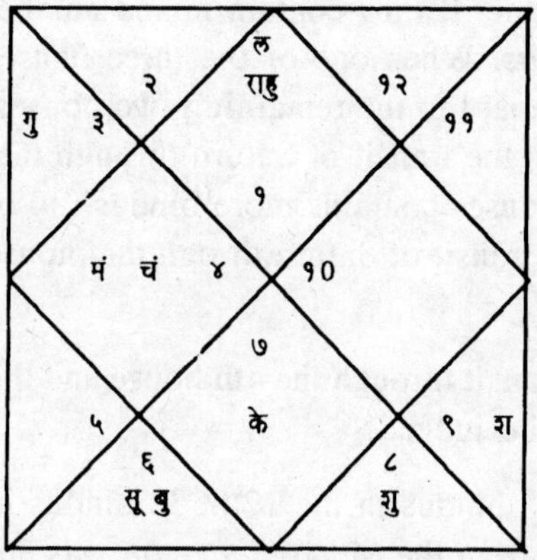

Chart No. 7
Rasi

	Ascd. Rahu		Jup
			Mars Moon
Sat	Ven	Ketu	Sun Mer

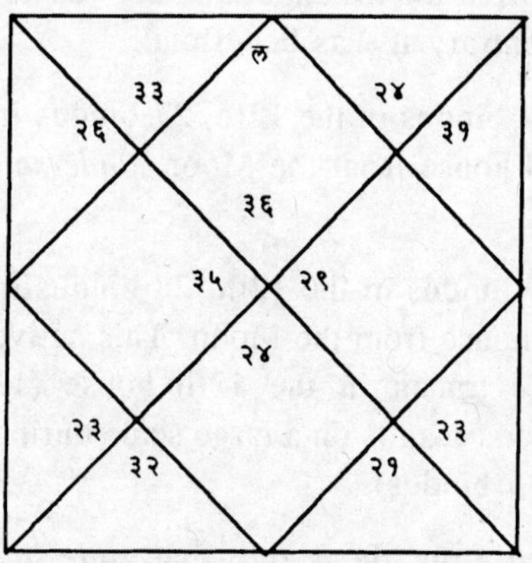

Samudaya
A.V.

24	Asc. 36	33	26
31			35
29			23
23	21	24	32

The Ascendant 36 bindus; the Ascendant lord (Mars) 35 bindus; and Karaka the Sun 32 bindus.

The native is well built, fairly tall and enjoys sound health, with no major sickness so far.

(4) Samudayashtakavarga and sade-sati :

The common man fears the mention of *sadesati*—7 1/2 years Panoti—in the south it is known as "*elarata*".

What is it? The transit of Saturn through the 12th, 1st and 2nd houses from the Moon is known as *sade-sati*. During this transit Saturn gives bad results to the native.

If the said houses contain more than 30 bindus each, the person suffers less troubles, miseries, etc., and he obtains good results on a very large scale, depending on the number of bindus in the said houses. If these three houses contain less than 25 bindus each, the person suffers miseries, etc., on a very large scale. If they contain mixed number of bindus, there are mixed results. When one of the three houses contains very few bindus as compard to the remaining two houses, the person suffers heavily during the transit of Saturn through that house. If one of the said three houses contains more bindus (30 or over) than the other two houses, transit of Saturn throgh that house will give good results.

In the same way Saturn's transit through the 4th house and the 8th house from the Moon may be judged.

In Chart No. 2, there are 33 bindus in the 12th, 33 bindus in the 1st and 28 bindus in the 2nd from the Moon. *Sade-sati* was not bordom to this native; on the contrary it was beneficial.

In Chart No. 4, there are 24 bindus in the 12th, 27 bindus in the 1st and 25 bindus in the 2nd house from the Moon. *Sade-sati* gave bad results to this native.

In Chart No. 5 there are 19 bindus in the 12th, 28 bindus in the 1st and 35 bindus in the 2nd house from the Moon. This native suffered heavily during Saturn's transit in the 12th house (19 bindus) while he obtained very good results on a large scale during transit through the 2nd house (35 bindus).

Thus, it would be observed from the above that *sade-sati* effects, good or bad, are correlated with the number of bindus in the respective houses from the Moon.

(5) Samudayashtakavarga and death : It has been observed, in practice *that at the time of death of a native*, generally Saturn transits a house containing the least number of bindus, or the next lowest house. It is also observed, that during such transit, the death of a nearer elderly relative takes place.

(a) Chart No. 8 : Born on 30-6-1961 are 00h 05m (a.m.) at Anand :

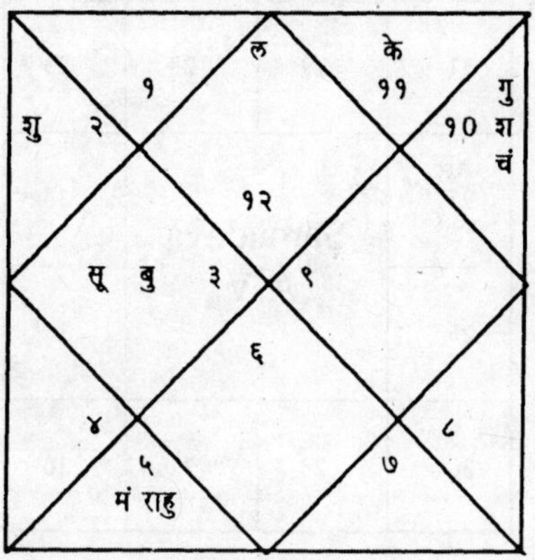

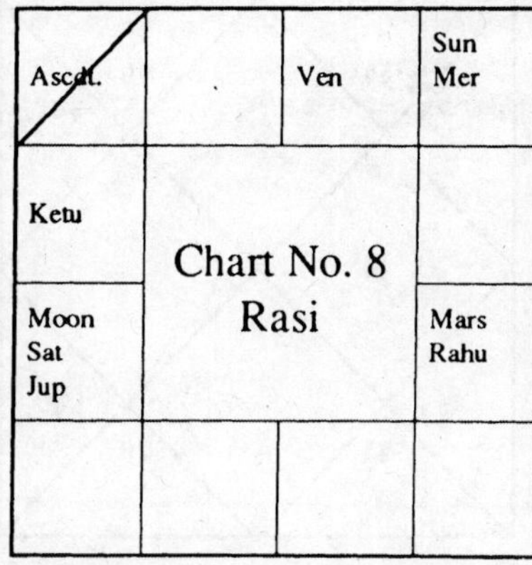

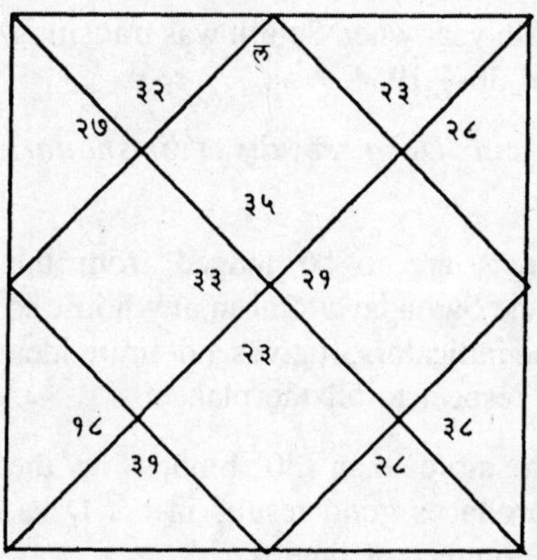

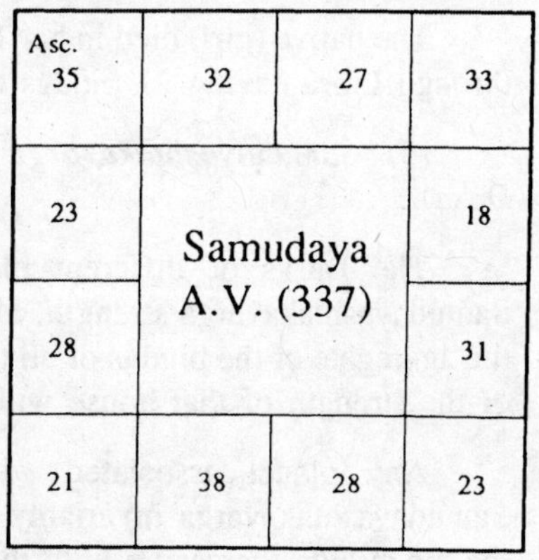

The boy died in his 16th year when Saturn was passing through Cancer having 18 bindus, on 20-10-1976.

(b) Refer Chart No. 6 (above). The young gentleman died in his 29th year, when Saturn was transiting Aquarius (16 bindus).

(c) Chart No. 9. Born on 5-12-1942 at 12h 54m at Bombay.

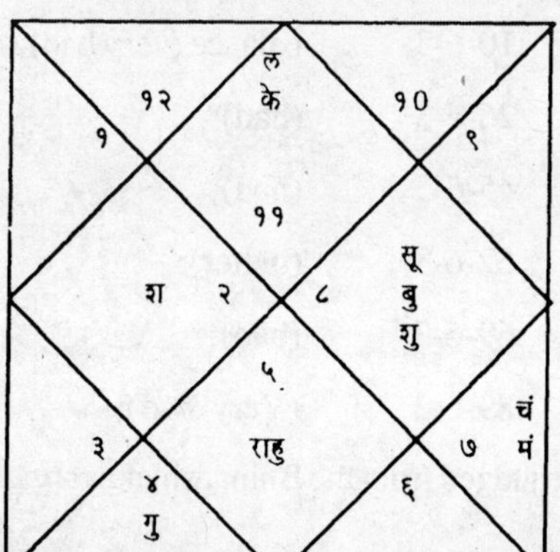

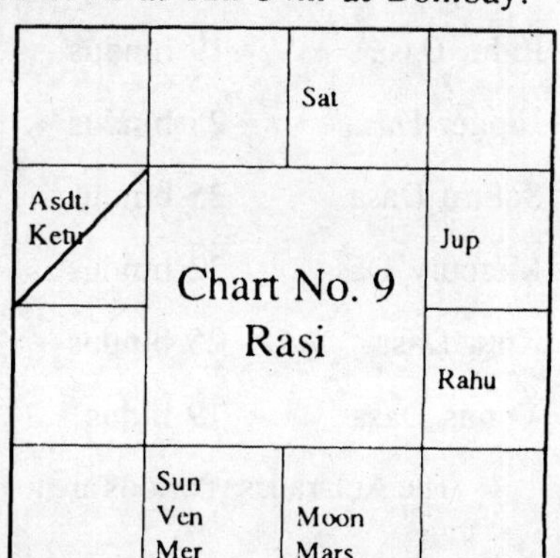

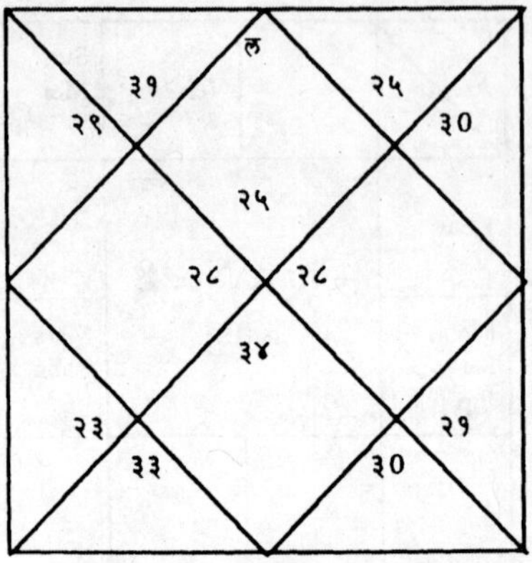

31	29	28	23
Asc. 25	Samudaya A.V.		33
25			34
30	28	21	30

The native (girl) died in her 12th year when Saturn was transiting through Libra having 21 bindus on 30-4-1954.

(6) Samudayashtakavarga and Dasa results (Vimshottari Dasa) :

The Dasas of different planets are to be judged from the Samudayashtakavarga strength. Since Samudaya total in any house is the aggregate of the bindus of all the indicators, it gives a definite idea of the strength of that house with respect to all the planets.

Any planet associated with more than 30 bindus in the Samudayashtakavarga invariably produces good results in his Dasa, the magnitude increasing with the number of bindus.

Kindly refer to Chart No. 2 (above)

Vimshottari Dasa balance 10 year, 6 months and 3 days (Rahu).

		Y—M—D	
Rahu Dasa	19 bindus	10-6-3	balance (very bad);
Jupiter Dasa	25 bindus	26-6-3	(bad);
Saturn Dasa	25 bindus	45-6-3	(bad);
Mercury Dasa	32 bindus	62-6-3	(better);
Ketu Dasa	25 bindus	69-6-3	(bad);
Venus Dasa	19 bidus	89-6-3	(Very bad);

The Antaradasa periods are to be judged from the Bhinnashtakavarga of the main Dasa lord.

Mercury Dasa from 45 years, 6 months and 3 days to 62 years, 6 months and 3 days (17 years).

Mercury's A.V. (54 bindus) :

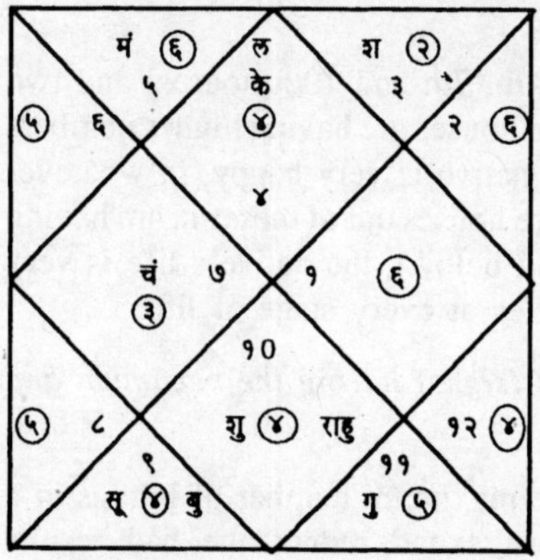

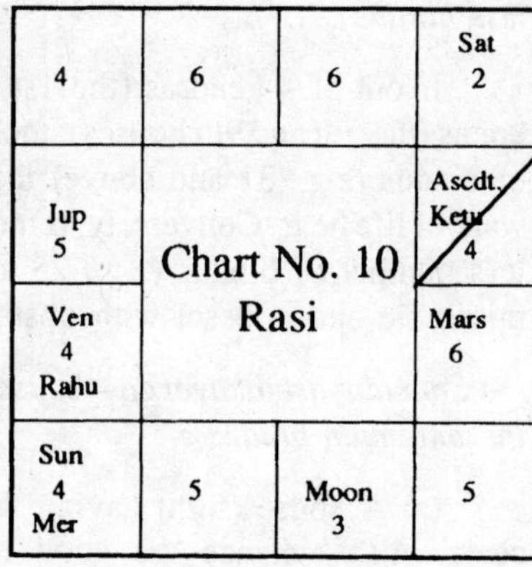

Antardasa Phalam :

Mercury is	associated	with 4	bindus	—	Medium
Ketu	do	" 4	do	—	"
Venus	do	" 4	"	—	"
The Sun	do	" 4	"	—	"
The Moon	do	" 3	"	—	Bad
Mars	do	" 6	"	—	Better
Rahu	do	" 4	"	—	Medium
Jupiter	do	" 5	"	—	Good
Saturn	do	" 2	"	—	Worse

The (Antara) period of a planet is auspicious if the planet is associated with 5 or more bindus in the house occupied by him in the Binnashtakavarga of the planet whose Dasa is under consideration. The effect reaches the maximum when the number of bindus is '8'; when the number is less than '4', the period proves inauspicious.

Rahu and Ketu are to be similar to Saturn and Mars respectively in their effects. As they are not included in the Ashtakavarga consideration, their *Antardasa periods* may be judged from the Ashtakavarga of Saturn (for Rahu) and Mars (for Ketu); but taking Rahu and the house occupied by him in lieu of Saturn and Ketu and the house occupied by him in lieu of Mars respectively.

(7) Samudayashtakavarga—houses (signs) associated with more or less bindus :

If out of 4 kendras (the 1st, 4th, 7th and 10th houses) and two konas (the 5th and 9th houses), more houses are having higher numbers of bindus (*e.g.*, 31 and above) the native is very happy, in whatever walk of life he is. Conversely, if more houses out of these six are having less number of bindus (*e.g.*, 25 and below), the native's life is very miserable and is beset with obstacles at every stage of life.

(8) Samudayashtakavarga—houses (signs) having the maximum and the minimum bindus :

(a) A house (sign) having the maximum number of bindus in a chart will enhance the good results and reduce the bad results pertaining to that house, while a house having the minimum number of bindus will enhance the bad results and reduce the good results of that house (no doubt, depending on the difference in the number of bindus).

For example, if the 4th house has the maximum 40 bindus, the native will have much landed property (land and buildings), many vehicles, will be very happy, etc., while the 4th house having the minimum 20 bindus, the native will have no accommodation of his own, no landed property, will sell away landed property if at all inherited and will be very unhappy.

(*b*) Similarly, a planet, malefic or benefic being associated with the maximum number of bindus in a chart, will produce good results on a very large scale, pertaining to the planet's *Karakatva*, ownership and occupation; while in contrast a planet being associated with the minimum number of bindus will produce unfavourable results on a very large scale, pertaining to the planet's *karakatva*, ownership and occupation.

The above rule will immediately show, at first sight, the intrinsic worth of a horoscope, as to how many planets are associated with higher number of bindus.

It may be pointed out that the horoscopes of renowned persons in different walks of life such as trade, commerce, industry, politics, learning, publishing, fine arts (music, singing, dancing, etc.,) painting, sports, medicine, scientific research, etc., will have at least one planet associated with 6, 7, or 8 bindus in Bhinnashtakavarga and more than 32 bindus in Samudayashtavarga in the house (sign) occupied by him. The type of vocation may be inferred from the position, ownership and *karakatva* of the planet or planets observed, *e.g.*, In horoscope of :—

(1) Dr. B.V. Raman—the Moon in the 4th house is associated with 6 bindus in Bhi. A.V., and 33 bindus in Samu A.V. : Saturn in the 4th house is associated with 4 bindus in Bhi. A.V., and 33 bindus in Sam. A.V.

(2) Amitabh Bachchan (Chart No. 3)—Jupiter associated with 7 bindus in Bhi. A.V. and 42 bindusin Samu A.V.

(3) K.M. Kharegat (Ref. page 507, A.M. June 1985)—The Moon in the 11th house is associated with 7 bindus in Bhi. A.V. and 39 bindus in Sam. A.V.; Jupiter in the Ascendant is with 5 bindus in Bhi. A.V. and 34 bindus in Sam. A.V.; Mercury in the Ascendant is with 6 bindus in Bhi.A.V., and 34 bindus in Sam. A.V.

(*c*) An easy and quick estimation of a horoscope, with respect to the good and bad effects to the native and his relatives, is as follows :

Observe the house having the maximum number of bindus and also the house having the minimum number of bindus in chart. Then, in the order of the *karakatva,* Ascendant for self, the Sun for father, the Moon for mother, Mars for brother, Venus for wife, etc., reckon from the house occupied by the *karaka* planet to the houses of the maximum and the minimum bindus. Observe the house positions indicated (from the *Karaka* Planet) by those houses and interpret the results with reference to those houses.

(*d*) If, in a chart, the disparity between the maximum and the minimum bindus is very little, *i.e.,* all the twelve houses are having bindus ranging betwen 26 to 30 only, such a native will have speedy progress in life with no great upheavals or downfalls.

(9) *Samudayashtakavarga and Vargottama planet :*

A Vargottama planet in any house with 30 or more bindus enhances the good results of the house to the greatest extent, in proportion to the higher number of bindus.

Quite the reverse is the case, when a Vargottama planet is associated with less number of bindus.

(1) A native has Venus in Pisces (Vargottama) in the 12th house with 20 bindus—he is fond of unnatural sex.

(2) Another native has Jupiter in Cancer (Vargottama) in the 5th house with 20 bindus—he is unhappy on account of the misdeeds of his daughters.

(10) *Samudayashtakavarga and Navamsa strength :*

Planets posited in the Rasi chart get their effects enhanced or reduced by their placements in Navamsa. If a planet in a particular house, associated with higher number of bindus in Rasi chart, happens to be associated with higher number of bindus in Navamsa sign also, the results of that house are magnified greatly; while the same planet if associated with less number of bindus in Navamsa sign bestows moderate results of the said house.

If a planet, associated with less number of bindus in Rasi chart happens to be associated with higher number of bindus in Navamsa sign, it bestows moderate results of that house; while the same planet has lsss number of bindus in Navamsa sign also, it bestows unfavourable results.

Kindly refer Chart No. 3 (above). Mars in the 8th house is associated with 20 bindus in Rasi chart while in navamsa Mars is in sign Cancer, which has 42 bidus. Hence Mars bestows moderate results.

(11) *Samudayashtakavarga—Phalam (results) at the age represented by the number of bindus :*

A native will get a royal vehicle, wealth, son, much knowledge, etc., after attaining the age represented by the number of bindus in the Ascendant.

Results at the age represented by the number of bindus in the house (sign) occupied :

(1) by Jupiter—one may expect birth of a child, wealth, etc.;

(2) In the case of Venus—one may expect marriage or marital happiness at the corresponding age;

(3) in the case of Mercury—learning of science, intellectual expansion and praise from scholars may be expected at that age;

(4) in the case of Mars—injury by weapons may be expected;

(5) in the case of Saturn—there will be sickness, sorrow, etc.;

(6) in the case of Rahu—if posited in the 6th, the 8th or the 12th house, snake bite or suffering from food poison;

(7) in the case of Ketu—accident or physical injury or operation would take place.

The above effects will take place only when there are indications capable of giving such results and not otherwise.

(12) *Samudayashtakavarga Comparison of bindus in certain pairs of houses :*

If there are more bindus

1. In the 5th house as compared to those in the 7th house, the native will be an aggressive husband/wife.
2. In the 4th house as compared to those in the 6th house—one gets more help from relatives.
3. In the 11th house as compared to the 10th, more earnings against less efforts.
4. In the 11th house as compared to the 12th, more earnings, emassing wealth and landed property.
5. In the 10th house—independent vocation
6. in the 1st house—reputation
7. in the 11th house—vehicle
8. in the 9th house—fearful nature
9. in the 2nd house—truthful
10. in the 5th house—intellectual and learned
11. in the 1st house—impressive personality
12. in the 7th house—over-sexed
13. in the Ascendant—long life and sound health
14. in the sign occupied by the Moon—same as item 13.

If there are more bindus

1. in the 7th house than the 5th house the native will be a henpecked husband/wife
2. in the 6th house than the 4th house it indicates more trouble from enemies
3. more bindus in the10th less earnings in proportion to efforts
4. more bindus in the 12th more expenses than income, more expenditure on worldly pleasures
5. more bindus in the 6th house—service under some superiors
6. in the 8th loss of prestige; bad name
7. in the 4th house—no vehicle
8. in the 3rd house—fearfulness
9. in the 3rd house—a liar
10. in the 2nd house—fluent speech and oratary
11. in the 3rd house—non-executive post in Government services
12. in the 3rd house—inclined towards unnatural lust.
13. in the 8th house—medium age (Madhyayus), ill-health
14. in the 8th house from the Moon—same as item 13.

19

Use of Bhinnashtakavargas in Prognostication

Ashtakavarga, unerringly indicates the nature of events which are likely to occur in future and the time of their fruition. In all standard works on Indian Astrology nowhere much importance is given to the transits of planets, in their *Bhinnashtakavargas* as in *Saravali*.

Devakerlam (Chandrakala Nadi), perhaps the most outstanding and unique contribution of Kerala, introduces some such techniques of delineation of transits results, not found in other classical texts on Astrology. *Devakeralam* was published by Government Oriental Manuscripts Library, Madras in two volumes (1951 and 1956).

बुधाष्टवर्गं निक्षिप्य हीनबिन्दुषु राशिषु ।
स्फुटयोगं गते सौम्ये तत्रिकोणे निशाकरे
अतीव क्लेशकार्याणि देहायासं विनिर्दिशेत् ।। V 618-618$\frac{1}{2}$
(Dev. Vol. II Part I page 74)

Meaning : Find a sign containing the lowest number of *bindus* in Mercury's *Bhinnashtakavarga*. When Mercury transits *that sign* over the degrees of natal Mercury, the native will suffer much mental agony on account of quarrels and physical afflictions. Similar will be the results, when the Moon transits trine signs *i.e.*, the 5th or the 9th sign from the natal sign of Mercury.

The Example Horoscope :

Birth details : 31st December, 1915 at 7.44 p.m. (IST) at 23° 2' N, 72° 37' E.

Planetary Longitudes :The Sun 256° 10'; The Moon 192° 13'; Mars 127° 9'; Mercury 265° 13'; Jupiter 329° 29'; Venus 283° 14'; Saturn 80° 42' (R); Rahu 287° 06'; Ketu 107° 06'; Herschel 291° 00'; Neptune 99° 13'; Ascendant 98° 53'; M.C. 04° 08'; Balance Rahu Dasa : 10 years 6 months 3 days.

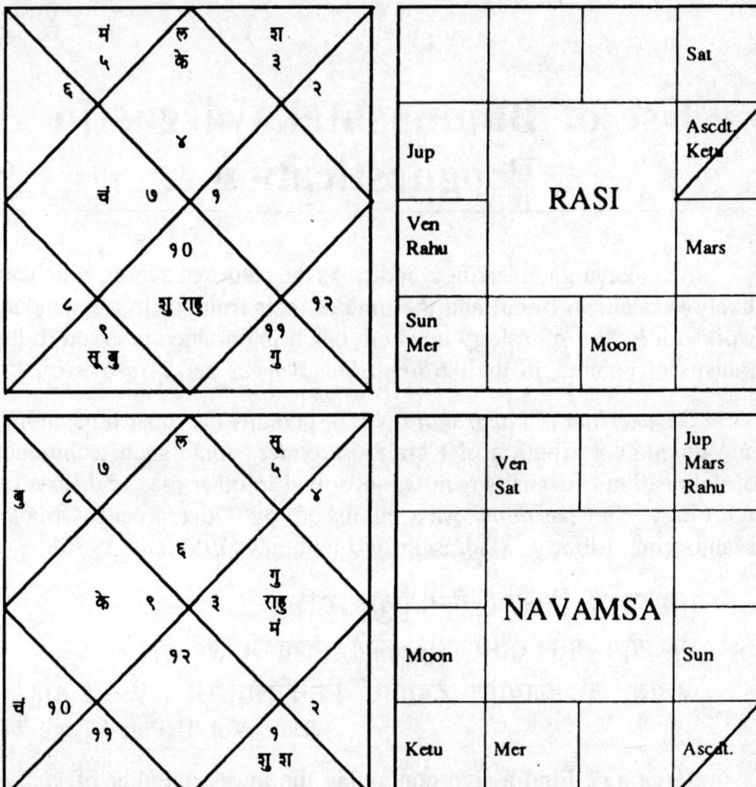

Mercury's *Bhinnashtakavarga* (54 *bindus*)—

Gemini has 2 *bindus* (the lowest). When Mercury transits 25° 13' in Gemini, the native will suffer the above unfavourable results. Mercury will take nearly a month or so, to transit Gemini and during that period when the Moon will transit Aries and Leo (trine signs from natal Mercury), similar results are likely to take place. The quantum of results will increase if the sign under consideration has 1 or 0 *bindu*.

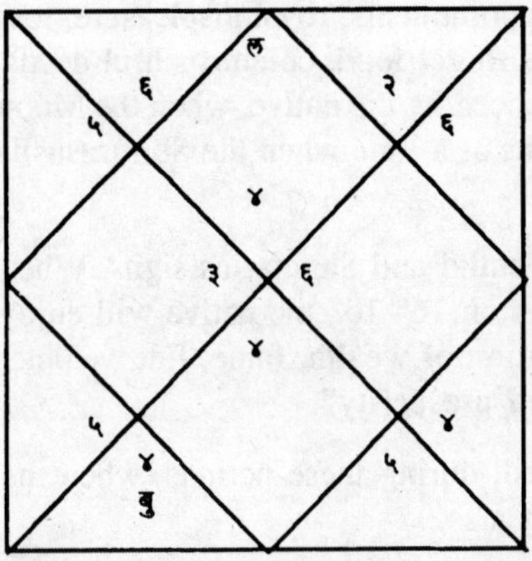

4	6	6	2
5			Ascdt 4
4	**Mercury**		6
Mer 4	5	3	5

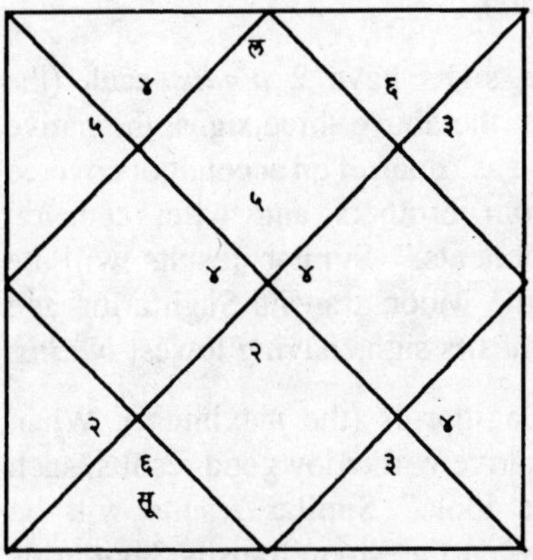

4	4	3	6
3			Asdt 5
2	**The Sun**		4
Sun 6	2	4	5

Conversely, one can find out signs having the higher number of *bindus* in Mercury's *Ashtakavarga.* In the example horoscope there are 6 *bindus* each in Aries, Taurus and Leo. When Mercury transits through these signs on 25° 13', the native will enjoy—"success in all undertakings; and will have capacity to grasp and accomplish easily the most intricate and abstruse problems". Similar results will be enjoyed by the native, when the Moon transits through Aries and Leo signs, at a time when Mercury transits those signs *viz.,* Aries, Taurus and Leo.

This is a mere indication. One can apply these rules to all the remaining planets' *Ashtakavargas,* except that of the Moon.

The Sun's *Bhinnashtakavarga* (48 *bindus*)—

Scorpio and Capricorn have 2 *bindus* each (the lowest). When the Sun trasnsit 16° 10' in Scorpio and Capricorn, the native will suffer unfavourable results such as "disappointments, royal displeasure, loss through theft, calumny, difficulties to get food, commit sinful deeds, etc." Similar results will be experienced by the native, when the Moon transits through Aries and Leo signs at a time when the Sun trasnsits Scorpio and Capricorn signs.

There are 6 *bindus* each in Gemini and Sagittarius signs. When the Sun transits through these signs on 16° 10', the native will enjoy favourable results such as "acquisition of wealth, fame, fine vehicle, success in undertakings, valour and prosperity".

Similar results will be enjoyed, during these periods, when the Moon transits Aries and Leo signs also.

Mars' *Bhinnashtakavarga* (39 *bindis*) :

Cancer, Libra and Capricorn signs have 2 *bindus* each (the lowest). When Mars transits 7° 9' in the above three signs, the native will suffer unfavourable results, such as "quarrel on account of coveted things and money, separation from brothers and wife; censure; dishonour from enemies and opponents." Similar results will be experienced by the native, when the Moon transits Sagittarius and Aries signs, at a time when Mars transits signs having lowest *bindus*.

There are 5 *bindus* in sign Sagittarius (the maximum). When Mars transits 7° 9' in this sign, the native will enjoy good results, such as "pleasing behaviour; handsome look." Similar results will be enjoyed, during the above period, when the Moon transits Sagittarius and Aries signs also.

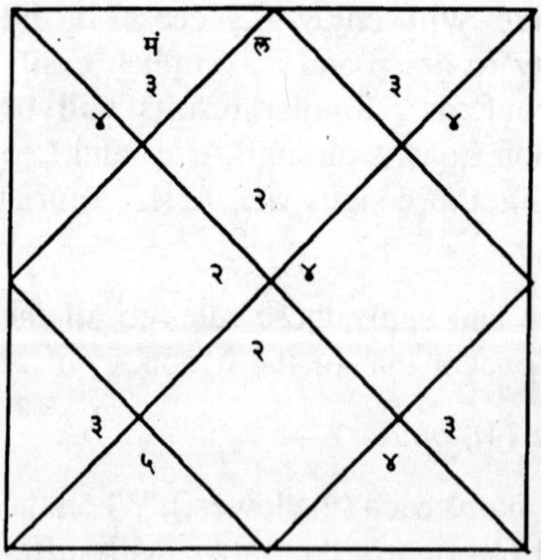

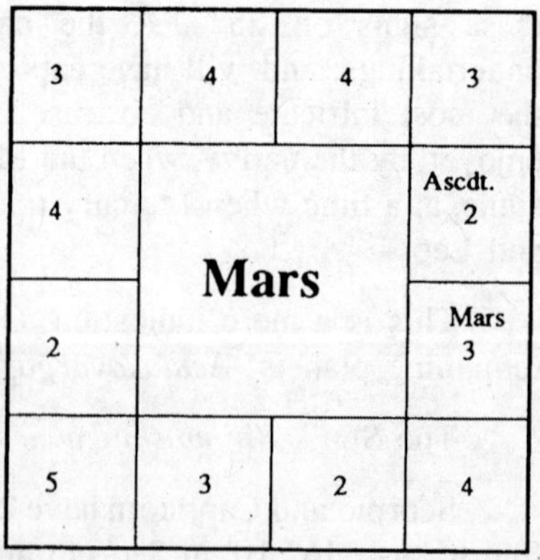

Jupiter's *Bhinnashtakavarga* (56 *bindus*):

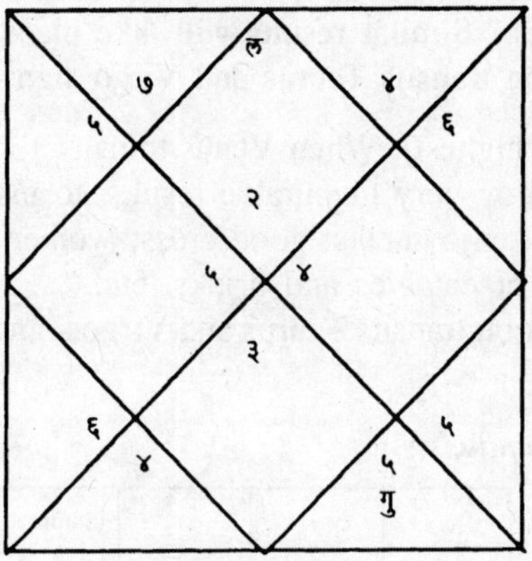

5	4	6	4
Jup 5	**Jupiter**		Ascdt. 2
3			7
4	6	5	5

Cancer sign has 2 *bindus* (the lowest). When Jupiter transits 29° 29' in this sign, the native will suffer unfavourable results such as "displeasure from ruling powers; loss of wife, children (their sickness) or landed property." Similar will be the case, *every month*, when the Moon transits Gemini and Libra signs, throughout the year till Jupiter transits sign Cancer.

There are 7 *bindus* in sign Leo (the highest). When Jupiter transits 29° 29' in this sign, the native will enjoy nice results such as "various kinds of wealth, general happiness,or birth of a child." Similar results will be experienced, when the Moon transits, every month, Gemini and Libra signs throughout this period of one year, till Jupiter transits Leo sign.

Venus' *Bhinnashtakavarga* (52 *bindus*) :

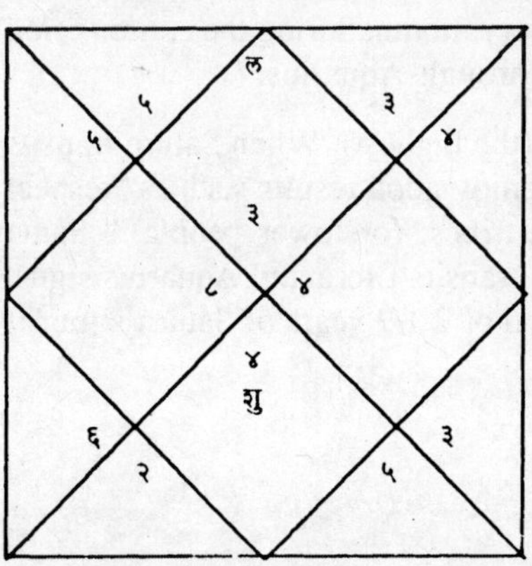

3	4	4	3
5	**Venus**		Ascdt. 3
Ven 4			5
2	6	8	5

Sign Sagittarius has 2 *bindus* (the minimum). When Venus trasnsits 13° 14' in this sign, the native will suffer bad results such as "degradation, sickness, wanderings." Similar results will take place, *during that period,* when the Moon transits Taurus and Virgo signs.

Libra sign has 8 *bindus* (the highest). When Venus transits 13° 14' in this sign, the native will enjoy very favourable results, to *the maximum extent,* such as "gets all enjoyments; good dress; women; sweet smelling flowers; varieties of eatables and drinks, etc. ...." Same will be the case, when the Moon transits Taurus and Virgo signs during that period.

Saturn's *Bhinnashtakavarga* (39 *bindus*) :

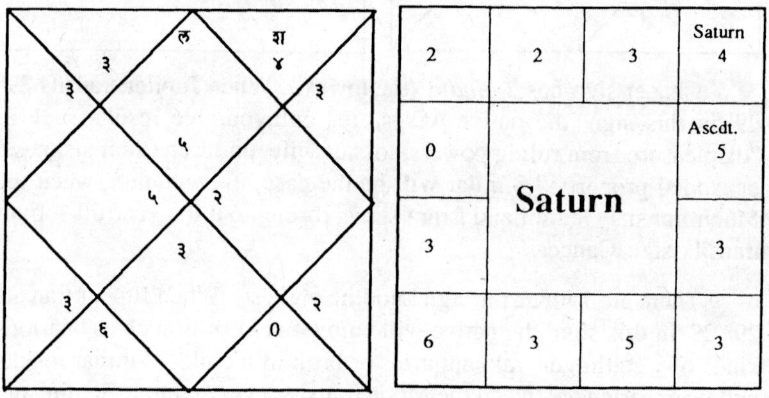

Aquarius sign has 0 - nil *bindu* (the minimum). When Saturn transits 20° 42' in this sign, the native will suffer unfavourable results, *to the maximum extent* such as "loss of everything; possibility of death (failing, severe sickness)." Similar will be the results, when the Moon transits Libra and Aquarius signs every month, during the entire period of 2 1/2 years of Saturn's transit through Aquarius.

Sign Sagittarius has 6 *bindus* (the highest). When Saturn transits 20° 14' in this sign, the native will enjoy good results such as "respect from leaders of thieves and forest tribes; (or lower people)." Same results will follow, when the Moon transits Libra and Aquarius signs, every month, during the entire period of 2 1/2 years of Saturn's transit through sign Sagittarius.

Table as below (of example horoscope) will be very useful

Planet	Associated *bindus* in the sign occupied by the planet in *Bhinnashtakavarga*	Associated *bindus* in the sign occupied by the planet in *Samudayashtakavarga*	Signs having highest number of *bindus*	Signs having lowest number of *bindus*
Sun	6	32	6—Gemini and Sagittarius	2—Scorpio and Capricorn
Moon	6	33	6—Aries, Virgo and Libra	1—Capricorn
Mars	3	31	5—Sagittarius	2—Cancer, Libra and Capricorn
Mercury	4	32	6—Aries, Taurus and Leo	2—Gemini
Jupiter	5	25	7—Leo	2—Cancer
Venus	4	19	8—Libra	2—Sagittarius
Saturn	4	25	6—Sagittarius	"0" (*nil bindu*) Aquarius

This table shows what will happen, when it will happen and in what proportion. If a sign has 0 nil *bindu* (the minimum), the proportion of adverse results will be the maximum; conversely, if the sign contains 8 *bindus* (the maximum), the proportion of favourable results will be very high. **The natives having horoscopes with 8 and 0 *bindus* in any *Bhinnashtakavargas*, will have rises and falls in their lives.**

If at a particular period of life, two, three,four or more planets transit, in their individual *Bhinnashtakavargas*, simultaneously, through signs, having lowest number of *bindus*, big calamities will have to be encountered; conversely, if more planets transit through signs, having highest number of *bindus* simultaneously, very favourable results will take place.

An intensive use of the above method will pinpoint most of the favourable or unfavourable periods and events in a native's life.

One can easily prepare annual readings of charts as per the above rules, meaningfully.

20

Interpreting Bhinnashtakavarga

The Bhinnashtakavarga (B.A.V.) provides certain keys for judging the worth or utility of some signs containing '0' or '8' *bindus* and also for evaluating the potency of transits through them. '0' or nil *bindu* sign means a sign without any benefic place (point or *bindu*). In Bhinnashatakavarga (B.A.V.) of any planet, if any sign is without a *bindu* it has some special significance. When the B.A.V. of any planet is prepared, each sign is to be observed carefully. A sign may contain from '0' to '8' *bindus.*

In B.A.Vs of Mercury (54 *bindus*), Jupiter (56 *bindus*) and Venus (52 *bindus*), one can find a sign having eight *bindus*, but to have a sign without a *bindu i.e.*, '0' is rare. On the contrary, 8 *bindus* in any sign in B.A.Vs of Mars and Saturn is a rarity, while '0' *bindu* sign is found very often in them.

One point is to be made clear in the beginning. Each planet from the Sun to Venus (six planets) gives a *bindu* to the sign occupied by himself. The result is that each of them can be associated with minimum 1 *bindu* and maximum with 8 *bindus*. While, Saturn does not contribute a *bindu* to sign occupied by himself, as such Saturn can be associated with minimum '0' *bindu* and with maximum, 7 bindus only and never 8.

Transit of Planets Through '0' Bindu Sign

When each of the seven planets beginning with the Sun to Saturn transits through a sign in their respective B.A.Vs having '0' *bindu* the results are as follows :

(1) Death or its equivalent troubles;

(2) Sorrow; anxiety, unexpected death;

(3) Stomach-ache; fainting; eye disease; death;

(4) Loss of everything (through enemy intrigues), consequent death;

(5) Loss of wealth or relations or children; becoming dull;

(6) All kinds of calamities; and

(7) Loss of everything; probability of death.

Death should be a certainly, if on a day, the sum of the *bindus* associated with the seven planets in the signs transited by them (in their respective B.A.Vs) be very little.

Results of Houses having '0' Bindus in any B.A.V. :

The various houses (signs) in any B.A.V. having '0' *bindu* give the following results to the native : In the 1st house - one suffers from serious disease; the 2nd - very poor; the 3rd - weak-bodied; not daring;' the 4th - unhappy; the 5th - evil-minded; the 6th - successful (victorious); the 7th - without marital happiness, loss ofwife; the8th - healthy, long-lived; the 9th - doing sinful deeds; the 10th - without honour, inactive; the 11th - a beggar, withiout income; and the 12th wealthy.

The above results are often found to be very accurate. In Chart 1, in Saturn's B.A.V., in the 8th house (from the Ascendant), there is no *bindu.* The native today is running the 75th year of life and is hale and hearty. In Chart 2 in Jupiter's B.A.V., the 12th house (from the Ascendant) has no *bindu.* The native, though born in a middle class family, was well-to-do when he died recently. In Chart 3, in Saturn's B.A.V., the 7th house has no *bindu.* Native's wife is not keeping sound health. She is always complaining about her health.

Phaladeepika XV - 12 :

खेटो बिन्दुशून्यर्क्षयुक्तः ।
तत्तत्पाके मूर्तिभावादिकानां नाशं ब्रूयाद्दैववित्प्राश्निकाय ॥

meaning "....The destruction of a Bhava from the Ascendant onwards should be predicted by the astrologer to a querist, during Dasa or Bhukti of a planet which occupies a house (sign) where there is no *bindu*."

Chart 1 : In Saturn's B.A.V., there is no *bindu* in Aquarius sign (the 8th house) which is occupied by Jupiter. So Jupiter's dasa (or Bhukti) should destroy the 8th house or be adverse to the native as far as health is concerned.

From research point of view, the converse (opposite) should be considered, *i.e.*, enhancement of a Bhava should be predicted, during the Dasa (or Bhukti) of a planet which occupies a house (sign) where there are 8 *bindus* in B.A.V. of any planet. In Chart 1, in Venus' B.A.V. there are 8 *bindus* in Libra sign (the 4th house) which is occupied by the Moon. So, the Moon's Dasa or Bhukti should enhance the good results of the 4th house.

Horoscope of C.S. Patel : Born on 31-12-1915 at 7.44 p.m. (IST) Lat. 23-2 N, Long. 72-39 E.

Rasi : The Sun 256-10; the Moon 191-13; Mars 127-9; Mercury 265-13; Jupiter 239-29; Venus 283-14; Saturn 80-42 (R); Rahu 287-06; Ketu 107-06; and Ascendant 08-53. Balance of Rahu Dasa at birth : 10 years, 6 months and 3 days.

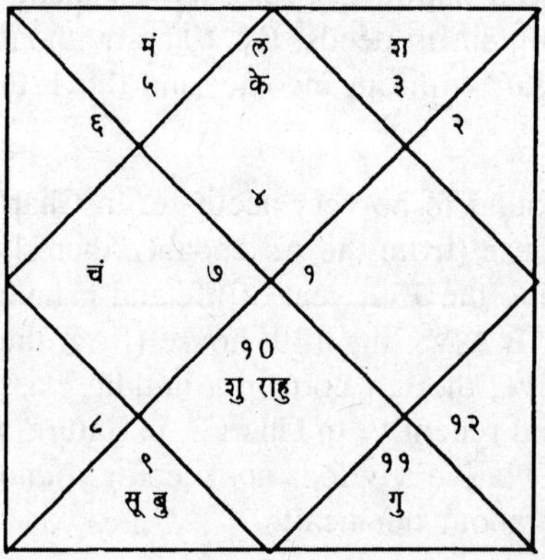

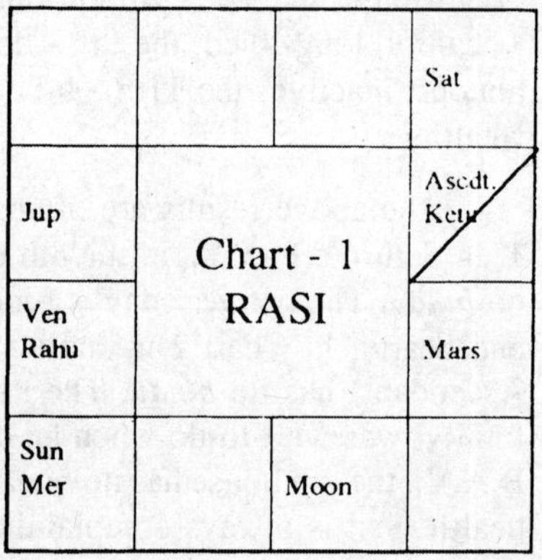

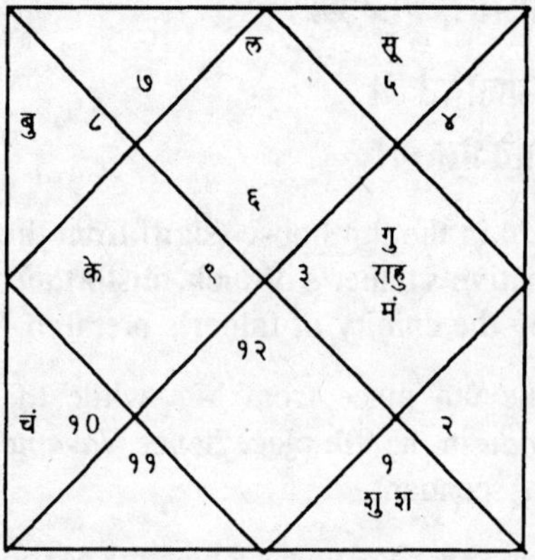

	Ven Sat		Jup Mars Rahu
	NAVAMSA		
Moon			Sun
Ketu	Mer		Ascdt.

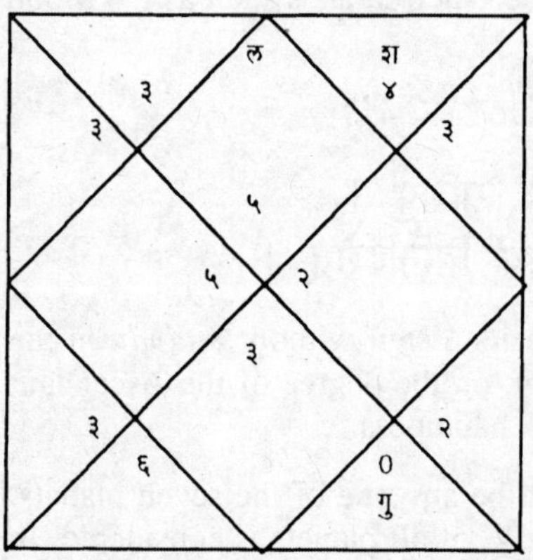

2	2	3	Saturn 4
Jup 0	Saturn B.A.V. *(39 Bindus)*		Ascdt. 5
3			3
6	3	5	3

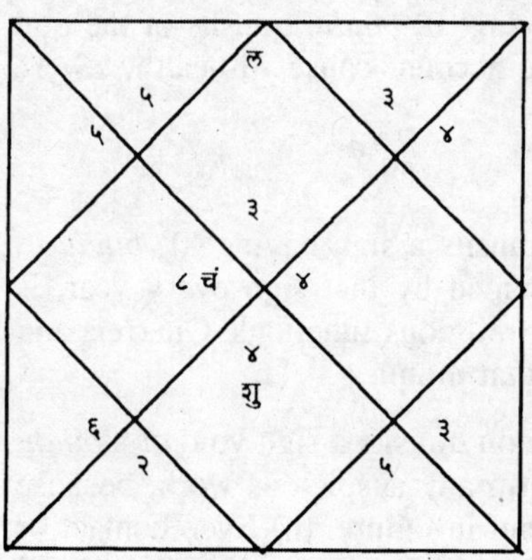

3	4	4	3
5	Venus B.A.V. *(52Bindus)*		Ascdt. 3
Ven 4			5
2	6	Moon 8	5

The unfavourable results, pertaining to the 8th house, during Jupiter Bhukti in various Dasas and favourable results pertaining to the 4th house during the Moon's Bhuktis in various Dasas, were more or less actually experienced by the scribe.

Chandrakala Nadi, Vol. II, Part I, V. 439.

सूर्याष्टवर्गे नवमे बिन्दुशून्ये प्रजायते ।
पितृव्यद्वेषमूलेन स्वपित्ररिष्टमादिशेत् ॥

meaning : "If there is '0' *bindu* in the 9th house (sign) from the Ascendant in the Sun's B.A.V., the native's father's ill-luck, misfortune, injury, loss or calamity is caused by the enmity of father's brethren."

The Sun gives a *bindu* in the 9th place from him while the Ascendant does not contribute a *bindu* in the 9th place hence *Navame* is interpreted as the 9th from the Ascendant.

This principle can be applied to other karakas such as the Moon for mother and Venus for wife.

Chandrakala Nadi Vol. II, Part I, V. 417;

भिन्नाष्टवर्गे लग्नेशे फलहीनस्य राशिषु ।
स्फुटयोगं गते जीवे त्वल्पसौख्यं विनिर्दिशेत् ॥

meaning : "When Jupiter transits a sign without a *bindu* in the B.A.V. of the lord of the Ascendant, on the degree of the Ascendant (Sphutayogam) the native has little happiness."

The lord of the Ascendant can be any one of the seven planets. It seems Jupiter's transit in the B.A.V. of all planets is considered. In the B.A.V. of the Sun, in a sign having '0' *bindu*, transits of the Sun and Saturn, concurrently taken into account cause ill-health, severe sickness and perhaps death.

B.A.Vs from the Sun to Saturn

1. *The Sun :* When the Sun transits a sign having '0' *bindu* in his B.A.V. the solar month, represented by that sign every year, is inauspicious for marriage and other religious functions. Quarrels and other miseries will happen during that month.

2. *The Moon :* (a)When the Moon transits a sign void of a *bindu* in her B.A.V. one should not perform any auspicious work, because all functions undertaken then will end in failure. (b) Even contact or association with persons having their Moon in a sign containing '0' *bindu* (in the Moon's B.A.V.) a first look at them in the morning will result in great disaster.

3. *Mars : Vararuchi*. Ch. IV, V. 21;

कुजाष्टवर्गे ...... सोदरे बिंदुहीने च भ्रातृहीनो भवेन्नरः ॥

meaning ; (a) "If the 3rd house from Mars in his B.A.V. is without a *bindu* the native has no brother (or sister), (b) When Mars in his B.A.V. transits through a sign without a *bindu,* brother or sister of the native, will suffer miseries, ill-health, injury etc".

4. *Mercury :* If the 2nd house from Mercury in his B.A.V. contains not even one *bindu* the person born will be dumb.

5. *Jupiter :* Practically all standard texts on Astrology refer to the 5th house from Jupiter to fix the number of children. But Balabhadra refers to the 9th house from Jupiter in the following verses;

Hora Ratnam, Part II, P. 354, Verse 1;

गुरोरष्टकवर्गेषु सन्तानमपि कल्पयेत् ।
गुरोः स्थितः शुभस्थाने यावता विद्यते फलम् ॥

In support of this view, refer to Chart 2. In the 9th house from Jupiter, in his B.A.V., there is no *bindu.* The native had no children at all and he died recently on 2-6-1990 (running 67th year) when Jupiter was transiting the 12th house (Gemini sign) without a *bindu.* No doubt, as referred earlier, the native, having '0' *bindu* in the 12th house from the Ascendant, was wealthy. Further research on this count (point) is necessary.

Chart 2 : Born July 28th 1923 at 5.48 a.m. (IST) Lat. 23 N 2, Long. 72 E 39. *Rasi :* The Sun. 100-50; the Moon 280-1; Mars 104-8; Mercury 108-27; Jupiter 196-57; Venus 90-5; Saturn 171-50; Rahu 140-30; Ketu 320-30; and Ascendant 94-33. Balance of Moon Dasa at birth : 9 years 10 months and 1 day.

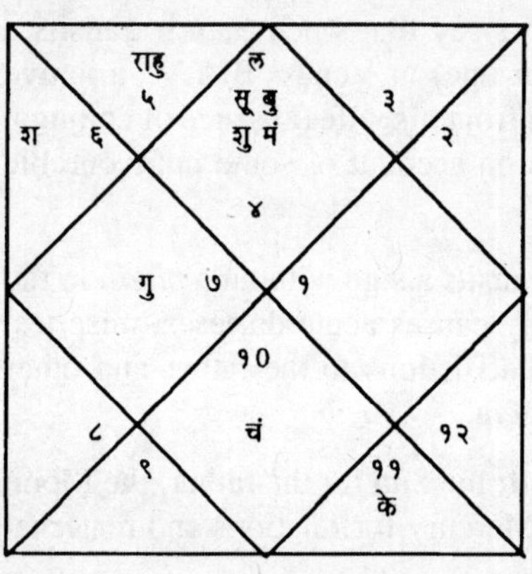

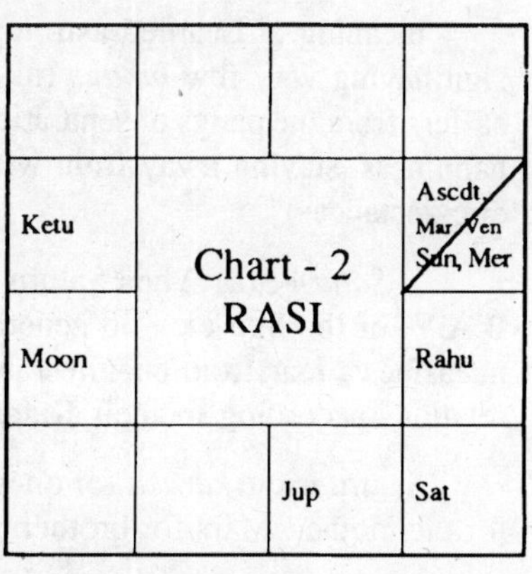

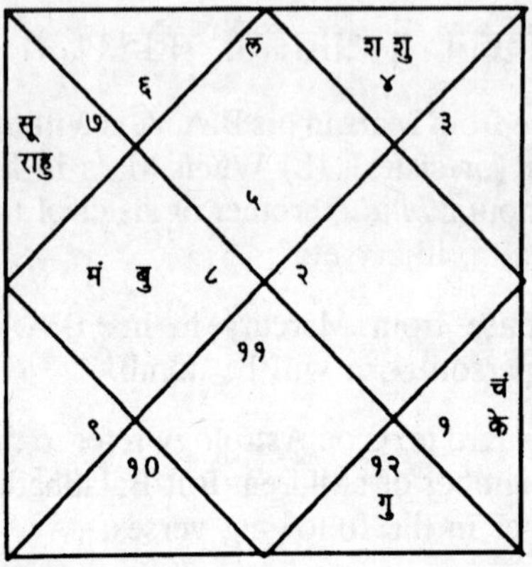

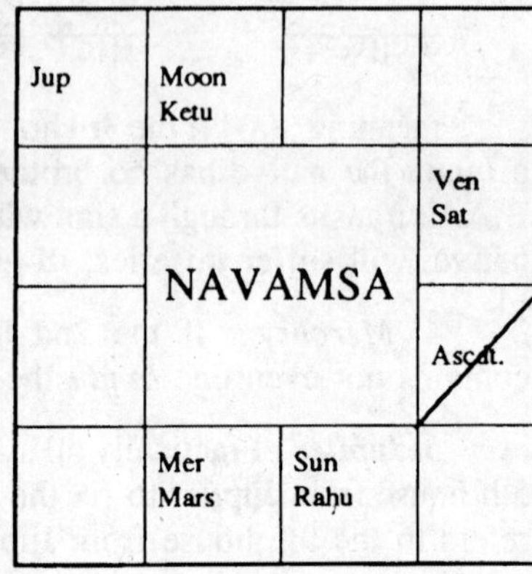

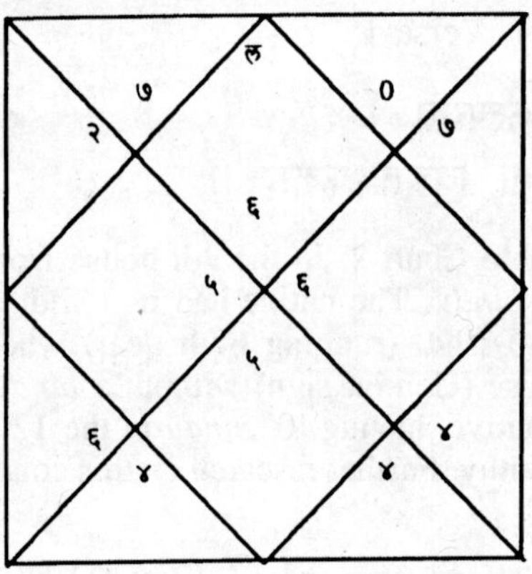

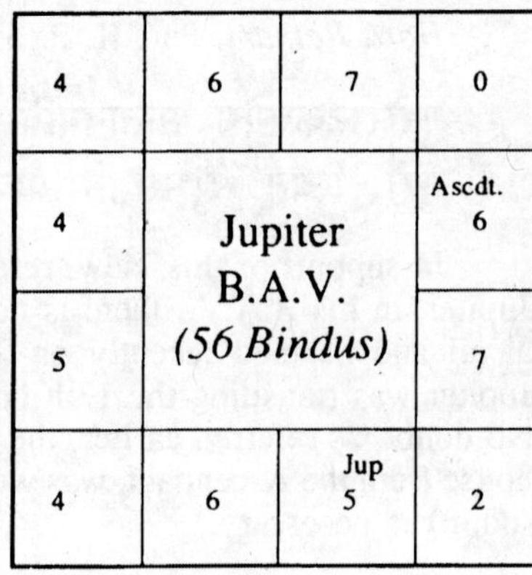

7. *Venus : Hara-Nava-Nitan*

अल्परेखान्विते शुक्रवर्गराशिगते शनौ ।
नारीवियोगजं दुःखं तदा वाच्यं सुरिभिः ॥

meaning : "Learned astrologers say that when Saturn transits a sign having very few *bindus* (nil or one) in Venus' B.A.V., a native suffers from the pangs of separation from his wife (absence of conjugal happiness, staying away from wife on account of some unfavourable circumstances)".

7. *Saturn :* (a) When Saturn transits a sign without a *bindu* in the B.A.V. of the Sun etc., he generally causes acute diseases, miseries, uneasiness, fear from enemies and afflictions to the father and other relations according to their Karakatva.

Saturn is the *karaka* for oneself; the Sun for the father, the Moon for the mother, Mars for brothers; Mercury for relations and maternal uncle/aunt; Jupiter for the children and Venus, for the wife.

(b) *Vararuchi*, Chap. IV. Vs 62-63 :

दुष्टस्थानाधिपते मंदे दुष्टस्थानास्थितोऽपि वा ।
अल्पबिंदुसमायाते जातौ दैन्यमवाप्नुयात् ।
रोगी भवति दुष्टात्मा बिंद्वाभावे मरिष्यति ॥

meaning; "If Saturn, occupying or owning the 6th, the 8th or the12th house, passes through a sign without a *bindu* the native suffers poverty. When Saturn passes through that house with '0' *bindu* (in the natal chart) the native is a wicked man or suffers from diseases or dies a premature death."

(c) Narada says : "If Saturn is associated with '0' *bindu* in his B.A.V. in any sign in the natal chart, short life will result or the native will lose all his wealth."

In Chart 3, Saturn, lord of the 6th house, is in the 7th house. In the B.A.V. of Saturn the 7th house has no *bindu*. So Saturn is associated with '0' *bindu*. The native, though born in a rich family, is passing through dire circumstances. He has lost greater part of his paternal wealth in the last four or five years.

Born October 7th, 1935, at 5.10 a.m. Lat. 23 N 2, Long 72 E 39. *Rasi* : The Sun 168-45; the Moon 280-18; Mars 230-28; Mercury 189-45 (R); Jupiter 210-30; Venus 134-20; Saturn 311-27 (R); Rahu 264-34; Ketu 84-34; and Ascendant 149-30, with a balance of Moon Dasa; 9 years, 9 months and 6 days.

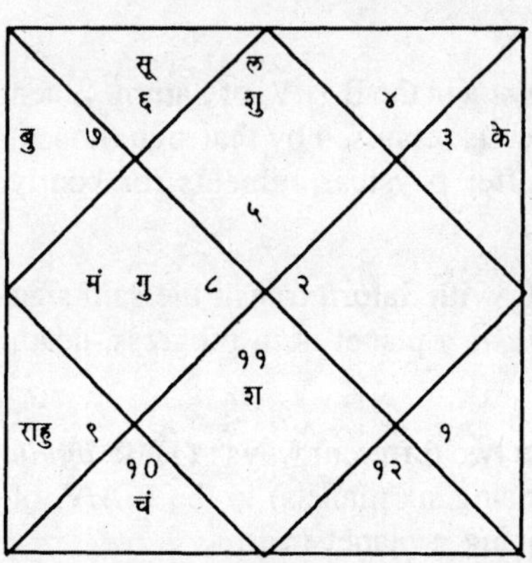

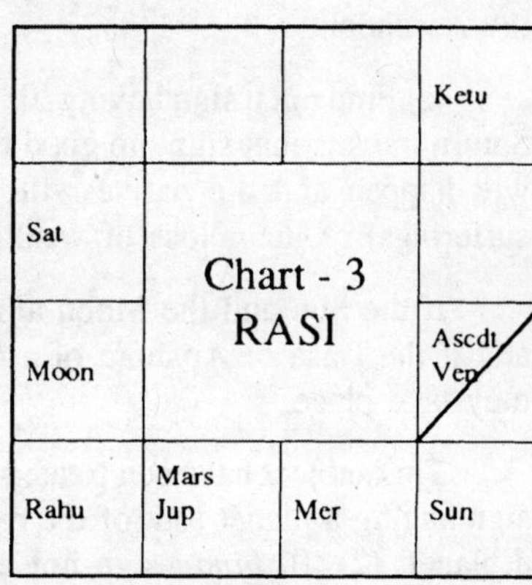

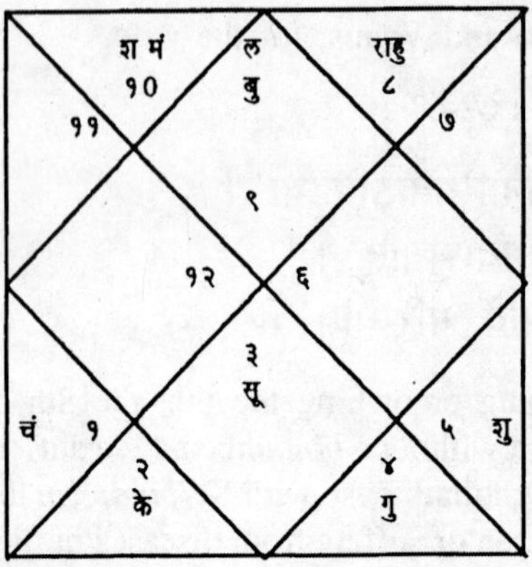

	Moon	Ketu	Sun
	NAVAMSA		Jup
Mars Sat			Ven
Ascdt. Mer	Rahu		

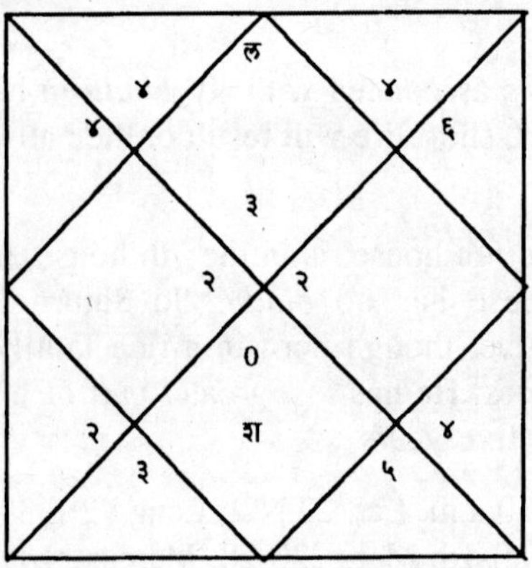

5	4	2	6
Sat 0	Saturn B.A.V. *(39 Bindus)*		4
3			Ascdt. 3
2	2	4	4

(d) Find which house (sign) has the minimum number of bindus in the B.A.V. of Saturn. Some kind of trouble will be happening daily at the time when that sign rises in the East (*i.e.*, when that sign becomes the Ascendant).

(e) Find out a sign having '0' *bindu* in the B.A.V. of Saturn. When Saturn transits that sign, no good results promised by that sign (house) will happen and the native will suffer physical ailments (or bodily sufferings) or incur loss of wealth.

If the Sun and the Moon along with Saturn transit the said sign and if the Dasa or Apahara of a *Makara* planet is in progress, death may take place.

This subject has been treated in two different ways : (1) '0' *bindu* sign having a planet (out of the remaing six planets) in the B.A.V. of a planet; (2) '0' *bindu* sign not having a planet in it.

Further research can be made in the direction :

(1) '8' *bindu* sign in any B.A.V.;

(2) '8' *bindu* sign in any B.A.V. having a planet therein out of the remaining six planets;

(3) A planet himself being associated with '8' *bindus* (Saturn 7 *bindus* only) in his own B.A.V.

In all the above three possibilities the results will be par excellence.

21

Use of Rekhas in Prognostication

When the scribe, joining hands with a friend, was collecting material to compile an exclusive and comprehensive English work on *Ashtakvarga,* he came across only one reference regarding the use of *rekhas* for delineations during the years 1954-55 and 1956. The said book *Ashtakavarga* by Patel and Aiyar was published in February 1957*. That single reference was taken from **Shambhu Hora Prakasha,** Chapter IX, verse 39, 2nd line and included in the said book in Chapter XIV, verse 39, 2nd line on page 193. Afterwards during the authors' further studies they came across two chapters on the use of **rekhas (Brihat Parasara Hora Shastra—** *Uttara Khanda,* Chapters XVI and XVII, Venkateshwara Press, Bombay).

It may be noted that in the northern part of our country, astrologers call *rekha* a benefic point and *bindu* a malefic one; while in sourthern states (e.g., Kerala, Tamil Nadu, Andhra and Karnataka) they call *bindu* a benefic point and *rekha* a malefic one. **Shambhu Hora Prakasha** follows the former view. In **Brihat Parasara Hora Shastra,** Parasara calls (स्थान) (Sthana) a benefic point and (करण) (Karana) a malefic point. In this article the scribe follows the second view, i.e., *bindu* for a benefic point and *rekha* for a malefic one.

Ashtakavarga Chapter XIV Verses 37-38-39 pages 192-193;

भावं विलोक्य सदसत्फलदायकं तु तद्राशिसंभवफलैश्च तदुक्तपिंडम् ।
निध्नंभभक्तपरिशेषकभे प्रयाति सौरिस्तदा भवति भावफलस्यनाशः ॥

* Reprint in 1996 by Sagar Publication, New Delhi.

पूर्वैरुक्तं सौरिनक्षत्रकाले रिष्टं राशौ विश्वनाथस्तमाह ।
पिंडेरेखा ताडिते भावशेषे राशौ तस्मिन्याति सौरिः समायाम् ॥

Verses 37-38.

To find the good or bad effects of a particular Bhava at a particular period take the Sodhya-pinda of Samudayashtakavarga bindu *(S.A.V.). Multiply it by the corresponding figure for that particular Bhava and divide the productby 27 to find the remainder.*

When Saturn passes through the asterism indicated by the remainder (counted from Aswini) there will be destruction of the effects of that Bhava.

Verse 39- 1st line;

यस्यां तत्तद्भावहानिं च विंद्यात्प्राहुर्वर्षे वाऽथवा तत्त्रिकोणे ।

The same product when divided by 12 and the remainder counted from Aries gives the Rasi and its trines which when transited by Saturn spoils the effects of the Bhava under consideration.

Verse 39 - 2nd line :

कृत्वा बिंन्दुभ्यस्तु कालं सुधीमान् तस्माद्वाच्यः प्राप्तिकालः शुभत्वे ॥

Repeat the same process with the S.A.V. of rekhas *(malefic points) and find out the asterisms and the Rasis as above. When Saturn transits them good effects promised by that Bhava are experienced.*

Example

The horoscope of Mr. Chandulal Sakaralal Patel (scribe) : Born 31-12-1915 at 7.44 p.m. (IST) at 23 N 02, 72 E 39.

Rasi : The Sun 256-10; the Moon 192-13; Mars 127-9; Mercury 265-13; Jupiter 329-29; Venus 283-14; Saturn (R) 80-42; Rahu 287-06; Ketu 107-06; Ascendant 98-53; and M.C. 04-08 with a balance of 10 years 6 months 3 days of Rahu Dasa.

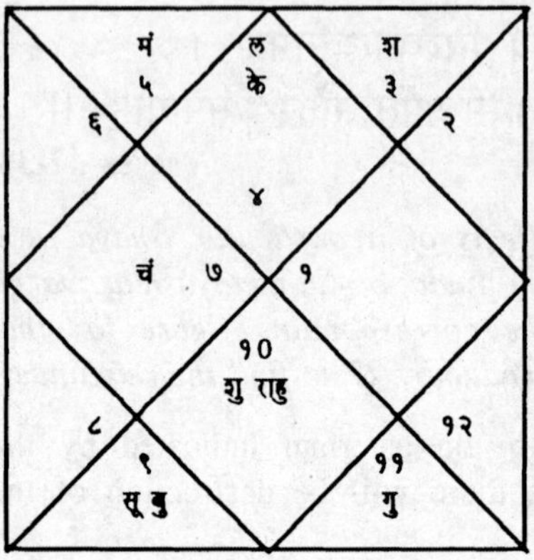

			Sat
Jup	RASI		Ascdt. Ketu
Ven Rahu			Mars
Sun Mer		Moon	

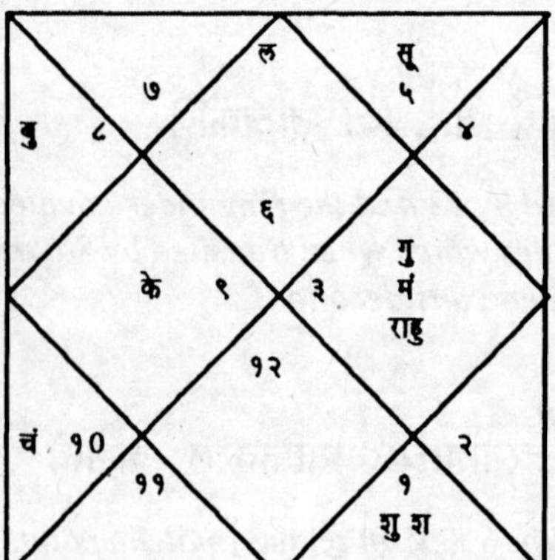

	Ven Sat		Jup Mars Rahu
	NAVAMSA		
Moon			Sun
Ketu	Mer		Ascdt.

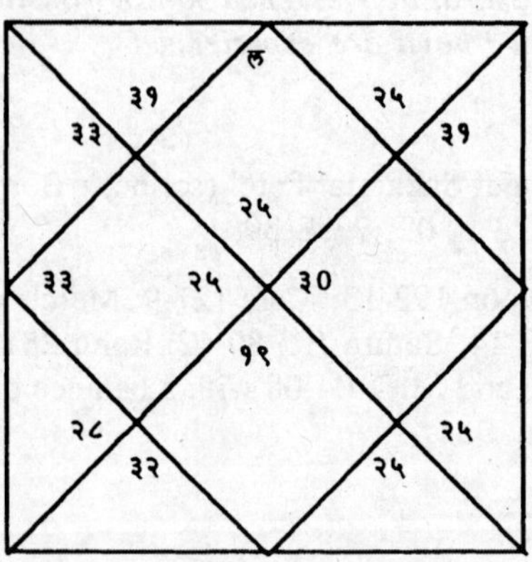

25	30	31	25
25	S.A.V. of Bindus (337)		Ascdt. 25
19			31
32	28	33	33

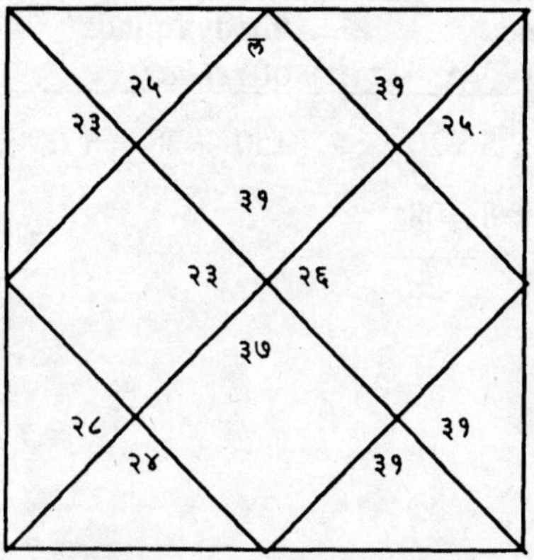

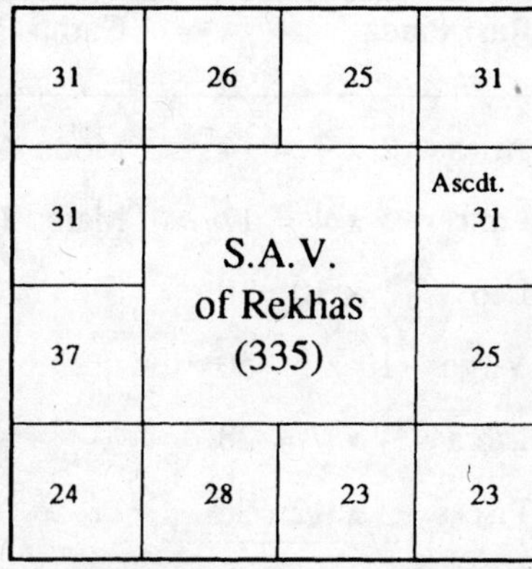

Deduct the number of *bindus* of each Bhava from 56 (total figure of *bindus* and *rekhas* in a house) to get the required number of *rekhas* in each Bhava, i.e.,

Ascendant 56-25 *bindus* = 31 *rekhas.*

In the example horoscope the 10th Bhava has 26 *rekhas*, Shodyapinda of S.A.V. *rekhas* 178 x 26 (*rekhas* in the 10th Bhava) = 4628, divided by 27 leaves remainder 11. Purvaphalgui, Purvashada and Bharani are the asterisms for Saturn's transit to cause good effects promised by the 10th Bhava.

Similarly, the figure 4628, divided by 12 leaves remainder 8, Scorpio, Pisces and Cancer are the Rasis for Saturn's transit to give some good results.

In the same manner calculations should be made for the remaining Bhavas to find Nakshatras and the Rasis for Saturn's transit to get good effects.

This point of using Shodyapinda in respect of S.A.V. of *rekhas* has been referred to by Dr. B.V. Raman in his book **Ashtakavarga System of Prediction** (1981 edition) on pages 108-109 under item 35 which may be referred.

Planets	Ascd. Ketu	Mars		Moon		Sun Mer	Rahu Ven	Jup.				Sat.
Bhavas represented bu Rasis	4	5	6	7	8	9	10	11	12	1	2	3
Rekhas	31	25	23	23	28	24	37	31	31	26	25	31
Mandala Reduction– Cycles of 12	7	1	11	11	4	0	1	7	7	2	1	7
Trikona Shodhana	3	1	10	4	0	0	0	0	3	2	0	0
Ekadhipatya Shodhana	3	1	10	4	0	0	0	0	3	2	0	0

Shodyavasishta 23; Grahapinda 28; Rasipinda 150; Shodyapinda 178.

Rasi Pinda		Garha Pinda		Shodya pinda of *rekhas*
Aries	2 x 7 = 14	Moon	4 x 5 =20	150 + 28 = 178
Cancer	3 x 4 = 12	Mars	1 x 8 =08	
Leo	1 x 10 =10		28	
Virgo	10 x 5 =50			
Libra	4 x 7 = 28			
Pisces	3 x 12 =36			
	150			

The XVII chapter of **Uttarakhanda of Brihat Parasara Shastra** deals with monthly results (Masacharyaphalam) :

तत्वमाकृतिरंकाक्षिच्छंदस्तत्वं चतुस्त्रयः ।
एकोनविंशतिच्छन्दो नवाक्षी षट्त्रयस्तथा ॥ 4 ॥
वेदेषवो नृपाः स्थाने भावसंख्याः प्रकीर्तिताः
(1st line of verse 5)

The statutory minimum *bindus* prescribed for the twelve Bhavas are as follows :

The Ascendant 25; 2nd Bhava 22; 3rd Bhava 29; 4th Bhava 24; 5th Bhava 25; 6th Bhava 34; 7th Bhava 19; 8th Bhava 24; 9th Bhava 29; 10th Bhava 36; 11th Bhava 54; and 12th Bhava 16. Grand total 337.

If one puts all the 7 planets in the Ascendant and prepares the S.A.V., the total *bindus* in each Bhava will be the same as above = the time of Mahapralaya.

एकत्रिशत्त्रयत्त्रिशंद्धानि त्रिंशन्तथैव च । ॥ 5 ॥
एकत्रिंशद् द्विनेत्रे च मुनिरामाः खपावकाः ।
भानि विंशतिरेकद्वौ खवेदाः करणस्य तु ॥ 6 ॥

The statutory minimum *rekhas* prescribed for the twelve Bhavas are as follows :

The Ascendant 31; 2nd Bhava 34; 3rd Bhava 27; 4th Bhava 32;

5th Bhava 31; 6th Bhava 22; 7th Bhava 37; 8th Bhava 32; 9th Bhava 27; 10th Bhava 20; 11th Bhava 2; and 12th Bhava 40. Grand total 335.

विषमायां क्रमादोजे युग्मे स्यातां शुभाशुभे ।
समायां भवतस्तद्वत्पापसौम्यफले क्रमात् ॥

If in an odd sign, the number of bindus is odd, it is auspicious and if the number of rekhas is even, it is inauspicous. Similarly, in the even signs, if the number of bindus is even, it is inauspicious and if the number of rekhas is odd, it is auspicous.

Natal Positions

	Aries	Gemini	Leo	Libra	Sagittarius	Aquarius
Bindus	30	25*	31*	33*	32	25*
Rekhas	26**	31	25	23	24**	31
	Taurus	Cancer	Virgo	Scorpio	Capricorn	Pisces
Bindus	31	25	33	28*	19	25
Rekhas	25*	31*	23*	28	37*	31*

* Auspicious; ** Inauspicious

Nine signs are auspicious and three signs are inauspicous.

It may be noted that in each Bhava, if *bindus*, are even, the *rekhas* will also be even; and if *bindus* are odd, the *rekhas* will also be odd.

Transit Results

This important technique has been taught by Lord Shiva to Parvati, as stated in **Brahmayamala.** On any Sankranti solar ingress day (Masacharyaphalam), find the number of *bindus* and *rekhas* associated with all the seven planets in respective Bhinnashtakavarga *bindu* and *rekhas* (B.A.V.) in odd and even signs and total them separately, in order to make use of the following verses. In the absence of comparative literature on this point elsewhere, the scribe is not in a position to explain fully the utility of this technique. The students may try themselves to make headway into it.

ओजो व्याधिः समे हानिर्यावत्तु दशकं भवेत् ।
परतः पंचकं चौजे समे व्याधिरथान्यथा ॥

यावत्तु दशकं प्राग्वत्ततस्तद्वत्फलं वदेत् ॥

In odd signs upto the number of 10 bindus *or* rekhas *the result is sickness, and in even signs it is loss. When the number of rekhas is between 10 to 15, the result is sickness in odd and even signs; beyond that upto 25 (*bindus *or* rekhas*) it shows sickness in odd signs and loss in even signs.*

शिरोरोगाक्षिरोगाश्च रक्तासृक्कामलाज्वरः ।
ग्रहणी शीतको मेहप्लीहो गुल्मलतः क्रमात् ॥

The following are the results in odd and even signs for the *bindus* and *rekhas* beginning with

(a) In odd signs : 26 - Afflictions to head; 27 - diseases of the eye; 28 - blood tumours; 29 - jaundice; 30 - fever; 31 - diarrhoea (dysentery); 32 - disease of cold; 33 - urinary disease; 34 - enlargement of spleen; and 35 - diseases of liver and spleen.

रत्नैर्धान्यैश्च हेमैश्च गोभिः क्षेत्रैश्च राजभिः ।
दासैश्च महिषैरुष्ट्रैर्गजाश्वैर्वृद्धयः स्मृताः ॥

(b) In even signs : 26 - procurement of precious stones; 27 - accumulation of good harvest and grain; 28 - getting gold or things made of gold; 29 - gain through cows and their products; 30 - gain of lands; 31 - gain through royal favours; 32 - gain through servants; 33 - gain of buffaloes; 34 - gain of camels; and 35 - increase in elephants and horses (Gain of animals may be interpreted in modern sense as acquiring transport vehicles - e.g., bicycle, two-wheeler; car, etc.)

जात्या देशस्य कालस्य स्वानुरूपं फलं वदेत् ।
तत्तद्भावानुसंज्ञं च ग्रहाद्भावात्फलं वदेत् ॥

The results signified by the various Bhavas and planets should be predicted, bearing in mind the caste (socio cultural), national and age factors.

Chapter XVII of **Uttarakhanda of Brihat Parasara Hora Shastra** (dealing with daily results - Dinacharyaphalam) :

Prastara-ashtakavarga (P.A.V.) is a spread out or a detailed B.A.V. Draw the P.A.V. table and mark the *bindus* for the Sun's A.V.

in respective Kakshyas (30° + 8 = 3° 45') of those planets which have donated *bindus* in all the twelve Bhavas. Similarly prepare P.A.V. table for the remaining six planets.

When the Sun passes through a Kakshya which has a *bindu* in his P.A.V., in any Bhava, he produces beneficial effects; if he is passing through a kakshya withoiut a *bindu* (i.e., a Kakshya having a *rekha*), the result is adverse. On a particular day note how many planets out of seven planets, transit through Kakshyas having *bindus* or Kakshyas having *rekhas*.

The following verses indicate a composite result of four or more planets transitting Kakshyas having *bindus* or *rekhas* on a particular day and a particular time.

अर्केन्दुगुरवः शुक्रः क्रमादन्ये बलक्रमात् ।
भवंति स्थानदाः खेटाश्चत्वारश्च यदैकदा ॥

धनादीनां यथा लब्धिः पंचचेत्पूज्यतायुतः ।
आरोग्यं वस्रलाभश्च षट्सु पट्टस्य बन्धनम् ॥

सप्त चेद्राज्यलाभः स्यादेवं करणदा यदि ।
धनहानिस्ततो व्याधिस्ततस्तु विपदादयः ।
सप्तमिर्मरणं प्रोक्तमक्षाभावे मृतिर्भवेत् ॥

1st line of 4th verse

When the Sun, the Moon, Jupiter and Venus pass through Kakshyas having bindus *in their respective P.A.Vs., they produce gain of wealth; these four planets and one more planet (out of the remaining three planets) will bestow great honour; these five planets and one more planet (out of the remaining two planets) the native will have very good health, god dresses and be honoured with robes (in modern time, titles, awards etc.) and when all the seven planets transit through Kakshya having bindus, the native will gain kingdom (great profit, dignified position and the like).*

Similarly, if four planets (the Sun, the Moon, Venus and Jupiter) transit through kakshyas having rekhas, there will be loss of wealth; if five planets as above there will be disease; if six planets, great calamity etc., will fall on the native; and if all the seven planets transit alike, death (of some near relation) is likely. If at that time some planets transit signs having no bindu *(Aksha Abhava) or minimum* bindus *in their B.A.V. in native's death be expected.*

Research on the *rekha's* utility is being carried out and any further development will be published in future articles. Meanwhile, the scribe, requests research sholars and ardent students to make studies in this old technique.

22

On Foreign Residence

Nowadays, people of developing countries have a craze to go to the States, United Kingdom, Australia, West Asia, Africa and other far off countries where the standard of living is very high, for the bettrerment of their prospects.

Now, a man born in Amritsar and staying in Islamabad or born in Rameshwaram and staying in Colombo, where the distance between the places is hardly 100 kilometres or so, is said to be a foreign resident. Yes, because both the countries are separate and independent ones. A doctor born in Trivandrum (South-Kerala) goes to Jammu (North-Kashmir) for medical practice, a man born in Rajkot (Gujarat) goes to Gauhati (Assam) for business or a man born in Moscow (Russia) goes to Vladivostok (Russia far east) for service is not said to be staying in foreign country, even though the distance between the respective places is more than 4000 KM or so.

For the purpose of this article, foreign residence is to be loosely interpreted as staying at a very very far off place from one's birth place, may it be his own country or a foreign country.

Uttara Kalamrita considers the 7th house for journeys to foreign countries; the 9th for travelling abroad and the 12th for going to foreign lands. Jataka Parijata partially suports these views.

Modern astrologers consider the 7th for foreign journeys; the 9th house for long journeys and the 12th for journeys for permanent stay.

In short, the 7th, 9th and the 12th houses play an outstanding role to indicate permanent foreign residence.

When somebody comes for consultation, it is the scribe's practice first to prepare the S.A.V. (Samudaya Ashtaka Varga) of the Rasi chart and place the Bindus in the respective houses, along with Navamsa chart.

Three houses containing higher number of SAV Bindus and lesser number of Bindus are marked with different identifications.

One day about five years back, one gentleman came for consultation with the horoscopes of his brother and brother's wife, both staying in the States. The SAV Bindus for both the charts were prepared and immediately the scribe's attention was drawn towards less, lesser and the least Bindus in the 7th, 9th and 12th houses (Chart No. 1 and 2). If an astrologer is used to prepare the charts according to north-Indian style, one's attention is immediately drawn to the three houses, if they obtain less, lesser and the least Bindus. This gave an inkling to make further probe into the subject. In the course of last four or five years, nine such charts have been collected whose natives are staying in foreign countries since many years.

Average Bindus for any house are 28 (337 divided by = 12). The statutory minimum Bindus for the 7th house, the 9th house and 12th house are respectively 19, 29 and 16. Neither average nor statutory minimum Bindus are taken into account for this article. Only less, lesser and the least Bindus in the 7th, 9th and the 12th house in any order are considered.

Arrange the SAV Bindus of the chart numerically in descending order with their house numbers in Romans. The last three houses will have to possess less, lesser and least Bindus. Lesser, least and less Bindus are marked by "x" in the SAV diagrams hereof. These three houses will be in any order forming a pattern as follows :

(a) 7th, 9th, 12th

(b) 7th, 12th, 9th

(c) 9th, 12th, 7th

(d) 9th, 7th, 12th

(e) 12th, 7th, 9th

(f) 12th; 9th, 7th

Examples charts in all are nine.

The Ashtaka Varga Bindus are considered as per the work "Ashtaka Varga" by Patel & Aiyar, and "Prasna Marga".

The scribe's clients, husband and wife, having the least number of Bindus in the 9th house stayed in the States for about 7 years. Both were in service. The husband being highly qualified had a good job. He, being a business-minded person, went on purchasing some manufactured goods and articles from the States, which would fetch higher prices and started exporting those items to India. At the same time, through agents in Bombay, he started purchasing commodities from India which would fetch higher prices there. Within four years, after earning a lot in such transactions, he shifted his headquarters permanently to Bombay. Casually, both of them visit the Sates to renew their greencards or otherwise. In sort, their's having minimum SAV Bindus in the 9th house only, they terminated their foreign residence and returned to Bombay.

The above considerations about foreign residence are to be observed only when the said conditions (less Bindus in the 7th, 9th and the 12th) are satisfied in the natal chart. One should not expect conversely as to why such a combination is not present in the charts of the persons who are having foreign residence.

The scribe (in his 80th year of life) will be very happy if a group of young research scholars would try to find out the results, if there are high, higher and the highest number of SAV Bindus in the said houses e.g., the 7th, 9th and the 12th houses.

Chart Particulars :

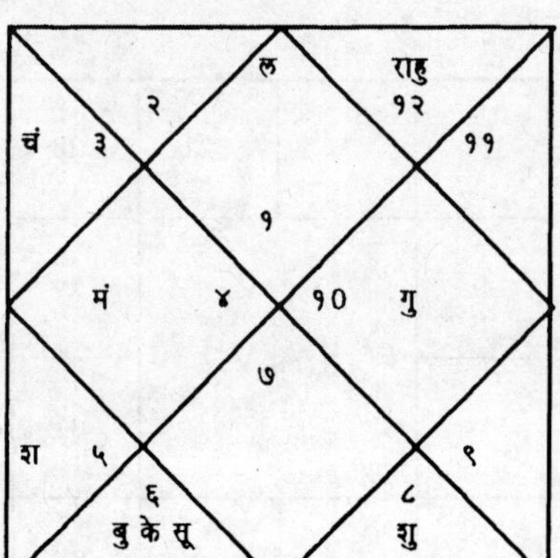

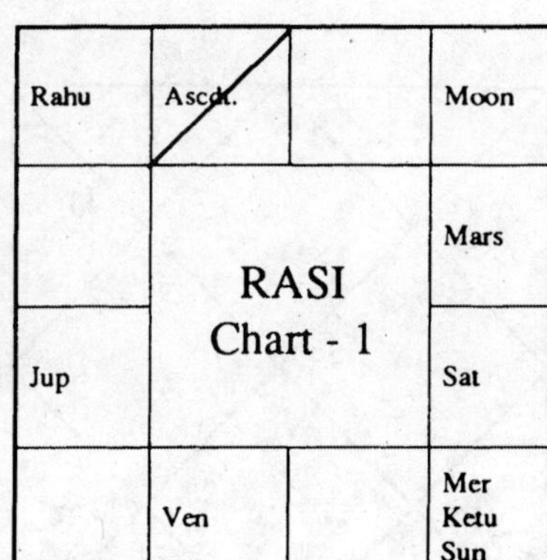

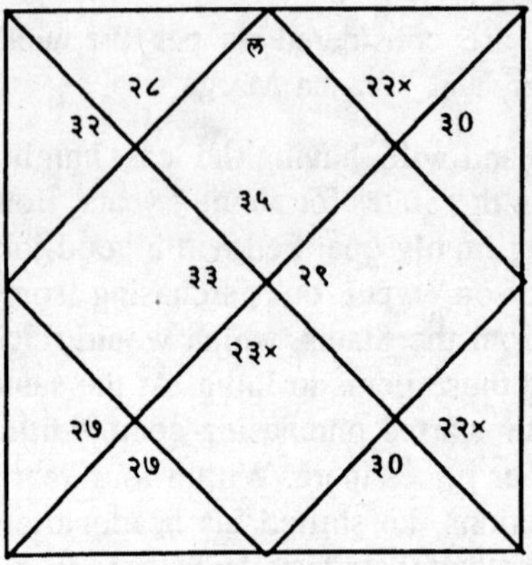

22 x	Ascdt. 35	28	32
30	S.A.V.		33
28			27
22 x	30	23 x	27

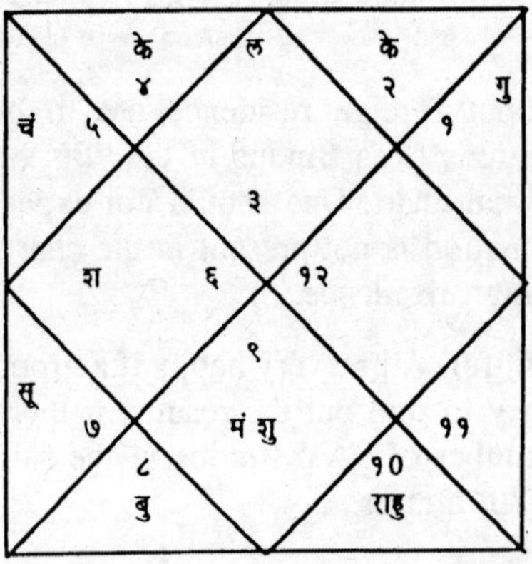

	Jup		Ascdt.
	RASI Chart - 2		Ketu
Rahu			Moon
Ven Mars	Mer	Sun	Sat

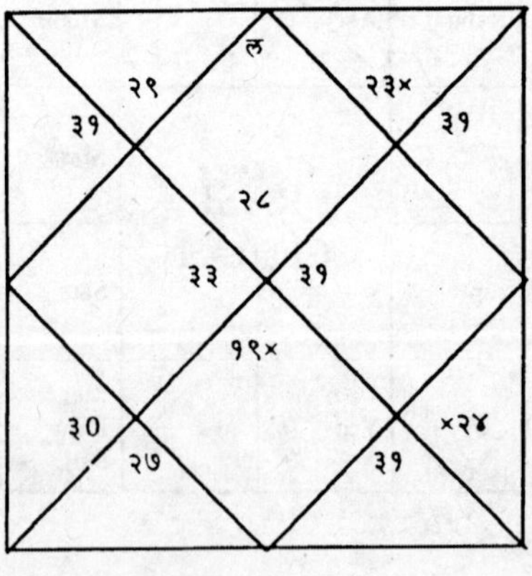

31	31	23x	Ascd. 28
24x	S.A.V.		29
31			31
19x	27	30	33

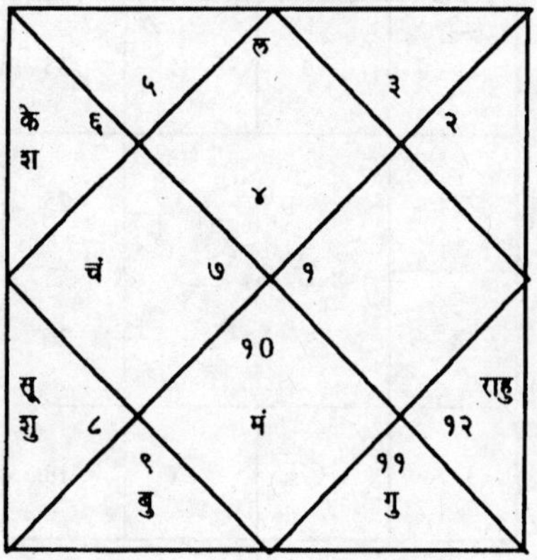
ल
५
३
के
६
२
श
४
चं
७
१
१०
सू
राहु
शु
८
मं
१२
९
११
बु
गु

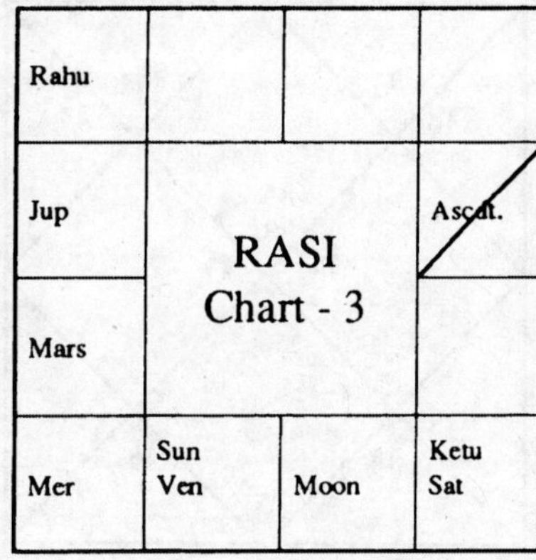
Rahu
Jup
Ascdt.
RASI
Chart - 3
Mars
Mer
Sun
Ven
Moon
Ketu
Sat

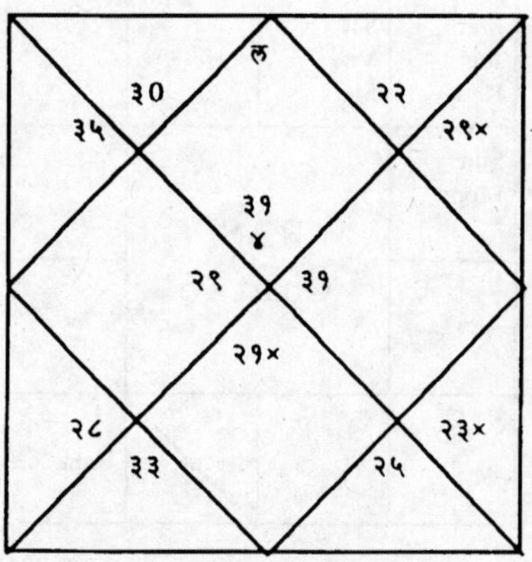
ल
३०
२२
३५
२९×
३१
४
२९
३१
२१×
२८
२३×
३३
२५

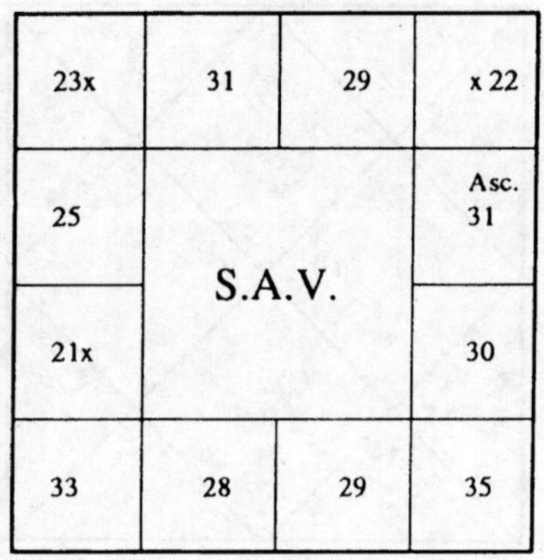
23x
31
29
x 22
25
Asc.
31
S.A.V.
21x
30
33
28
29
35

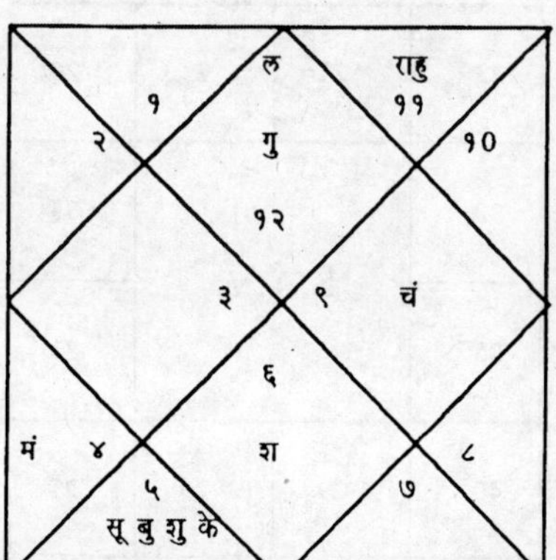
ल
राहु
१
११
२
गु
१०
१२
३
९
चं
६
मं
४
श
८
५
७
सू बु शु के

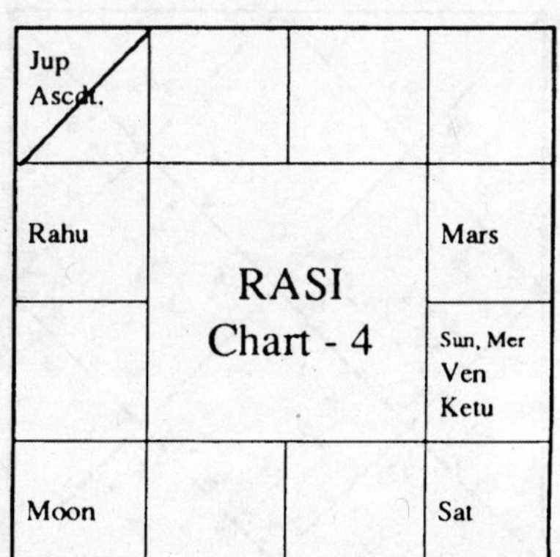
Jup
Ascdt.
Rahu
Mars
RASI
Chart - 4
Sun, Mer
Ven
Ketu
Moon
Sat

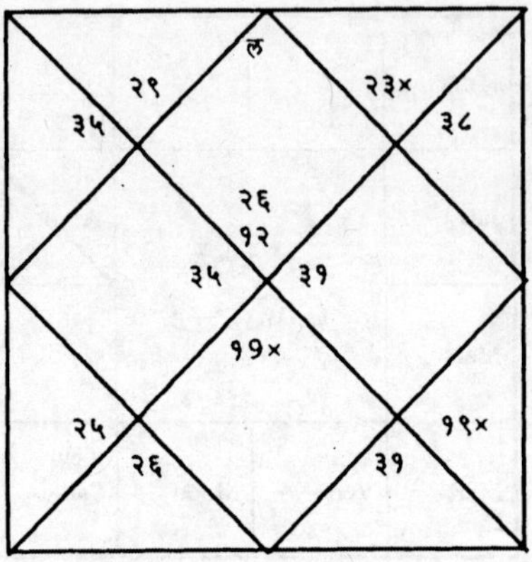
ल
२१
२३×
३५
३८
२६
१२
३५
३१
११×
२५
१९×
२६
३१

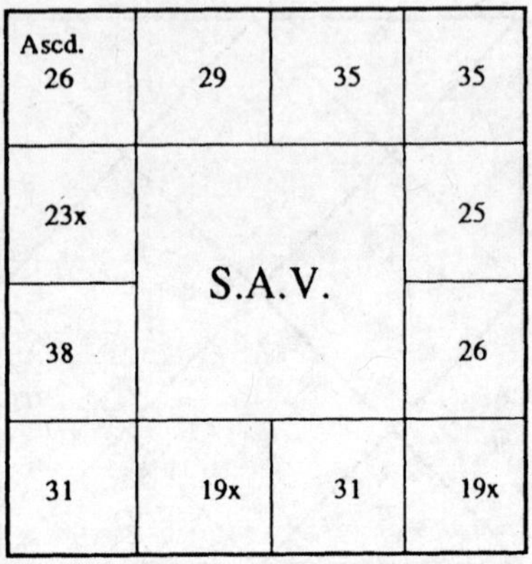
Ascd.
26
29
35
35
23x
25
S.A.V.
38
26
31
19x
31
19x

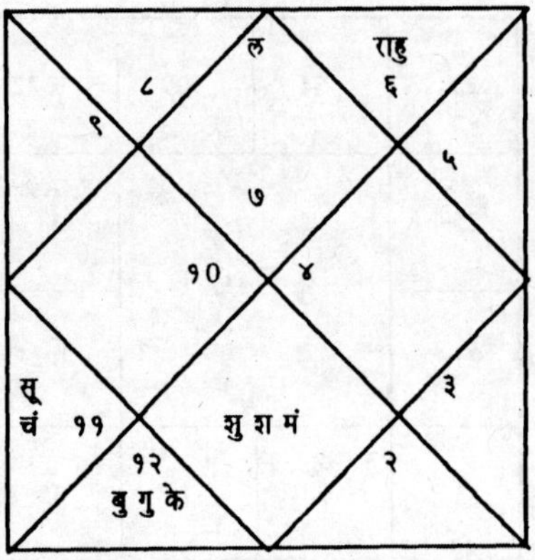
ल
राहु
८
६
९
५
७
१०
४
सू
चं
११
शु श मं
३
१२
२
बु गु के

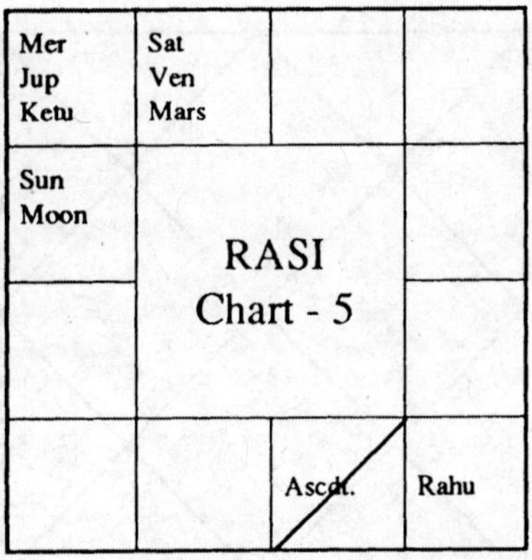
Mer
Jup
Ketu
Sat
Ven
Mars
Sun
Moon
RASI
Chart - 5
Ascdt.
Rahu

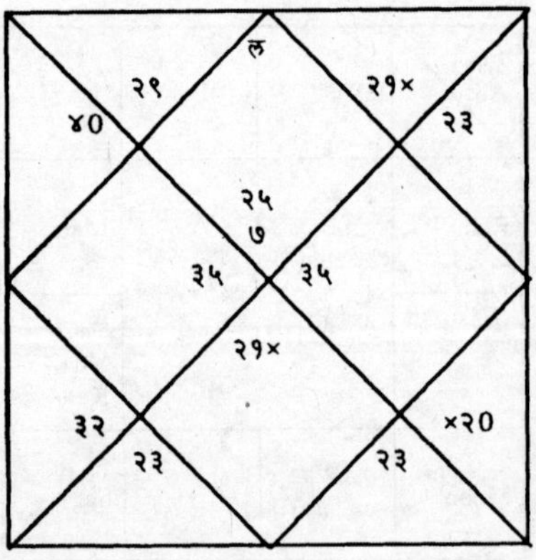
ल
२१
२१×
४०
२३
२५
७
३५
३५
२१×
३२
×२०
२३
२३

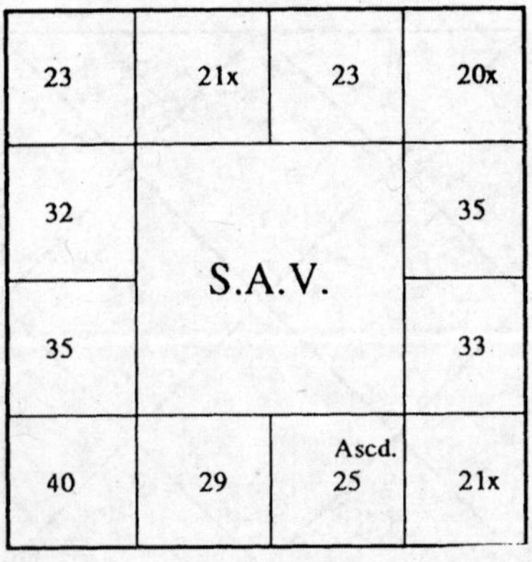
23
21x
23
20x
32
35
S.A.V.
35
33
Ascd.
40
29
25
21x

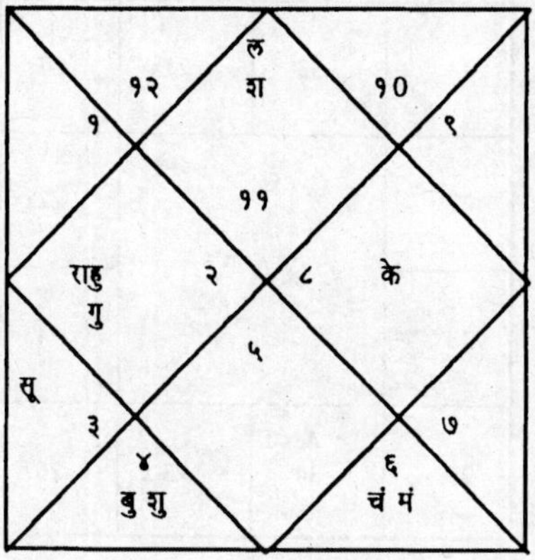
ल
१२ श १०
१ ९
११
राहु
गु
२ ८ के
५
सू
३ ७
४ ६
बु शु चं मं

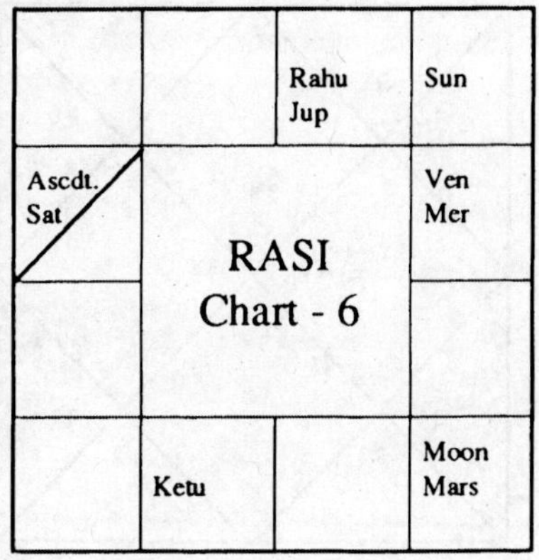
Rahu
Jup
Sun
Ascdt.
Sat
Ven
Mer
RASI
Chart - 6
Ketu
Moon
Mars

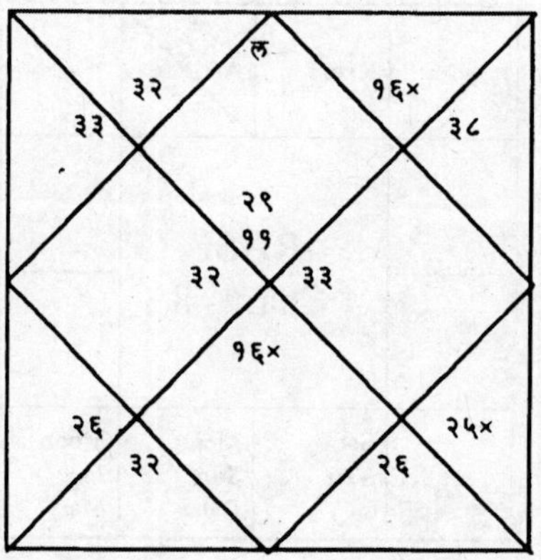
ल
३२ १६×
३३ ३८
२९
११
३२ ३३
१६×
२६ २५×
३२ २६

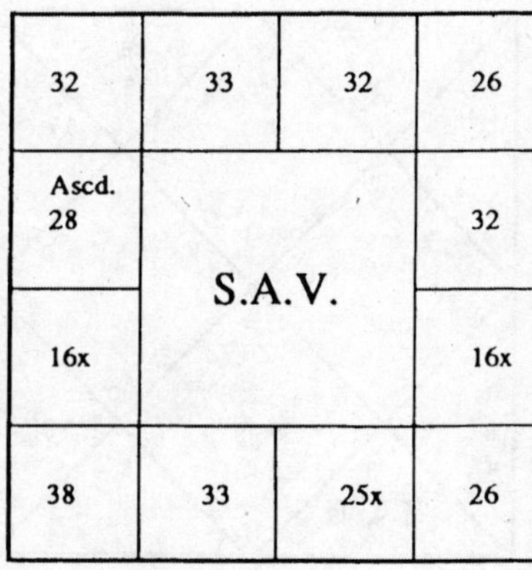
32
33
32
26
Ascd.
28
32
S.A.V.
16x
16x
38
33
25x
26

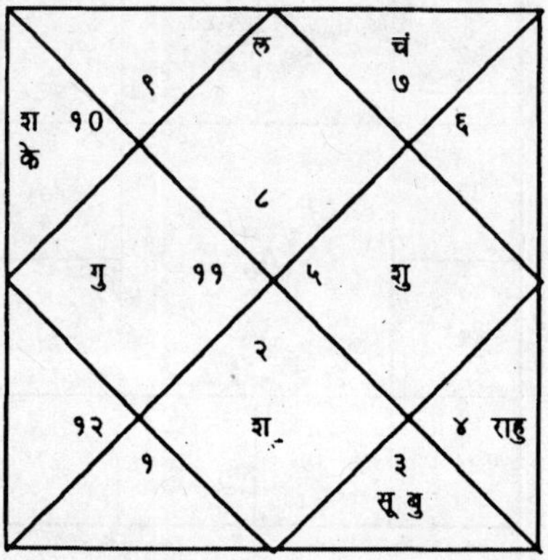
ल चं
९ ७
श १० ६
के
८
गु ११ ५ शु
२
१२ श ४ राहु
१ ३
सू बु

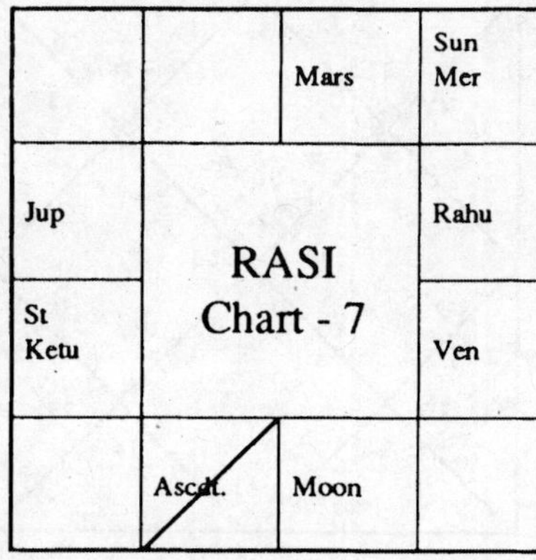
Mars
Sun
Mer
Jup
Rahu
RASI
Chart - 7
St
Ketu
Ven
Ascdt.
Moon

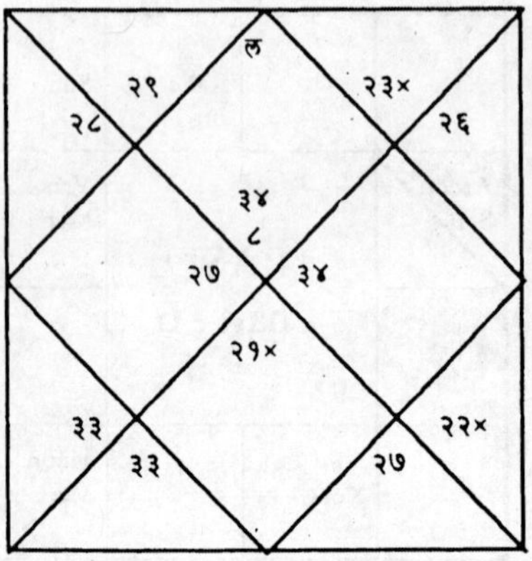
ल
२९
२३×
२८
२६
३४
८
२७
३४
२१×
३३
२२×
३३
२७

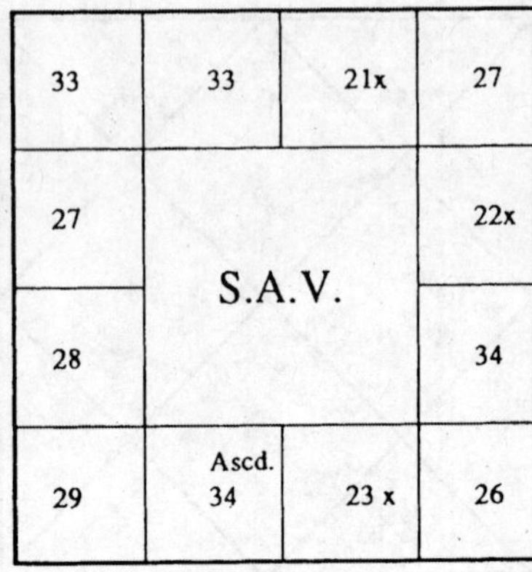
33
33
21x
27
27
22x
S.A.V.
28
34
29
Ascd.
34
23 x
26

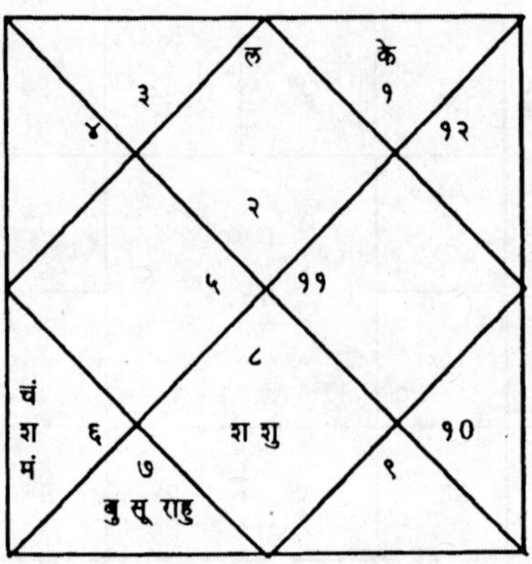
ल
के
३
१
४
१२
२
५
११
८
चं
श
मं
६
श शु
१०
७
९
बु सू राहु

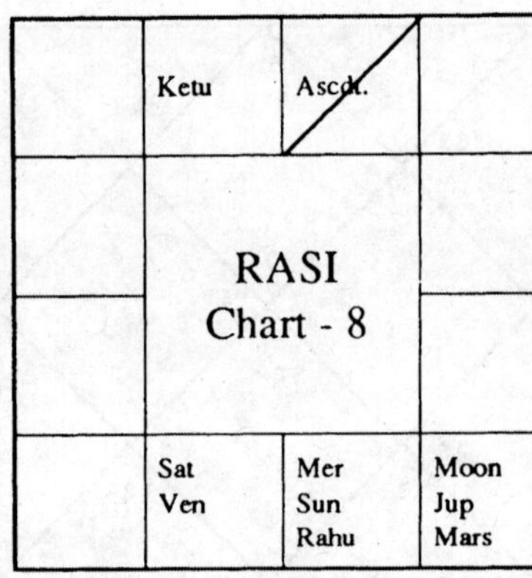
Ketu
Ascdt.
RASI
Chart - 8
Sat
Ven
Mer
Sun
Rahu
Moon
Jup
Mars

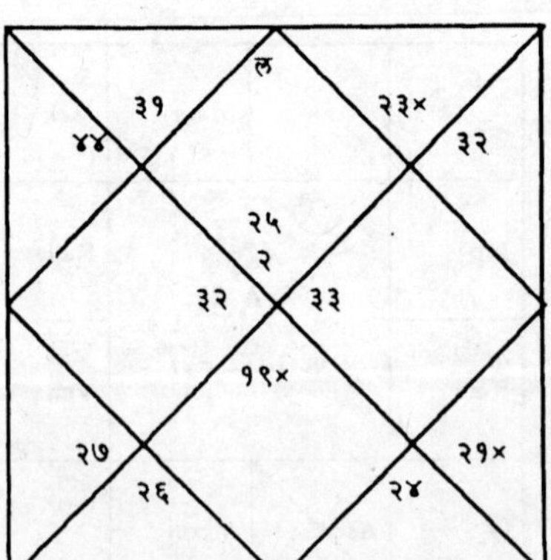
ल
३१
२३×
४४
३२
२५
२
३२
३३
१९×
२७
२१×
२६
२४

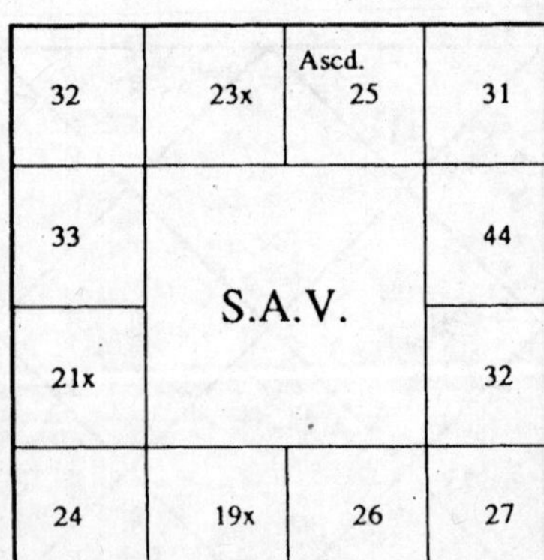
32
23x
Ascd.
25
31
33
44
S.A.V.
21x
32
24
19x
26
27

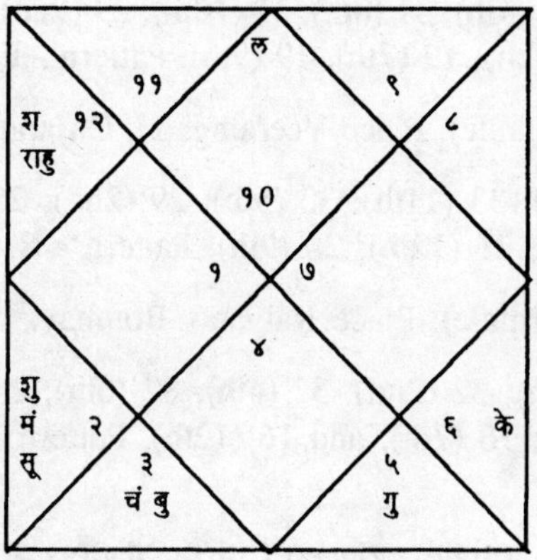

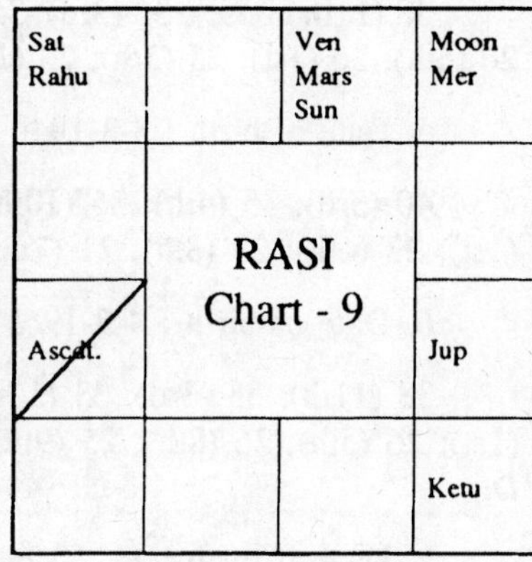

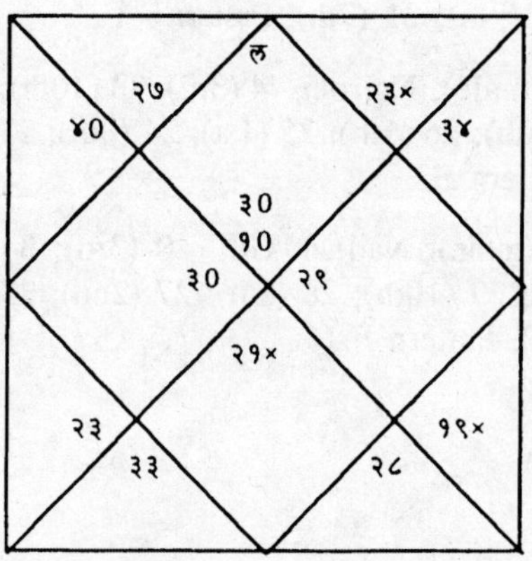

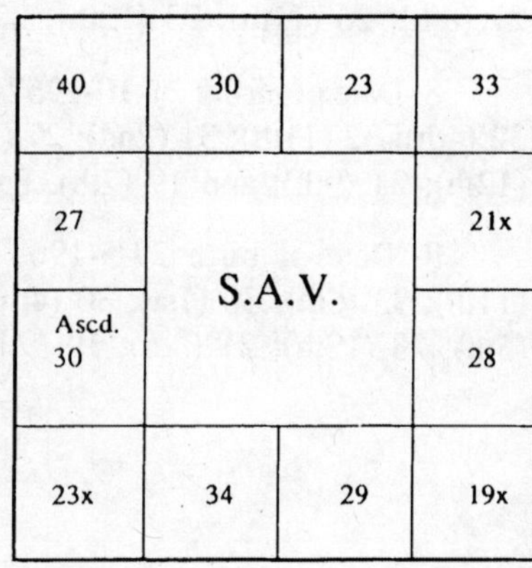

1. Date of birth : 13-10-1949, Bombay, SAV bindus in descending order are 35 (1st house), 33 (4th); 32 (3rd); 30 (11th); 30 (8th); 28 (10th); 28 (2nd); 27 (5th); 27 (6th); 23 (7th); 22 (9th); and 22 (12th). Pattern - A.

2. Date of birth : 11-11-1952 (female). Bombay.

33 (4th); 31 (10th); 31 (11th); 31 (8th); 31 (4th); 30 (5th); 29 (2nd); 28 (1st); 27 (6th); 24 (9th); 23 (12th); and 19 (7th). Pattern - C.

3. Date of birth : 6-12-1950 (female). Place : Sojitra. Near Baroda.

35 (3rd house); 33 (6th); 31 (10th); 31 (1st); 30 (2nd); 29 (11th); 29 (4th); 28 (5th); 25 (8th); 23 (9th); 22 (12th); and 21 (7th). Pattern - C.

4. Date of birth : 9-9-1951 (female). Place : Nadiad, Gujarat.

38 (11th house); 35 (3rd); 35 (4th); 31 (8th); 31 (10th); 29 (2nd); 26 (6th); 26 (1st); 25 (5th); 23 (12th); 19 (7th); 19 (9th). Pattern - E.

5. Date of birth : 8-3-1940 (male). Place Veeramgaon, Gujarat.

40 (3rd); 35 (4th); 35 (10th); 33 (11th); 32 (5th); 29 (2nd); 25 (1st); 23 (6th); 23 (8th); 21 (7th); 21 (12th); 20 (9th). Pattern - B.

6. Date of birth : 4-7-1965 (male). Place Kalyan - Bombay.

38 (11th); 33 (3rd); 33 (10th); 32 (2nd); 32 (4th); 32 (6th); 28 (1st); 26 (5th); 26 (8th); 25 (9th); 16 (7th); and 16 (12th). Pattern - D.

7. Date of birth : 11-7-1962. (male). Place of birth Madras.

34 (10th); 34 (1st); 33 (5th); 33 (6th); 29 (2nd); 28 (3rd); 27 (4th); 27 (8th); 26 (11th); 23 (12th); 22 (9th); 21 (7th). Pattern - F.

8. Date of birth : 21-10-1957 (male). Nairohi 44 (3rd); 33 (10th); 32 (4th); 32 (11th); 31 (2nd); 27 (5th); 26 (6th); 25 (1st); 24 (8th); 23 (12th); 21 (9th); and 19 (7th). Pattern F.

9. Date of birth 29-5-1968 (male). Nadiad. Guj. 40 (3rd); 34 (11th); 33 (6th); 30 (1st); 30 (4th); 29 (10th); 28 (8th); 27 (2nd); 23 (5th); 23 (12th); 21 (8th); 19 (9th). Pattern F.

23

Samudaayashtakavarga

Of all various chapters of Ashtakavargas, the most important one for prognostication pusposes, is Samudaayashtakavarga (the collective Ashtakavarga).

In Vaidyanatha's book 'Jaataka Paarijata' the following verse (Chapter X Verse 64) is of special importance :

yatyatchavimsatimukhastridasaanta samkhyaa bandhusthita-navamasaasikbindavascha.

yadhyashtakenasaha vimsativatsaraanaamamte pare saradi vanaravaahanaadyaha (64 Chapt. X).

There are quite a few verses in Sanskrit astrological classics whose correct import has eluded the grasp of even seasoned astrological scholars. The above verse is one such example, which has not been translated correctly in any edition, eg., Sanskrit, Hindi, English etc. Kashi Sanskrit Grandhamala (No. 10) translates "should the 4th and the 9th houses carry 25 to 30 bindus each, the native will become very rich at or after his 28th year." There can be any number of horoscopes having 25 to 30 bindus in the 4th and 9th houses, which makes this yoga very common. The same error has been committed in English Edition of Bangalore. We (M/s C.S. Patel and C.A.S. Aiyer) in our book 'Ashtakavarga' have made some improvement in interpretation but have wrongly interpreted 'tridasa' to mean '33' which should be '30'. Commentator of 'Sri Ranaveera-jyotirmahaanibandhaha' has also made similar error.

The correct meaning of the said verse is as follows :

"If the number of bindus in each of the houses beginning with the 4th and ending with the 9th (i.e., including all the six houses) is between 25 to 30, the person will be carried in palanquin borne by men, i.e., will be as rich as Kubera, after completing 28 years of age."

Under the above said conditions only, this yoga becomes a rarity. In my study of last 38 years, I have come across, only 15 horoscopes fulfilling the conditions laid down.

The verse refers to houses from the 4th to the 9th (in all 6 houses) consecutively. None of them can have less than 25 bindus or more than 30 bindus, this evidently indicates that the house(s) containing-maximum number of bindus in the chart, will fall in the other half of the horoscope, (i.e., from the 10th house to the 3rd house, which include the 10th—Karma, the 11th—labha, the Ascendant—beginning of the active life, the 2nd—wealth, and the 3rd—adventure etc.).

The total number of Samudaya bindus is 337, divided by 12 houses, gives quotient 28, an average of bindus for a house. As such the seer has mentioned that prosperity will commence after the 28th year.

The parents, who are looking for matching the horoscope for their son or daughter, should take advantage, if in the horoscope the bride or bridegroom, the above yoga is found even at the cost of some minor negative points in their horoscopes.

Let us illustrate this Yoga.

(A) Chart of a gentleman—born on 14/15-6-1913; time 3-10 a.m. Place : Bombay.

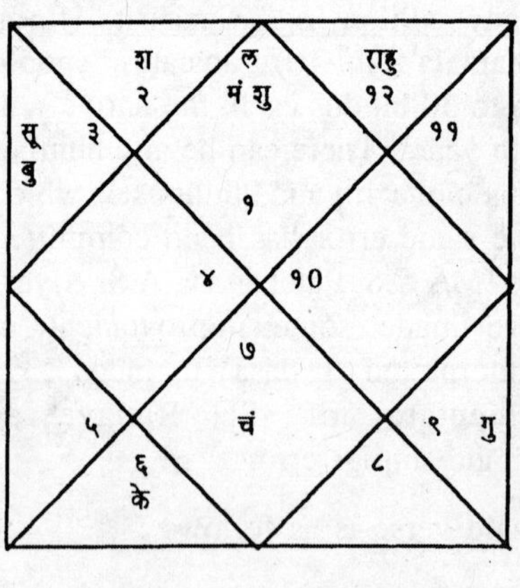

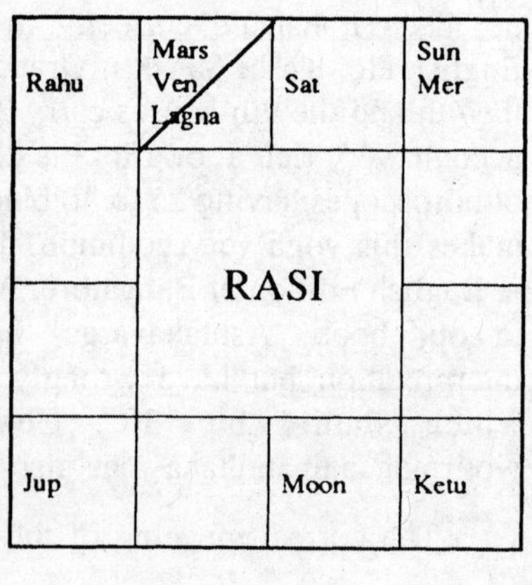

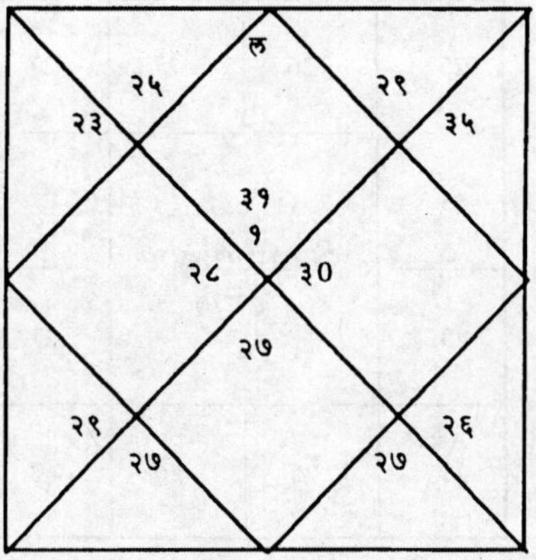

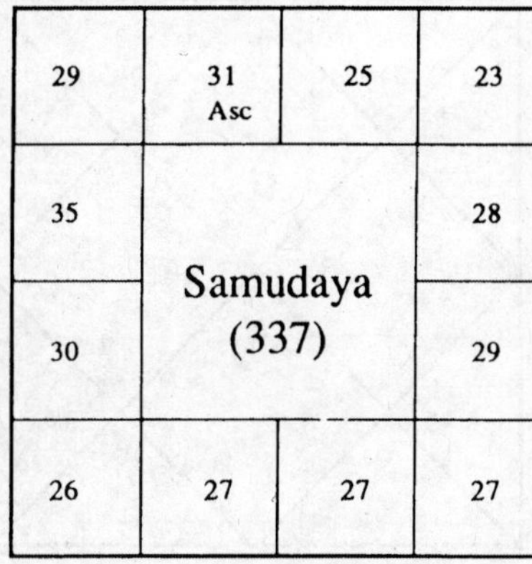

The native, at present, running 73 years, is known to the (author) since last 15 years. He was an ordinary person earning salary, little more than his monthly needs. Since 1941 (i.e., during the 2nd World War) he started his own business and prospered much thereafter. He earned lakhs of rupees in speculation and share investments. Today at 73 he is hale and healthy and very well off.

He has 28 bindus (in the 4th house) 29 (in the 5th); 27 (in 6th); 27 (in the 7th); 27 (in the 8th); and 26 (in the 9th). It may be noted, the native has maximum 35 bindus in the 11th house.

(B). Chart of lady—born oN 19-11-1926; time 9-10 a.m. Place : Ahmedabad.

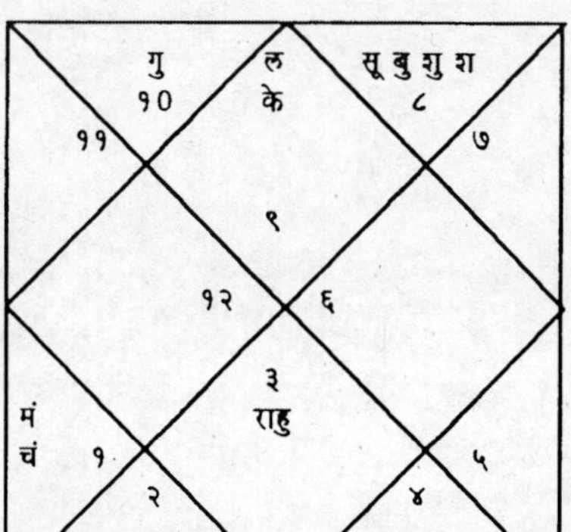

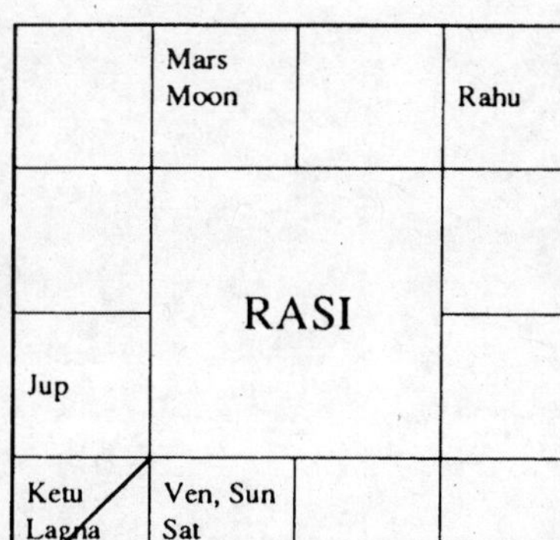

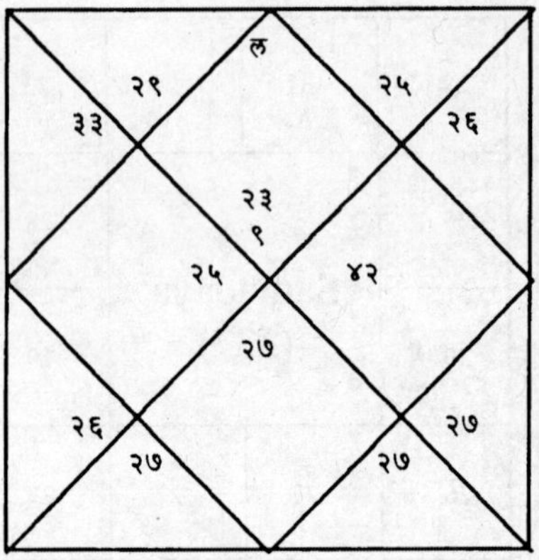

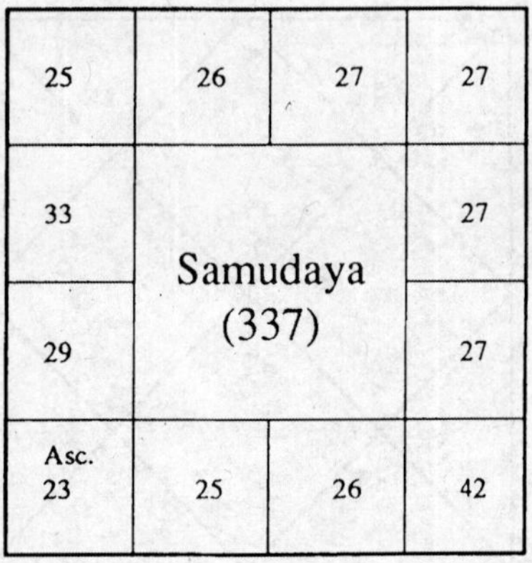

The writer knows her since childhood. She has lost her parents before she was 10 years old. At the age of 21 (in 1947) she got married to a well to do person, but not very rich. After her age of 28, i.e., from 1954 her husband started earning more and more. To-day she is very rich having bungalows, cars etc., and her husband is having income from many sources.

She has 25 bindus (in the 4th house); 26 (in the 5th); 27 (in the 6th); 27 (in the 7th); 27 (in the 8th); 27 (in the 9th). It may noted, she has got maximum 42 bindus in the 10th house.

The count of Bindus is according to, two important verses, "Balo Balishto lavangametsaro........" etc.......... .

24

Transit Results from Signs occupied by Planets

Most astrologers consider transit results of planets from the sign occupied by the Moon, while others from the sign occupied by the Ascendant or the Sun. Almost all the standard texts take the Moon-sign as the starting place. The western astrologers give preference to the Sun-sign for transit results. But, very few astrologers give importance to the transit results of each planet from the sign occupied by that same planet in the natal chart.

This is known as Nijakrantaraasiphala, i.e., transit results of planet from the sign occupied by him in the chart. Our ancient authors have weighted the good and bad places carefully for all the planets and have specified only one house (sign) each for the best results and one house each for the worst results.

Suppose, Jupiter gives good results during his transit from the sign occupied by him, in some six different signs. Out of these six good signs, which sign is the best one? Here it is the 5th house-sign from his positioin. Similarly, out of the remaining six unfavourable signs which one is the worst? It is the 3rd house-sign from his position. In short, Jupiter during his transit will give very good results when he transits the 5th sign from the sign he occupies, while the most unfavourable results will follow during his trasit through the 3rd sign from his natal position. Similarly, the ancient authors have given good and bad signs for all the remaining planets.

Scarcely is this subject dealt with by ancient authors. The scribe has come across very few verses on this subject in standard texts.

Jaataka Parijata - Chap. XVII Vx. 34-35-36;

भ्रातृस्थानगतो जीवो दारस्थानगतः कुजः ।
तथा जन्मगतो मन्दो राहुर्नवमराशिगः ॥
चन्द्रोऽष्टमगृहं यातः सूर्योरिःफगृहं गतः
बुधः सप्तसभावस्थो भार्गवः शत्रुराशिगः ॥
इत्येवं मरणस्थानं तस्मिन् पापयुतेऽथवा ।
पापदृष्टेऽरिनीचस्थे दुर्बले दुःखमाप्नुयात् ॥

meaning, "Jupiter in the 3rd place from the sign occupied by him; Mars in the 7th sign; Saturn in the first sign; Rahu in the 9th sign; the Moon in the 8th sign; the Sun in the 12th sign; Mercury in the 7th sign and Venus in the 6th sign—each of these signs are death-inflicting. When such a sign in natal chart is occupied or aspected by a malefic planet, or that sign falls in inimical or depression house or is destitute of strength and when that particular planet transits that sign, the native comes to grief."

Phaladeepika Chap. XXVI - Vs. 34

चन्द्रोष्टमे च धरणीतनयः कलत्रे
राहुः शुभे कविररौ च गुरुस्तृतीये ।
अर्कः सुतेऽर्किरुदये च बुधश्चतुर्थे
मानार्थहानिमरणानि वदेद्विशेषात् ॥

meaning, "the period when transit Moon is in the 8th sign from her natal sign; Mars in the 7th sign; Rahu in the 9th sign; Venus in the 6th sign; Jupiter in the 3rd sign; the Sun in the 5th sign; Saturn in the 1st sign (Saturn over Saturn) and Mercury in the 4th sign, they will bring about loss of honour and wealth and in most cases will cause danger to one's life also (if many planets transit such afflicted signs simultaneously)."

It may cause danger to one's life or of some close relative. In the scribe's chart (referred many times earlier) transit Saturn (2s 20° 30') was passing degreewise over natal Saturn (2s 20° 42') on 24-1-1975 when his wife expired. On that day the Moon was also passing through the 8th sign (Taurus) from the natal Moon-sign (Libra).

Unfvourable results such as sickness of near relatives or one's own, physical injury, worries; debt, quarrels, insult, humiliation, legal proceedings, hindrances in service, loss in business or trade, theft, fear from fire or poison etc., are experienced when slow-moving planets transit through afflicted signs. When the afflicting planets in transit become powerful by position, retrogression or otherwise, the evil efftects multiply on a large scale.

There are parallel verses in **Prasna Marga** on this topic with slight variations and additions.

Prasna Marga Chap. X Vs. 56-57:

चन्द्रस्तु निधनं प्राप्तः सप्तमं बुधलोहितौ
व्दादशं भास्करः षष्ठं भृगुपुत्रः समाश्रितः ॥
तृतीयं देवमन्त्री च राहुकेतुशनैश्चराः ।
जन्मस्थाः प्राणसन्देहं कुर्वन्त्येते न संशयः ॥

meaning, "the period, when transit Moon is in the 8th sign; Mercury or Mars in the 7th sign; the Sun in the 12th sign; Venus in the 6th sign; Jupiter in the 3rd sign from their occupied signs; and Rahu or Ketu or Saturn passes through his occupied sign (*Janmasthaah* in whichever signs they are) should be considered as most fatal".

Comments : It is very difficult to understand as to why **Jataka Parijata** has included the above 3 verses in Chapter XVII dealing with Kalachakra Dasa. Perhaps, these inflicting signs falling on Deha or Jeeva sign, may cause evil effects of greater magnitude. The **Phaladeepika** has included this parallel verse in Chapter XXVI on "Gocharaphala" while **Prasna Marga** has included similar verses in Chapter X on "Timing Death".

In some Tamil manuscripts Jyothisha Pala Grantha by Krishna Murti Siddhanti, Ketu is said to give worst results during transit through 2nd sign from his natal position.

Saturn in the third round, Jupiter in the 6th round and Rahu in the 4th round, transit their afflicted signs, from 57th year or so upto 62nd year or so of life. When two or three of these slow-moving planets simultaneously transit the afflicted signs, the native has to face many troubles at a time. Physical inability; retirement from service; education, marriage and employment of grown-up children or death or severe sickness of near relative; paucity of funds etc., will be experienced by the native during the transit of these three planets.

When a slow-moving planet completes its transit through the

afflicted sign and crosses over the next sign, the evil effects, troubles etc., caused by that planet come to an end. The scribe has successfully observed this change for the better in the lives of many nativities.

The ancient scholars have weighted the unfavourable places carefully for all the nine planets and have allotted only one place each for every planet covering nine different places for nine different planets as follows :

Saturn in the 1st house	(from his natal position)
Ketu in the 2nd house	do
Jupiter in the 3rd house	do
Mercury in the 4th house	do
The Sun in the 5th house	do
Venus in the 6th house	do
Mars in the 7th house	do
The Moon in the 8th house	do
Rahu in the 9th house	do

Mrs. Indira Gandhi : Born 19-11-1917 at 11-11 p.m. (IST)at 25 N 27, 81 E 51 (Ref. A.M. August 1966, p. 761).

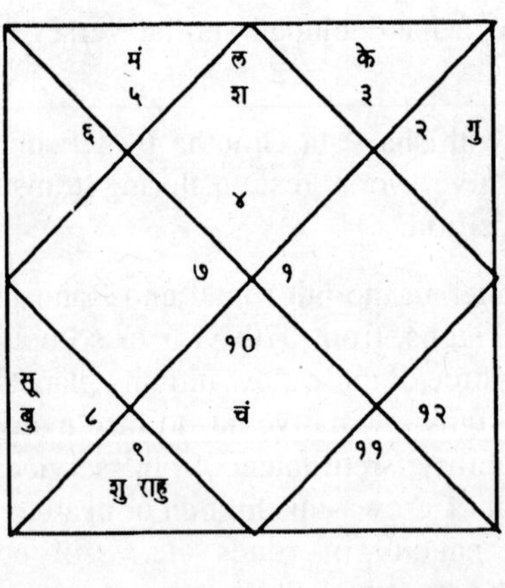

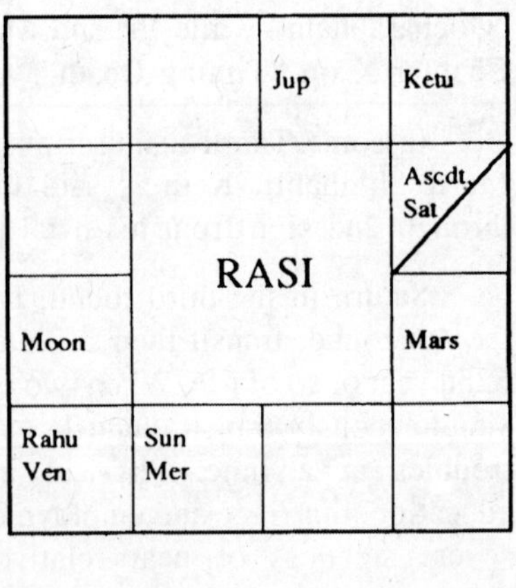

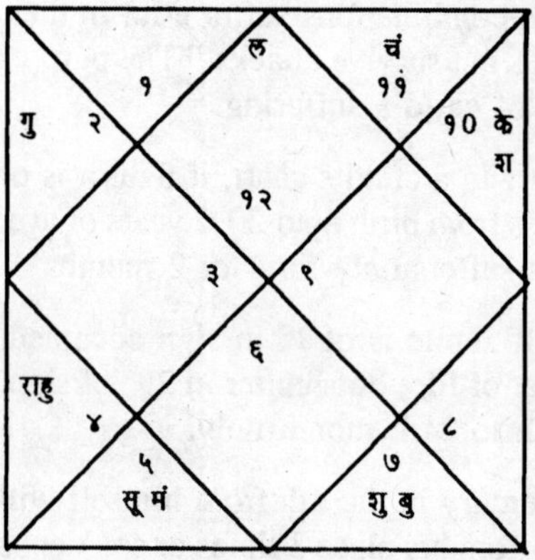

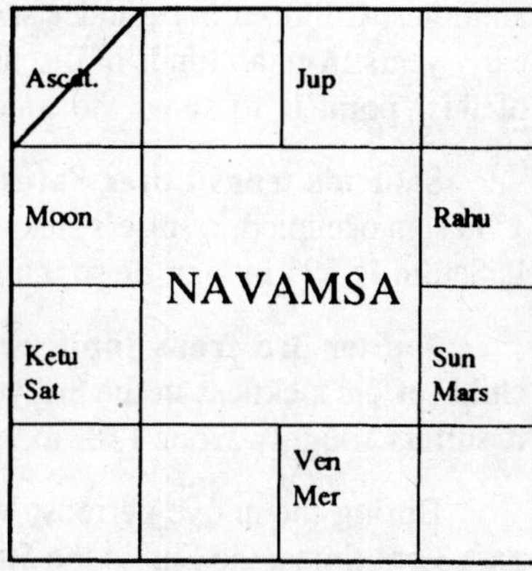

Rasi : The Sun 214-08; the Moon 275-37; Mars 136-23; Mercury 223-15; Jupiter 45-1; Venus 261-00; Saturn 111-47; Rahu 250-33; Ketu 70-33; Herschel 297-21; Neptune 104-18; Asendant 117-3; M.C. 00-25 with a balance of 1 year, 11 months and 20 days of Sun Dasa. Saturn was in Cancer (Saturn over Saturn — 3rd round) from 23-7-1975 to 7-9-1977; Jupiter in Cancer (3rd from Jupiter in Taurus—6th round) from 5-7-1978 to 29-8-1979; Rahu in Leo (9th from Rahu in Sagittarius—4th round) from 18-11-1978 to 6-6-1980.

Indira Gandhi declared new elections to Lok Sabha when transit Saturn was degreewise transiting natal Saturn. She lost the election and resigned on 22-3-1977. Most unfortunate event such as expulsion from Parliament (January 1979), warrant for her arrest, being driven to Tihar Jail (round about 19-12-1978)—all these events took place during the period of two months i.e., from 18-11-1978 to 20-1-1979. In short all the above events took place when Saturn was transiting natal Saturn; Rahu was transiting the 9th from natal Rahu and Jupiter was transiting cancer, 3rd from his natal position. The concurrent transits, both of Rahu and Jupiter from 18-11-1978 to 29-8-1979 through their respective afflicted signs was the worst period full of insults and humiliation etc.

Balaristhta (Infant Mortality)

A child dies before it is 4 years old on account of sins committed by its mother; between 5 and 8 years on account of sins committed by the father and between 9 and 12 years for its own sins committed in previous births. This is an old dictum.

"In certain charts evil affliction will be available indicating early death to the infant but certain other configurations try to act as antidotes. Children born under such combinations suffer a lot in their early years from all kinds of diseases but survive attacks." The purport of this point is to show the time of child's suffering.

Saturn's transit over Saturn : In a child's chart, if Saturn is of 1° in sign occupied, it suffers sickness from birth upto 2 1/2 years of age. If Saturn is 29° in sign or so, child suffers only for 1 or 2 months.

Jupiter 3rd from Jupiter : If Jupite is of 1° in sign occupied, child suffers sickness in the 3rd year of life; but Jupiter in 29° of sign, it suffers roughly from 13th month to 24th month only.

During the above periods, Mercury in the 4th from himself will pass 3 o:4 times; the Sun in the 5th from his place 3 times or so; Venus in the 6th from his own place 3 or 4 times; Mars in the 7th from natal Mars at least twice. Thus the period of 4 years from birth is conductive to health hazards in childhood. When transits of slow-moving and fast-moving planets concur the child suffers much.

Jyotish-Tattvam by Mukunda Daivagna - Vol. I. Chapter X Vs 25-26.

अङ्गरको यद्धगतो जनौ ततस्तुर्येऽनृजुर्भूफलदो विशेषतः ।
सूरिः स्वतः सूनुफलं सुते दिशेज्ज्ञः स्वाम्बुभे सौरव्यफलं मघाभवः ॥
कान्ताफलं कामगृहे शनैश्चरः स्वतः शुभे गोचरके विधेः फलम् ।
विधुः स्वतोऽर्थे फलं तु वैषुवे फलं खगानां बलतारतम्यतः ॥

meaning, "Mars when retrograde transits the 4th house from the sign occupied by him at birth will specially bestow land; Jupiter will similarly favour with birth of a child during transit through the 5th house; Mercury will bestow happiness during transit through the 4th house; Venus will confer conjugal bliss during transit through the 7th house; Saturn will cause luck (Bhagyodaya) during transit through the 9th house; while the Moon will bestow wealth during his transit through its 2nd house provided that period is Vishuva Kala (when it passes Equinoctial Point). The effects above described will come to be felt according to the strength or othewise of the planets concerned."

Comments : All the above results are from the occupied places of the planets (*Nijakranta Rashahe Phalam*). These two verses of **Jyotish Tattvam** lead the scribe to interpret other verses of the article on the above line. One should note that in verse 25, result of the Sun is missing and Mercury's transit in the 4th sign gives good results while in **Jataka Parijata** and **Phaladeepika,** Mercury confers bad results in the same sign. **Prasna Marga** refers to the 7th sign for Mercury for bad results.

There is a parallel verse in **Sanketa Nidhi.**

Sanketa Nidhi. Chap. VI - Vs 102;

बलाबलविवेकतः फलमिहोदितं कोविदैः
कुजो निजचतुर्थभूफलविशेषदो वक्रगः ।
स्वतः सुतफलं गुरुः सुखफलं बुधः स्त्रीफलं
सितो नियतिजं शनिर्धनफलं विधुर्वैषुवे ॥

Vidya Madhaveeyam Part II, Chap. VIII. Vs 50 (P. 223);

वयसि बुधस्सहजे कुजमन्दौ भृगुतनयो निधने विधुरस्ते ।
द्विषति रविश्च भवेद्यदि दिष्ट्या परिणयने शुभदः किल योगः ॥

meaning, "Fortunately at the time of Panigrahana (marriage in the charts of bride or bridegroom) transit Mercury is in the 4th sign; Mars or Saturn in the 3rd sign; Venus in the 8th sign; the Moon in the 7th sign; or the Sun in the 6th sign **from their respective occupied signs**, marriage is really beneficial."

Sage Vashishta adds Jupiter's position in the Ascendant also (*Vilagnastho Bhavajeeva*). If more planets transit in the respective places in the charts of the bride groom at the time of marriage, the couple will have Dharma, Artha and Kama; will see their sons and grandsons and will live upto hundred years, so says Vashishta.

The above verse has been referred by Mrs. Gayatri Devi Vasudev on page No. 539 of The Astrological magazine July 1993.

The scribe hopes that research scholars will agree with this deviation in interpreting the verses mentioned here.

25

Conjunctions of Planets in Transit — I

At the time of Shri Ramachandra's investiture ceremony, King Dasharath said to Sri Rama (Valmiki Ramayana) : My star is afflicted by transit - conjunction of three malefic planets, the Sun, Mars and Rahu.

This astronomical reference from the earliest Epic, is sufficient testimony to the basis used by ancient astrologers for prediction in those days - namely "transit - conjunctions". Stellar conjunctions of planets are more effective than those of sign conjunctions.

"The Concise Oxford Dictionary" defines the word "conjunction" as "apparent proximity of two heavenly bodies". Two planets are said to be in "close conjunction" or "rapt conjunction" when they occupy same degree of the zodiac. There are conjunctions of planets in sign(s) in natal chart. There are also conjunctions of planets in transit. Conjunction of two planets lasts as long as one of them leaves the sign during forward or backward motion. This article deals with "transit-conjunctions" only, e.g., Mars in first degree of Aries and Saurn 29° in Aries are said to be in sign conjunction, even though they are about 28° away from each other. Mars 1° in Aries and Saturn 29° in Pisces are not said to be in conjunction in a sign, eventhough the longitudinal distance between them is only 2 degrees. They may form a house conjunction. While examining conjunction, one has to take into account, *which planets* are conjunct and also *the sign in which* they are together (representing a particular house). Besides this, one has to bear in mind the *relative strength* of the conjunct planets at that time.

Chandra Kala Nadi - Vol. II, Part II, P. 71 verse 3272;

Meshe chhapamsage sukre kuleera cha prajaayathe / jeeve Kujayuthe kaale bahuvittayutha sukhee //

Meaning - "a native born in Cancer Ascendant, with Venus occupying Sagittarius Navamsa in Aries sign (both of neutral planets), will have much wealth and be happy, during the preiod of conjunction in transit of Jupiter and Mars."

Comments : The study of this verse led me to make deep research on results of transit conjunctions of two or more planets in a chart and hence this write-up. Note that Venus, a benefic planet is posited in the 10th house, occupying Pushkara Navamsa (Sagittarius Navamsa in Aires sign). Why, the author Sri Achyuta has taken into account the conjunction of Jupiter and Mars only? It may be noted that Mars is the sign dispositor (Aries) and Jupiter is Navamsa dispositor (Sagittarius) of Venus. These two planets whenever in transit conjunct, they produce certain favourable results to the native. Venus in Cancer Ascendant, is the lord of the 11th house and the 4th house, hence he bestows wealth (the 11th house) and happiness (the 4th house) as per houses owned by him. The sign conjunction between Jupiter and Mars takes place roughly once in every two years (i.e., 24 months). This period of conjunction varies from 1 1/2 months to 6 months, depending on their speed. Conjunctions of Jupiter and Mars in Cancer, Sagittarius, Pisces, Aries, Scorpio and Capticorn signs are productive of more good results, because either of them becomes powerful in each of these six signs. Only in sign Cancer or Capricorn, one is exalted and the other is debilitated, simultaneously.

One research scholar has successfully applied this principle of Navamsa dispositor and Rasi dispositor of Mandi and confirmed the demise of Mahatma Gandhiji in the Dasa of Rasi lord Venus and in Bhukti of Navamsa lord Jupiter. *In application of this rule to Dasa Bhukti, I think stellar-dispositor of a planet be taken into account for inclusion of Dasa / Bhukti of Rahu and Ketu. A rule can be deduced from the above verse;*

"Two planets, one Navamsa dispositor (Jupiter, in this case) and the other Rasi (sign) dispositor (Mars in this case), during their conjunction in transit produce results pertaining to sign(s) houses owned by the disposited planet. (Venus in this case).

How many possibilities :

Venus in different signs	12
—do— Navamsas;	9
Twelve different ascendants :	12
Seven planets :	7

= 12 x 9 x 12 x 7 = 9072

There can be 9072 different possibilities of results, taking into account, all the seven planets, in different signs, Navamsas and Ascendants.

Kerala Nadi (University of Mysore) p. 205 (my copy)

Vyaadhipaanthare kaale vyayese paapasamyuthe / Daarapeedaam manasthapam sisupeedmithi smrutham //

meaning, when the lord of the 12th house conjuncts a malefic in transit, during the Antara (Bhukti sub period) period of the lord of the 12th house, mental anguish to the native, trouble (sickness, etc.) to wife and to child are indicated.

Comments : Vyayasthan is the 12th from the Ascendant, (mental anguish to the native) - is 6th from the 7th house (sickness to wife) - is 8th from the 5th house (sickness to child). This principle can be applied to the conjunction of a planet owning benefic house (e.g., the 9th house) and a benefic planet (e.g., Jupiter), during the Bhukti period of the lord of that house (namely the 9th house lord).

Jatakadesh Marg - Chap. XVI - V.25.

Jeevapathya vilgnajan - mapatayah putreswararudhabhel puthre vaa athatathostrikona bhavane va samchareyuryad II yoge va vanita vilagnatanayesanam trayana,m yada santhathyaa jananam tatha khalu nrunaamityeva satsrodithamlI

meaning : Astrologers declare that the birth of a child may take place when (1) Jupiter (2) the lord of the 5th house (3) the lord of the Ascendant and (4) the lord of the Moon - sign transit the house occupied by the lord of the 5th house or 5th house itself or the trine signs of these two houses.

The same event (birth of a child) may also be expected when the owners of the 7th, the 1st and the 5th houses, conjoin together *in any house* during their transit.

Comments : In the above verse, two different yogas (possibilities) are discussed. It is rare to have a conjunction of three planets in transit in a sign, and it is still rarer to have a conjunction of four planets in a sign. In the first yoga, the 5th house and its trine signs are accounted while the second yoga considers conjunction in any house. My experience says that even a conjnunction of three or two planets in a sign as referred above will give the desired results.

Application of the 2nd yoga the details of birth of my five children are in the table on next page.

In my chart the 7th lord is Saturn, the Ascendant lord is the Moon and the 5th lord is Mars.

There is a conjunction of two planets in case of three children out of five born as stated in the verse. This is just to explain the application of the Yoga.

Phaladeepika - Chap. XVI V. 33

Lagnaanatha yoge tu lagnesaddurale ripau I tada tadvasagh tru viparietamatho anyatha II

meaning : Whenever the lords of the Ascendant and the 6th house come in conjunction during transit, the native's enemy will come under his control, if the lord of the 6th house is weaker than the lord of the Ascendant. Otherwise, the contrary will happen.

Comments : Sometimes it may so happen, the Ascendant lord becomes powerful and the lord of the 6th house is weak during transit/ conjunction. At some other time, reverse may be the case. For Leo Ascendant, the Sun ascendant lord and Saturn, the lord of the 6th house conjoin together in transit in the 9th house (Aries), where the Sun is exalted and Saturn is debilitated, the enemy of the native will come under his control. At some other time when they (the Sun and Saturn) conjunct in transit in the 3rd house (Libra) where the lord of the 6th house Saturn is powerful and the Sun is weak, *the same native* will come under the control of his enemy.

Phaladeepilka Chap. XVI, V. 35.

Lagnesayadbhavapayostha yoga I yada tada tatphalasiddhi kaalah II bhavesa veerye subhamanyathanyallagnaachcha chandradapi chintaneeyam II meaning : whenever the Ascendant lord comes in conjunction (during transit) with lord of any particular Bhava under consideration, the success of that Bhava may be expected, if the lord of that Bhava is strong. Otherwise the effect will be different. Similarly one may reckon the bhavas from the Moon instead of from the Ascendant.

Comments : In this verse, Mantreshwar has expanded the application of the principle explained in the previous verse i.e., the transit conjunction of the lord of the Ascendant with the lord of any house, out of the remaining eleven houses, success of that Bhava, whose lord is powerful vis-a-vis the Ascendant lord, is expected during transit conjunction. The author also, recommends to apply this theory from the Moon-sign, i.e., the lord of the Moon sign vis-a-vis the lord of the remaining eleven houses.

Birth date	Saturn in sign	The Moon in sign	Mars in sign
1st child 31-12-36	11	4	7
2nd child 27-07-38	12	4	4*
3rd child 05-12-42	2	7	7*
4th child 19-11-45	4	2	4**
5th child 05-11-54	7	11	10

*Moon & Mars ** Saturn & Mars

Ashtakavarga - Chap. XIV, V. 8

Ekatra bhave bahavo yadaneemukthankagascharavasad vrajanthi I Pushnanthi tadbhava phalani samyak tatharakaththanu purvabhave.II

meaning : When a Bhava is transited by many planets simultaneously and if that Bhava contains the greater number of Bindus, these planets multiply the good effects of that Bhava. The nature of the effects will be according to the Bhava positon of this house from the houses occupied by the transiting planets at birth and their Karakatva.

Comments : Evidently, when a Bhava containing least or less number of Bindus in transited simultaneously by many planets, the bad effects of that Bhava will multiply, accordingly, to a great extent.

To illustrate above principles of "transit-conjunctions" of two or more planets, three most outstanding events in my life are astrologically examined for the benefit of reserch students.

Horoscope of C.S. Patel :

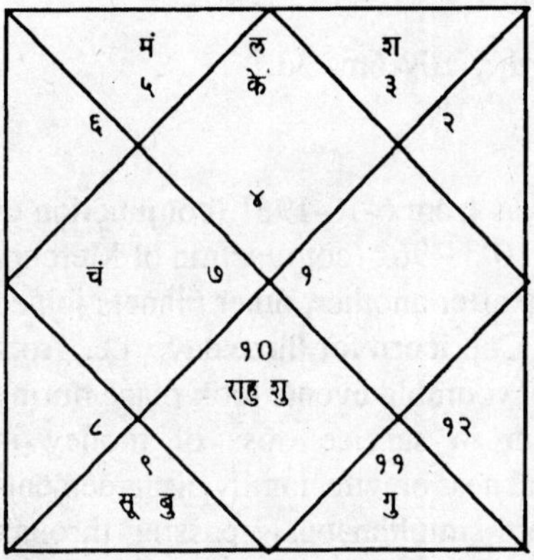

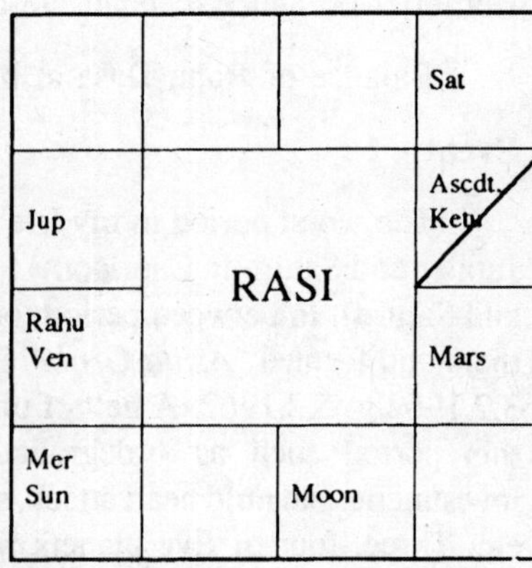

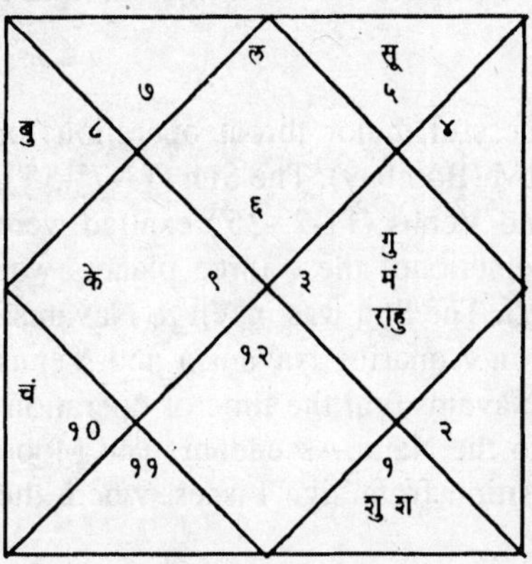

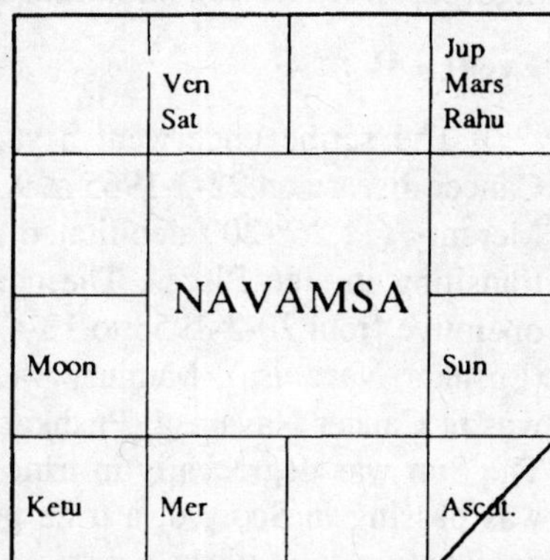

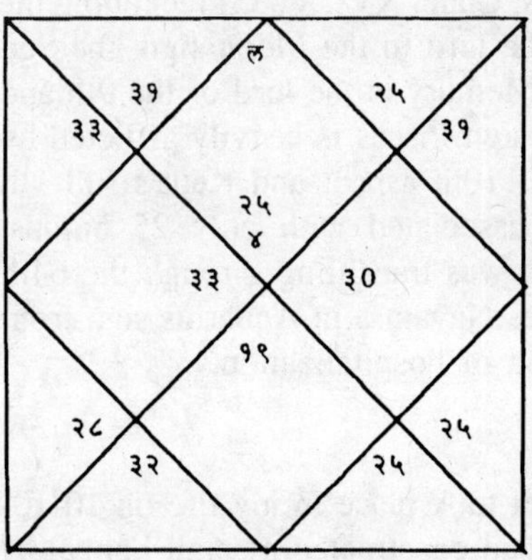

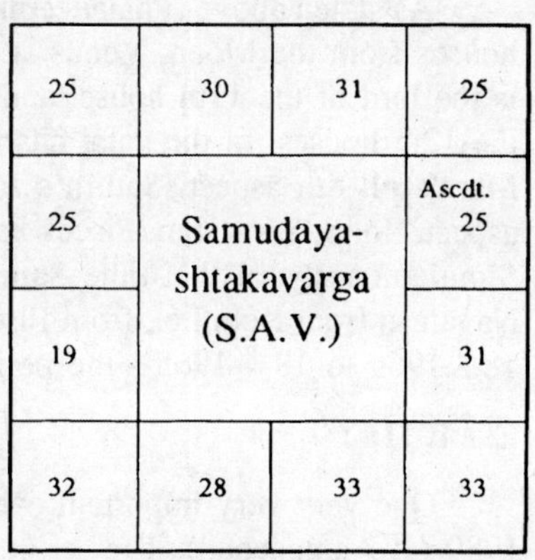

Born on 31-12-1915 at 7.44 PM (IST), Lat, 23-2N Long 72-39E, Rasi : The Sun 256-10; the Moon 192-13; Mars 127-9; Mercury 265-13; Jupiter 329-29; Venus 283-14;; Saturn 80-42 (R); Rahu 287-06; Ketu 107-06 and Ascendant 98-53.

Balance of Rahu Dasa at birth : 10y 6m, 3d.

Event - I :

The worst period in my life was from 6-10-1961 (conjunction of Jupiter and Saturn in Capricorn) to 10-3-1962 (conjunction of Mercury and Saturn). In between period, one after another, other planets joined them and formed "*Ashta-Grahi*" in Capricorn for three days, i.e., from 3.2.1962 to 5.2.1962. A hell of unfavourable events took place during this period such as - degradation in service, loss of money in investments and mild heart attack, sickness of wife, family disagreements etc. Three, four or five planets were simultaneously passing through sign Capricorn having minimum 19 bindus in S.A.V. in the 7th house.

Event - II :

The scribe underwent a successful major throat operation for Cancer disease on 22-3-1965 at 9 AM (Bombay). The Sun (11-7°-55'), Mercury (11.26°-20') debilitated and Venus (11-2°-35') exalted were transiting in sign Pisces. The conjunctionof these three planets was operative from 20-3-1955 to 13-4-65. The Sun was in Virgo Navamsa (Pushkar Navamsa), Mercury was in Aquarius Navamsa and Venus was in Cancer Navamsa (Pushkar Navamsa) at the time of operation. The Sun was degreecally in trine to the Natal Ascendant. The Moon was passing in Scorpio, a trine position from sign Pisces, where the conjunction took place.

As stated above (Phaladeepika, Chap. XVI, V. 35) reckoning the houses from the Moon, Venus is the lord fo the Moon sign, the Sun is the lord of the 11th house, and Mercury is the lord of the 9th and the 12th houses. In the natal chart sign Pisces is heavily afflicted by Mars' full 8th aspect, Saturn's full 10th aspect and Ketu's full 9th aspect. In S.A.V. sign Pisces is associated with only 25 bindus. Simultaneously, at that time Saturn was transitting through the 64th Navamsa from Ketu i.e., from Pisces Navamsa in Aquarius sign from 18.3.1965 to 18-4-1965 - the period of hospitalization.

Event III :

One very very important event took place in my life on 10-10-1989 (at Ahmedabad). The scribe had constructed a small bungalow atAhmedabad in 1970 and rented it to a tenant immediately. Now-a-days, in big cities, tenants are not vacating occupied premises when required by the landlord. Mine is an exceptional case in a city like Ahmedabad. The tenant vacated it after 19 years of occupation, on Tuesday 10-10-1989 at 12-40 PM. This event gave me extra-ordinary pleasure i.e., as good as birth of a child to wife after many years of married life. Its present value goes to several lakhs of rupees.

In example chart :

1. Mars - Karaka for landed property is posited in the 2nd house (sign Leo).

2. Sign dispositor of Mars is the Sun.

3. Navamsa dispositor of Mars is Mercury.

A transit conjunction of these planets - Mars, the Sun and Mercury was in operation from 16-9-1989 to 17-10-1989, in sign Virgo - which is Udita Navamsatulya sign or Navamsa ascendant sign (also a Puskara Navamsa). The event took place, when the Moon was passing through sign Capricorn - Chandra Navamsa tulya rasi trine to sign Virgo - in which the conjunction of three planets took place. It may be noted that one of these three planets, Mercury was powerful, occupying his own sign Virgo, which has maximum 33 bindus (in S.A.V.).

Four guiding principles discussed in the article are "transit conjunctions" of -

1. dispositor of Rasi (sign) and dispositor of a Navamsa of a planet;

2. lord of a house and a malefic planet;

3. lord of the ascendant/the Moon sign and each lord of the remaining eleven houses; and

4. lords of certain specified houses.

Thus, it can be seen that there is a vast field of Hindu astrology, containing gems of rules for the timing of events, hitherto unnoticed. Some of these gems are uncut and require polishing. If systematic research is carried out, many wonderful rules can be found out and put to use for better and accurate predictions.

26

Conjunctions of Planets in Transit - II

After posting the first article on this count for publication to The TOA in February 1991, (which appeared in June 1991 issue) Chapter-25, the scribe tried to scan rare publications and *Nadi Granthas* and met with a partial success. The result is this write up - II.

Dhana Prapthi Kaalah (The time when one gets "wealth") : "*Jataka Parijata*" Ch. XI verse 51 :

"Dhanapayathah prathamo atha darsee graho dwitiyo dhanapostruteezya I tatpaakabhuktav dhanalabhamethi kramena tatkaraka graha mulath II

meaning : note, first the planet occupying the 2nd house; next the planet aspecting that house and thirdly the planet owning the 2nd house. A native will gain wealth during Dasa and/or periods (bhukti) through sources indicated by these planets (Karakas) in their order, (Ref. Chart No. 2).

Comments : Sri Vaidyanatha has given importance to planet (1) posited in the 2nd house; (2) aspecting the 2nd house and (3) its lord in order. The time of fruition is during the Dasa and bhukti of these planets. The native does get some wealth (worldly possessions) during these periods. But to acquire more wealth at a time. *Daivagnabharanam* has a added one more condition to the above one. (Ref. chap. X Verse 74, p 92, GOML Madras, 1954)

"dhanadrusthadhanasthasya dhanesasya dasásu cha I dhanakarakasamyoge dhanam bahu san-snuthe II

meaning : note the planet aspecting the 2nd house; the planet occupying the 2nd house and also the lord of the 2nd house. The native will acquire much wealth during their Dasa (and or periods - bhuktis) provided a conjunction in transit of any two (or more) planets takes place simulataneously (*Dhanakarakasamyoga*) during that period.

Comments : The author of Daivagnabharanam gives importance firstly to planet(s) aspecting the 2nd house; secondly to planet(s) posited in the 2nd house and thirdly to the lord of the 2nd house. The time of fruitation is during Dasa (bhuktis) periods of these planets. The author further restricts this priod of occurance to certain periods caused by conjunction of Dhanakaraka planets in transit during concurrence of Dasa/Bhuktis to garner more wealth. Dhanakaraka planets as implied in this verse are those planets which aspect, occupy or own the 2nd house as against those usual Dhanakarakas such as Jupiter and Venus. The Dhanakaraka in this case may be benefic(s) and/or malefic(s) (Ref. Ch. No. 1, 2 and 3).

Maximum Dhanakaraka planets in a chart can be all seven planets and minimum there can be only one planet. In such nativities, where the major Dasa(s) of dhanakarakas are not likely to come during his life time, the periods (bhuktis) in various Dasas are definitely going to give "results of course during transit conjunctions as mentioned above.

About 90% of the world population earns its bread by working in fields, or factories or other places, or in service by daily, weekly, fortnightly or monthly wages, salaries, pensions, etc. The wealth (*Dhanam*) as mentioned in the above verse, does not refer to the above sources of income, earned by labour. The wealth referred to above is easy-money and other properties acquired through sources such as legacy, inheritance, will, theft, gift, dowry, hidden wealth (underground), lottery, races (jackpot etc.) gambling, loot, cheating, speculation, bribery, misappropriation of funds; betting in matches (cricket, football, hockey ... etc.). In short this wealth is acquired or poured upon native by sheer luck, i.e. wealth acquired without any physical exertion, (*Dhanasya labbdhih aayatnatah*). This kind of wealth may be in from of hard cash, gold, silver, jewels, shares, landed property, etc. or any *kind of such property (worldly possessions)* which can be converted into hard cash.

This type of wealth is freely spent away by the native in various ways. Unless and until there are some "yogas - strong combinations" in the natal chart, there are more chances of this wealth being spent away or lost in risky ventures or nefarious activities or wasted for nothing.

This verse is just a parallel to one referred to in the first article(June 1991 issue) wherein importance is given to a running bhukti and a transit conjunction of two malefic planets, both concurrently.

Chart No. 1 : Date of birth 31-21-1915. Time : 7.44 PM Lat 23° 2' (N); Long 72° 37' (E). Balance Dasa : Rahu 10y 6m 3d.

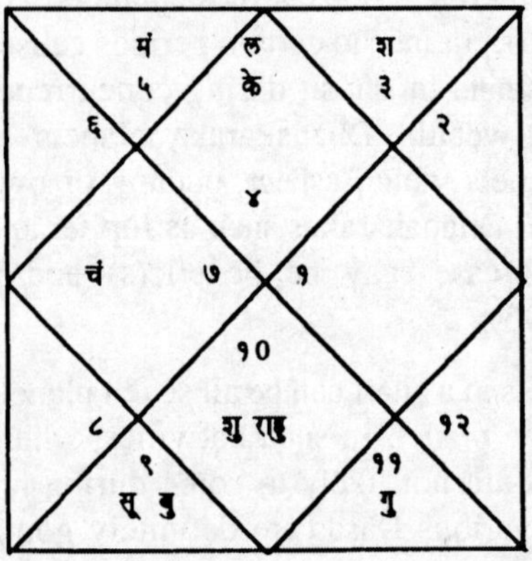

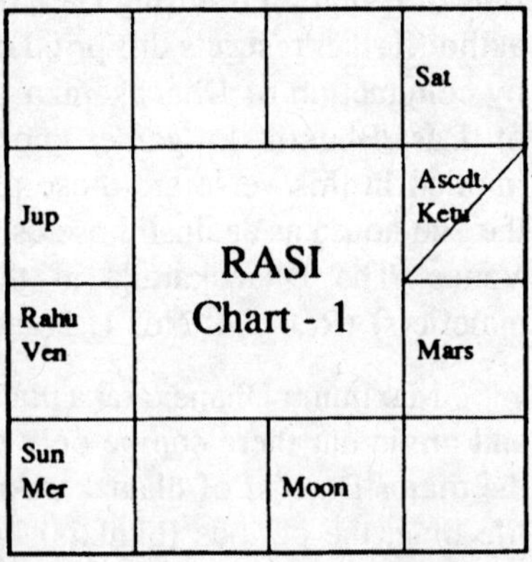

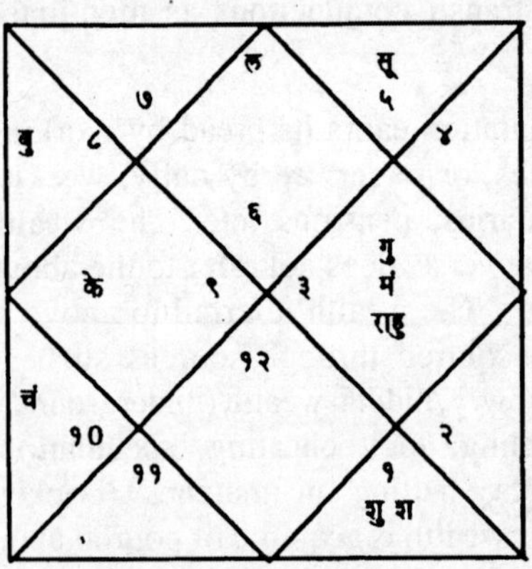

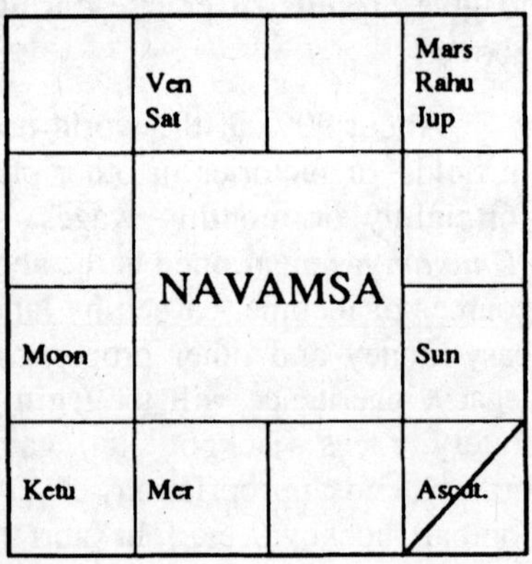

Dhanakaras - (Signifiers of wealth)

1. Jupiter and Saturn aspect the 2nd house;
2. Mars is posited there;
3. The Sun, lord of the 2nd house.

So, there are four Dhanakara planets. The native had earned a good deal of money from speculation many times during his life. Only most outstanding two periods are stated below :

1. During Jupiter Maha Dasa (from 6.7.1926 to 6.7.1942). Mars bhukti (from 6.3.1939 to 10.2.1940) and also during conjunction in transit of Mars and Jupiter (in sign Pisces) from 24-12-1939 to 4-2-1940 - fat amount ranging to five figures was earned by the native from speculation in cotton (running age 25-26).

2. During Saturn's Maha Dasa (from 6.7.1942 to 6.7.1961); Jupiter's bhukti from 23.12.1958 to 6.7.1961) concurrently during transit of 3 planets - Mars, Jupiter and Saurn in sign Sagittarius i.e., from 8.1.1960 to 15.2.1960. Again a fat amount ranging to five figures was earned from speculation in shares. In both events transit Jupiter was powerful being in own sign.

This is just to explain concurrent application of bhukti period and transit conjunction of dhanakara planets :

Chart No. 2 : Date of birth : 23-7-1978; Time 6.00 AM Lat; 23° 2' (N); Long. 72° 37' (E). Balance Dasa of Rahu 4-3-11.

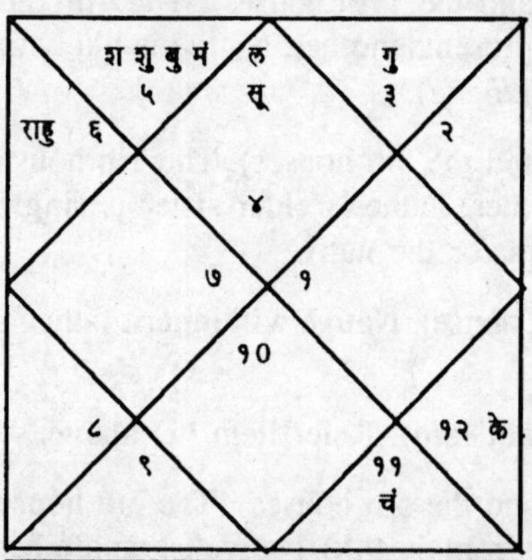

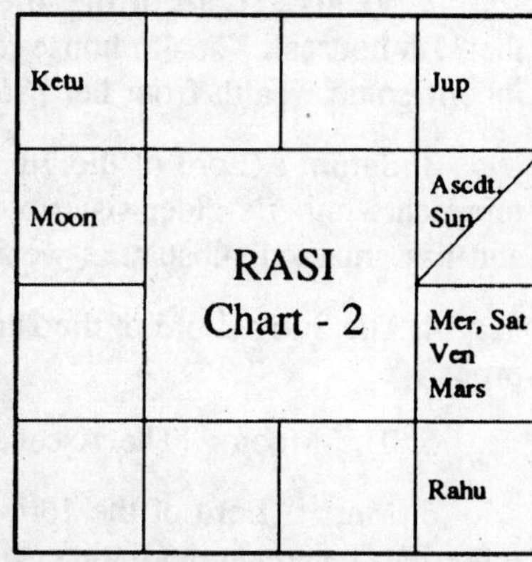

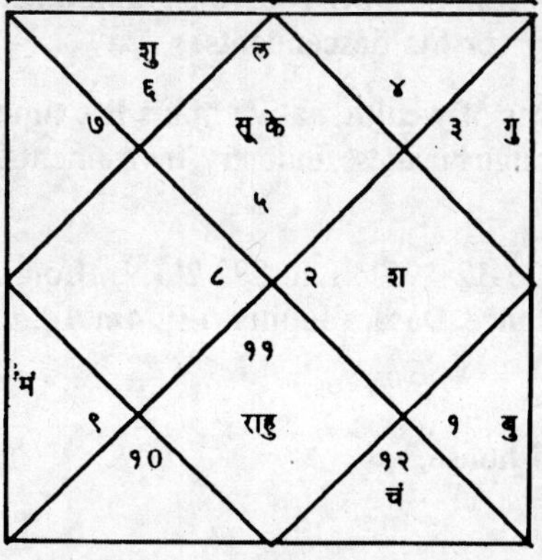

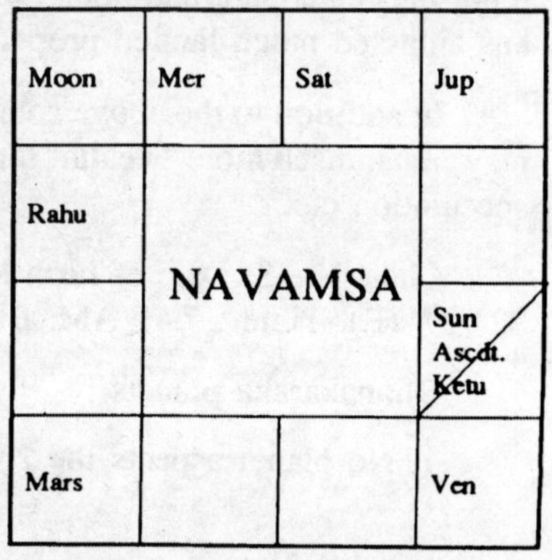

This is the chart of a close relative of the scribe-just completed 13 years.

Dhanakaras :

1. 4 planets - Mercury, Saturn, Venus and Mars in the 2nd house.

2. The Moon aspects the 2nd house.

3. The Sun the - lord of the 2nd house.

So, there are six Dhanakara planets in this chart. Maximum there can be seven Dhanakara planets and minimum one planet only (ref. Chart No. 3).

Sources of "wealth" indicated by Dhanakarakas :

1. Mercury : (Lord of the 3rd and the 12th houses). The 12th house represents *(Matamahah* - mother's father. Native is likely to inherit some landed property from his maternal grandfather.

2. Venus : (Lord of the 4th and the 11th houses). The 4th and the 11th houses). The 4th house represents mother. Native is likely to inherit some wealth from her *(Stridhana)*.

3. Saturn : (Lord of the 7th and the 8th houses). The 7th house represents father's elder sister/brother. Father's elder sister is single and has amassed substantial wealth for the native.

4. The Sun : (Lord of the 2nd house). Native will inherit father's property.

5. The Moon : (The Ascendant lord). Refer item (2) above.

6. Mars : (Lord of the 10th and the 5th houses). The 5th house represents paternal grandfather (9th from the 9th). Native's grandfather has amassed much landed property for his descendants.

In addition to the above sources of wealth, native in his life time may earn himself more "wealth" through business, industry, investments, speculation etc.

Chart No. 3; Date of birth : 25-12-1951; Lat. 23° 2' (N); Long. 72° 37' (E). Time : 7.41 AM. Balance Dasa : Jupiter 13y 4m 1d.

Dhanakaraka planets :

1. No planet aspects the 2nd house.

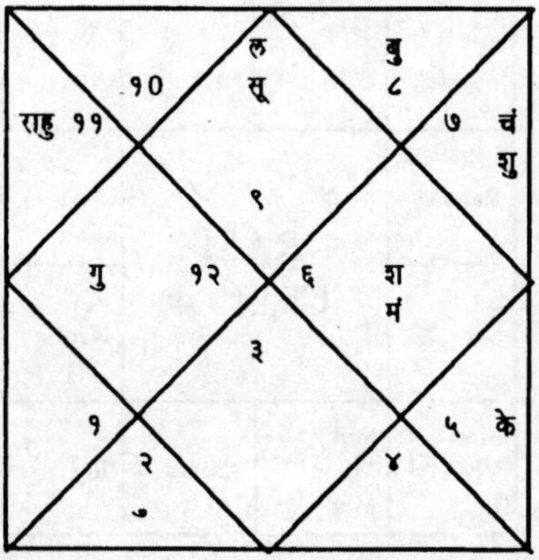

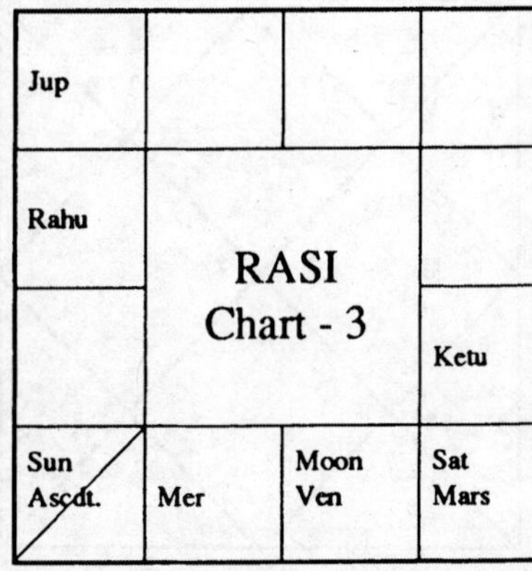

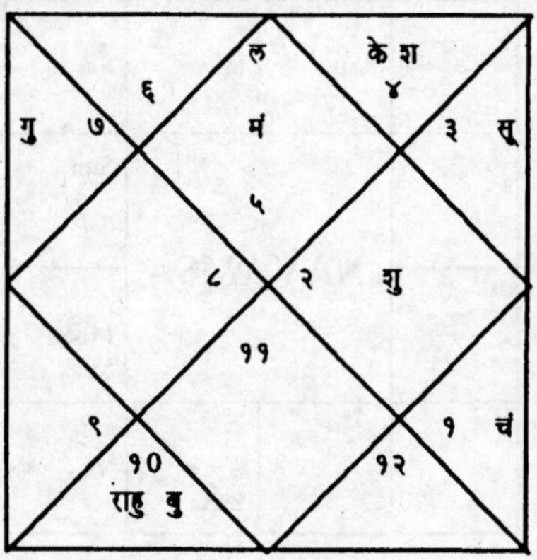

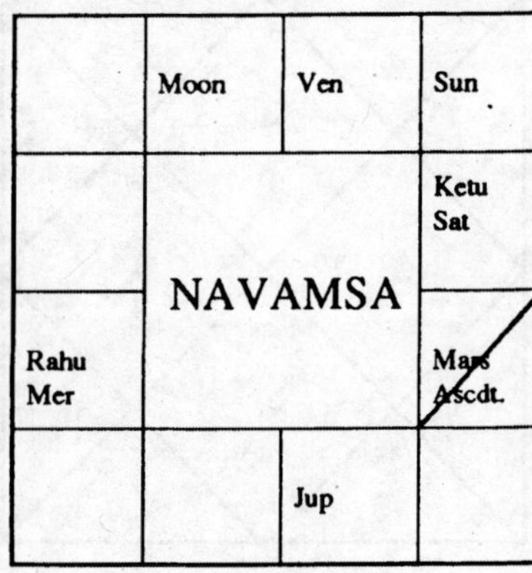

2. No planet is posited there.

3. Saturn the lord of the 2nd house.

There is only one Dhanakaraka planet in this chart. Native may get some wealth during Mahadasa and Bhuktis of Saturn.

Chart No. 4 : Date of birth 17/18.11.1933; Time : 4h 38m AM; Lat. 23° 8' (N); Long. 72° 3' (E). Balance Dasa : Saturn 14y 10m 12d.

Dhanakaraka planets :

1. No planet aspects the 2nd house.

2. The Sun, the Moon and Mercury posited in the 2nd house.

3. Mars the lord ofthe 2nd house.

There are four Dhanakaraka planets in this chart. This native has

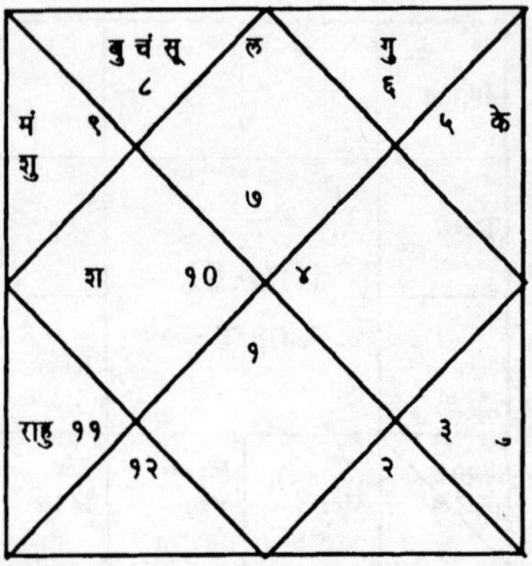

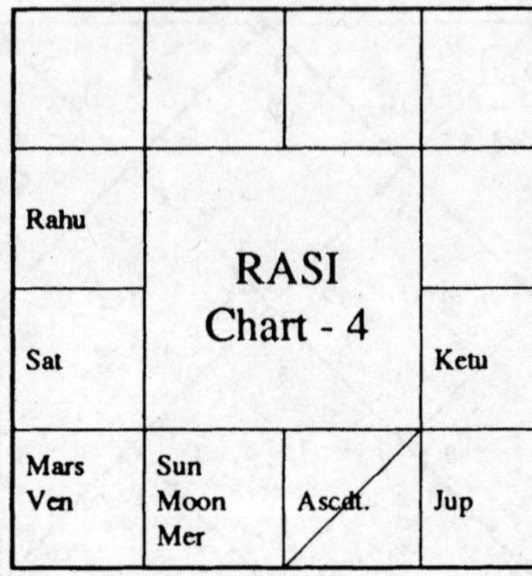

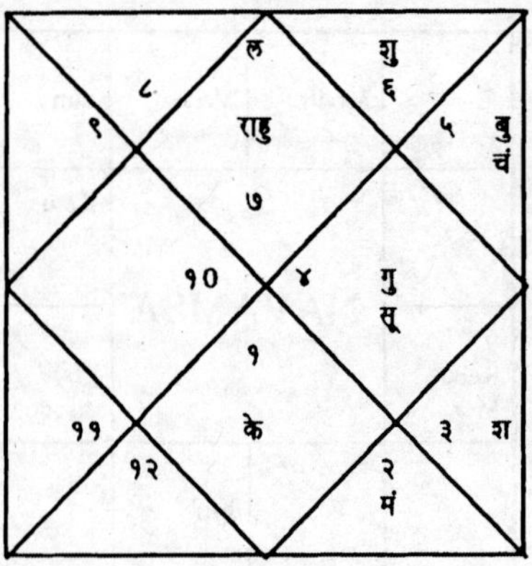

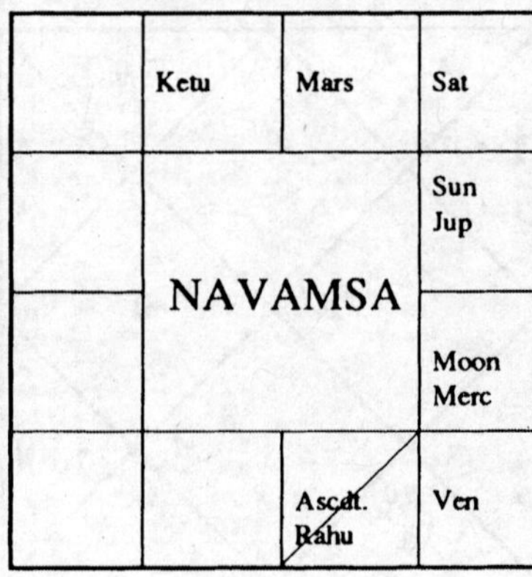

recently inherited on 14.5.1991 a large amount of wealth including much landed property.

During Venus Maha Dasa (from 30.9.1972 to 30.9.1992), Mercury Bhukti (from 30.9.1988 to30.7.1991), Transit conjunction of three Dhanakaraka planets viz. the Sun, the Moon and Mercury took place on 14.5.1991 in sign Aries (the Sun exalted).

Chandra Kala Nadi. Vol. II, Part II p. 183 V. 1286/87 :

"Dehe papagrahairyukte deha peeda vinirdiseth / Jeeve yote jeeva badha dasaa sandhau muhad vipath // 4286 / Chakra sandau manassthaapam yojayeth kalavittamah /

Meaning : When many malefics (three or more) transit Deha Rasi simultaneously, the native suffers from much bodily afflictions (some serious disease;while Jeeva Rasi afflicted likewise, it confers extreme mental apprehension and great calamitiy, much more so, if at that time, there is change of major Dasa (Dasa-Sandhi). An astrologer should indicate great mental anguish, if at that time, same Jeeva Rasi happens to be one of the Chakra Sandhi signs.

(Pisces-Aries; Cancer-Leo; Scorpio-Sagittarius are Chakra Sandhi signs).

Comments : Kala Chakra Dasa system has its own special methods of interpreting results. One outstanding feature of this system is the importance given to 'Deha' and 'Jeeva' rasis. The first Dasa Rasi is Deha and the 9th Dasa Rasi is Jeeva for Savya Nakshatras. In Apasavya Nakshatras, the first Dasa Rasi is Jeeva Rasi while the 9th Dasa Rasi is Deha.

When benefic planets transit through 'Deha' and 'Jeeva' rasis some outstanding auspicious results are promised or are likely to take place.

If both, Deha and Jeeva rasis are transited by malefics only, or by benefics only simultaneously, the consequent bad or good results are multiplied to a great extent.

If more points are found out during further research, the scribe will write "third article" on this subject. Meanwhile, the scholars are requested to refer to the following references for additional information on transit conjuinctions of planets :

1. Phaladeepika Ch. XII, Verse 26 and Ch. XVI, V. 31.

2. Jatakadesa Marga Ch. X, V. 4; and

3. Chandra Kala Nadi Vol. II, Part, II, p. 91, V. 3456 - *Sanyangaarakasamyoge*........... where Sri Achyuta has referred to transit conjunction of Rasi lord (Mars) and Navamsa lord (Saturn) of the Ascendant of the chart discussed.

Readers may find that some hint is mentioned in classicl texts viz. Phaladeepika, Jatakadesa Marga and in Nadi Granthas like Chandra Kala Nadi and significantly in Devagnabharanam with regard to conjunction of planets in transit. Only in Chandra Kala Nadi the significance is brought out with respect to timing due to Dasa Bhukti and also Dasa Sandhi and lastly but not the least in

Chakra Sandhi signs.

Discerning scholars may apply the above principle of Karaka planets with regard to any other bhava just as Dhanabhava shown in this write-up.

27

Conjunction of Planets in Transit - III

The conjunctions of planets in transit are of three types :

1. Sign conjunctions
2. Star conjunctions
3. Navamsa conjunctions

In article 1 (June 91) Chapter-25 and II (Dec. 91) Chapter-26 sign conjunctions only were discussed. Similarly in the present article (III) only sign conjunctions of planets are considered. Almost all the verses are taken from Deva Kerlam Vol. I & II.

In article I, a mention of the epic Ramayanam was made. The scribe had been able to procure the original text of Valmiki Ramayana and the relevant sloka is quoted below for perusal of students :

Valmiki Ramayana - Ayodhya Khanda 4th Sarga, Verse No. 18 -

"Avashtabdam cha meRama nakshamam daaruna grahaih / Avedayanthi daivagnah Suryangaraka rahubhih //

meaning - King Dasaratha says -

"Oh Rama, astrologers communicate that my birth star is afflicted by transit conjunction of malefic planets viz. the Sun, Mars and Rahu."

In article IV, to follow, the scribe proposes to discuss effects produced by conjunctions of planets in transit through Navamsa only i.e., within an arc of 3° 20'.

Deva Keralam Chandra Kala Nadi. Vol. II Part II p. 16, verse 2787 states :

"Yada hi mandena yutascha ketusada bhaved bhoopathi glora yuthan / Tatha mave taskara sainkairva daahaadikratyam jana nasanam cha//"

meaning : "When transit Ketu conjuncts Saturn in transit, a horrible war takes place between two kings, devastating fires etc. and destruction of human beings are caused by thieves and soldiers."

Note : Conjunction between Ketu and Saturn takes place roughly once in every 12 years.

Saturn - Ketu conjunctions -

a. In sign Aries on 14.1.1940

b. In sign Virgo on 19.10.1950

c. In sign Capricorn on 15.10.1962

d. In sign Gemini on 13.9.1973

e. In sign Scorpio on 4.1.1985

Exactly opposite results will be experienced when Rahu conjuncts Saturn.

1. The second world war was started in Sep. 1939 - Ketu (0s - 8° 30) conjuncts Saturn (0s - 7° - 40'). It ended in May/June 1945- Rahu (2s-18°-00') and Saturn (2s-17°-00').

2. China invaded India (North - East Assam) on 15.10.62 (Ketu conjunct Saturn).

3. Israel declared war on Egypt round about Sep/Oct 1973 (Ketu Saturn conjunction).

Ketu is a war-monger and Rahu is a peace maker. It is not out of place to mention here a Tamil Verse -

Rahuvaippol koduppan ilai
Ketuvaippol keduppan illai

2. Deva Keralam Chandra Kala Nadi Vol. I p. 46, V. 471 :

"Aticharagathe Jeeva Sanau Vakratvamagathe / Hahaahaa karam janatsarvam visehaad dakshinadisa //"

meaning - at the time when Jupiter is in accelerated motion and Saturn in retrograde motion the entire world will be wailing aloud in grief, particularly the southern region.

Notes : When Jupiter is accelerated, he is mostly in conjunction with the Sun and Saturn in retrogression is generally in the 6th, 7th from the Sun. In May/June 1989 Jupiter was in accelerated motion in conjunction with the Sun (in sign Taurus) and Saturn was in retrogression (in sign Sagittarius). Thousands of students who agitated were killed in China's capital, Beijing.

This position occurs once in 20 years.

3. Deva Keralam - Chandra Kala Nadi, Vol. II, Part I, p. 222, V. 2054.

"Meenasthe Vrischikanthecha yugme simhe cha madhyame / Yaavath sthithau manda jeevau taavad durbhiksham adiseth//"

meaning - When Saturn and Jupiter conjunct in the end (last few degrees) of signs Pisces and Scorpio and in the middle" (round about 15°) of signs Gemini and Leo, famine takes place.

Note : This conjunction would take place roughly once in 20 years provided it falls in the above referred degreecal position.

4. Deva Keralam Chandra Kala Nadi, Vol. I, p. 140, v. 1479.

"Keete chapanchaana karkatesh - varkissavakro asana bhithidah syaath / Sri CholaPandye Vrisha - bhachalese yuddham nripanam para chakramahuh //"

meaning - Transit Saturn in conjunction with Mars in sign Scorpio or Leo or Cancer causes invasion of armies and consequent war takes place between the Kings of Chola, Pandya and Vrishabhachala.

Note : *"Arkih savakrah"* is interpreted as Saturn together with Mars. These conjunctions take place four or five times during Saturn's period of 30 years cycle.

5. Deva Keralam Chandra Kala Nadi Vol. II, Part I, p. 124, V. 1091.

"Guru Rahu yuthe kaale rajamathya janavadhi / rajanya jana santhapobrahmananan mahadhhayam //"

meaning - When Jupiter and Rahu conjunct, there will be

replacements of rulers and ministers; some distress in government, people, and great fear in Brahmin community.

Notes : This conjunction takes place roughly once in 7 to 8 years.

6. Eclipses :

Eclipses are nothing but transit conjunctions of two or three planets at a time in a sign out of the four planets the Sun, the Moon, Rahu and Ketu.

a. The Sun conjunct the Moon conjunct Rahu, in opposite sign Ketu- eclipse of the Sun. The Sun conjunct the Moon conjunct Ketu, in opposite sign Rahu-eclipse of the Sun.

b. The Sun conjunct Rahu - in opposite sign - the Moon conjunct Ketu - eclipse of the Moon;

and the Sun conjunct Ketu in opposition to the Moon conjunct Rahu - Eclipse of the Moon.

Natural calamities such as earth quakes, cyclones etc. are ascribed to occurrence of eclipses.

If the degree of an eclipse falls on native's Ascendant degree or planetary position, it creates some event favourable or unfavourable, all of a sudden in his life.

The conjunction is good or bad which depends on the two planets involved in conjunction, whether they are benefics or malefics by nature or by lordship or by situation in certain houses. Experience shows that too much importance should not be attached to natural benefics or malefics. Two conjuncting benefic planets produce good result and two conjuncting malefic ones produce evil results. If, one of them is benefic and the other is malefic, the result is mixed.

Conjunctions of fast moving planets do not cause long lasting effects, while those of slow-moving planets indicate turning points in mundane (or political) astrology.

The ultimate result of a conjunction depends on the houses ruled by the conjuncting planets and the sign or star in which the conjunction takes place.

28

Conjunction of Planets in Transit - IV

In the previous three articles (June 1991 Chapter-25; December 1991 Chapter-26; and November 1992 Chapter-27) "Conjunctions of Planets in Transit" through a sign (30°) were discussed. In the present and the last instalment, it is proposed to highlight the results of conjunctions of planets during transit through one Navamsa (3° 20' = 200 minutes of arc) only.

Conjunctions of planets in Navamsa chart are of two types :

(i) Conjunctions of planets in Navamsa sign, posited in Rasi chart at a distance of 40°, 80°, 120°, 160°, 200°, 240°, 280° or 320° (known as nonile aspect).

(ii) Conjunction of planets in Navamsa sign, posited in one Navamsa of 3° 20' i.e., those same planets having conjunction in sign in Rasi chart and the same planets conjuncting in one Navamsa in Navamsa chart also.

The present article deals with the second type of conjunction.

a. Vidyamadhaviyam Part - III P. 175 : "In any sign; if the Sun and Saturn be in conjunction in Navamsa (in transit), and at a time when that Navamsa is rising in the East, it is beneficial to purchase (or acquire) black-iron (quality of iron available in olden days). Under similar position of Venus and Ketu, one should buy and store chariots (vehicles) and armaments for future benefits."

b. Vidamadhaviyam Part III P. 175 : "In any sign, if Venus and

Ketu be in conjunction in a Navamsa (in transit) and at a time when that Navamsa is rising in the East, it is beneficial to acquire (purchase) and store Chhatra (an umbrella - an emblem of honour), chariots (vehicles) and armaments.

c. Vidyamadhaviyam Part - III p. 174 : "In own or Mulatrikona sign, if Venus and the Sun be in conjunction, in a Navamsa (in transit) and at a time when that Navamsa is rising in the East, one should purchase and store silver, so its price would go up day by day (in course of time).

d. Vidyamadhaviyam Part - III p. 174 : "In any sign, if the Moon and Venus be in conjunction in a Navamsa (in transit) and at a time when that Navamsa is rising in the East, one should purchase cereals, clothes and silver, so their prices would go up later on."

e. Vidyamadhaviyam Part - III p. 174 : "In any sign, if the Sun and Rahu be in conjunction (barring eclipse time) in a Navamsa (in transit) and at a time when that Navamsa is rising in the East, one should take possession of land (purchase etc.) so that its price would go up later on."

f. Vidyamadhaviyam Part III p. 187 : "In any sign, if Jupiter and Venus be in conjunction in a Vargottama Navamsa (in transit) and at a time when that Navamsa is rising in the East, one should have conversation with an enemy, so that they (native and enemy) would become mutual friends."

g. Vidyamadhaviyam Part - III Page 181 : "In any sign, if Jupiter and Ketu be in conjunction in a Navamsa (in transit) and at a time when that Navamsa is rising in the East, one should see his master or enemy or anyone else, that person will become his friend.

h. Vidyamadhaviyam Part - III P. 181 : Comments : One Navamsa is 3° 20' : time taken by an arc of one Navamsa to rise in the East is about 13m 20s (3° 20' x 4 minutes). The Navamsa conjunction of fast moving planets lasts hardly for a few days : that of slow moving planets e.g., Jupiter, Ketu etc. lasts for a longer period i.e., 10, 15, 20, 30 or even more days.

In the previous three articles on "Conjunctions of Planets in Transit" rules for timing future events have been discussed, in the present one the rules explained are to be put to use for future monetary gains and other advantages. These rules are discussed in Vidyamadhaviyam Part - III in main text as well as in reference verses.

There are still more vcrses of the kind, but only selected ones have been included in the write-up. For more and varied details scholars can refer to Part - III of this book.

Commercial astrologers may find useful hints for their research as to when to buy commodities; shares and stock; silver; gold etc. They can also use their brains to find out rules based on the above principles as to when to sell their purchased items.

29

Transits - Good & Bad Phases as per Deva Keralam

Deva Keralam introduces many rare concepts and techniques which are not traceable in other classical texts. In this write up an attempt is made to bring to the notice of every serious student and researcher, one such hitherto unknown technique.

Adba means a year and yearly transit refers to Jupiter's transit only. Masa means a month and monthly transit refers to the Sun's transit only. Krura abda means transit of Jupiter through Krura sign. Krura masa means transit of the Sun through Krura sign.

The transit of Jupiter through Subha sign is said to be Shubha abda and transit of the Sun through a Subha sign is said to be Shubha masa.

The usual Krura signs owned by malefic planets and Subha signs owned by benefic planets are not referred in this technique.

Venkatesa - the author of Volume II, Part I and Part II (Deva Keralam) has defined Krura rasi in unique manner, only at one place and that too in two lines out of a total of 9182 verses :

In Deve Keralam, Volume II part I verses 1774 1/2 and 1775 1/2.

रन्ध्रेशाक्रान्तभवनदृष्टराश्यंशकोणगाः ।
क्रूरमासा इति ख्याताः क्रूराब्दे योजयेत् क्रमात् ॥

Meaning - "The sign occupied by the lord of the 8th house and its trines - sign or signs aspected by him and the sign identical with Navamsa occupied by him (the 8th lord) and trines thereof, are said to be Krura signs. Transits of the Sun through them are known as Krura months and transit of Jupiter is said to be known as Krura year."

In six Ascendants from Aries to Virgo (Ist group) the lords of the 8th signs (houses) therefrom are Mars, Jupiter, Saturn, Saturn, Jupiter and Mars respectively. These three planets have two more extra aspects in addition to the usual 7th house aspect. As such Krurasigns for them will be more as compared to the remaining six Ascendants. In ascendants from Libra to Pisces (2nd group) the lords of the 8th sign (houses) therefrom are Venus, Mercury, the Moon, the Sun, Mercury and Venus respectively. These four planets have only one full aspect. i.e., the 7th house aspect, so the total number of krura signs will beless in this case.

Chart I - the scribe's chart with Cancer Ascendant.

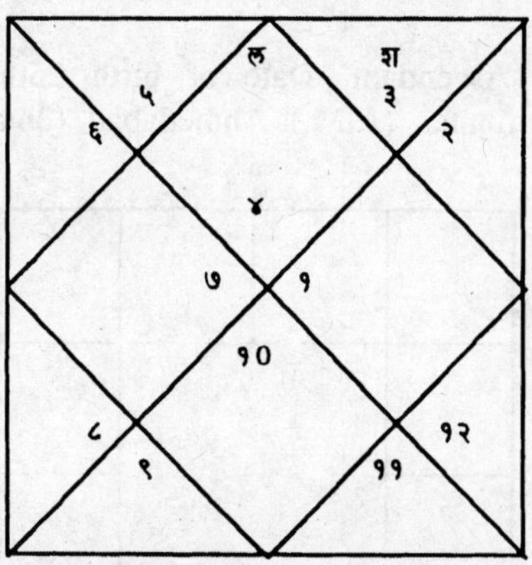

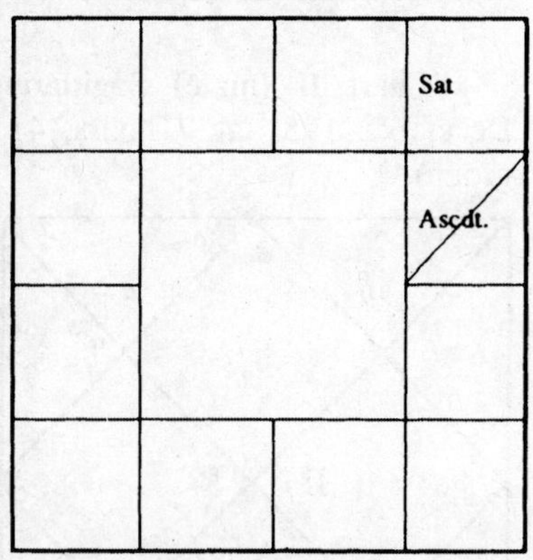

Date of birth : 31st December 1915 at 7 hours 43 minutes (PM) Ahmedabad (Ist group).

The lord of the 8th house Saturn (2s 20° 42') is in Gemini, its trines are Libra and Aquarius; Saturn's aspected signs are Leo, Sagittarius and Pisces, Saturn is posited in Aries Navamsa and its trines are Leo and Sagittarius.

8th lord Saturn's and trines 3-7-11, 8th lord aspected signs 5-9-12;

8th lord Navamsa sign and trines 1.5.9.

In short 1 - 3 - 5 - 7 - 9 - 11 and 12 are Krura signs for the native. The remaining five signs are Subha signs.

From the above table it can be observed that the deaths of scribe's close relatives had taken place during the transits of Saturn and Jupiter through Krura signs only.

Dates of demise of scribe's close relatives	Transit Saturn	Transit Jupiter
Daughter 29th April 1954	Libra 7	Gemini 3
Mother 30th November 1965	Aquarius 11	Gemini 3
Father 15th June 1968	Pisces 12	Leo 5
Wife 24th January 1975	Gemini 3	Aquarius 11
Sister (1) 25th September 1989	Sagittarius 9	Gemini 3
Sister (2) 23rd August 1994	Aquarius 11	Libra 7

Chart II (male) Sagittarius Ascendant. Date of birth 25th December 1951 at 7 hours, 41 minutes (A.M.) Ahmedabad (2nd group).

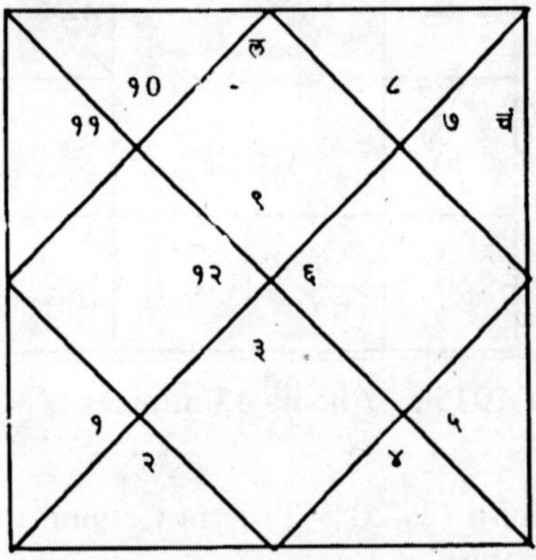

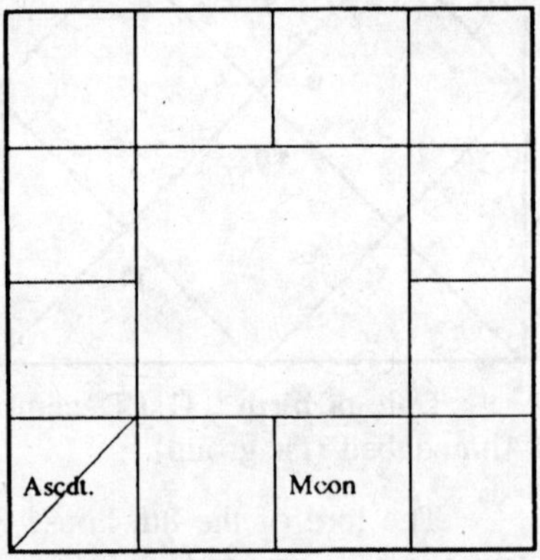

The lord of the 8th house, the Moon (6 - 22° - 13') is in Libra and its trines are Gemini andAquarius. Her aspected sign is Aries. She is in Aries Navamsa - trines are Leo and Sagittarius.

8th lord, the Moon and trines 7-3-11 The 8th lord aspected signs - 1

8th lord Navmsa sign and trines 1 - 5 - 9.

In short 1 - 3 - 5 - 7 - 9 and 11 are Krura signs for the native. The remaining signs 2 - 4 - 6 - 8 - 10 and 12 are Subha signs.

According to this principle Jupiter's transit through his own signs Sagittarius and Pisces; exalted sign Cancer and kendra and kona houses will not give favourable results, if these signs happen to be Krura signs in a nativity.

On the contrary, Jupiter's transit through his enemies' signs, debilitation sign (Capricorn) and evil houses (6th, 8th and12th), will bear favourable results if these signs happen to be Subha signs.

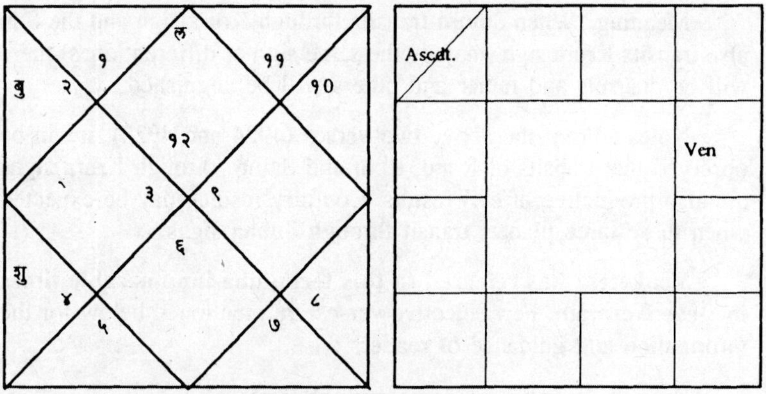

Deva Keralam, Volume II Part I verse - 4923.

कुलीरसिंहालिझषे कुम्भे नक्रे दिवाकरे ।
क्रूरराशिमिति प्रोक्तं क्रूरमासं तथैव च ॥

Meaning ; "Cancer, Leo, Scorpio, Pisces, Aquarius and Capricorn are said to be Krura signs and transit of the Sun (through any one of them) is said to be Krura month."

Verse No. 4923 (above is from Pisces - Ascendant - shitalaamsa).

The lord of the 8th house Venus is in Cancer. Aspected sign is Capricorn and Scorpio and Pisces as trine signs from Venus. her Navamsa position is not mentioned in the text. Leo andAquarius signs are not accounted, perhaps they are the 2nd and the 8th signs from Venus (2nd group).

8th lord Venus and trines - 4 -8 - 12

8th lord Venus aspected sign - 11

Navamsa trines not mentioned in the text.

गोचरे क्रूरराशीषु राहुकेतुशनैश्चराः ।
स्फुटयोगं गतास्तत्र स्वजनादिप्रपीडिताः ।। V. 4924.

Meaning - "When Rahu, Ketu and Saturn transit through such Krura signs, over certain degrees, close relatives will be anguished."

स्वपिताक्रूरमासेषु क्रूरराशौ शनैश्चरे
सञ्चारकाले क्लेशं च पित्रादीनां मनोव्यथा ।। V. 4925.

Meaning "When Saturn transits through Krura sign and the Sun also transits Krura sign (may be the same sign or different ones) there will be quarrels and father and others will be anguished."

Notes : From the above two verses (4924 and 4925), it can be observed that transits of Rahu, Ketu and Saturn through Krura signs are also productive of evil results. Contrary results may be expected when these three planets transit through Subha signs.

Venketesa has referred to this technique innumerable times in Deve Keralam. Few selective verses are mentioned below for the information and guidance of readers :

विपद्धाये पित्ररिष्टं वृश्चिकान्त्यांशगे गुरौ ।
अथवा मकरे मृत्युः क्रूराब्दे क्रूरमासगे ।।

Meaning - "During third Dasa Jupiter's transit through the last Navamsa of Scorpio or through Capricorn, will prove fatal to the native's fatheror a near relative; Jupiter's transit through Krura sign and the Sun's transit also through similar sign at a time will cause death."

विवाहोत्सवकार्याणि स्वपितुर्भाग्यकालगे ।
शुभाब्दगे शुभं नित्यं क्रूराब्दे व्याकुलं महत् ।।

Meaning - "Marriage festivities will take place, during the father's fortunate period. During Jupiter's transit through Subha sign (Shubha abda) happiness will continue to prevail; while during adverse transit of Jupiter (Krura-abda) native will be in great trouble."

सुतराशिदशाकाले क्रूराब्दे क्रूरमासगे

अपमृत्युभयप्राप्तिः शान्त्या शान्तिं प्रयास्यति ॥

Meaning - "During the dasa of the 5th sign (Capricorn - in Virgo, Ascendant) Jupiter and the Sun's transits through Krura sign or signs will cause untimely death, suitable remedies be performed."

लाभाधिपदशाकाले शुभाब्दे शुभमासगे ।
राजयोगाभिवृद्धिः स्यात् सदा राजप्रसादवान् ॥

Meaning - "In the Dasa ruled by the 11th lord (Jupiter in Aquarius Ascendant) during Jupiter and the Sun's transits through Subha sign or signs, the native will see increased prosperity and will continue to receive royal favours."

रन्ध्राधिपदशाकाले वेधकग्रहभुक्तिषु ।
क्रूराब्दे क्रूरमासे च स्वजनारिष्टशोकवान् ॥

Meaning - "During the Dasa of the 8th lord and in the sub-period of an obstructive planet, the native will incur grief on account of troubles to his men, when Jupiter and the Sun transit Krura sign or signs."

षष्ठाष्टमाधीशदाये दुःस्थानग्रहभुक्तिषु ।
क्रूराब्दके शत्रुभीतिर्दानं कुर्याद्विचक्षण ॥

Meaning- "During the Dasa of the 6th lord or the 8th iord and in sub-periods of planets placed in evil houses (6th, 8th or 12th), coinciding with Jupiter's transit through Krura sign, fear from enemies will strike. To overcome such an evil, charities be given away."

क्रूराब्दगे महाकष्टं विप्लवेन धनव्ययम् ।
शुभाब्दगे धनप्राप्तिं प्रबलोद्योगभाग्यवान् ॥

Meaning - "The native will be subjected to great trouble during Jupiter's transit through Krura sign; he will have loss of wealth in revolution (or public outrage). He will obtain wealth and will be lucky to have prosperous industry during Jupiter's transit through Subha sign."

The scribe fervently hopes that ardent students of sidereal astrology will make further research on this technique.

30

Importance of Deha and Jeeva Rasis

The Kalachakra Dasa system has its own special methods of horoscopic interpretation. One outstanding feature of this system is that it gives much importance to Deha and Jeeva Rasis. The first Dasa Rasi is Deha and the 9th Dasa Rasi is Jeeva for Savya Nakshatras. In Apasavya Nakshatras the first Dasa Rasi is Jeeva Rasi while the 9th Rasi is Deha one.

Instead of going through a cumbersome procedure to find these Rasis, one should refer to some books giving ready-made tables and find out the Deha and Jeeva Rasis form the Nakshatra-pada or the quarter occupied by the Moon at birth.

Deha Rasis in Savya and Apasavya Nakshatras are seven signs only viz., Aries, Taurus, Cancer, Libra, Scorpio, Capricorn, and Aquarius and their lords are only four planets viz., The Moon, Mars, Venus and Saturn. Jeeva Rasis in both sets of Nakshatras are only four signs viz., Gemini, Virgo, Sagittarius and Pisces and their lords are two planets only i.e., Mercury and Jupiter.

The sign Leo does not come into the picture, so the planet Sun, cannot be either Deha or Jeeva Rasi lord. Students should bear in mind this point very well, while studying Kalachakra Dasa system.

In short, these Deha and Jeeva Rasis are very sensitive ones, and placement of planets in these signs in the birth chart, as well as transit of all the 9 planets, malefic or benefic, through them are productive of certain peculiar results (given at the end of this article).

The natal placement of benefic planets only in them indicates important developments (rises in life) and of malefic planets only indicates dreadful diseases, fall in life ets., in the native's life. When Deha Rasi is occupied by a malefic (e.g. Saturn, Rahu, Ketu or Mars), there will be disease, bodily afflictions etc. When Jeeva Rasi is afflicted likewise, calamity, mental anguish, extreme fear, apprehension, great risk etc., are indicated. Natives having no planets in these signs have normal lives.

Frist of all, one should find out whether Deha or Jeeva Rasi in a chart is occupied or unoccupied by planets. There can be only three possibilities:

(i) Both Rasis are vacant;

(ii) One Rasi is vacant and the other is occupied by planets; and

(iii) Both Rasis are occupied by the planets as in the case of example chart.

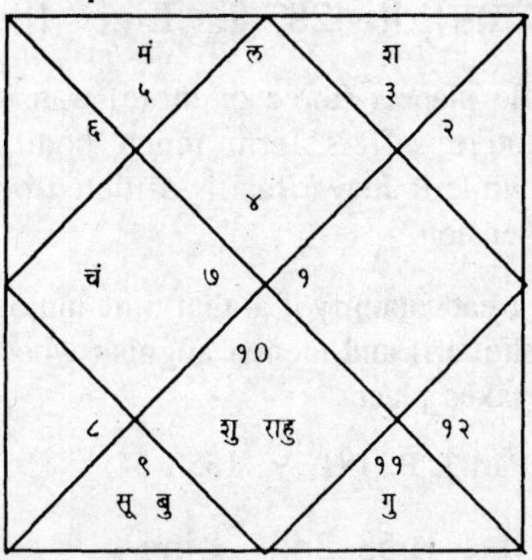

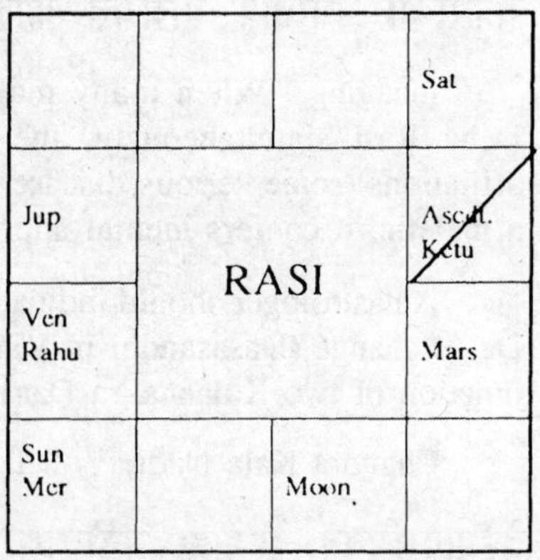

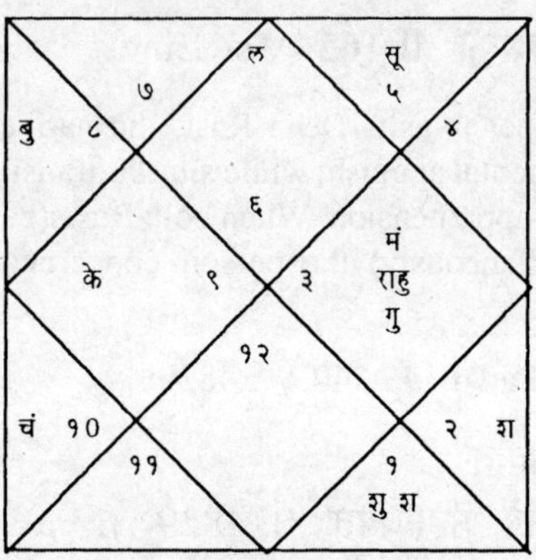

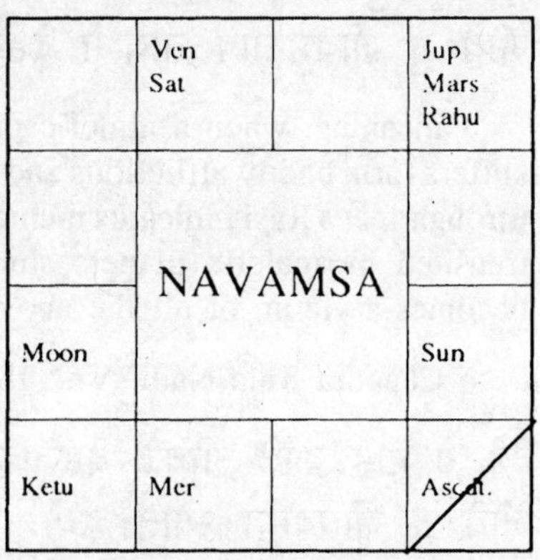

C.S. Patel: Born on 31-12-1915 at 7-44 p.m. (IST) at 23-2 N, x 72-39 E.

Rasi: The Sun 256-10; the Moon 192-13; Mars 127-9;Mercury 265-13; Jupiter 329-29; Venus 283-14; Saturn (R) 80-42; Rahu 287-06; Ketu 107-06; and Ascendant 98-53 with a balance of 10 years, 6 months and 3 days of Rahu Dasa at birth.

The Moon is 6^s 12^0 13^1(Swati Star 2nd Pada - Capricorn Navamsa). Deha Rasi Capricorn sign and Jeeva Rasi is Gemini Sign, whose lords are Saturn (Dehadhipati) and Mercury (Jeevadhipati) respectively.

Chandra Kala Nadi Vol. II - Part II, P. 183, Vs. 4286 and 4287 (1st line)

देहेपापग्रहैर्युक्ते देहपीडां विनिर्दिशेत् । जीवे पापे जीवबाधा दशासन्धौ महाविपत् । 4286
चक्रसन्धौ मनस्तापं योजयेत् कालवित्तमः ।। 4287 1st Line ।।

meaning, "When many malefic planets (three or more) transit Deha Rasi simultaneously, the native suffers form much bodily afflictions (some serious disease), while if Jeeva Rasi is afflicted by a malefic, it confers mental apprehension.

An astrologer should indicate great calamity if at that time major Dasas change (Dasasandhi in Vimshottari) and mental anguish when junction of two Kalachakra Dasas takes place."

Chandra Kala Nadi, Vol. II, Part I, P. 181, V, 1653-54:

देहेपापेसंयुक्ते देहपीडा मनोव्यथा ।। 1653 2nd Line
जीवे तु जीवसन्तापं तावुभौ देहनाशकौ ।। 1654 1st Line

meaning, when a malefic planet transits Deha Rasi, the native suffers form bodily afflictions and mental anguish; while similar transit through Jeeva Rasi indicates mental apprehension. When both Rasis(be transited by malefic planets simultaneously) the person concerned becomes a victim of all the above.

Chandra Kala Nadi, Vol. II, Part II, P. 240, V. 4829:

देहे पापग्रहे काले गोचरे देहजाड्यकृत्
जीवे तु जीवबाधा स्यात् द्वयोः पापे महाविपत् ।। 4829 ।।

Compare - Chandra Kala Nadi, Vol. I, P. 100, V. 1060:

देहे पापग्रहे काले गोचरे देहजाड्यकृत् ।
जीवे तु जीवबाधा स्यात् व्ययस्थे च महाविपत् ।। 1060 ।।

In the above three verses the first three padas, indicate more or less the same results. In the fourth pada (V. 1060) the author refers to one more point. He says if Deha Rasi or Jeeva Rasi falls in the 12th house in natal chart, the native suffers form great calamity. Scholars should make deep research on this point i.e.in which house (i.e. in the 6th 8th or the 12th house) Deha or Jeeva Rasi falls. In some cases both Deha and Jeeva Rasis fall in the 8th and in the 12th houses, e.g., in Leo Ascendant, with the Moon in Revati 4th pada, Deha Rasi, Cancer and Jeeva Rasi, Pisces will fall in the 12th and the 8th houses respectively. With change in the Ascendant, the houses in which these Rasis fall, will change. In Scorpio Ascendant, the same Moon, Revati 4th pada, Deha Rasi Cancer and Jeeva Rasi Pisces will fall in the 9th house and in the 5th house respectively (both Kona houses). this will cause a lot of change in results to the native for the better.

Chandra Kala Nadi, Vol. II, Part II, P. 240, V. 4830:

जीवराशिगते भौमे जन्माब्दे जन्मदायगे ।
मान्द्यज्वरव्रणादीनि नेत्रपीडा क्वचित् क्वचित् ।। 4830 ।।

meaning, "When Mars transits Jeeva Rasi druing the first Dasa (Jamadayage) in the first year of life, the child suffers from indigestion, fever, ulcer (wounds) etc. and sometimes eye disease as well".

Comments: Note the effects produced by the fast moving planet Mars. When slow-moving planet (namely Saturn, Rahu, Ketu or Jupiter) transits through Deha or Jeeva Rasi, events unfavourable or favourable take place. Simultanceously, transit of fast moving planets (namely, the Sun, Mars, Mercury or Venus) through either Rasi will pin-point the probable period of occurrence of events to a month or so.

Chandra Kala Nadi: Vol. II, Part II, P. 194, V. 4396, 2nd line:

देहे जीवे राहुयुते ह्ययमृत्युभयं क्वचित् ।। 4396 ।। 2nd line

Meaning, "When Rahu transits either Deha or Jeeva Rasi sometimes fear of untimely death is there."

Simultaneous Transits of Planets :

Jataka Parijata, Chapter XVII, Verse 14, second line and Verse 15, 1st line:

देहजीवे यदा राहु केतुर्भौमो रविः स्थितः ।। 14 ।। 2nd line
तदा तस्मिन् भवेन्मृत्युर्देहे रोगः प्रवर्तते ।। 15 ।। 1st line

meaning, "When Rahu, Ketu, Mars and the Sun transit through both Deha and Jeeva Rasis, there will be death consequently. If they transit Deha Rasi alone disease is the result."

Jataka Pariata, Chapter XVII, V. 15, 2nd line and Verse 16:

देहजीवगृहं यातः सौम्ये जीवश्चभार्गवः ।। 15 ।।
सुखसंपत्करं सर्व शोकरोगविनाशनम् ।
मिश्रखेचरसंयुक्ते मिश्रं फलमवाप्नुयात् ।। 16 ।।

meaning, "When Mercury, Jupiter and Venus transit simultaneously Deha and jeeva Rasis, everything leads to happiness and prosperity, sorrow and sickness come to an end. When Deha or Jeeva sign is transited by a mixture of planets (benefic and malefic), the result will be of mixed nature."

Prasna Marga, Chapter X, Verse 10:

देहजीवेशयोरेकस्यासद्योगो गदप्रदः ।
द्वयोस्सह स चेन्मृत्युर्दशा चेदशुभादृढम् ।। 10 ।।

meaning, "If an evil planet, conjoins during transit, with the lord of Deha or Jeeva Rasi, it causes sickness; and if both Deha and Jeeva lords be simultaneously conjoined with malefics and should the Dasa at that time also prove unfavourable, it will cause death."

Comments : A similar verse is found in Jatakadeshamarga (Chap. XII verse 26) with minor variations in text, e.g. there is तयोः in place of द्वयोः and ध्रुवम् in place of दृढम् in the second line. Whether, the transit referred to in the verse takes place through any other sign or through Deha or Jeeva sign, is not clear. The scribe thinks that transit shoud be either through Deha or Jeeva sign or through both signs.

In the example chart, there can be four possiblities:

(1) Saturn (lord of Deha sign) and a malefic planet in one sign;

(2) Mercury (lord of Jeeva sign) and a malefic planet in one sign;

(3) Saturn, Mercury and a malefic planet in either Deha sign (Capricorn) or in Jeeva sign (Gemini):

(4) Saturn, Mercury and a malefic planet in any sign out of the remaining 10 signs.

In this and the next verse the author refers to one more point i.e., the lords - Dehadhipati and Jeevadhipati are considered.

Prasna Marga, Chapter X, Verse 17:

देहजीवेशयोर्योगराशिगोऽपि बृहस्पतिः।
पापग्रहाश्च तत्रस्था नृणां मरणदायिनः ॥ 17 ॥

meaning, "Death can also take place when Jupiter transits the Rasi arrived at by adding the longitudes of the lords of Deha and Jeeva signs, provided other malefics also pass through the same sign simultaneously".

Comments : In the example chart Deha sign is Capricorn whose lord is Saturn (80° 42') and Jeeva sing is Gemini whose lord is Mercury (265°13') i.e. resultant sign is Pisces in this case (345 ° 55') . This sign can be any sign out of the twelve signs. It can be even Deha or Jeeva sign in some cases.

When Jupiter transits this sign Pisces along with other malefics, unfavourable results may take place as indicated. It may be noted that even Jupiter's (a first-rate benefic planet) transit causes death.

The following are the results suggested in standard texts when planets occupy Deha or Jeeva Rasis:

(1) The Sun - Adversities of various sorts; loss of wealth; disease, fever; risk from enemies; loss of position; bilious complaints; spleen; diarrohoea; consumption; ear-troubles; loss of brother, cattle and relations.

(2) The Moon - Association with one's own kith and kin; acquisition of virgin girl as a help-mate; good health; armaments; luxurious apparel; respect from rulers; giving charities; visting pilgrim places; baths in holy waters and pleasant meals.

(3) Mars - Inflammation of body; disease; dread of fire and robbers; quarrels with kindred; death of dear realtion; loss of land and treasure; fall from position; colic; piles; leprosy; danger form poison; enemies and reptiles; fever; small pox; biliousness; tumour; fire; weapons; fear form robbers and foes.

(4) Mercury - Favours from benevolent and trusty persons; knowledge of science; good menners; insight into Vedas; philosophy; acquistion of women; progeny; wife; royal ornaments; cattle, elephants; increase of wisdom, wealth, intellect and fame.

(5) Jupiter - Joys of affluence; eminent rank; esteem of rulers and similar honours; family life; armaments; abundant food; wealth, health, fame; victory and helping others.

(6) Venus - Sexual delight; society of elite women; interest in art; riches; good clothes; cattle; vehicles; precious stones; musical concerns; dancing parties; good fame; charity and company of virtuous persons.

(7) Saturn - Quarrels; physical pain; deaths; trouble from relatives; dread of fire, enemies and ghosts; trouble from venomous reptiles; loss of honour, wealth and self-respect; deprivation of affection form wife and children; loss in agriculture, trade, wealth and of place.

(8) Rahu - Trouble from enemies; relations in trouble; aimless wanderings; afflicted with palsy and fear from the ruler.

(9) Ketu - Troubles from thieves and fire; bleeding, poverty; loss of relations, wealth and place.

Notes: In the example chart Deha Rasi is Capricorn and Jeeva Rasi is Gemini.

Saturn's transit through Capricorn form 20-3-1990 to 5-3-1993 Rahu's transit through Capricorn form 20-9-1989 to 13-3-1991; and Ketu's transit through Gemini form 13-4-1991 to 30-10-1992.

The scribe had suffered a hell of calamities such as death of sister; quarrels with relatives and friends; sickness to self (four times); great loss of wealth and self-respect; trouble from enemies; relations in great trouble; loss of money in fixed deposit receipts (being not honoured); mental apprehension is still going on. All these troubles will continue till 30-10-1992 (Ketu) and 5-3-1993 (Saturn).

Analysis of Deha and Jeeva Rasis :-

Out of 27 Nakshatras, 15 are savya ones and 12 are Apasavya ones. Each Nakshatra has four padas (Navamsa), as such there are in all 108 padas for Deha Rasi and 108 padas for Jeeva Rasis. Only four planets, the Moon, Mars, Venus and Saturn are allotted each 27 padas for Deha Rasi. Mars own two signs; Aries allotted 18 padas and Scopio 9 padas, Venus owns two signs; Taurus allotted 18 padas and Libra 9 padas, Saturn owns two signs; Capricorn allotted 18 padas and Aquarius 9 padas, so there are double chances for Aries Deha Rasi, Taurus Deha Rasi and Capricorn Deha Rasi as compared to Scorpio, Libra and Aquarius Deha Rasis respectively.

Only two planets Jupiter and Mercury are allotted each 54 padas for Jeeva Rasis. Jupiter owns two signs; Sagittarius allotted 27 padas and Pisces also 27 padas both equally. Mercury owns two signs. Gemini allotted 36 padas while Virgo 18 padas only. So there are double chances for Gemini Jeeva Rasis as compared to Virgo Jeeva Rasis.

31

Use of Rahu/Ketu in Prognostication

Why is so much importance being given to Rahu/ Ketu? Rahu and Ketu (the Moon's ascending and descending nodes) are not visible planets, nor bodies of matter, they are merely points of interesection in space of the celestial ecliptic and the orbit of the Moon. The northern point of inter-section is known as Rahu (ascending node-Dragon's head) and the Southern one as Ketu (Descending node - Dragon's tail). They are always retrograde and in continuous motion. The time taken by them to complete one round of the zodiac is 18.6 years (18y 7m 6d) The line joining the Nodes is called Nodal Axis (abbreviated as N.A.). Earlier much importance was not given to these Nodes by the Western astrologers, but of late a good many books have been published in Western countries on Rahu and Ketu. Utility of Nodes in predicitve astrology has been a special feature of Hindu astrology since time immemorial. This is the main feature of this article.

Rahu-Moon Midpoint :-

Many students are unaware of the principles adopted in Nadi astrology, some of which are not found in standard texts. One such principle is prediction of transit results of a planet on an imaginary midpoint between Rahu and the Moon which is known as Bhrigubindu.

This point is very sensitive. When any planet benefic or malefic (including Rahu and Ketu) during transit aspects or conjuncts this midpoint some favourable or unfavourable event takes place.

However, it should be borne in mind that the effects of transit by conjunction are more potent than those by aspect. Jupiter usually fulfills long cherished desires depending on age, sex, status in life etc. of the native.

The transit of Rahu or Ketu will cause favourable or unfavourable results all of a sudden, on a very large scale and from unexpected sources.

Sometimes, it happens that two or three benefic planets simultaneously transit over or aspect this midpoint, incresing the mangitudeof the favourable result to a very great extent.

Similarly, two or three malefic planets, simultaneously, transit over or aspect this point, increase the magnitude of the unfavourable result to a very great extent.

(For futher details and examples, refer to the article "New Predictive Technique Based on Nadi Astrology " Chapter-13.

The Sun-Mercury-Venus Arc :-

In the zodiac, these three planets are posited very near to each other. The angular distance between the Sun and Mercury may very upto 28 degrees and that between the Sun and Venus may very upto 48 degrees. The maxmum distance between Mercury and Venus (being on either side of the Sun) will be about 76 degrees.

This arc of the zodiac formed by the Sun, Mercury and Venus in a natal chart, when transitted by Rahu gives highly beneficial results in matters of profession and earnings, promotions in service, rise in political life etc. to a native. While tranist of Ketu through the sam arc after about 9 years and 3-1/2 months will give major setbacks in professional field and to earnings thereform, troubles in service, and reversals in political life.

This predictive techinque is helpful in giving snap-shot predictions based on transit of Rahu and Ketu alone and does not take into account the Vimsottari Dasa or Ashtakavarga or the Ascendant.

Even in case the actual time of birth is unknown and date of birth only is known, this technique will be useful to give snapshot predictions.

In actual practice, the scribe has found, the effect of transit starts the moment Rahu and Ketu enter a sign in which this arc is formed. But, intensity of effects increases when Rahu or Ketu is about 6° 40' away form the arc point. Actual major events take place round about the dates when Rahu or Ketu degreecally traverses over the Sun - Mercury or Venus in whichever order they are in a chart.

(Refer to the article "Transit of Rahu and Ketu and the Fortunes of Politicians" by Shri R. G. Krishnan; December 1988 issue of the TOA, P. 14.)

Placement of planets in Rasi chart on either side of Nodal Axis: (Ref. Fig.1)

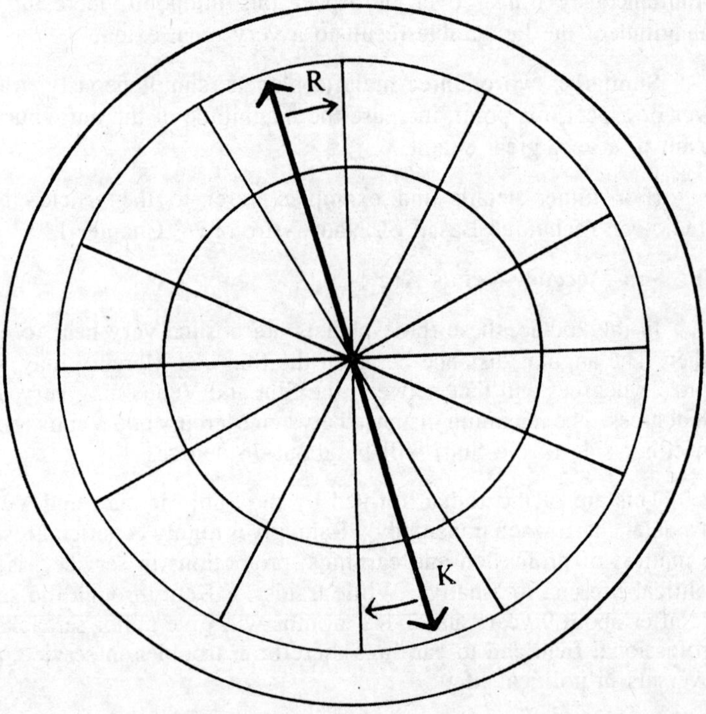

1. In a birth chart if Mars is on one side and Venus on the other side of the Nodal-Axis, the native's married life will not be smooth and happy. If both planets, are on one side of the axis, married life will be harmonious.

2. If the Moon and the Sun are on the same side of the nodal Axis, the native will have little help from his parents and/or brethren; if they are in opposite halves, help from them will be forthcoming.

3. If Saturn, and Jupiter are on opposite sides of Rahu-Ketu axis,

the native is employed far away from his native place and has to struggle his way through to come to a position.

4. If Saturn- Mars conjunction (in a sign) is on one side of the Nodal-axis and Venus-Jupiter conjuction (in a sign) is on the other side, the native will be involved in great calamity in his 49th year of life.

5. If the Nodal Axis falls between Mercury and Jupiter the children of native very often disagree with him.

6. If the N.A. falls between the Moon and Saturn there is disagreement with mother.

7. If the N.A. falls between the Sun and Saturn there is disagreement with father.

8. Five planets, viz. the Sun, Venus, Jupiter, Mercury and Saturn are on one side and the remaining two viz. the Moon and Mars are on the other side of the N.A., the elders in the native's family went abroad (far away place) and amased great wealth.

Transit results of Nodal Axis :-

In a circular chart, draw a line joining Rahu (R) with Ketu (K). This line joining the Nodes is called Nodal Axis. Draw a line at right angle to this NA as shown above. Rahu's and Ketu's transits in backward directions and the direction of motion is shown by the curved arrows. Upper point (A) indicates Rahu's results while lower point (B) indicates Ketu's results (Ref. Fig.2).

In short when point (A) (for Rahu) touches a natal position (in a birth chart) of a planet degreecally good results occur.

Suppose needle (A) touches the Sun's position in the birth chart, good results will be pertaining to (a) the father (Karaka); (b) the bhava karaka (c) house owned by Sun (lordship); and (d) the house position of the Sun.

In the same way, when the needle (A) touches other natal positions of planets during transit favourable results appropriate to them will be experienced. (Please refer Figure 2).

When needle (B) (for Ketu) touches the Moon bad results pertaining to :

a) the mother

b) the house lordship of the Moon.

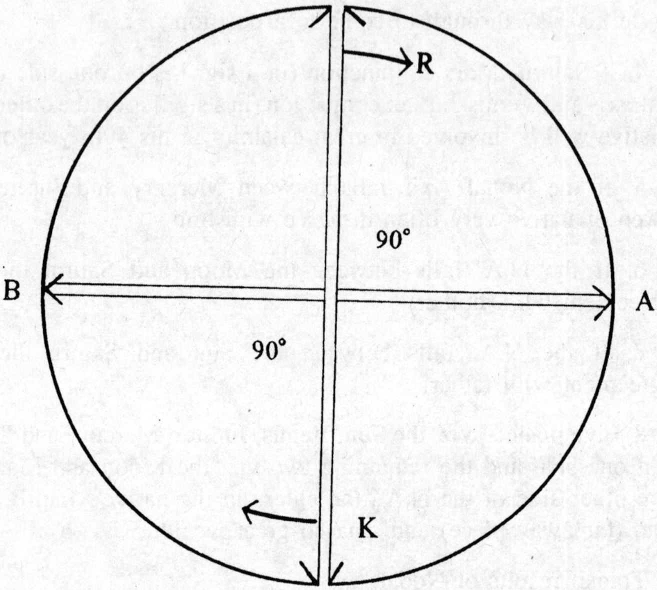

c) the house position of the Moon and

d) bhava Karaka.

In the same way when needle (B) touches other natal positions of planets unfavourable results appropriate to Karakahood, its lordship, and occupation etc. will occur. E.g. :

Our late Prime Minister Smt. Indira Gandhi took decision to hold a fresh Lok Sabha election on 18.1.1977. On that day needle (B) touched her natal Moon (lord of the Ascendant) 9s 5·30'. On that day in her chart Rahu was 6s 5° 27' and Ketu was 0s 5° 27'. Result was she lost majority in Lok Sabha.

Separation/Divorce in Married Life. :-

If, Venus or the lord of the 7th house is in conjunction with or in trine to Ketu in birth chart, there is a potential problem in married life. Native's married life is not happy and harmonious. This position has been found to be holding good in several cases where separation or divorce has alredy taken place.

If, however, the spouse has at least Venus or the lord of the 7th house in trine or in conjunction with Rahu in his or her chart, the ill-effects will not materialise.

(For more details refer to the article. "Some Research Findings on Divorce" by Shri R.G.Krishnan in The TOA April/May 1988 p. 12-13.)

Saturn/Ketu Conjunction :-

When transit Ketu conjuncts Satrun in transit a horrible war takes place between two Kings (countries); or devastating fires etc. and destruction of human beings are casued by thieves or soldiers.[1]

Notes: Conjunction between Ketu and Saturn takes place roughly once in every 12 years.

Saturn conjunction Ketu:-

a) In Aries on 14.1.1940

b) In Virgo on 19.10.1950

c) Capricorn on 15.10.1962

d) In Gemini on 13.9.1973 and

e) In Scorpio on 4.1.1985

Exactly, opposite results will be experienced when Rahu conjuncts Saturn. It is also observed in experience that similar results are repeated when Ketu or Rahu trines (at 120° or 240°) Saturn. Wide field is open for research to test conjunction or trine results between Ketu or Rahu and other planets.

1. The second world was started in septemeber 1939 Ketu (0s-8° 30') conjunct Saturn (0s 7° 40') it ended in May/June 1945 (Rahu 2s 18° 00') and Saturn (2s 17" 00').

2. China invaded India (North-East Assam) on 15.10.1962 (Ketu conjunct Saturn).

3. Israel declared war on Egypt round about September-October 1973 (Ketu conjunct Saturn).

Ketu is a war-monger and Rahu is a peace-maker.

Signs Owned by Rahu and Ketu :-

Ketu is the lord of the 4th sign counted from the sign occupied by the Sun; while Rahu is the lord of the 4th sign counted in the reverse order. (e.g. if the Sun is in Sagittarius-the 4th sign from it is Pisces, owned by Ketu; while the 4th sign counted backwards from Sagittarius is Virgo, owned by Rahu). When Saturn transits through sign Pisces bad results follow; and when he transits through sign Virgo, good results will be experienced by native born with the Sun in Sagittarius sign. Transit results of other planets through signs be judged in the same way.

Many texts express the owner-ship, exaltation and deblitation of Rahu and Ketu as particular Rasis, but they differ amongst them-selves having no single agreement. However "Krishneeya" authoritatively states so.

Rahu's Benefie Results/Ketu's Malefic Results. :-

Rahu and Ketu are considered as first rate malefic planets in Hindu Astrology. The following points made the scribe to revise or reconsider Rahu as bestowing benefic results:-

1. Rahu is Sudhapayi (one who had drunk nectar)

How can he be malefic?

2. "Spiritual Astrology" by E. Krishnamacharya - pages 212 - 213. " Any planet apparently in conjunction with one of the nodes will influence the earth in a particular manner. The vibrations of the planet will be intensified in their negative and positive expressions. A planet in conjunction with the ascending node (Rahu) proves highly positive and beneficial. A conjunction with the descending node (Ketu) intensifies the negative and evil influence of the planet".

3. Some Western astrologers consider Rahu as a benefic equal in effect to Jupiter and Venus combined; Ketu as a great malefic equal in effect to Saturn and Mars together.

4. Rahu in transit through "The Sun - Venus - Mercury" arc gives favourable results.

5. Rahu in transit through "Rahu - Moon" midpoint also gives rise to favourable events.

From the above reasons the writer considers Rahu as a benefic planet.

Use of true Rahu/Ketu positions helps to pinpoint the probable time of events. The use of mean Rahu/Ketu be avoided.

1. यदा हि मन्देन युतश्च केतुस्तदा भवेद् भूपतिघोर युद्धम् ।
तथा भवे-तस्करसैनिकैर्वा दाहादिकृत्यं जननाशनं च ॥
(Vide Chandra Kala Nadi, Vol. II. Part II, P.16-V2787)

2. दिवसकरस्य पुरस्तात्चतुर्थ राशीश्वरो भवति केतुः ।
राहुरपि पृष्ठतः किल चतुर्थ इष्टोऽर्कचारवशात् ॥

32

Vimsottari Dasa

Government Oriental Manuscripts Library (Madras) had published a book 'Bhargava Nadika' (1950), (भार्गव नाडिका) which is out of print, since long. This book deals with onlyVimshottari Dasa, Bhukti, Antaraantara, Sookshma and Prana results. It comprises about two thousand verses, mostly in Anushtup metre. The author's name is not known. He deals with Dasa and Bhukti results, in verses composed by him and then he has added many verses from other standard texts, stating "Granthantare ग्रन्थान्तरे".

In the text, the Dasa lord's position is discussed as under:-

1. Arohini-Avarohini;

2. Own sign, friendly sign, enemy's sign, Moola trikona sign; exaltation or debilitation sign;

3. Associated with or aspected by benefic and or malefic planets;

4. Bhava positions from Lagna to Vyaya bhava;

5. Rasi position from Mesha to Meena.

6. Bhava position of Bhukti lord from Dasa lord;

7. Planet in retrograde or direct motion;

8. Subhamsa, Papamsa, Ripuamsa, Nichamsa, Uchchamsa or Swaamsa etc.,

One single planet, may confer some good results under three or more conditions mentioned above and simultaneously confer bad results under other conditions. It is very very difficult to come to a definite, clear-cut conclusion. Sometimes favourable as well as unfavourable events happen more or less within a few days from each other.

Deva Keralam (Chandra Kala Nadi) introduces many rare concepts and techniques, such as, assessment of certain yogas, interpreting Navamsa and Rasi dispositors, Ashtamamsa and Nidhanamsa, Pushkara Navamsa, Rasitulya Navamsa and Navamsa-tulya Rasi, Navamsa transit and many more, hitherto not found in other classical texts.

One such very useful clue about the Dasa Bhukti results of a planet occupying a particular constellation in a Rasi in the natal chart is hidden in the following verse. That very planet in the same Rasi in other star behaves differently:-

See Deva Keralam (Chandra Kala Nadi) (O.M.L.) Madras) Vol. 1, Verse. 3043, P. 304 and Deva keralam (Chandra Kala Nadi), Book II, English translation R. Santhanam, Vol. II, Verse. 3043, P.37:

ऋणचोरभयप्राप्तिं व्रणोपदवरुग्भयम् ।
शन्याराक्रान्ततारेशदशायामन्तरेषु वा ॥

Meaning :- Debts, theft, fear, ulcer, troubles, disease will follow, during the Dasa or Bhukti denoted by the Nakshatra lord occupied by Saturn or Mars at brith."

Very useful clue is stated in the above verse about Saturn's and Mars' natal positions.

At birth, Saturn will be in a particular constellation, which in turn will relate to a Dasa. For example, Saturn in Asvini will mean that Ketu's Dasa will be adverse; in Bharani, Venus Dasa will be adverse, in Krittika the Sun's Dasa will be adverse, so on and so forth. Similarly the Dasa Bhukti results of all remaining eight planets be inferred from the ruler of the constellation occupied by each of them.

Example chart - Male born on 31-12-1915 at 07.44 p.m. (IST), Ahmedabad, Latitude 23° N 2'; Longitude 72° E 39'.

Rasi: The Sun 256-16; The Moon 192-13; Mars 127-9; Mercury 265-13; Jupiter 329-29; Venus 283-14; Saturn 80-42 (R); Rahu 287-06; Ketu 107-06 and Ascendant 98-53.

Balance of Rahu Dasa at birth:-

10y-6M-3d.

Table of Nakshatra lords:-

Planets	Star (Pada):-	Lord
Sun	P. Ashadha (1)	Venus
Moon	Swati (2)	Rahu
Mars	Makha (3)	Ketu
Mercury	P. Ashadha (4)	Venus
Jupiter	P. Bhadra (3)	Jup
Venus	Sravana (1)	Moon
Saturn	Punarvasu (1)	Jup
Rahu	Sravana (3)	Moon
Ketu	Aslesha (1)	Merc.
Lagna	Pushya (2)	Saturn

In the example chart, Saturn is posited in Purnarvasu (Ist pada) owned by Jupiter. So Jupiter's Data from 06-07-1926 to 06-07-1942 should prove adverse. In fact, the native suffered a lot during that period, encountering many hindrances, troubles and difficulties in his studies, family matters, quarrels, employment etc... When Jupiter's Dasa was over and Saturn's Dasa started from 06-07-1942 onwards, the whole picture changed for the better.

Jupiter's Bhuktis in various other Dasas, had also proved baneful, socially, financially, health-wise, deaths etc.

(1) In Saturn's Dasa-Jupiter's Bhukti- i.e., from 32-12-1958 to 05-07-1961 deaths of grand mother, paternal and maternal uncles took place.

(2) In Mercury's Dasa-Jupiter's Bhukti i.e. 20-07-1973 to 26-10-1975- death of wife on 24-01-1975.

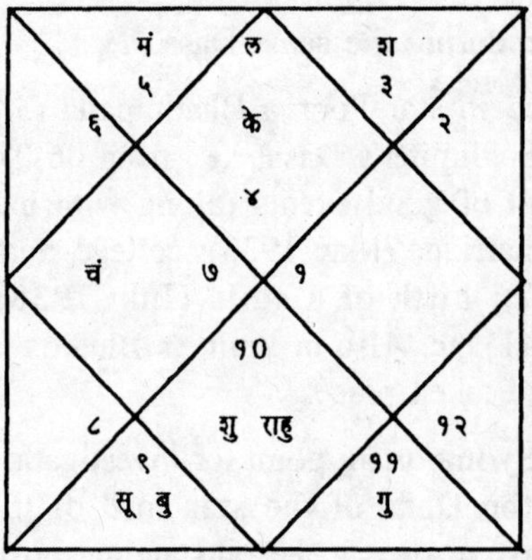

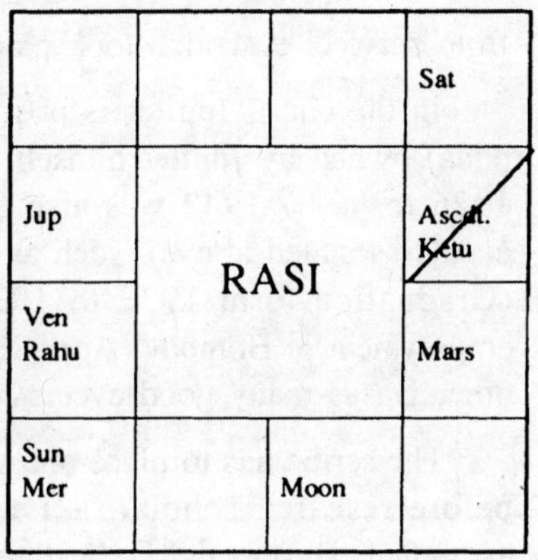

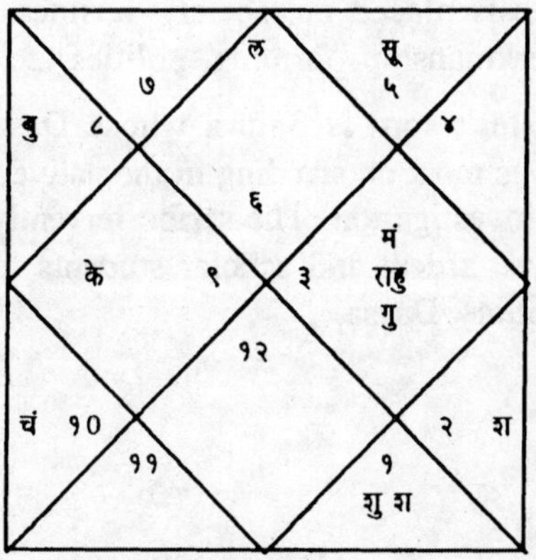

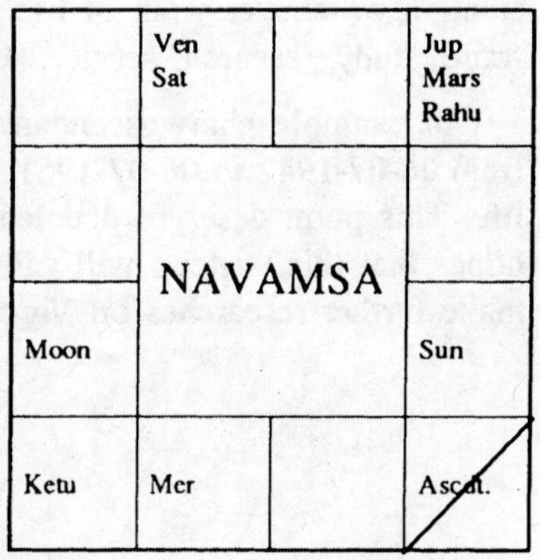

(3) In Ketu's Dasa - Jupiter's Bhukti i.e. from 23-06-1982 to 31-05-1983 - No death of a close relative, but other troubles about health and finance were there.

(4) In Venus' Dasa - Jupiter's Bhukti to rule from 04--9-1995 to 05-05-1998 - may turn out to be unfavourable - the native will be running 83rd year of life, health may suffer. Mars, the yoga karaka for Cancer ascendant is placed in the star makha (3rd pada) owned by Ketu. In fact Ketu's Dasa i.e. from 05-07-1978 to 05-07-1985 - was full of honours, respect, appreciation of researches, fame etc. (astrological studies and researches).

Ketu, posited in star Aslesha (Ist pada) will mean that Mercury's Dasa, i.e. from 05-07-1961 to 05-07-1978 should be the most adverse. The native had lost his mother on 30-11-1965; father on 15-06-1968 and wife on 24-01-1975 and had Cancer - operation on 22-03-1965. Great losses in business, trade, speculation, investments, retirement from service, etc., also took place during the same Dasa.

In the chart, Jupiter is posited in star Poorva Bhadrapada (3rd pada) owned by Jupiter himself. So Jupiter's Dasa, i.e., from 06-07-1926 to 06-07-1942 was also full of good events (along with bad events as stated above), such as marriage (May 1933); college-study (Graduation-form 1933 to 1937); birth of a child (July 1938), employment in Bombay (April 1941) etc. Also in Jupiter's Bhuktis in other Dasas many good events had taken place.

The scribe has to place one very important point for investigation before research scholars - i.e. the Dasa of the star lord of the ascendant. During the Dasa, the native rises to an outstanding position, in whichever walk of life he is placed i.e. society, business, trade, study, research, service, workmanship, farming, politics etc.

In example chart ascendant star's lord is Saturn whose Dasa from 06-07-1942 to 06-07-1961 was most outstanding in the native's life. This point deserves detailed investigation. The scribe fervently hopes that this writeup will enthuse ardent and scholar students to make further researches on Vimsottary Dassa.

33

Viparita Raja Yoga

Lords of evil houses spoil the signification of the houses they occupy as of the planets they are associated with. But, when they are placed in evil houses, they can bestow beneficial results and give rise to Viparita Raja Yoga.

Deva Keralam Book 2 page 88-Vs 95 (translated by R. Santhanam) states :-

रन्ध्रेशे व्ययषष्ठगे रिपुपतौ रन्ध्रे व्यये वा स्थिते ।
रिःफेशेऽपि तथैव रन्ध्ररिपुगे यद्वा त्रयः स्वर्क्षगाः ।।
सर्वेऽ न्यौन्य गृहाश्रिताः यदि ग्रहा युक्तेक्षितास्तत्र हि ।
जातो भूमिपतिः प्रशस्तविभवो राजाधिराजस्तुतः ।।

Meaning-"The 8th lord in the 6th or 12th, the 6th lord in the 8th or 12th, and the 12th lord in the 6th or 8th or these three planets in their above specified own houses in mutual aspects only between them (to the exclusion of other associations)-this Yoga will make one a king, endowed with distinct wealth and be praised by the king of Kings."

There is more or less a parallel verse in Uttara Kalamrita of Kalidasa.

Uttara Kalamrita, Khanda, IV, V. 22, (page 100) states as under.

रन्ध्रेशे व्ययषष्ठगो रिपुपतौ रन्ध्रे व्यये वा स्थिते ।
रिःफेशेऽपि तथैव रन्ध्ररिपुभे यस्यास्ति तस्मिन्वदेत् ।
अन्योन्यर्क्षगता निरीक्षण युताश्चान्यैरयुक्तेक्षिता
जातोऽसौ नृपतिः प्रशस्तविभवो राजाधिराजेश्वरः ।।

Meaning-"In any one of the following three yogas, viz.-

(a) lord of the 8th occupying the 12th or 6th;

(b) lord of the 6th occupying the 8th or 12th;

(c) lord of the 12th occupying the 8th or 12th;

(d) the said three lords being connected in any way, by mutual interchange of places, mutual aspect or conjunction and are at the same time free from such relation with other planets, the person born will become a great king lording over other kings and blessed with fame and wealth.

There are only four possibilities of this yoga :-

(1) the lord of the 8th should be in the 6th or in 12th;

(2) the lord of the 6th should be in the 8th or in 12th;

(3) the lord of the 12th should be in the 6th or in 8th;

(4) the lords of the 6th, 8th and 12th houses may exchange their houses or be together or have aspects (mutual) over each other.

In short, in all these cases, these three planets should not have any relation with other planets. Viparita Raja Yoga should be pure and any relation with other planet nullifies this yoga. So, an unblemished Viparita Raja Yoga complying fully with the definition of Kalidasa appears to be a rarity.

All conditions of this Yoga are to be satisfied before any such yoga is declared to be present. There is no partial yoga. Either, there is full yoga satisfying all required ingredients or there is no yoga.

Example Chart : (of the Scribe) :-

D.O.B. 31-12-1915 at 7-44 P.M. (I.S.T.), Sat 23N2, Long 72E39-Rasi The Sun 256-10; the Moon 192-13; Mars 127-9; Mercury 265-13; Jupiter 329-29; Venus 283-14; Saturn 80-42(R); Rahu 287-06; Ketu 107-06 and Ascendant 98-53.

Balance of Rahu Dasa at birth 10Y, 6m, 3d. Condition of the 6th lord Jupiter in the 8th house is satisfied but the 6th house is aspected by Saturn from the 12th; The 8th lord Saturn is in the 12th, but this 8th house is aspected by Mars from the 2nd. The 12th lord is in the 6th but the 12th house is aspected by two planets viz. Jupiter from

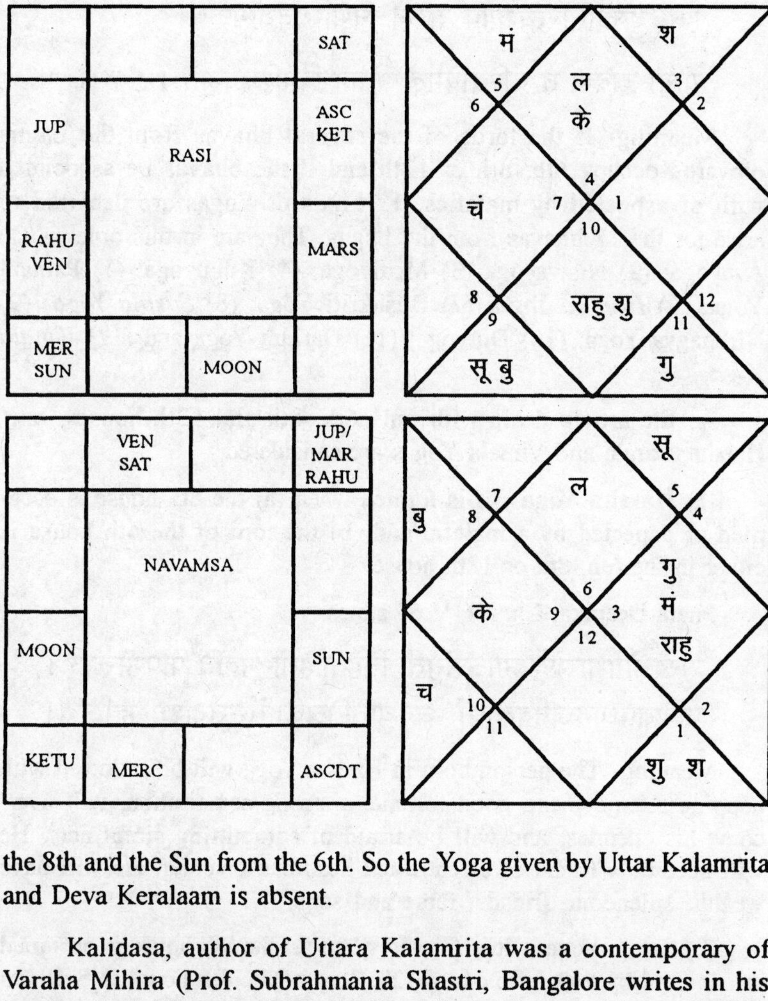

the 8th and the Sun from the 6th. So the Yoga given by Uttar Kalamrita and Deva Keralaam is absent.

Kalidasa, author of Uttara Kalamrita was a contemporary of Varaha Mihira (Prof. Subrahmania Shastri, Bangalore writes in his introduction). Whatever it may be, Uttar Kalamritam and Deva Keralam verses seem to have been composed prior to Phala Deepika of Mantresvara, which is a further development of the Viparita Raja Yoga principle.

Phala Deepika, Ch. IV, V. 57 (p. 68) (English translation by V. Subrahimanya Sastri) States :

दुःस्थैर्भावगृहेश्वरैरशुभसंयुक्तेक्षितैर्वा क्रमाद्भावैः स्युस्त्ववयोगनिः स्वमृतयः प्रोक्ताः कुहूः पामरः ।

हर्षो दुष्कृतिरित्यथापि सरले निर्भाग्यदुर्योगकौ

योगा द्वादश ते दरिद्रविमले प्रोक्ता विपश्चिज्जनैः ।।57।।

Meaning-"If the lords of the several bhavas from the Lagna onwards occupy 6th, 8th or 12th and if the bhavas be associated with or aspected by malefics, 12 kinds of Yogas are declared to arise for the 12 bhavas from the Lagna. They are in this order :- (1) Avayoga; (2) Niswayoga (3) Mritiyoga; (4) Kuhuyoga; (5) Pamara Yoga; (6) *Harsha Yoga;* (7) Dushkriti Yoga; (8) *Sarala Yoga;* (9) Nirbhagya Yoga; (10) Duryoga; (11) Daridra Yoga and (12) *Vimala Yoga.*

As the article deals with only 6th, 8th and 12th houses, only Harsha, Sarala and Vimala Yogas are considered.

(1) Harsha Yoga : If is formed when (a) the 6th house is occupied or aspected by a malefic and (b) the lord of the 6th house is either in the 6th, 8th or 12th house.

Phala Deepika, Ch. VI, V 63 states :-

सुखभोगभाग्यदृढगात्रसंयुतो निहताहितो भवति पापभीरूकः।

प्रथितप्रधानजनवल्लभो धनघुतिमित्रकीर्तिसुतवांश्च हर्षजः ।।

Meaning-"The person born in Harsha Yoga will be endowed with happiness, enjoyment, good fortune, a strong constitution, will overcome his enemies, and will be afraid of committing sinful acts. He will become a friend of a renowned headman or chief. He will have wealth, splendour, friends, fame and sons."

(2) Sarala Yoga :- It is formed when (a) the 8th house is occupied or aspected by a malefic and (b) the lord of the 8th house is either in the 6th, 8th or 12th house .

Phala Deepika, Ch. VI, V 65:-

दीर्घायुष्मान् दृढमतिरभयः श्रीमान्विद्यासुतधनसहितः।

सिद्धारम्भो जितरिपुरमलो विख्याताख्यः प्रभवति सरले ।।

Meaning-"One born in Sarala Yoga will be long-lived, resolute, fearless, prosperous, and will be endowed with learning, children and riches. He will achieve success in business at the very outset, overcome his foes be pure and widely celebrated."

(3) Vimala Yoga :- It is formed when (a) the 12th house is occupied or aspected by a malefic; and (b) the lord of the 12th house is either in the 6th, 8th or 12th house.

Phala Deepika Ch. VI V. 69 :-

किंचिद्व्ययो भूरिधनाभिवृद्धिं प्रयात्ययं सर्वजनानुकूल्यम् ।
सुखी स्वतन्त्रो महनीय वृत्तिर्गुणैः प्रतीतो विमलोद्भवः स्यात् ।।

Meaning-"The person born in Vimalayoga will spend little and save much money. He will be good to everybody. He will be happy, independent and will hold a respectable position and be renowned for his good qualities."

Scribe's example chart is a peculiar chart wherein all the above three yogas are formed satisfying all conditions.

(A) Harsha Yoga :-

(1) The 6th house is aspected by Saturn from the 12th house and (2) Jupiter, the lord of the 6th house, is posited in the 8th house.

(B) Sarala Yoga :-

(1) The 8th house is aspected by Mars from the 2nd house and (2) Saturn the lord of the 8th house is situated in the 12th house.

(C) Vimala Yoga :-

(1) The 12th house is aspected by the Sun from the 6th house; and (2) Mercury, the lord of the 12th, is placed in the 6th house.

Thus, it is observed, that all the three yogas-Harsha, Sarala and Vimala-are formed as per Mantresvara. The good results mentioned in these three verses of Phal Deepika-Ch. VI-Verse 63, Verse 65 and Verse 69, are more or less really enjoyed by the scribe till today who is running the 81st year of his life. The scribe's chart is a unique one, imbibing all the three negative Raja Yogas in one chart.

Scribe's own experience :

The native born under Viparita Raja Yoga enjoys its fruits by his own efforts and that too after hard labour while one born with normal Raja Yogas (due to Kendra Kona relations etc...) enjoys their fruits life-long and mostly created by relations or somebody else

Viparita Raja Yoga natives are generally self-made persons Rises in their lives are sudden, steep and unexpected, but last only for a limited period.

The scribe has enjoyed all three Dasas :-

of (1) 6th lord Jupiter from July 1926 to July 1942; of (2) 8th lord Saturn from July 1942 to July 1961; and of (3) 12th lord Mercury from July 1961 to July 1978.

34

Gain and Loss—Determining Specific Years

The whole world is moving round the pivot of wealth and all people, rich or poor, except a few who have renounced the world, often consult astrologers, as to when and how much wealth they are likely to get.

The scribe, in the course of his studies and research in astrology of about fifty years, has come across only two strange and unnoticed verses, indicating only one fixed year of life for inflow of wealth and similarly, only one fixed year for outflow of wealth. On application of these principles to the charts of people he knows well, he has found them verified beyond doubt. The verse for the inflow of wealth is from Manasagari Paddhati and the one for outflow of wealth is from Lagnachandrika.

According to Subhashitarthabhandaram (page 64, V. 5) "Megha (dark clouds) and Dhana or wealth—from where they come, where the clouds rain, how long the wealth remains and where they go away are not traceable; so strange are their movement."

When dark clouds coming from any direction are in the sky people expect good rainfall. But in no time, clouds are swept away by the wind and consequently, there is no rain. Similarly from which source, wealth comes to a native, how long it remains with him, and when and where it goes, are not easily known. The author has compared wealth with the clouds for its source of coming and mode of disappearing.

According to Manasagari Paddhati (V-9, page 328) "Note the

lunar day (Tithi) on which a native is born; in the year (age of native) represented by the number of Tithi, wealth definitely accrues (in the family)."

The Tithi current at a native's birth is noted. Suppose, a child is born on Panchami of the bright half of the Hindu month. Its birthday (Tithi) is the 5th. Another child is born on Full Moon day and its birthday will be the 15th. The 3rd child is born on the Saptami of the dark half of the month, its birthday is 15 + 7 = 22nd. The fourth child is born on Amavasya day and its birthday is the 30th. In the current year of a child, representing the numbers of the running Tithi of birth, some extra wealth (property etc.) is earned or procured by the child's family.

As per Lagna Chandrika (V. 206 page 80), "For a native born with the Moon in any Navamsa from Aries to Pisces (in any sign), there will be loss (destruction, etc.) of family wealth (Vyayah) in the years of his life represented by the following numbers respectively viz., Aries - 8 नाग; Taurus - 9 गो; Gemini - 24 सिद्ध; Cancer - 22 जाती; Leo - 5 षु; Virgo - 1 क्षमा; Libra - 4 ब्ध्य; Scorpio - 2 क्षि; Sagittarius- 20 नखा; Capricorn - 38 धृति; Aquarius - 21 क्षमाश्वि; and Pisces - 10 दिव्ट; Note the Moon's Navamsa Rasi of the native. In the running year of life mentioned above against each Navamsa Rasi, ranging from Aries to Pisces, some loss (or destruction, theft, fire, spending, celebration, marriage, festivities etc.) of family wealth (or property, takes place. Suppose a child is born with the Moon in Virgo Navamsa. In the very first year of the child's life, some family wealth will be lost or reduced. Another child is born with the Moon in Gemini Navamsa, the family's wealth or property will be lost or reduced or destroyed in the 24th year of its life. Similarly, the critical years for the Moon's position in other Navamsas can be arrived at for different nativities.

Case 1 : Born 31-32-1915 at 19th, 46m, at Ahmedabad.

(a) Month of birth - Margasirsha Dark half; Tithi 10 or 15 + 10 = 25th day. The 25th year from 31-12-1939 to 31-12-1940 saw more earnings in cotton speculation.

(b) The Moon in Libra 12° 13' in Capricorn Navamsa i.e., 38th year.

In the 38th year from 31-12-1952 to 31-12-1953, he suffered great loss in share transactions.

Case 2 : Born 27-7-1938 at 16th. 47m. at N 30, 72 E 04.

(a) Month of birth-Sravana bright half; Tithi = 1. In the first year of life from 27-7-1938 to 27-7-1939, there were profits in speculation to father.

(b) The Moon-Cancer 15°8', Scorpio Navamsa i.e., 2nd year from 27-7-1939 to 27-7-1940 saw substantial amount of money spent on repairs and alterations of family residence.

Case 3 : Born 19-11-1945 at 21h. 30m. at Ahmedbad.

(a) Month of birth-Kartika dark half; Tithi (1). In the 15 + 1 = 16th year from 19-11-1960 to 19-11-1961, the native's father made huge profits in stock exchange.

(b) The Moon in Taurus 4°20' in Aquarius Navamsa i.e., 21st year from 19-11-1965 to 19-11-1966 saw the father suffer great loss in oil business.

Case 4 : Born 5-11-1954 at 16h. 10m. at Ahmedabad.

(a) Month of birth - Kartikay bright half; Tithi - 10.

In the 10th year from 5-11-1963 to 5-11-1964, the native's father earned well in the stock exchange and went in for purchase of land in Ahmedabad and a residential block at Bombay.

(b) The Moon in Aquarius 8° 33' in Sagittarius Navamsa. The 20th year from 5-11-1973 to 5-11-1974 saw her mother very sick with heavy hospital and medical expenses.

From the above two verses, it can be observed, how much importance was given by the ancient authors to Tithi of birth and the Navamsa Rasi of the Moon, barring aside any other condition for gaining or losing wealth respectively.

35

On Kartari Yoga

If both, the 2nd and the 12th houses from a particular bhava or a planet, are occupied by :

(i) benefic planets if causes Suubha Kartari and

(ii) malefic planets if causes Papa Kartari.

There are a number of Kartari Yogas, such as :

(1) Lagna Kartari

(2) Bhava Kartari

(3) Subha Kartari

(4) Papa Kartari

(5) Uchha Kartari

(6) Neecha Kartari

(7) Mitra Kartari

(8) Shatru Kartari

(9) Sama Kartan

Durudhara yoga.

Ubhayachari Yoga : Planets, other than the Moon (i.e. Mars, Mercury, Jupiter, Venus and Saturn) in the 2nd and the 12th houses from the Sun will cause Ubhayachari Yoga.

There may be Subha, Papa or Misra Kartari.

The Sun having Mercury in the 2nd, Venus in the 12th = Subha

The Sun having Mars in the 2nd, Saturn in the 12th = Papa.

The Sun having Mars in the 2nd, Venus in the 12th = Misra.

Lagna Subha - Papa-Kartari :

When the 2nd and the 12th bhavas from the Ascendant are occupied by benefics or malefics, the Yoga is Lagna Shubha Kartari or Lagna Papa Karatari as the casemay be.

Results :

A native with Lagna Subha Kartari will be eloquent; handsome; amicable; worthy; lustruous; wealthy; strong; devoted to his wife; affable in address; prosperous; a leading citizen; long-lived; very enthusiatic; chief member of his clan etc.

A native with Lagna Papa Kartari will be lustful, wicked; criminal; impure; eating begged food; decietful; depraved in his speech; tormented; shortlived; low-minded; fickle; deprived of some limb; will live in a foreign country (distant place); will have risk from poison, fire or weapon.

(Refer *Jataka Parijata* VII-vs-125-126-127; *Jatakadesa Marga,* VIII-Vs-26-27-28.)

There is a verse in *Jyotisharnava Navanitam;* P. 90 V. 202 (English translation by R. Santhanam).

पापमध्यगते शुक्रे जामित्रेशेऽथवा पुनः।
जामित्रे पापमध्ये (च) जायारिष्टं वदेद् बुधः।।

Meaning : "The learned speak of early death of spouse, in case Venus is hemmed between malefic havenly bodies; while in addition, the 7th house or its lord is also similarly placed (in between the malefics)".

Venuse (Karaka) : Mars in the 2nd Saturn in the 12th

7th lord : Mars in the 2nd, Saturn in the 12th

7th house : Mars in the 2nd, Saturn in the 12th

One can say :-

शुभमध्यगते शुक्रे जामित्रेशेऽवा पुनः।
जामित्रे शुभमध्ये (च) जायासौख्यं वदेद बुधः।।

There is a parallel mention in Uttara Kalamrita Khanda, IV/V-12-P. 89-first line only.

भावो भावपतिश्च कारकखगस्ते पापमध्यस्थिताः ।

———————————————— भावहानिं वदेत् ।।

Meaning : "If a bhava, its lord, and its karaka planet-these three-be surrounded by malefics the destruction of that Bhava be declared."

One can say : "भावो भावपतिश्च कारकखगस्ते शुभमध्यस्थिताः ।

———————————————— भाववृद्धिं वदेत् ।।

Naval use of Papa Kartari is made three times in one and the same verse the 7th house (Jamitrasthana); Karaka for the 7th house (Venus) and the lord of the 7th house, all these three can be Papa Madhya. This is simply wonderful.

In the scribe's chart, with Mercury in the 6th house; Venus in the 7th house and Jupiter in the 8th house, two points are covered, i.e. Bhava (7th house) and Karaka Venus are hemmed between benefics. His marital life was enviable. This kind of triple use of Kartari malefic or benefic is rarely found in standard texts.

It is found only in Jyotisharnava Navnitam and Uttara Kalamritam.

Neecha Uchcha Kartari :

There are two types of Kartari Yogas : Bhava Neecha Kartari and Neecha-Kartari. Similarly there are Bhava-Uchaha Kartari and Graha-uchha Kartari.

Deva Keralam or Chandra Kala Nadi Book (3) p. 241. sloka No. 5260 (English translation by R. Santhanam) :-

लग्ने नीचे व्यये पापे स्वोच्चांशे नीचकर्तरी ।

उग्रकार्यपरो नित्यं महारोगेन कर्शितः ।।

Meaning : "The ascendant occupied by a debilitated planet and a malefic in the 12th house with an exalted Navamsa and a debilitated planet in the 11th house cause Neecha Kartari Yoga. One having this combination will ever perform fierce deeds and be emantiated due to a dire disease."

12th house Simha : Saturn is exalted Navamsa i.e. 4s 20" 0° to 4s 23° 20' : Lagna-Kanya-Venus, 11th house-Cancer Mars.

Neecha Kartari : There are only four possibilities :-

(1) Bhava/sign Simha : Cancer-Mars, Kanya Venus;

(2) Bhava/sign Dhanus : Kanya Venus, Vrishichika Moon.

(3) Bhava sign Dhanus : Vrishchika Moon, Makara-Jupiter.

(4) Bhava sign Kumbha : Makara-Jupiter, Meena-Mercury.

Jupiter becomes debilitated i.e. enters sign Makara on 26-12-96 and remains there for one year.

(i) From 13-3-97 to 26-3-97, Mercury is also debilited in Meena. There is Neecha Kartari Yoga for Kumbha sign as far a planet therein. (ii) During Jupiter's transit through Makara, whenever the Moon transits sign Vrishchika (every month for two and half days i.e. twelve times during the year), there is Neecha-Kartari Yoga for sign Dhanus/or for a planet therein.

Uchcha Karatari Yoga - there are only four possibilities :-

(1) Bhava sign Simha : Meena-Venus, Vrishabha-Moon.

(2) Bhava sign Mithuna : Vrishabha Moon, Karkataka Jupiter.

(3) Bhava sign Kumbha : Makara Mars, Meena-Venus.

(4) Bhava sign Simha : Karkataka-Jupiter, Kanya-Mercury.

Results will be very good, quite opposite of the Neecha Kartari as above. Till date, scribe has come across only one verse for Neecha Kartari i.e. in *Deva Keralam.*

Mitra Kartari, Shatru Kartari and Sama Kartari.

Bhava Prakasa (Jeeva Nath) IX - verse (1).

दशास्वामिनो मित्रखेटान्तरेऽपि प्रशस्त रिपोरप्रशस्तं समस्तम् ।

समानं समस्यात्र वर्गानुसारात् फलं संवदेत् प्राणीनामार्यवर्यः ।।

If the Dasa lord is between :

(i) Friendly planets-good results;

(ii) Inimical planets-bad results;

(iii) Neutral (Sama) planets-mixed results will follow to all nativities according to their positions in life, so say the learned seers.

(i) Saturn/Dhanus : Mercury-Vrishchika, Venus-Makara = Friendly planets.

(ii) Mars/Dhanus : Venus-Vrishchika, Saturn - Makara = Sama-neutral planets.

(iii) Jupiter/Dhanus : Mercury-Vrischika, Venus-Makara = Enemy planets.

A planet getting hemmed in between malefics, not only becomes weak thereby, but the efforts of the house/s over which the planet has lordship and all the significations of the planet get destroyed.

Bhaskara Bhava Deepika - Verse 21.

(i) If the lord of ascendant is hemmed in between planets who are inimical to him, the native will be troubled by his enemies.

(ii) If such lord of the ascendant (hemmed in between inimical planets) is conjunct or aspected by a benefic, the native will be free from enemy trouble.

Some useful verses :-

Hora Ratnam - Part-1 P. 785, V. 85 (English translation, by R. Santhanam) :-

द्यूनचतुरस्रसंस्थे पापद्वयमध्ये शशिनि जातः।

विलयं प्रयाति नियतं देवैरपि रवितो बालः।।

Early death : Even gods cannot save the child from early death who has its Moon in the 7th, 4th or 8th house between two malefic planets.

P. 786-V-90.

पापद्वयमध्यगते होरासप्ताष्टसंस्थिते चन्द्रे।

सौम्यैः सबलैः खेटैरनीक्षते च ध्रुवं म्रियते।।

Early death : The Moon in the ascendant, 7th or 8th in between two malefic planets and unaspected by strong benefics will cause immediate death.

P. 795. V. 135 :

पापमध्यगते सूर्ये लग्नस्थे शत्रुवेश्मनि।

जातश्चरोगपीडार्तः परमायुर्ऋषित्रयम्।।

21 years of life : The Sun in the ascendant in an inimical sign, and being between malefic planets will bring forth death at 21, apart from troubles from diseases.

P. 814. V. 216 :-

सौम्यान्तरगतैः पापैः शुभैः केन्द्रत्रिकोणगैः ।
सद्यो नाशयते रिष्टं तद् भावोत्थं फलं न तत् ।।

Cancellation of evils of father : Malefics placed between benefic planets, and benefics occupying angles and trines (with reference to the Bhava under consideration i.e. the 9th) will instantly eliminate all the evils and will bring forth good concerning that Bhava i.e. concerning 9th Bhava (father).

P. 814, v. 217 :-

चतुर्थदशमे पापः सौम्यमध्ये यदा भवेत् ।
पितुः सौख्यकरो योगः शुभैः केन्द्रत्रिकोणगैः ।।

Happiness to father : Even though there may be malefics in the 4th and 10th, their placement between benefics and the angles and trines in occupation by benefics will cause happiness to father.

P. 823, V. 259 :

सौम्यद्वयान्तरगतः संपूर्णः स्निग्धमण्डलः शशभृत् ।
निःशेषरिष्टहन्ता भुजङ्गलोकस्य गरुड इव ।।

Meaning : If the full Moon is placed between two benefics, evils will be destroyed just as Garuda destroys the world of snakes.

संतानदीपिका :–

P. 6. Verse 18 :

पुत्रस्थानगते भानौ नीचे मन्दांशके स्थिते ।
पार्श्चयोः क्रूरसम्बन्धे पितृशापात् सुतक्षयः ।।

Meaning : There will be loss of progeny due to patenal curse, if the debilitated Sun is in the Navamsa of Saturn and is placed in the 5th house and flanked in by two Krura planets.

P. 6, Verse 19 :-

पुत्रस्थानाधिपे भानौ त्रिकोणे पापसंस्थिते ।
क्रूरान्तरे पापदृष्टे पितृशापात्सुतक्षयः ।।

Meaning : The native will lose his progeny by paternal curse; if the Sun, as the lord of the 5th house, together with a malefic, is posited in the 5th or 9th house, is between malefic planets, aspected by a malefic.

P. 10, Verse 32 :

पुत्रस्थानाधिपे चन्द्रे नीचे वा पापमध्यगे।
हिबुके पंचमे पापे मातृशापात् सुतक्षयः।।

Meaning : The native will lose his progeny by maternal curse, if the 5th lord the Moon is debilitated or is placed between the malefics and there is a malefic in the 4th and 5th house.

P. 12, Verse 40 :

पापमध्यगते लग्ने क्षीणे चन्द्रे च सप्तमे।
मातृपुत्रे राहुमंदौ मातृशापात्सुतक्षयः।।

Meaning : The ascendant hemmed in between malefics, the waning Moon in the 7th house: with Rahu and Saturn respectively in the 4th and 5th houses, will cause loss of children due to maternal curse.

P. 16, Verse 54 :

पापमध्यगते लग्ने सुतभे पापमध्यगे।
नाथाच्च कारको दुःस्थे भ्रातृशापात्सुतक्षयः।।

Meaning : The ascendant and the 5th house both between the malefics and Karaka Jupiter is placed in the 6th, 8th or the 12th house from the lord of the 5th, will cause loss of progeny by brotherly curse.

Jataka Tatva (V.S. Shastri, Bangalore) :

P. 285, item 58 :

खेशे शुभान्तरे गुरुशुक्रयुते पितृसुखम्।

"If the lord of the 10th house be between benefics or be conjoined with either Venus and Jupiter the native will become happy through his father."

P. 285, item 64 :

खेशे पापसम्बन्धे पापान्तरे पितृदुःखम्।

"If the lord of the 10th house be related with a malefic and be also between malefics the native will be unhappy due to his father (may lose him in his childhood).

Most of the ancient authors have made use of this technique in their books on Astrology. Some verses from **Hora Ratnam** - part (by R. Santhanam), Santana Deepika and Jataka Tatva are referred in the write up for their variety of uses and guidance of the students. Deva Keralam, Chandra Kala Nadi has used many of these techniques in innumerable verses. It is no use mentioning them here.

Readers will learn a lot from this innovative article.

36

Diseases and Injuries—Caused by Planets

The Ashtakavarga is recognised as an outstanding system of prediction among the many advocated in the standard works of astrology. In such three ancient texts, one and the same topic is included in the chapters on Ashtakavarga, Hora Makaranda (Gunakar) - 1200 A.D. P. 111-Vs. 15-16-17: (Chap XII):

शीर्षास्ययोस्तिग्मरु चिर्विभुत्वं करोति चंद्रो हृदये संकठे।
क्रोडे स्पृष्टे तनयो धरित्र्याः शाखासु सूनुः शशलांछनस्य।।१५।।
कट्यां सुरेज्यो जधनस्थले च भृगोः सुतो मुष्कयुगे सगुत्ये।
स्फिजोरपाने तपनस्य पुत्रो जन्मन्यमी चारवशेन यद्वा।।१६।।
दुःस्था निजांगेषु रुजं विदध्युः स्वकीय दोषेण नभश्चरेन्द्राः।
निजे च धाता विदमादरेण प्रश्नप्रयाणादिषु चिन्तनीयम्।।१७।।

जातकाभरण (Dhundhiraja - 1538 A.D. pg. 216-Vs-27-28-29):

शिरःप्रदेशे वदने दिनेशो वक्षःस्थले चापि गले कलावान्।
पृष्ठोदरे भूतनयः प्रभुत्वं करोति सौम्यश्चरणे च पाणौ।।२७।।
कटिप्रदेशे जधने च जीवः कविस्तु गुह्म स्थलमुष्कयुग्मे।
जानूरुदेशे नलिनीशसूनुश्चारेण वा जन्मनि चिन्तनीयम्।।२८।।
यदा यदा स्यात् प्रतिकूलवर्ती स्वाङ्गेऽस्य दोषेण करोति पीडाम्।
इदं तु पूर्व प्रविचार्य सर्वे प्रश्नसूत्यादिषु कल्पनीयम्।।२९।।

I shall consider my labour amply rewarded if this work proves helpful in enabling students and practitioners to make predictions with greater confidence and greater success than otherwise.

September 1996
29-D, 3rd floor,
Gandhi Market,
Ghatkopur (E)
Mumbai-400077

C.S. Patel

जातकसारदीप (Nrisimha-17th century A.D. p. 586 : V - 20):

This verse has been included in our book **Ashtakavarga** (1957) Chap. XIII V. 4 pg. 159.

शीर्षाऽस्य सूर्य इह कंठहृदिंदुरारः पृष्टोदरेंऽघ्रि वित्कटि जंघ जीवः।
मुष्कोरु गुह्यसित आर्किरपानकस्फिगेते निजे विदधते किल
दोषपीडाम् ।।

Meaning, when (1) *the Sun is in an unfavourable position he causes afflictions to the head and face due to impurities in bile;*

(2) the Moon in a similar position afflicts the heart and neck due to phlegm;

(3) Mars afflicts the back and belly portions due to blood disorders.

(4) Mercury, the joints of limbs such as arms and legs, nervous afflictions due to excess of bile, phelgm and wind;

(5) Jupiter affects the loins and shanks due to excess of phlegm;

(6) Venus, the thighs, private parts and scrotum due to excess of bile and phlegm; and

(7) Saturn affects the buttocks and anal parts due to wind troubles.

In **Horamakaranda,** Verses 15 and 16 convey the same matter as in **Jatakasaradeepa.** In verse 17 it is said that a planet will give diseases or troubles in the respective part of the body by bile, phlegm or wind disorders or accident. In **Jatakabharana** in verse 29 same reasons and results are stated. The time of occurence is indicated as to when a particular planet is unfavourable (प्रतिकूलवर्ती).

During last few years, the scribe was thinking seriously as to why the above topic had been included in the chapter on Ashtakavarga. It has to do something with Ashtakavarga methodology.

The Pratikulagraha or unfavourable planet may mean :-

(1) A particular planet transiting a sign having O-nil or the minimium *bindu* in his B.A.V. or a sign having the minimum *bindus* in S.A.V.

* B.A.V. = Bhinnashtakarvarga;
* P.A.V. = Prastarashtakavarga;
* S.A.V. = Samudayaashtakarvarga;

This would happen once every year or so for the fast moving planets and for Jupiter, once in every twelve years and for Saturn, once in every thirty years and that too in every cycle (Paryaya);

(2) A planet associated with 1 *bindu* in his B.A.V. (the Sun to Venus) or with O-nil *bindu* Saturn.

Recently the scribe came across the following verse from **Deva Keralam** (Chandrakala Nadi) Part II, Vol. II, pg. 119-V. 3711. Scorpio Ascendant.

D.K. (3) p. 128-v. 3711

पूवार्धे बुधभुक्तौ च करपादेषु रोगवान् ।

देहायासमवाप्नोति शान्त्या शान्तिं प्रयास्यति ।।

Meaning : *in the first half of the running Dasa (particular), during the period of Mercury, the native will have diseases or injury on hands and legs. To ward off bodily sufferings one should resort to propitiatory measures.*

In this verse Venkatesha, the author, has indicated three points, namely, (i) suffering on account of Mercury will be on hands and legs; (ii) the suffering will be during Mercury's period; and (iii) Mercury is the 8th lord for Scorpio Ascendant.

Example : Born February 4/5th, 1944 at 2-52 a.m. (I.S.T) at 23 N 34 72 E 45.

Rasi : The Sun 79-36; the Moon 242-2; Mars 122-29; Mercury 83-36; Jupiter 122-48; Venus 81-44; Saturn 68-48; Rahu 95-15; Ketu 275-15; and Ascendant 16-45 with a balance 5 years 11 months 7 days of Ketu Dasa.

One fine Sunday morning (29-7-1984), this native went to Lonavala, about a 100 kms away from Mumbai, to take an open bath under falling waters from an overflowing Dam. Round about 11-30 a.m. he slipped from a big stone and the thigh bone was fractured in the upper part. He was brought to Mumbai and operated for injuries i.e., a steel rod was inserted in the thigh. After about two and a half months, he was discharged from a private clinic. Even after 12 years a slight difference is observed in the mode of his walking.

The native was having Moon Dasa Venus Bhukti from 11-4-1984 to 12-12-1985. Venus is a double Marka, being the lord of the 2nd

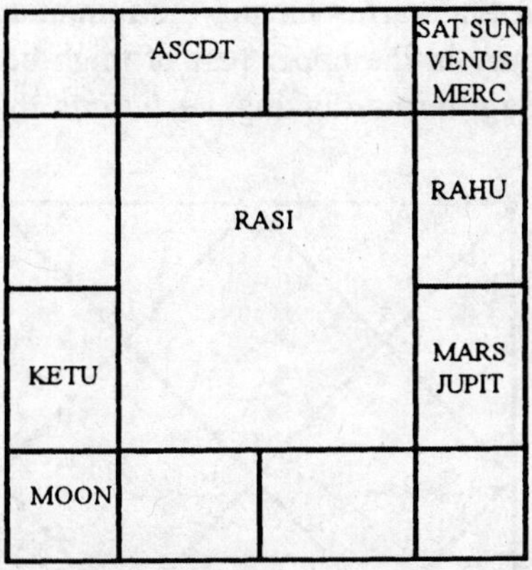

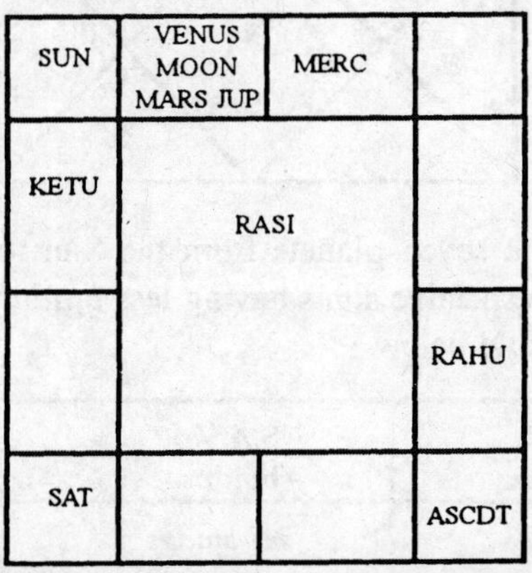

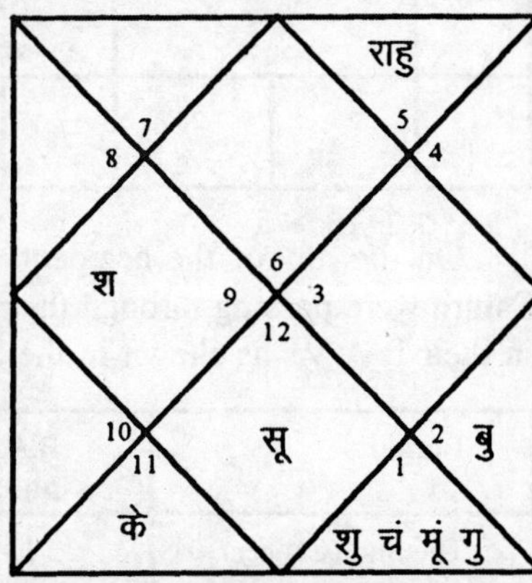

Signs	Aries	Tau.	Gemini	Cancer	Leo	Virgo	Libra	Scorpio	Sagi.	Capri,	Aqua.	Pisces	Total
Sun's A.V.	5	4	5	3	2	5	2	3	4	4	6	5	48
Moon's A.V.	5	3	5	0	5	6	5	3	5	4	4	4	49
Mars' A.V.	5	4	4	1	3	3	3	4	1	4	4	3	39
Mercs' A.V.	6	5	5	5	3	5	4	4	1	5	6	5	54
Jupi' A.V.	5	4	5	4	6	5	6	5	2	3	6	5	56
Venus' A.V.	8	3	4	4	5	2	5	4	3	5	5	4	52
Sat's A.V.	5	4	4	4	1	2	3	3	3	5	3	2	39
Total	39	27	32	21	25	28	28	26	19	30	34	28	337

Ashtakavarga as per Prasna Marga allocation of *bindus*.

and 7th houses and the Moon is in Sagittarius having the minimum *bindus* (S.A.V.). The native had injury in the upper part of thigh because Jupiter is the lord of sign Sagittarius, having 19 *bindus* the minimum in S.A.V.

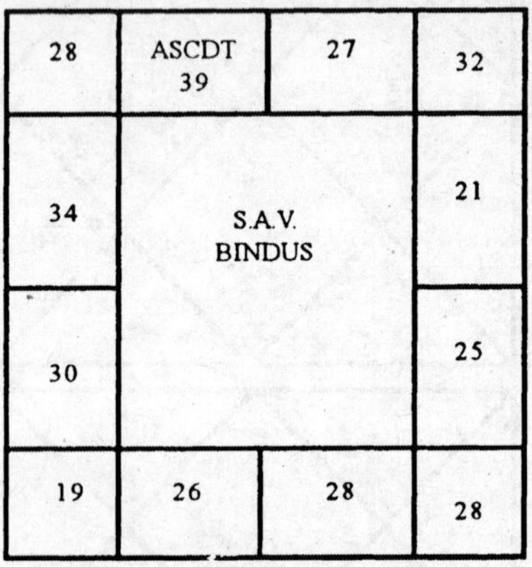

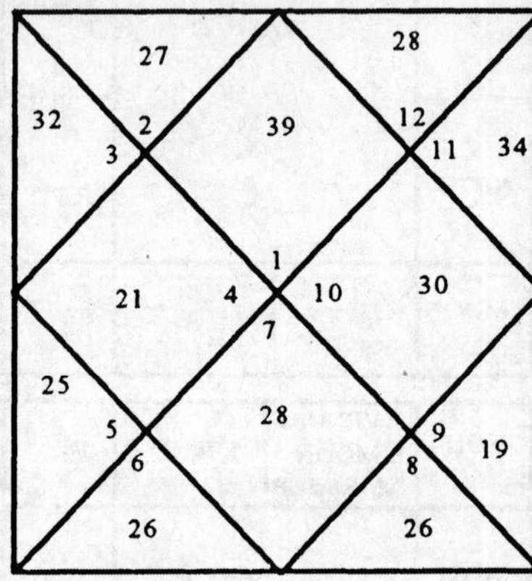

On the day of the accident, the seven planets from the Sun to Saturn were passing through their respective signs having less *bindus* in their B.A.V.s as shown in the Table below.

Planet	**B.A.V. bindus**	**S.A.V. bindus**
The Sun (Cancer)	*3 bindus*	*21 bindus*
The Moon (Cancer)	*0 bindus*	*21 bindus*
Mars (Libra)	*3 bindus*	*28 bindus*
Mercury (Leo)	*3 bindus*	*25 bindus*
Jupiter (Sagittarius)	*2 bindus*	*19 bindus*
Venus (Cancer)	*4 bindus*	*21 bindus*
Saturn (Libra)	*3 bindus*	*28 bindus*
	18 bindus	

The Total number of *bindus* for the transiting seven planets in the individual B.A.V.s were 18 only, far less. Three planets, the Sun, the Moon, and Venus were transiting through sign Cancer having 21 *bindus* (S.A.V.) and Jupiter through Sagittarius having 19 *bindus*, the minimum in the chart.

From such examples the scribe has come to the following conclusions.

(1) Find a sign containing the minimum number of *bindus* in S.A.V. and its lord. The part of the body indicated by that planet will be affected.

(2) At the time of the event or period all the seven planets should transit signs having less number of *bindus* in their B.A.Vs and or in S.A.V. also.

(3) There must be one sign having O-nil *bindu* in any B.A.V.

(4) Dasa and Bhukti also should be unfavourable.

If the above conclusions are satisfied, the inclusion of the above verses in chapters on Ashtakavarga is justified. Research students are requested to find horoscopes of some aged or dead persons fulfilling the above conditions. The scribe will feel happy and satisfied, if they meet with success.

37

Techniques of Vimsottari Dasa

Deva Keralam (Chandra Kala Nadi) introduced many rare concepts and techniques, such as, assessment of certain Yogas, interpreting Navamsa and Rasi dispositors, Ashtamsa and Nidhanamsa, Pushkara Navamsa, Rasi Tulya Navamsa and Navamsa Tulya Rasi, Navamsa transit, Vimsottari Dasa Bhukti results and many more hitherto not found in other classical texts.

An attempt is made to collect some such concepts and techniques about Vimsottari Dasa from Deva Keralam and standard texts, not referred in scribe's articles previously published in this Magazine.

Deva Keralam Book 3, p. 212 Vs. 4853-54 (in 3 volumes with Mr. R. Santhanam's. English translation):

लग्नाधिपस्य यः शत्रुस्तद्भक्तौ सर्वदायगे।

अतीव क्लेशकार्याणि मित्रभुक्तौ धनागमम्।।

समग्रहान्तरे काले शुभाशुभफलं समम्।

तात्कालिकमित्रग्रहस्यान्तर्दाये शुभाधिकम्।।

"The sub-period of a planet that is an adversary to the lord of the ascendant will in various Dasas cause much anguish in one's undertakings. The sub-period ruled by a friendly planet will lead to acquisition of wealth. A planet that is neutral to the ruler of the ascendant will only produce such effects which are just neutral. The sub-period of a planet which is temporary friend to the lord of the ascendant will give exceedingly auspicious results in various ways."

Deva Keralam, Book 2, Page 105, Verse-245.

लग्नेशस्थांशराशीशे दारेशस्थानगेऽथवा।
सुतेशस्थांशराशीशभुक्तिकालेमहत्सुखम् ।।

"Great happiness will come to pass in the sub-periods of the following planets :-

(1) of the Navamsa dispositor of the natal ascendant lord;

(2) of a planet posited in the sign together with the 7th lord; or

(3) of the Navamsa dispositor of the 5th lord.

In the horoscope of the scribe :-

(1) the Navamsa dispositor of the natal ascendant lord is Saturn (Makara Navamsa).

(2) No planet in conjunction with the 7th lord Saturn in the 12th house;

(3) the Navamsa dispositor of the 5th lord is Mercury (Mithuna Navamsa).

In scribe's life not only the sub-periods of Saturn and Mercury in various Dasas were favourable but their entire Dasas were outstanding.

Deva Keralam 3 P. 135-Verse 3806 :-

जन्मे शनिस्थिथे काले नानाव्याकुलसंभवम्।
कुजभुक्तौ फलं सत्यं राहुभुक्तौ विशेषतः ।।

"Saturn coming in transit on the sign occupied by the Moon will cause various types of anguish in the sub-period of Mars and much more so in the sub-period of Rahu."

Janma Sani generally means transit Saturn on the natal Moon sign. The above rule can be applied in general to all ascendants. Saturn's evil transit and malefic sub-period simultaneously produce intense anguish.

Deva Keralam 1 P. 174-V. 1956.

उत्कृष्टधर्मसिद्धिः स्याल्लग्नदृष्टि ग्रहान्तरे।

"The sub-period ruled by the planet aspecting the ascendant will be significant, in respect of religious attainments, Yatras etc.—In the scribe's chart two planets Venus and Rahu are aspecting the ascendant from the 7th house.

Uttara Kalamrita, Khanda 2-P 257-Verse 102 (English translation V. Subramanya Sastri).

शुक्रे राहुयुते च केतुमुखतो भाग्यव्ययं निर्दिशेत् ।।

"If Venus be conjoined with Rahu, there will be decline in native's prosperity from the period (dasa) beginning with Ketu's."

Cf = भृगुनाडी P. 446 :-

शुक्रे राहुयुते दृष्टे योगभङ्ग पदे पदे ।

Deva Keraḷam, Book 3, P-122-V. 3611 :-

निधनस्थानदोषेण शुभभुक्तौ मनोव्यथाम् ।
पापभुक्तौ महत्सौख्यं गृहे गोधनसंकुलम् ।।

During the dasa of a planet, because of his 8th house occupation :-

(i) The sub-period of a benefic planet will cause mental distress;

(ii) the sub-period of a malefic planet will bring forth happiness and cause acquisition of quadrupeds and wealth for the family.

In the scribe's chart, Jupiter is posited in the 8th house (Dasa for 16 years i.e. from 6.7.1926 to 6.7.1942):-

Outstanding events in sub-periods of Jupiter's Dasa (occupying 8th house) :-

(1) Sub-period of Jupiter - death of younger brother;

(2) Sub-period of Saturn - won scholarship in competitive examination;

(3) Sub-period of Mercury - father's sickness and retirement from service;

(4) Sub-period of Ketu - got married and joined college for further studies;

(5) Sub-period of Venus - birth of a daughter who died soon, wife's sickness;

(6) Sub-period of the Sun - passed B.A. father prospered in business and came to Mumbai for Post graduation studies.

(7) Sub-period of Moon - father lost his cousin sister, who was ailing.

(8) Sub-period of Mars - earned a fat amount of money ranging to five figures in speculation.

(9) Sub-period of Rahu-joined service in Mumbai from April, 1941.

The scribe has come across the above verse for the first time during his study of Deva Keralam. There is no mention to this effect in the standard texts, studied so far by him.

First birth Dasa :-

Deva Keralam, Book 3, P. 232 V. 5140 :-

स्वर्क्षे मीनांशगे चन्द्रे गुरुभुक्तौ प्रजायते।
बालारिष्टभयं किञ्चच्छनिभुक्तौ न संशयः।।

"For the native born with the Moon in Cancer with Pisces Navamsa:-

(i) in Jupiter sub-period, there is fear of infantile mortality.

(ii) in Saturn's sub-period, there is definite infantile mortality.

There is some misprint in text. It should be न संशयः in place of प्रजायते (in the last quarter). The Moon being in Pisces Navamsa in sign Cancer can have Mercury's Dasa i.e. the last quarter period, covering Jupiter's and Saturn's sub-periods.

Jyotisharnava Navanitam (English translation by R.Santhanam) P. 102 - Verse 245 :-

लग्नपे मृत्युपे वाऽपि जन्मकालदशा यदि।
कष्टातिकष्टं विज्ञेयं तत्केन्द्रे मरणप्रदम्।।

First-birth Dasa :-

"Should a person born in the dasa of either ascendant lord or the

8th lord, that dasa will produce intense difficulties. Both these planets posited in Kendra from each other will cause early death."

Dasa/periods of Rasi and Navamsa dispositors :-

It may be noted that dispositorship of Rasi and Navamsa lords is linked with Dasa and Bhuktai effects.

Deva Keralam, Book 3, page 222 - verses 4992½ to 4995½:-

अष्टमाधिपतौ लग्ने मेषांशे चापाराशिगे।
मूसुतस्य दशा केत्त्कशमपरार्धे महाविपत्।।

Dasa of Navamsa Dispositor :-

"Should the lord of the 8th house (in Dhanur Lagna - the Moon) be in the ascendant in sign Dhanus with Mesha Navamsa, the dasa of Mars will be a sourse of anguish. Great calamity will result in the 2nd half of dasa".

सिंहे चापांशगे राहौ धनुर्लग्नसमुद्रवः।
गुरुभुक्त्यन्तमारभ्य राहुदाये सुयशैग्वान्।।

"Rahu in Simha with Dhanu Navamsa, for one born in Dhanus Lagna, will cause much prosperity, right from the end of the sub-period of Jupiter in Rahu Dasa (i.e. from the beginning of the sub-period of Saturn in Rahu dasa).

शुक्रभांशगते चन्द्रे कीटे चापांशगे शनौ।
धनुर्लग्ने प्रजातस्तु गुरुभुक्तौ श्रियान्वितः।।

Bhukti of Navamsa Dispositor :-

"The Moon in Rasi and Navamsa of Venus, while Saturn in Vrischika with Dhanu Navamsa for one born in Dhanur Lagna, the sub-period of Jupiter will produce wealth."

Example-1 :

An interesting chart of a boy (15 years old) appended below is worth studying. He met with a fatal jeep accident while crossing road on 2.6.1994 (running 15 years of life) at 9.15 P.M., Ghatkopar, Mumbai. He breathed his last on the way before reaching hospital.

Birth details :-

Date of birth 14th November, 1979-Wednesday on 0h - 20 m A.M. A.M. (IST), Long 72°50' E, Lat. 18°56' N) The Sun 6s 27°13'; the Moon 4s 19°55'; Mars 4s 3° 36'; Mercury 7s 10° 48', Jupiter 4s 13°54'; Venus 7s 17° 00'; Saturn 5s 0° 56'; Rahu 4s 10° 53'; and ascendant 3s 26° 48'; Ayananda 23°-34'-23" Dasa balances of birth. Venus 10.1.12.

Lord of the ascendant the Moon is in sign Simha, whose Rasi dispositor is the Sun and Navamsa dispositor is Mercury. The boy was having the Sun's dasa from 25.12.1989 to 25.12.1995. The Navamsa dispositor Mercury's period was current from 13.10.1993 to 19.8.1994. It may be noted that Rasi and Navamsa dispositors of the ascendant lord have caused havoc in this case on 2.6.1994.

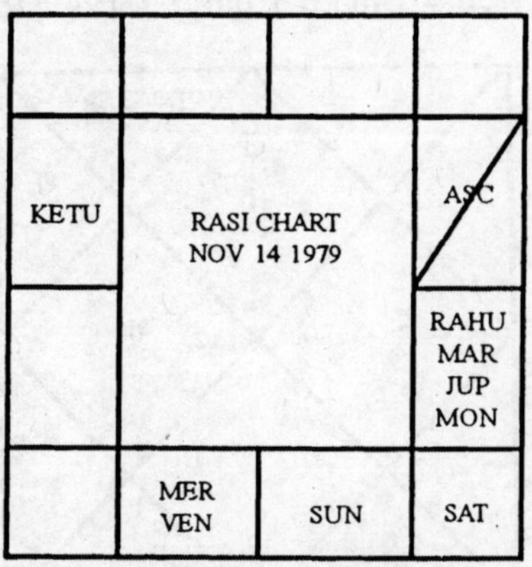

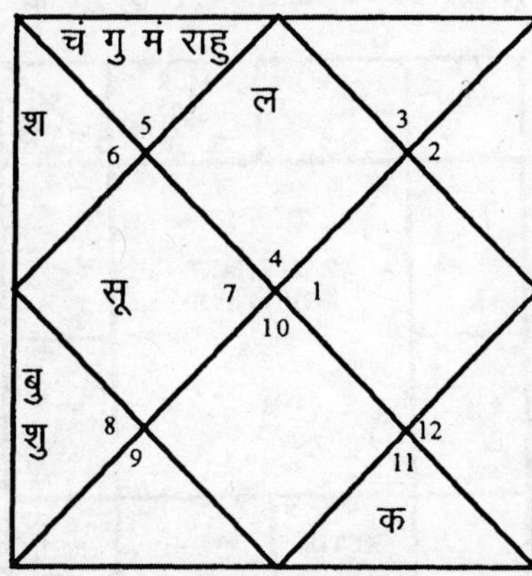

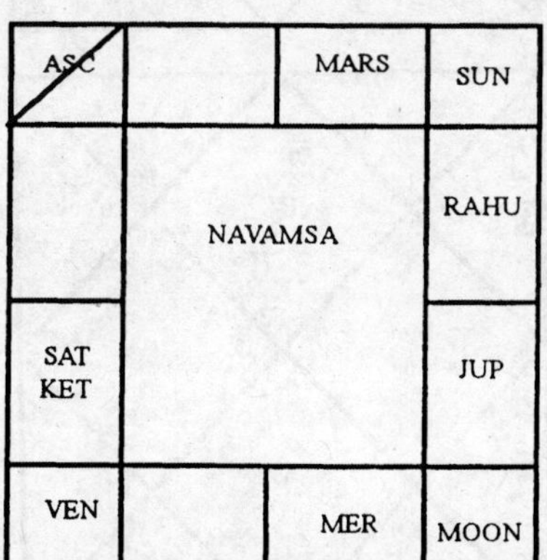

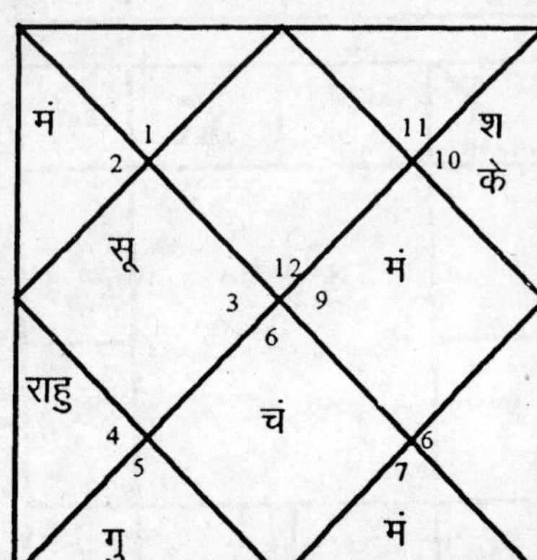

Example-2 :

Nathuram Vinayaka Godse :

Birth details Long 73° 52' E; Lat. 18° 31' N

Date of Birth 19.5.1910 at 8.29 A.M. (IST).

The Sun 36° 41'; the Moon 160°43'; Mars 79°16'; Mercury 45° 39'; Jupiter 163° 44', Venus 351°42'; Saturn 9° 4'; Rahu 37° 17'; Ketu 217° 17'; and Lagna 79° 16';

Ayanamsa 21° 1;. Dasa balance at birth Moon 9.5.16.

Lord of the ascendant is Mercury and Navamsa ascendant lord is Jupiter. Nathuram Godse murdered Mahatma Gandhi on 30.1.1948. He was executed on 15.11.1949. He was having Jupiter Dasa (5.11.1944 to 5.11.1960) and Mercury Bhukti from 5.7.1949 to

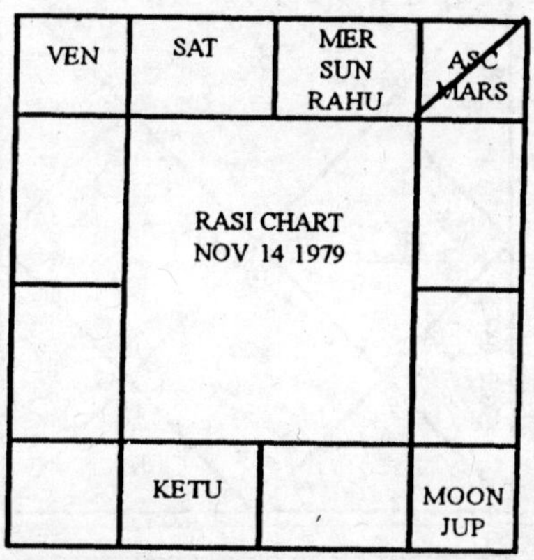

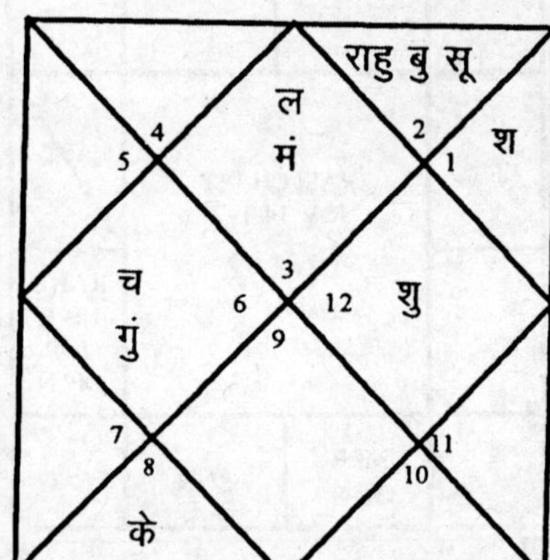

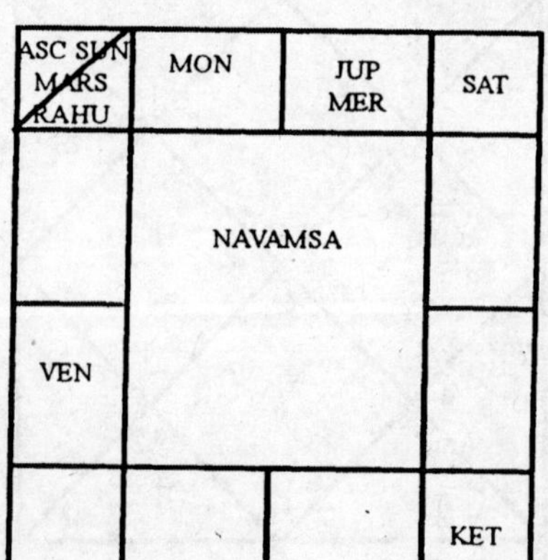

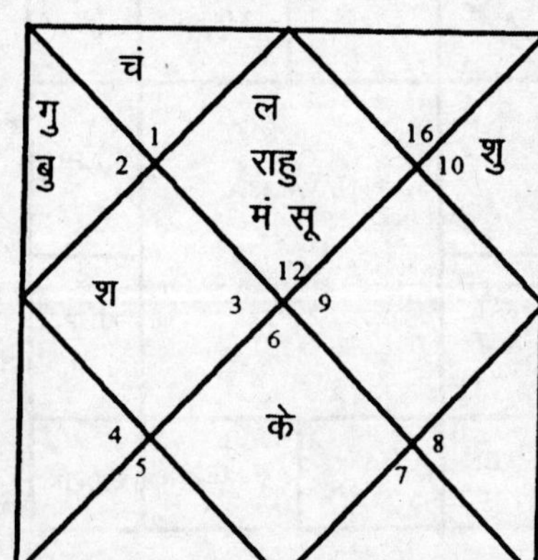

16.10.1951. It may be noted that he was executed during ascendant lord Mercury's period, in Navamsa ascendant lord Jupiter's Dasa. Rasi dispositor and Navamsa dispositor of the ascendnat itself have caused the execution on 15.11.1949.

The scribe has to draw the attention of the sholars to the following important point for research i.e. the Dasas and Bhuktis of Rasi dispositors-versus the Bhaktis and Dasas of Navamsa dispositors of all the seven planets be studied to arrive at correct timing of fruition of all outstanding good and bad events in one's life.

For Example :-

In scribe's chart ascendant lord the Moon-is in Makara Navamsa in Tula Rasi-hence the Dasa of Venus x Saturn Bhukti (i.e. from 5.5.1998 to 5.7.2001) has better potential of inflicting final blow. Moreover, the 7th lord Saturn is ill-placed in the 12th house, aspected by the 2nd lord Sun, has better inflicting power (both Marakas)

The scribe hopes that this write-up will enthuse the ardent scholars to make further researches on dispositors of Rasi/Navamsa.

38

Gemini Astrology—Lagna-Aarudha

Maharashi Jaimini (author of Poorva Mimamsa) extensively dealt with this Arudha pada system of astrology. Though sage Paarasara has originally sown seeds in B.P.H Sastra chapters 29 to 33; later on Jaimini deep and located many pearls out of his wisdom and intuition. Thus the system has become to be known by the name of jaimini astrology rather than Paarasara.

Right from Vridhha Yavan (150 B.C.) till 18th century none of the authors of standard texts had touched this subject of "Arudha" except the following authors;

1. **'Hora-Sara'** Chap iv verse 2; Chap. xxvii verses 23-24-25;
2. **'Prasna Marg'**

   Both the authors in aforesaid works referred to this **"Arudha pada"** for Prasna only.
3. **"Uttara-Kala-Mrita"**- Khand V verses 34-40 deal with Jataka results.

Arudha Lagna is not confined to Jaimini system of astrology alone, but it is extensively used even in Paarasari system.

Prof. K.V. Adhyankara writes in his book "The Upadesh Sutra of Jaimini-1951"

"Jaimini has paid special attention to the aspects of planets especially to the way in which they aspect their own signs. Apparently, there was a peculiar belief that the reflection was as good as the original, the reflecting medium being furnished by a planet as in the case of the Pada or Upapada, or by a sign as in the case of 'Bahya Rasi.' The old astrologers at the time of *Jaimini* believed that *along with the sign he ruled, a planet aspected, with the same attention, another sign which had the same angle of incidence as the sign ruled by him, had with the sign in which he was placed.* In other words, a sign had its reflection in its ruler planet and the sign corresponding to the reflection was as powerful as the original one. The sign agreeing with or corresponding to the reflection was called "*Pada*" or '*foot*' by *Jaimini and his colleague astrologers.* The 'Pada' of the ascendent or Lagna Pada is taken by Jaimini as the basis in determining the monetary prospects of an individual. The seventh, the eleventh and the twelth houses from the 'Pada' give special results by means of the planets present therein or aspecting. The remaining houses (and their Padas) give results just in the same way in which houses from the sign occupied by the significatory Planets do."

[R. Santhanam's B.P.H.S. pages 293-294]:-

The Pada (or Arudha) of the ascendant will correspond to the sign arrived at by counting so many signs from the ascendant lord as he is away from the ascendant. A chart with this "Arudha Lagna" is called "Arudha Chart". This Arudha Lagna is a magnetic point of the horoscope. Similarly, Padas (or Arudhas) for the remaining eleven houses be known through their lords. The word "Pada" exclusively denotes the Arudha for Ascendant (Lagna-Arudha or Lagna Pada).

In calculating the Arudha for various houses, one has to proceed as under. First of all one should understand the 12 Arudhas thus :-

Name		Arudha of the House
1.	Lagna Pada-Lagna Arudha or Simply Pada or Tanu	1st
2.	Dhana Pada	2nd
3.	Vikrana-(Bhatru) Pada	3rd
4.	Sukha Pada	4th
5.	Putra-(Mantra) Pada	5th
6.	Roga (Satru) Pada	6th
7.	Dara-(Bharya) Pada	7th
8.	Marana-(Ayu) Pada	8th
9.	Pitru-(Bhagya) Dharma Pada	9th
10.	Karma Pada	10th
11.	Labha-(Aya) Pada	11th
12.	Vyaya Pada	12th

In calculating the "Arudha Pada" for (a house), note number of signs its lord moved away from that particular sign. Count so many signs from the lord in question. The sign so arrived will be the Arudha for that house.

There are three exceptions to this general rule :-

1. When the Pada falls in the same house, the 10th therefrom be treated as its 'Pada.'

2. When the 7th house becomes Pada of a house, the 4th from the original house be treated as its "Pada".

3. If the ruler of a Bhava (house) be in the 4th from the Bhava, then the very house occupied by that planet be noted as its 'Pada'.

Scriber's Chart : D.O.B. 31-12-1915, at 7.44 p.m. (IST) of 23-02' N; 72-39' E (other details not necessary).

In the chart, Lagna lord, the Moon is in the 4th house from the Lagna. So the Arudha Pada for the Lagna is Tula (Put Roman numbered 1 in Tula).

The 2nd house lord, the Sun is in the 5th house from the 2nd, so the 5th house from Dhanus i.e. sign Mesha is Dhana-Arudha. mark-II in sign Mesha.

In 3rd house lord Mercury is in the 4th house from Kanya, so Vikrama-Arudha falls in itself. Mark VI in sign Dharma

The 5th house lord Mars is in the 10th house from the 5th house, hence the 10th house from Simha i.e. sign Vrishabha is Putra-Arudha. Mark V sign Vrishabha.

The 6th house lord Jupiter is in the 3rd house from the 6th house, so the 3rd house from Kumbha i.e.sign Mesha is Roga-Arudha. Mark VI in sign Mesha.

The 7th house lord Saturn is in the 6th house from the 7th house, so the 6th house from the Mithuna i.e. sign Vrischika is Dara-Arudha. Mark VII in Vrischika.

The 8th house lord Saturn is in the 5th house from the 8th house, so the 5th house Mithuna i.e. sign Tula is Marana-Arudha. Mark VIII in sign Tula.

The 9th house lord Jupiter is in the 12th house from the 9th house, so the 12th house from Kumbha i.e. sign Makara is Bhagya-Arudha. Mark IX in sign Makara.

The 10th house lord Mars is in the 5th house from the 10 house, so the 5th house from Simha i.e. sign Danus is Karma-Arudha. mark X in sign Dhanus.

The 11th house lord Venus is in the 9th house from the 11th house, so the 9th from the sign Makara sign Kanya is Labha-arudha. mark XI in sign Kanya.

The 12th house lord Mercury is in the 7th house from the 12th house, so the 4th house from Mithuna i.e. sign Kanya is Vyaya–Arudha. mark XII in sing Kanya. (Ref. 3rd exception to general rule).

Rules for application to Pada/Arudha Lagna : Income

1. If the 11th from the Pada Lagna has one or more planet/s, or if it is aspected by one or more planet/s, the person becomes wealthy.

Date of Birth : 31 December 1915
Time : 7.44 P.M.
23-02' N; 72-39' E

PLN	RASI	DEGREE	LRD	NAK	SUB	SS	CUSP	RASI	DEGREE	LRD	NAK	SUB	SS
SUN	SAG	16:14:44	JUP	VEN	MON	MON	1	CAN	09:02:17	MON	SAT	VEN	RAH
MON	LIB	12:16:59	VEN	RAH	SAT	JUP	2	LEO	03:54:20	SUN	KET	MON	RAH
MAR	LEO	07:13:53	SUN	KET	RAH	SUN	3	VIR	02:20:44	MER	SUN	JUP	VEN
MER	SAG	25:19:58'	JUP	VEN	MER	RAH	4	LIB	04:25:26	VEN	MAR	VEN	SAT
JUP	AQU	29:31:53	SAT	JUP	MON	MON	5	SCO	07:39:06	MAR	SAT	KET	MAR
VEN	CAP	13:19:03	SAT	MON	RAH	VEN	6	SAG	09:22:45	JUP	KET	SAT	SAT
SAT	GEM	20:47:07	MER	JUP	JUP	KET	7	CAP	09:02:17	SAT	SUN	VEN	JUP
RAH-R	CAP	15:44:56	SAT	MON	SAT	SAT	8	AQU	03:54:20	SAT	MAR	VEN	JUP
KET-R	CAN	15:44:56	MON	SAT	JUP	KET	9	PIS	02:20:44	JUP	JUP	RAH	MER
URA-R	CAP	21:02:11	SAT	MON	VEN	MON	10	ARI	04:25:26	MAR	KET	MON	MER
NEP-R	CAN	09:17:58	MON	SAT	VEN	JUP	11	TAU	07:39:06	VEN	SUN	KET	SAT
PLU-R	GEM	09:49:58	MER	RAH	JUP	VEN	12	GEM	09:22:45	MER	RAH	JUP	MER

FORTUNA : TAU : 05:04:32
AYANAMSA : 22:35:25
BALANCE OF DASA : RAH 10 YEARS 5 MONTHS 0 DAYS
Lagna Nirayana Bhava Chart

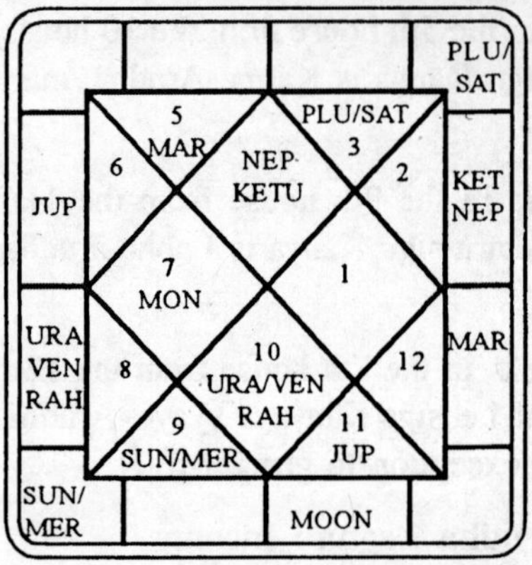

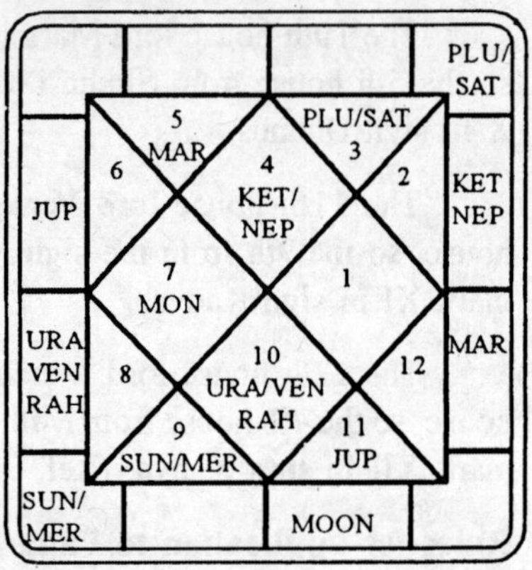

2. If all these planets are benefic, his acquisition is by virtuous means.

3. If the planets are malefic, his acquisition is by ignoble means.

4. If the planets in question be in exaltation or in own sign, or otherwise powerful, there will be plenty of happiness.

Notes : In the scribe's chart, the 11th from Pada Lagna i.e. sign Simha is occupied by Mars (a malefic) and aspected by Saturn (malefic-retrograde) from the 12th house and by Jupiter (a benefic) from the 8th house. The native had regular income from salary, as well as hazarous income from speculation, racing etc.

Expenses :

5. The person becomes a spendthrift, if the 12th house from the Pada Lagna has one or more planets or if it is aspected by one or more planets.

6. If the Sun, Rahu and/or Venus be in the 12th from Pada Lagna, the expenses are due to the king's demands i.e. taxes, fines etc.

7. If there is the aspect of the Moon in addition to the above mentioned, expenses occur definitely.

8. If there is Mercury in the 12th, the expenses arise due to fines etc, levied by caste people or due to quarrels.

9. If there is Mars and Saturn the expenses are due to brothers and the like.

10. If there is Jupiter in the 12th, the expenses are due to brothers and the like.

11. The causes of expenses given above (Rules 5 to 10) become in fact the sources of income in case these planets are in the 11th house from the Pada Lagna.

Others rules :

12. If there is Rahu or Ketu in the 7th house from the Pada Lagna, the person suffers from diseases of the stomach.

13. If there is Ketu in the 2nd house fiom the Pada Lagna, there occur signs of old age prematurely.

14. If there is the Moon, Venus and/oi Jupiter (in the 2nd house from the Pada Lagna) the person becomes rich.

15. If there is any planet in exaltation, the same is the result.

16. Other results should be understood on general lines as in the cases of various planets stationed at different distances from chief significator.

Additional rules :

17. If the Pada of the 7th house be in square (1st, 4th, 7th or 10th) or in trine (5th or 9th) from the Arudha Pada, the person becomes wealthy.

18. If it be elsewhere (i.e. in 2nd, 3rd, 6th, 8th, 11th, or 12th houses) the person becomes poor.

19. If the Pada of the 7th house be in Kendra or Kona or Upachaya from the Lagna Pada the husband and wife should remain friendly.

20. If the Pada of the 7th house be in the 6th or 8th or 12th from the Lagna Pada they dislike each other.

21. Even though, a planet is well placed in Rasi Chart i.e. either is an angle or in trine from the ascendant, yet that planet happens to

be placed either in the 6th, 8th or the 12th from the Arudha Pada, then its Dasa is said to give rise to adverse results.

Some rules from (B.P.H.S. Chap. 30 page 308-R. Santhanam's edition):-

Lagna-Arudha :

1. Rahu and Saturn in the 3rd or 11th from the Lagna-Pada will destroy the coborns of the native-in the 11th elder coborns and in the 3rd younger ones.

2. If Venus is in the 3rd/11th from Lagna Pada, there would have been an abortion to the mother earlier. Same is the effect if Venus aspects or is in the 8th house from the natal ascendant or from the Lagna Pada.

3. Should the Moon, Jupiter, Mercury and Mars be in the 3rd/11th from the Lagna Pada, there will be many valourous coborns.

4. Should Saturn and Mars be in the 3rd/11th from the Lagna Pada or lends aspects there to, younger and elder coborn will respectively be destroyed. If Saturn alone is in one of the said houses the native will be spared while the coborn will die.

5. Ketu in the 3rd/11th from the Lagna Pada, the native will have abundant happiness from his sisters.

6. If the 6th from Lagna Pada is occupied by a malefic and is bereft of conjunction/aspect of a benefic, the native will be a thief.

7. If Rahu is in the 7th/12th from the Lagna Pada or aspects one of the said houses, the native will be endowed with spiritual knowledge and be very fortunate. (In the seribe's Chart, the 12th house from Lagna Pada i.e. sign Kanya is aspected by Rahu).

8. If Mercury is in Lagna Pada, the native will lord over whole country while Jupiter will make him a knower of all things. Venus in this context denotes a poet/speaker.

9. If benefics occupy the 2nd from the Lagna Pada, the native will be endowed with all kinds of wealth and be intelligent.

Some novel uses of Arudha of the 12 houses mentioned in Deva Keralm-Chandra Katu Nadi-3 for further research :

D.K.. 3 P. 49 Verse 2665. :

भाग्यारूढ़े धनुर्लग्ने भाग्ये यावत् फलैर्युते ।
तावद्वर्षात् पर भाग्यं योगवान् कीर्तिमान् भवेत् ।।

Meaning : "One born in Dhanur Lagna will prosper after such number of years denoted by S.A.V. (Sarvastaka Varga) bindus in Bhygya-Arudha sign."

In the scribe's chart Bhagya-Arudha is sign Makara (7th house) which contains 19 S.A.V. binds. The scribe started earning even during college studies from the 19th year. This rule can be applied to any Ascendant.

D.K. 3 p. 187 (text variation-refer footnote of original text)-Vol III p. 205 verse 4494.

भाग्यारूढाधिपे भौमे कर्मरूढपसंयुते ।
भाग्ययोगमिति प्राहुः सत्कर्माचारबुद्धिमान् ।।

Meaning : "If Mars the lord of the *Bhagya-Arudha sign is in conjunction with the lord of the karma-Arudha sign, it makes Bhagya Yoga and the native undertakes the paths of good deeds and is an intellectual," In the scribe's chart, Bhagya-Arudha lord Saturn is aspected by Jupiter, who is Karmarudha lord. How wounderfully the Nadi author has taken into account, the conjunction of Bhagya-Arudha lord and Karma-Arudha lord.*

D.K. 3 p. 77 verse 3016.

चन्द्रलग्नाद् व्ययारूढे पापाक्रान्ते प्रजायते ।
लोकान्तर सुखं नास्ति गुरुदृष्टौ क्वकचित् क्कचित् ।।

Meaning : "If the Arudha Pada of the 12 house counted from the Moon is occupied by a malefic, the native will not be happy in the other world (i.e. after death). If Jupiter aspects the said sign, some happiness will be there."

The author takes into account Arudha from the Chandra Lagna. This is a novel point to be thought of.

D.K. 3 p. 49, vers 2666 (1st line oonly) :-

आरुढ़े राहुदोषण बाल्येऽल्पसुखबुद्धिमान् ।

Meaning : "Due to blemish of Rahu being in Lagna-Arudha, the native in childhood has limited happiness and limited intelligence"

The Arudha-Pada system is a peculiar one in which degrees of planets, transits, sixteen Vargas of signs etc, are not considered. Only Natal Rasi Chart is enough. The predictions promised by Lagna Pada and by various Bhava-Arudhas take place during the currency of periods of those planets in their Dasas.

This system of prediction is freely used in Nadi texts such as Deva Keralam and Bhargava Nadi, as against its use in standard texts.

39

Retrogression of Planets

The world which is comprehensible to our senses is three-dimensional. The celestial bodies (the Planets) are spherical i.e. three dimensional. If a planet is a body which is exercising its influence upon us then the quantity of its intensity must become greater if the planet is approaching the earth, and it must become smaller as it recedes.

Uttara Kalamrita-II Ves 6.

वक्री स्वोच्च बैलः।

"When a planet is retrograde in motion his strength is similar to that when in his exaltation."

Parasar :-

खेटाः पूर्णफलं दद्युः सूर्यात् सम्तमके स्थिताः।
फलाभाव विजानीयात् समे सूर्य नभश्चरे।।

Meaning : "Planets when nearest the earth i.e. retrograde give maximum results and when farthest from the earth i.e. combust give very little effects."

Roughly speaking, Saturn, Mars and Jupiter start retrogression (Vakra) when the Sun comes to the 5th sign from them. When the Sun comes to the 7th sign (180°), the maximum retrogression takes place i.e. it is 'ATI-VAKRA' retrogression planets move more slowly, ordinarily, than when they are in direct motion.

When the planets in their orbits come closest to the earth, they are retrograde and when they are farthest from the earth they are combust.

Retrogression days for :-

Mercury	23 days;
Venus	45 days;
Mars	76 days;
Jupiter	122 days;
Saturn	135 days;

The above rule holds valid for superior planets namely Mars, Jupiter and Saturn as well as for inferior planets viz. Mercury and Venus, whose orbits lie below the earth's orbit. Mercury and Venus, when they are closest to the earth (i.e. when retrograde) at inferior conjunction, they can't normally be seen at all, because their non-luminous sides are turned towards the earth.

Combustion :-

Five planets from Mars to Saturn and the Moon become combust when they are within certain degrees from the body of the Sun.

The Moon within 12° (on both sides).

Mars within 17° (on both sides).

Mercury (direct beyond the Sun) within 14° (on both sides);

Mercury (retrograde i.e. between the Sun and the earth) within 12° (on both sides);

Venus (direct beyond the Sun) within 10° (on both sides);

Venus (retrograde i.e. between the Sun and the earth) within 8° (on both sides).

Jupiter within 12° (on both sides); and

Saturn within 15° (on both sides)

When Mercury and Venus are retrograde, they are between the Sun and the earth, and within certain degrees they also become combust during retrogression. Distances of planets from the Sun (Heliocentric) :-

Mean distance (in millions of miles) :-

1.	Mercury (M)	36;
2.	Venus (V)	67;
3.	Earth (E)	98;

4.	Mars (Kuja-K)	142;
5.	Jupiter (J)	483; and
6.	Saturn (Paugu-p)	886

E=Earth; M_1 = Mercury beyond the Sun; M_2 = Mercury between the Sun and the earth, S = The Sun. The distances shown in this article are tentative and not actual as per measurement.

1. Mercury :-

E__________M2____________S______________M1

Mercury is about 36 millions of miles away from the Sun (SM1=SM2). Mercury beyond the Sun (M1) is at a distance of E.S. (98)+SM1 (36) = 134 millions of miles away from the earth, when in combustion. Mercury, when between the Sun and the earth is at a distance of ES (98) - SM 2 (36) = 62 millions of miles away when retrograde i.e. at the minimum distance from the earth.

2. Venus.

E_______V2_______(S)_______V1

Venus is about 67 million of miles away from the Sun (SV1-SV2). Venus beyond the Sun V1 is at a distance of ES(98) + SV1 (67=165) millions of miles away from the earth when in combustion. Venus when between the Sun and the earth is at a distance ES(98)—SV2=31 millions of miles when retrograde i.e. at the minimum distance from the earth. Venus is the only planet in the galaxy which comes nearest the earth (31 millions of miles) when retrograde.

3. Mars (Kuja)

K2__________E_________S__________K1

Mars (Kuja) is about 142 millions of miles away from the Sun (SK1 = SK2) Kuja beyond the Sun is at a distance of SK1. (142) + ES (98) i.e. 240 millions of miles away from the earth when in combustion Kuja when retrograde i.e. in the 7th from the Sun at a distance EK2(142)-ES (98) = 44 millions of miles away from the earth SK2. It may be noted that the distance of Kuja from the earth at the time of combustion is 240 million of miles. One can imagine the impact of effect of Mars upon the earth when retrogade. *This is probably the reason why retrograde planets are powerful.*

4. Jupiter

J2___________E__________(S)____________J1

Jupiter is 483 millions of miles away from the Sun (SJ1 = SJ2). Jupiter beyond the Sun is at a distance of SJ1 (483) + ES (98) = 581 millions of miles away from the earth when in combustion. Jupiter when retrograde i.e. in the 7th from the Sun is at distance of SJ2 (483)-ES (98) = 385 millions of miles from the earth.

5. Saturn (Pangu-P) :

Saturn (Pangu) is 886 millions of miles away from the Sun (SPI=SP2). Saturn beyond the Sun is a distance of SPI (886) + ES(98)=984 millions of miles awa from the Earth when in combustion. Saturn when retrograde i.e. in the 7th from the Sun, is at a distance SP2 (886)-ES(98) = 788 millions of miles from the Earth.

Naturally, planets when nearest to the Earth exert maximum effect (influence) i.e. when they are retrograde, they are very powerful, whether they give favourable or unfavorable results, it is immateial.

Attention of the readers is drawn to the following very important verse :- Deva Keralam-Chandra Kala Nadi=G.O.M.L.-edition Vol. I-P 46-wise 471.

= Delhi edition) (1) P-47) - verse 471

अतिचारगने जीवे शनौ वक्रत्वमागते ।
हाहाकार जगत्सर्व.विशेषाद् दक्षिणादिशि ।।

Meaning : "When Jupiter is an accelerated motion (combustion) and Saturn is in retrograde motion simultaneously, the whole world will be wailing aloud in grief, particularly waiting the southren region."

Notes : Jupiter's acceleration takes place when he is in combustion i.e. far away from the Earth so his benevolent rays on the earth meagre. Saturn, at the same time is very powerful to cause evil effects on an extensive scale being retrograde i.e. nearest the earth. This kind of Yoga takes place once in every 20 years i.e. Saturn Jupiter's opposition.

Round about 30-6-1989-Jupiter was in acceleration motion, covering about 4° of arc, in one month and Saturn was retrograde. In June end and beginning of July 1989-thousands of students who revolted against the government, were massacred by military in Beijing

(China's capital) at Tinaman Square.

Round about the same time in Bukharest also thousands of people who revolted were killed by the President's order.

After studying the article, it could be clear as to why retrograde planets are capable of maximum self-expression and the combust planets manimum. The scribe has tried to explain the subject matter astronomically.